# W
# Bright Idea
# Was That?

## GREAT FIRSTS OF
## WORLD HISTORY

**Matthew Richardson**

KODANSHA INTERNATIONAL

*New York · Tokyo · London*

Kodansha America, Inc.
114 Fifth Avenue, New York, New York 10011, U.S.A.

Kodansha International Ltd.
17-14 Otowa 1-chome, Bunkyo-ku, Tokyo 112-8652, Japan

Published in 1998 by Kodansha America, Inc.

First published in 1997 by Penguin Books Australia Ltd
with the title *The Penguin Book of Firsts*.

Library of Congress Cataloging-in-Publication Data

Richardson, Matthew.
Whose bright idea was that? : great firsts of world history /
Matthew Richardson.
p.   cm.
Includes index.
ISBN 1–56836–256–0
1. History—Miscellanea.   I. Title.
D10.R52   1998
909—dc21                                        98–16847
                                                        CIP

Manufactured in the United States of America

98 99 00 01 02    QFF    10 9 8 7 6 5 4 3 2 1

# CONTENTS

# INTRODUCTION

The biggest, the strongest, the furthest and the fastest all have a common destiny – second place. Sooner or later someone will outdo them, and relegate them to the archives. Being first is the one record which is unbreakable.

Even so, many holders of the title 'first' can be expected to lose it, because it is often bestowed in error.

Leonardo da Vinci did not design the first helicopter. Britain did not have the first empire on which the Sun never set – but electric lights were already shining in Britain while Thomas Edison, in America, burnt the midnight oil trying to invent them. The great explorer Vasco da Gama did not discover anything much, whereas explorers of the mind had identified the subconscious well before Sigmund Freud got out of his Oedipus phase.

People are often ready to declare something a first without worrying about accuracy. Plenty of others are determined to be first at something themselves without listening to common sense. Some have tortured and killed themselves in treks to the Pole, ascents of unclimbed mountains and singlehanded circumnavigations. Or, desperate to do something not already done, they accomplish preposterous feats like pushing a wheelbarrow around Australia. Partly because being first is such an effective claim to fame.

Copernicus was a great worker on many fronts, but his name is a household word only for the revelation that the Earth goes round the Sun. Columbus is feted as discoverer of America and founder of the round Earth theory. Most people only know Pythagoras for Pythagoras's Theorem, and Gutenburg as the first printer. Everyone admits the greatness of Galileo, but what can they tell you of his work? That he invented the telescope and discovered that bodies of different weight descend at equal velocity. Perhaps that he discovered the Moon shines with reflected sunlight.

As a matter of fact, all the claims to fame in the previous paragraph are false: these celebrated men were all beaten to the punch. Mostly they would have admitted it gladly enough, though not Columbus, who went to his grave denying that America exists.

The same distortions apply to nations as to individuals. It was not the

Scots who invented golf; the Chinese did not make the first abacus; nor did philosophy begin with the Greeks, or monotheism with the Jews.

*Whose Bright Idea Was That?* is frequently at odds with expert opinion and deliberately confronts the misconceptions of leading authorities. To inform sceptics and meet challenges I have prepared a separate book, *On the Sources of the Penguin Book of Firsts*\*, which may be obtained by contacting the author at Halstead Press, 19A Boundary St, Rushcutter's Bay, New South Wales, 2011.

*Whose Bright Idea Was That?* aims to throw out time-honoured claims and traditional assumptions (except where they are right) and to give trustworthy accounts of true firsts. This is really two aims and the first is a lot easier than the second. To undermine someone else's claim all you need do is point out a prior occurrence. To be sure that the prior occurrence is not preceded by yet another is the real problem. For instance, just because Henry Sinclair got to America before Columbus does not mean no one had been there earlier still.

In some cases the best we can finish with is a possible first based on an informed assessment of the circumstances. This difficulty does not justify the feeble position that 'first' means 'first known'. The challenge is to pursue knowledge to the point where it embraces the actual first. With the completion of this book, that challenge now passes to the readers – if any of them can ascertain that there is a precedent for a thing that is entered here as the first, the author and publishers will acknowledge them with gratitude in the next edition. In an ambitious book like this, mistakes are not only embarrassing, but inevitable. So the reader has an opportunity to serve the cause of knowledge, while relishing the author's discomfiture.

**Firsts in History**

World firsts reveal a pattern related to the human condition. They disclose little of the prehistoric period because the circumstances are mostly unknown. It was an era of comparative stability in lifestyles, punctuated by a small number of revolutionary inventions, such as agriculture.

In contrast, the earliest age of civilisation, beginning around 6000 years ago, brought a rapid spate of innovations, which introduced a lifestyle like the one most people live today.

After that, innovation slowed markedly, and in a thousand years, one will only find a few dozen significant novelties.

About the year 600B.C., the Classical Age dawned in Chinese, Indian and Western civilisation, giving us eight centuries of intense creativity, ideas and beliefs, political and social innovation and scientific revolutions.

Afterwards, from about 200A.D. to 1300, comes another period in which firsts appear comparatively rarely, interrupted by a spate of activity around the 11th century, associated mainly with China's Sung Dynasty.

Dark ages of varying length afflicted different parts of the world. Even the brilliant civilisations of the Middle Ages tended to repeat the innovations exhibited in the Classical Age.

From around 1300 there is a steady increase in the number of firsts being entered – for which Western Europe is mostly responsible. It culminates in the intense activity of the 19th and 20th centuries – two hundred years that furnish more entries than any earlier period of similar length.

However, even though the last 200 years supply many firsts in science, technology, war and sport, they are meagre contributors in other realms – literature, government, law, exploration, philosophy etc. It seems in these fields most of what could be done had been done already. That is why people like to say 'there is nothing new under the sun'.

A feature of this recent period is the contribution of places outside the traditional seedbed of Asia and Europe, due to the development of daughter cultures, like Australia and America. Considering the vastly increased populations contributing in this period, the necessary conclusion is that the human race has become less capable of new things than before. It is the natural result of so much having been done already.

This book is not an objective measure, because it concentrates on subjects which contemporary readers will wish to refer to. The camp mill, which mills grain while transporting it, was a remarkable invention in 400B.C., but from a modern perspective, it is not important enough to include. The LP record, on the other hand, is so familiar to contemporary readers that it earns a place, even though it is going the way of the camp mill. Also, the further back in time one goes, the more things have to be left out because nothing is known of their inception – another factor that masks the true proportion of ancient to modern firsts.

On the other side of the coin, technical developments now are more numerous, and less influential, than they once were. Modern-day firsts which are important enough for this book are a small minority of those which actually take place. While the rate at which a given population can come up with new things has declined, the resources which go into invention and discovery have burgeoned. Around the world, probably as much effort is dedicated in one week to technological innovation, as prehistoric man spared in a thousand years. As time passes, breakthroughs become harder and harder. It is now quite normal for a large research and development team to devote years to a single ordinary goal. And the fruit of the efforts expended is generally less significant than when the possibilities were fewer and simpler.

The management of fire was the most important new technology of its day. The silicon chip is perhaps the most important of the present generation. Controlled fires revolutionised the social order, being focal points for a new sort of organised group. They lengthened lives; they added cooked food to people's diets; they destroyed the old order of nature as hunters repeatedly fired vegetation to flush out prey; and they enabled the colonisation of the cold parts of the world which later became major population centres. Their invention required no costly resources, no special research facilities – and they were simple to make and install. But after their introduction, life was almost unrecognisably different.

Silicon chips, however, are things of ingenious complexity, the work of thousands of specialists labouring in stupendous research complexes. Yet living conditions immediately before them were very similar to what they have been since.

In the future it will only be possible to sustain the impact of technical innovation by committing an ever-increasing share of resources to the creation of new firsts.

In pursuits other than technology, the gains from past precedents can be consolidated, so that an end to new development does not doom society to a downhill slide. In philosophy for instance, once the truth is discovered, it is enough to make people understand and live by it: new philosophies are not needed to avoid degeneration. But if human society, as it now operates, were forced to live by existing technologies, it would be unable to meet its material requirements.

The reason is simple. While in theory the Earth can sustain life indefinitely, in practice the human species lives by using up resources. With an ever-growing population exhausting ever-shrinking resources, painful upheavals are inevitable, unless technology bales it out in time. For instance, when extraction of minerals began, people got exactly the raw material they required by scratching the surface. Thousands of years later, nothing is left on the surface. Demand is only met by ingenious technologies which make it possible to mine phenomenal distances below land and sea. Techniques are having to be developed at the same time to get yields from low and ever-lower grades of ore.

So technical progress – usually regarded as the agent of change – is mainly absorbed in preserving the status quo – in sustaining the provision of material needs. A vital question for the future is how long technological invention can continue at the rate we have learnt to rely on.

There is a tendency for the supply of firsts to dry up, as other fields demonstrate – for instance philosophy, global exploration and law. It isn't likely that technology will stagnate during our lifetimes. But sooner or later the crunch will come, and play havoc if society has not begun radical adjustment well ahead.

It is probably going to strike our descendants with much force too soon, when fossil fuels become hard to get. Then, perhaps, rather than sacrifice the prodigal habits they inherit from us, they will elect to run the world on nuclear energy and let their descendants count the cost.

An analysis of world firsts offers an opportunity to compare peoples and countries with each other. In early history, Egypt and Mesopotamia (present-day Iraq) repeatedly took the lead in almost every field. This is hardly surprising – since they had the first civilisations, most of the new things they did or had were being tried out for the first time. They also excelled in certain pursuits which are usually put down to much later times, as their record in government and thought demonstrates.

After about 1600B.C. the Mesopotamians remained important but not dominant contributors, until the Greeks took front place. From around 600B.C. onwards the Greeks and Chinese swept the field, each contributing more to *Whose Bright Idea Was That?* than any other peoples, past or present. It would be strange, of course, if the Chinese did not figure conspicuously, considering that historically China has usually been the most, or one of the most, populous, organised and affluent societies. Even allowing for this, Chinese innovation in ancient Classical times (up to about 200A.D.) was astonishingly vigorous. So was the Greeks' during the same epoch. These two peoples stand head and shoulders above any others – at times their inspired brilliance seems almost beyond logical explanation: like the Chinese talent for working out philosophical positions, miles ahead of modern capabilities; or the Greeks' gift of unlocking secrets, with minimal data and equipment – such as atoms and molecules, capillary blood vessels, climatic zones and the circumference of the globe. The Greeks would take an even more conspicuous place except that the records of their most brilliant age – the Hellenistic period from 323 to 44B.C. – have mostly been wiped out. So would the Chinese, but for the destructive work of the Chin Dynasty, which briefly held total power (221 to 206B.C.).

To work out what was so special about these bygone cultures might reward modern society. Part of the answer lies in their classical education methods which were well conceived to open the mind to multitudinous possibilities and make the student work out why each thing is right, before accepting it. The refusal of the ancient Greeks and Chinese to take fundamentals for granted is what contrasts most strongly with the sheep-like thinking of people nowadays.

They also differ from many nations by defining their societies as cultural units rather than ethnic units. The primaeval Chinese nation, small in numbers and territory, expanded the sway of its culture by incorporating neighbouring peoples without any thought for its racial purity. The Greeks were by disposition more exclusive than that, but history changed their destiny by spreading them thinly over the ancient West. From the French Riviera to the Persian Gulf, countries with a mere drop of Greek blood became Greek in their higher culture.

After the ancient Classical period, the Chinese went on accruing world firsts – in proportion to their great numbers and resources. In the early Sung era (960A.D.–1126) they even recaptured the disproportionate intensity of a thousand years earlier. The Greek impetus, however, was spent, and in the Dark Ages the Western World was divided by religious devotees, into Christendom and Islam. Islam's early dark ages were brief, and it soon proved a worthy successor to the intellectual culture of the Greeks. In this it had a long head start over Christian Europe, and one often hears the claim that some important first was an Islamic rather than a European achievement – algebra is a popular example. However most of these things had already been encompassed by the Greeks, or other early peoples. Islamic science improved the groundwork around the findings of ancient scientists but it was not so fruitful in opening new departments.

In the 1200s when Christian Europe began to emerge from ignorance, its science was centuries away from breaking ground not already cultivated by Greek and Islamic predecessors. Religion and exploration were the first important fields in which novel progress was made. In due course, however, it was progress in science that gave Europe its intellectual lustre, and ultimately progress in technology that gave it the opportunity to bestow or impose European ways on the whole world.

European firsts originated in Britain, in Russia and many countries in-between: no country dominated, but Britain was the most vigorous.

In the same period, the traditional sources of firsts further east more or less dried up. India and the Islamic countries no longer gave the world new things. China continued to generate firsts until the 20th century, but at no greater rate than several small European countries. Some of the firsts still coming from China are important, and a few – such as metric measurement and steam traction – were the fruit of co-operation between Europeans and Asians.

There is a difference between calling a society 'innovative' – in the limited meaning that applies in a book of firsts – and calling it 'advanced'. The Christian countries were backward and spent most of the modern period in rapid progress. Some of the old civilisations of Asia were much more sophisticated; all had become comparatively static, and ultimately they went into decline.

A society need not generate a torrent of world firsts for its civilisation to be at a high level. It can be static, or – like Japan – developing in the wake of precedents established elsewhere.

Since the 7th century A.D., at junctures in its history, Japan has adopted foreign institutions and developed them, sometimes with such vigour that the Japanese manifestations outstrip the home countries' best. As centuries ago Buddhism was more vital in Japan than in its Indian birthplace, today Japan's automated industry is superior to Britain's and her collapsing fans put China's to shame. Japan's gift for developing things which reach her shores could almost be said to have been given in place of a capacity to make firsts.

Those Asian cultures which formerly devised their own way in things are now in total eclipse. They have arrived at their dark ages by an even greater disintegration than Western civilisation suffered in Roman times. The only development they have known for over a century is either in reaction to Western influence or a direct adoption of Western ways. Elements in these societies recognise the harmful effect of dependency, but their concerns are translated into action in forms which underline the dark age conditions of their countries – such as political totalitarianism and religious fanaticism. The higher intellectual and creative powers are exercised within humble limits, and in accordance with Western models. It is now clear that most of these borrower societies gain less from 'modernisation' than they have lost by turning their backs on traditions and resigning their old vigour.

From 1500A.D. an important new bracket of societies has developed. Lying beyond the 'Old World' – as the ancient countries of Europe, Asia and Africa were designated – were sparsely populated lands which emigrants from the Old World settled in such numbers that their descendants now pre-dominate. Or, in a few cases – such as Peru – the settlers destroyed so much of a large indigenous population that they have since been able to prevail.

European offshoot societies today own a population greater than Europe's, and territory equal to Europe many times over. From their mother countries they gained in a moment the institutions, culture and education which arduous centuries had built up. From their new lands they derived resources in tremendous abundance. They had a head start unparalleled in the annals of the human race.

It is a wonder how little they contribute to our harvest of firsts. The discrepancy in output between the Old World and the New is the result of too many different causes in different places to examine minutely here; three regions will briefly illustrate it: Australia, Latin America and North America.

North America is in fact the home of many world firsts – primarily in religion, technology, travel, sport and warfare. But relative to its large population and prodigious resources, the number is small. Nevertheless, the United States leads more fields of technology and research than any other land. What is exhibited there, it seems, is a tendency similar to Japan's: a gift for adopting and improving things more potent than its gift for making entirely new things. The contrast is actually less marked than in Japan and a perusal of the following chapters will show that many more firsts come from America than Japan.

Former colonies of Spain and Portugal mostly seem to be in disarray and penury compared to their motherlands. The reasons for Latin America's plight must be complex, but having once fallen into the trap, it appears to be locked there by international debt as well as internal conditions. Evidently society in South and Central America and Mexico exhibits vitality in various departments; but in what is relevant to our book there is only paralysis. The region has given us less than any other major division.

On a simple head count Australia's performance is not disappointing. Yet Australia's advantages of material abundance, freedom from strife and social barriers, access to education, and unparalleled spare time should have produced more distinct results. But Australia is a handicapped society, because of its resolute and self-fulfilling conviction in its cultural and intellectual inferiority. It routinely expects to take its lead from Britain, America and Western Europe. In the face of contrary evidence, the people believe the myth that the characteristic Australian is a lowbrow drunken yobbo. They measure the success of their compatriots by how much esteem they win overseas. Because any achievement above a meagre level of sophistication has to be accomplished within international guidelines, Australian society is incapable of making its own way. Australians are doomed to remain asleep to the possibilities as long as this mortgagor vocation endures.

The malaise that stifles creativity in Australia is pronounced, but not unusual. Borrower cultures all over the world exhibit something similar. You will find it in Poland and Brazil, Canada, Iraq, Thailand and dozens of other places. It thrives where circumstances lend it a kind of logic, and where it is manifestly absurd. It comes and goes, and is strong today in China and Greece which were once so free of it. For the time being, it cannot be found in the United Kingdom and the United States, which means we, the handicapped, must wake up to ourselves, or expect to live increasingly on their terms in future.

To divine what makes certain societies more prolific than others in world firsts requires a complex and well informed analysis. It may not be worth the effort, given that firsts are not a particularly dependable index of creativity. But it is a very true generalisation that a society's expectations of itself determine of how innovative it is.

Undoubtedly cultural and geographical circumstances affect how creative a people will be. It is probably also true that innate ethnic characters differentiate races in their levels of achievement, and explain in part why some peoples 'burn out', reduced to gazing admiringly at their past or over their borders. However, most of the confident racist analyses of congenital traits are useless, because they ignore the historical and geographic circumstances which promote one race and restrict another.

For example, Australian Aborigines were stone age hunters until the time of European settlement. Noticing that they had no farms, towns, ceramics, metal, houses, nor any of the other amenities peculiar to farming peoples, observers find it easy to call them intellectually inferior. That overlooks the fact that Australia furnished no animals that could be herded, no cereal crops, no garden vegetables. The failure of European settlers to make anything economically significant of Australian native species helps demonstrate that animal husbandry and agriculture were not feasible for the Aborigines. Their stone age condition has nothing to do with intellectual inferiority, and everything to do with their geographic heritage.

## Tradition and Innovation

In identifying a first, no attention is given to whether it inaugurated an important tradition. For example, Sir Isaac Newton's statement of Newton's First Law has no place – even though Newton's work introduced it to his successors down to the present day. That law was known beforehand to British scientists and to Galileo, and to the Greeks much earlier still. Two and a half thousand years ago, the law was even stated by a Chinese philosopher. In *Whose Bright Idea Was That?* it is only the Chinese who count on this point, even though they took no advantage of their knowledge. Their statement, indeed, played no part in informing the Greeks and was unknown to Newton.

Some people ask, 'What can be the relevance of looking back to something that has no detectable influence on the modern world?'

There are two answers. Knowing when and where the human mind encompassed new things is necessary to understanding not just the things, but humanity and progress. Second, a remote precedent, for what is always deemed to be an innovation nearer at hand, challenges us to find out whether the idea has been transmitted from that distant source to our own time and place. Most observers are content to follow traditions back to a convenient and well known founder, and assume they have the origin. This is a practice fraught with error and misunderstanding.

For instance, everyone acknowledges Charles Darwin as founder of the theory of evolution in the 1850s. Remind his admirers that Darwin's British predecessors had fully expressed the idea beforehand, and they will hasten to assert that religious strictures prevented them from communicating such insights to the general public. Yet William Lawrence's book setting forth all the elements of 'Darwinism' was so popular that it went through many reprints early in the 19th century. Darwin himself admitted to reading about natural selection (the cornerstone of evolutionary theory) in an ancient Chinese encyclopaedia. Erasmus Darwin, Charles's grandfather, wrote of natural selection at some length. Erasmus's contemporary, David Hume, mentions it too, citing for his source the Roman author Cicero of the 1st century B.C. Cicero got it from a chain of Greek thinkers extending back centuries before his time.

So evolutionary theory – like most of the great breakthroughs in modern intellectual culture – is a tradition much older than modern Western civilisation, a tradition largely forgotten in the comparative ignorance of the 20th century.

This ignorance, which shrouds the sources of dominant ideas, also obscures the parentage of familiar practices. Immunisation is an example. It is popularly traced back to Edward Jenner, and his studies on British milkmaids in the 1790s. Point out that immunisation was commonplace in India and China much earlier, and some reply that because modern society did not learn it from there, it is to Jenner, and his independent discovery in Britain, that we are indebted.

Will they be prepared to question his originality, if informed that Lady Montagu's children, immunised in Constantinople before Jenner was born, were relatives of his? Our tradition of immunisation did not begin in Britain, nor indeed in Turkey – but further East, and longer ago than modern medicine.

Without knowing the many traditions of this kind, it is not possible to realise just how comprehensively Western culture and the modern way of life are derived from works and minds which are ancient and Asian. People who lack that understanding cannot be treated as authorities on their own world.

*Whose Bright Idea Was That?* only goes part way to remedying the deficit in knowledge which leaves people blind to their cultural background. Here only the remote points of origin are identified. Others can fill in the links between them and 20th-century society, or discover, in some cases, that there really has been a separate invention rather than a transmission.

### Verification

Discovering the circumstances of an episode from literary or archaeological sources is the minor part of ascertaining a first. The major part is establishing that there has been no prior occurrence of the same thing.

Books and papers on specialist topics usually contain reasonably clear attributions of the relevant first. However they can rarely be trusted. Fifty reputable books might concur in identifying something as the first, when really it is just the second or the sixtieth. Chapter 1 in a history of yachting will probably tell you that yachting was begun by Cleopatra. There is really no reason why Cleopatra should even be mentioned in the history of yachting. One day some authority credited her and that single mention has made her the customary founder, as the nonsense is copied from one book to the next.

Nor does language supply the answer. Many inventions and concepts come into existence before any name they are now recognised by, and the meaning of names is too changeable in any case. For instance, 'port' – which now designates a particular type of wine – was once the label of all reds shipped through Porto. The advent of the name does not indicate when port was invented.

Bogus firsts are readily accepted because one can research a posited first in detail, without becoming aware of the real first before it. This is particularly a problem when the actual first comes long ago, or from a non-Western society, while the supposed first is in more recent times, in the West.

Every supposed first has to be treated with scepticism, even when it could only have arisen in living memory. The electronic computer could not have been invented more than a short time ago, and required so much in resources and manpower that it could hardly pass unnoticed. Yet, the ENIAC computer of 1946 is said to be the first, and computers of the 1930s have been forgotten even by many computer experts.

Verification consists primarily of going back to the earliest possible starting point, and working through the records of activity and achievement, towards the posited first which is being checked. In the case of the electronic computer, this does not mean going back very far, because electricity generation is comparatively new. However many other innovations have to be looked for from the beginning of history or earlier.

Archaeology reveals a long list of familiar things from prehistoric times before writing began. For example, in the ruined town at Çatal Hüyük in Turkey are 8000-year-old traces of printed cloth, brick houses, egg cups, mirrors, lead, copper, beer and wine. Prehistoric Egyptian sites provide glass and paint, fine pottery and furniture of various kinds.

These finds cannot usually be relied on to establish a first. Seals were used at Çatal Hüyük, but they may already have been widespread elsewhere. Most prehistoric archaeology is limited in its usefulness here to tossing out bogus firsts posited for historic times. Occasionally it does narrow down the locale of an invention clearly enough; for example several representations of skis have been found in Scandinavia, thousands of years older than any evidence from elsewhere.

### Sources and Authenticity

Archaeological evidence, and artefacts and monuments, continue to be important sources for the historic period. For example, the bikini's origins are only known from Roman art, and Greek mechanical computers only because one turned up in an ancient shipwreck.

Another service of archaeology and relics is to corroborate what is recorded in old literature. Modern scholars usually refuse to take ancient books at face value when they speak of anything which is amazing, or which today's experts imagine could only have happened in modern times. For example the entire ancient history of China was written off by western scholars as an ingenious fabrication – until archaeology confirmed the discredited claims made by early Chinese historians. Ancient descriptions of the pyramids would be dismissed now as obvious nonsense, except that the pyramids themselves prove that the implausible tales of Greek writers are true.

Fresh finds repeatedly bear out what was previously known only from distrusted books. Still, most experts refuse to conclude that any ancient source is more reliable than they once allowed, in relation to issues on which archaeology is silent.

Szu Ma Chien, a Chinese historian of 100B.C., was corroborated in his account of the Sharng Dynasty by discoveries since the 1890s of Sharng bone inscriptions. In the 1970s, the famous grave of the First Emperor was opened, and found to be precisely as Szu Ma Chien describes, right down to the perpetual motion machinery which was the first of its kind (see p. 244). But Szu Ma Chien's history of the early Jo period – which lies between Sharng and the First Emperor – is still dismissed as an idealised misconception which he too credulously accepted; and the whole of his account of the pre-dynastic era is treated as pure mythology by modern experts. Were archaeology to come to Szu Ma Chien's support in relation to either of these periods, then and only then they will acknowledge that he was right. The position taken in compiling *Whose Bright Idea Was That?*, however, is that Szu Ma Chien is a historian with superior critical judgement, whose version is to be preferred to the version of his dogmatic modern critics.

The literary record is so copious that it is obviously impossible to comb it all. Inevitably some important things will have been missed. It starts with inscriptions and papyruses from Egypt and clay tablets from Mesopotamia. Unlike the earliest Chinese scribes, their authors used durable material, producing originals which have survived to prove that they already knew how to write, so their authenticity is not doubted. However, many firsts which probably belong to the Old Kingdom Egyptians will never be known. It is sad to ponder how losses have spoilt the chance to explore the intellectual heights reached 5000 years ago. One ancient writer, Clemens Alexandrinus (c. 150A.D.–c. 220), in his *Stromata*, speaks of a 42-volume early Egyptian compendium of factual knowledge. If just the six volumes it devoted to medicine alone had been saved, ideas about science in highest antiquity would be transformed radically.

Civilisation next arose in the Indus valley, but the script it developed has never been deciphered. Chinese history began in the 3rd millennium B.C., but the oldest Chinese literature only survives in copies made thousands of years later. This is what makes it so easy for modern experts to challenge its authenticity. Huarng Di, the earliest ruler to be regarded as historical by Szu Ma Chien, may indeed have lived before the time of written records, but there is no reason to suppose that an accurate and detailed oral tradition from his time did not reach a literate age following soon after – as we know has happened in other societies.

As a matter of fact, these records which experts call myth – and which I treat as history – disclose only a few world firsts, because of the lead the West had over China in those early times. Differences of opinion over authenticity become more of a practical issue in connection with the Classical Age, beginning about 2000 years later. Quite a few texts from this later period are passed as authentic by modern experts – because internal clues settle their dating. But let an author omit such accidental clues, and there is no way they will allow his work to belong to him. An important example is the *Dao De Jing*, which according to ancient tradition was the work of Lao Dzu, around 500B.C.

As the chief classic of Taoism, it is a bestseller in dozens of English translations. Its authenticity is vital in *Whose Bright Idea Was That?* because only if the traditional attribution is right can the *Dao De Jing* be declared the first exposition of a number of important beliefs.

Modern experts insist that it was written instead by multiple authors around 300 B.C. But when you look at their reasons, there is only broad assumption, circular argument and hot air. They add that we have no historical evidence to support the traditional attribution to Lao Dzu – despite the fact that it is attested by Szu Ma Chien, 2100 years closer to the event than they and by another book written soon after 300B.C..

To be fair to these sceptics, nothing in the text itself proves it older than 300B.C.; but since it has neither anything to prove it more recent than 600B.C., the ancient attributions are the only guides. Problems like this always beset undated texts which exist only in late copies, because the age cannot be proven by philological means nor archaeological dating.

The same thing occurs in the study of ancient Greek literature – for example, the argument over the authorship of Homer's works. It is fundamentally unscientific, flatly rejecting clear external evidence – like Szu Ma Chien's – when textual evidence supports neither point of view. This dodgy methodology is so popular in contemporary scholarship because of the self-image of modern experts. They fervently believe that they possess an enlightenment denied their predecessors centuries ago, and that only the modern scientific approach makes penetrating criticism feasible.

These experts have deep-seated prejudices about how the past ought to have been; they are prepared to rely on evidence when it lends them support, and to reject it when it runs contrary to their preconceptions. Their preconceptions become the balance in which all the evidence is weighed.

They use what an eminent English jurist called the 'goodness gracious me test' – by which you read down anything which is uncomfortably different from what you think it should be. Confronted with a tour de force, like Homer's *Iliad* or Lao Dzu's *Dao De Jing*, coming too early in history to fit one's comfortable scheme, it is the easiest thing to be sceptical about its age and authorship. When an ancient writer reports achievements which you don't think the period could have sustained, it is no trouble to label such reports exaggeration, mythology or idealisation. The ignorant scepticism of old women is easily passed off as the penetrating scepticism of objective scientists.

For the purposes of the present work, it is mostly Greek and Chinese literature to which these arguments apply; and only a minority of the firsts extracted from them comes into question as a result. However, foreseeing objections from readers who accept the goodness-gracious-me assumptions, I had to run over the conceptual issue rather bluntly. I have accepted corrections based on convincing philological argument, internal evidence as to authorship or trustworthy external evidence. These are valid criteria for assessing the accuracy of historical works and the authenticity of literary monuments, which have been applied by creditable critics ancient and modern.

In early ages, most firsts were the work of only a few societies; obviously with the passage of time, others rose to a position from which they could lead the world. Texts from Biblical literature, India, the Hittites and Persians were added to the material which has to be searched as, later, were works in Latin, Japanese, Arabic, etc.

There has been a great increase in the volume of written records in the last thousand years, and comparatively little of it has been destroyed. Compared to ancient literature, the proportion translated into English has decreased and the frequency with which firsts are revealed has slumped.

Together these factors mean it has not been feasible to survey recent texts with any semblance of comprehensiveness, and I have often had to rely on information in studies, compilations and works of reference. Because so much complete material survives from recent times, it is generally easier to search specifically for a subject. In consulting ancient sources, because most specialist books have been destroyed, one generally has to hunt down incidental references to special subjects in general books.

Obviously a book like this has to be based on hundreds of books and papers. A few of these I rely on over and over again, even more for the help they give in the verification process than for the subjects they supply for entries. There is the Roman author Pliny for instance, and the British scholar Joseph Needham. Needham's *Science and Civilisation in China* (Cambridge, Cambridge University Press), which will soon be more than twenty large volumes, is the foremost work of modern antiquarian scholarship – indispensable not only for information about China, but for the many comparisons it draws with other leading cultures. Other Needham admirers may notice how often I have departed from his conclusions. But in truth, it is his visionary work that gives people like me the opportunity to reach conclusions of our own, and it isn't easy to see how I could have written this book without access to his.

Most of the sources I have used are either very old or rather academic and specialised, and the best thing at this point is to refer the reader who wants more information to the booklet *On the Sources of the Penguin Book of Firsts*, mentioned above.

By way of acknowledgement, I should point out that compiling this book has only been possible because of the large and judiciously chosen collections in the great libraries of Canberra (especially those of the A.N.U.), Sydney and Melbourne. If only they had opening hours worthy of their contents, a mere dilettante might aspire to any feat of scholarship within their doors.

## Inclusions and Exclusions

Inevitably something has been left out which some readers are convinced should have been included. The selection criteria will help to determine whether the omission is consistent with the scheme of the book or due to the author's mistake or ignorance. Enlightenment and corrections from readers are warmly welcomed; please send them to me care of the publishers, P.O. Box 257, Ringwood, Victoria 3134, Australia.

All the entries are human firsts: firsts in natural phenomena are unknowable. There is also a major division of human innovation – artistic creativity – which cannot be itemised in firsts. Here it is just the categories that are entered – the novel, the pagoda, the feature film and so on – as well as techniques and approaches, like social realism and perspective.

Nothing has been included as a first if there is a known precedent for it, or even if it seems clear that there would have been a precedent. The reinvention of a technique, the rediscovery of a land, the restatement of an idea, and so forth, all have to be omitted. The famous inventors, explorers, philosophers and scientists who miss out because of this rule were sometimes no less creative in their achievements than the obscure predecessors we acknowledge – but this is a book of firsts, and seconds do not belong.

To be a first, the subject has to be distinguishable in its identity from anything that has gone before. Improvements, reconceptualisations, anything that is only different in degree, are passed over. In many cases the test imposed is how much qualification would be necessary in the title to make a first of it. For instance, the 'first flight around the world' belongs in here, but the 'first East–West flight around the world by a woman with only three stops' is too qualified. Exceptions are made where an arbitrary turning point has a special significance in people's minds – for example, the four-minute mile and the city with a million people.

Entries are not made for developments which are first only in a particular country, region, era or group of people. Again, there is a bracket of exceptions. Where, because of its character, a thing which is first only by reference to a locality or class has a world significance, it is entered. This exception is made for discovery and exploration of previously unknown lands, the first literature in the various languages and some great engineering breakthroughs.

Many subjects are left out because of the lack of clues. Frequently evidence which does not put matters beyond doubt has to be relied on, but by themselves guesswork and even educated speculation cannot support an entry. Many of these unavoidable omissions are referred to in the introductions to each section. Most go back to prehistoric times, and most cultures have myths, traditions and reconstructions, which anyone who needs an answer on such matters can consult. To incorporate such accounts into this book is not feasible because of the many disagreements in detail between prehistorians and mythographers, and within the ranks of each.

M.E. Richardson
Canberra, Dec. 1996

\* *Whose Bright Idea Was That?* was first published in Australia as *The Penguin Book of Firsts*.

# ACKNOWLEDGEMENTS

The author's most important debt is to writers and compilers of the sources on which this book is based. They are too numerous to name here but many are identified in the book *On the Sources of the Penguin Book of Firsts*, obtainable by contacting the author at Halstead Press, 19A Boundary St, Rushcutter's Bay, New South Wales, 2011.

People who facilitated the project by lending approbation to it or aid to its author include Georg Karlov and John Ferguson in Sydney; Clare Forster and Robert Sessions of Penguin Books; James Peterson, Dermid McGrath and Paul Hitchenson in Canberra; my wife Carolyn, and parents Grace and Jack. All who offered information or checked passages – amongst them Tim Sherratt of Australian Science Archives Project, Canberra, and Dominique Suet of Paris – deserve thanks for their contributions, but not the blame for errors or misjudgements, which are mine.

For her editing I thank Foong Ling Kong in Melbourne; for practical assistance with text and pictures, Nathalie Suet, Pauline Husen and Vanessa Hill of Halstead Press; Carolyn Conlon; Alison White, and Yong Chui Hsia. Apologies no less than gratitude go to those deserving acknowledgement whom I've accidentally overlooked.

# PICTURE SOURCES

*The Australasian Sketcher*, June 1879. **330.**

The Bodleian Library, Oxford. Ms. Bodl. 264. (Manuscript of 1338 A.D., probably originating in Bruges.) Fol. 22r. **335.**

The British Museum, London. Reference: 208. Neg. no. PS209027. **315.**

*Chin Ding Sho Shir Tung Kao*, 1742. **241.**

*Hsin Yi Hsiarng Yao*, by Su Sung, 1092 A.D. 7b-8a. **202.**

Jarng Dse Duarn's scroll "Going up River at Ching Ming Time", 13th century A.D., detail. **106.**

Dr. M. Lay, author of *Ways of the World*, Primavera Press, Sydney, 1993. Personal photo. **105.**

J. Lissarrague; previously published in P. Lissarrague, *Clément Ader: Inventeur d'Avions*, Editions Privat, Toulouse, 1990. **290.**

Lu Chi, *Ping Fu Tieh*. **4.**

The (former) Mawson Institute for Antarctic Research, Adelaide. BAE S. 14B. **308.**

National Archaeological Museum, Athens. No. 3477. **326.**

National Film and Sound Archive, Canberra. **37.**

*Pyrotechnia or, a Discourse of Artificial Fireworks*, by John Babington, Ralph Mab, London, 1635. **247.**

The Science Museum, London. **95.**

*Sport in Ancient Egypt*, by A. Touny and S. Wenig, Edition Leipzig, 1969, Pl. 12 (Steffin Wenig). **323.**

*Tien Gung Kai Wu*, originally published with illustrations in 1637. The illustrations used here are from a Ching Dynasty edition. **116, 120, 126, 234, 235, 239, 242.**

# SPELLING OF CHINESE NAMES

Nearly all sounds in Chinese are roughly similar to common sounds in English. However the Wade-Giles spelling system, which used to be the standard, departs from natural pronunciation in some confusing ways. The *pinyin* system, which has largely replaced it, makes gross departures from natural pronunciation and is only suitable for trained readers. So in this book, Chinese is spelt just as the letters are pronounced in normal English. (Pronouncing the 'u' as in 'put', 'ai' as in 'taipan', 'e' as in 'dated'). Familiar names that have long been standard in peculiar spellings retain those spellings in this book, e.g. Hong Kong, Szechuan, Confucius. The following list can be used to convert romanisation systems used in other books.

|  | WADE-GILES | PINYIN | NEEDHAM'S SYSTEM |
|---|---|---|---|
| arn | an | an | Needham's system is roughly |
| arng | ang | ang | the same as Wade-Giles. But |
| aw | o | e | 'h' is used instead of an |
| b | p | b | apostrophe. |
| ch | ch' | q, ch | |
| d | t | d | |
| ds | ts | z | |
| dzu | tzu | zi | |
| eh | eh | e | |
| erh | erh | er | |
| ew | ü | ü | |
| g | k | g | |
| hs | hs | x | |
| ien | ien | ian | |
| ir | ih | i | |
| j | ch | zh, j | |
| k | k' | k | |
| o | ou | ou | |
| p | p' | p | |
| r | j | r | |
| szu | szu | si | |
| t | t' | t | |
| ts | ts' | c | |
| tzu | tz'u | ci | |
| ung | ung | ong | |

## SPELLING OF ARABIC NAMES

Exceptions are made for very familiar spellings, e.g. Koran, Cairo.

| ARABIC LETTER | TRANSLITERATION | SHORT VOWELS | |
|---|---|---|---|
| ء | ' | | |
| ب | b | ´ | a |
| ت | t | ٴ | u |
| ث | th | ٍ | i |
| ج | j | **LONG VOWELS** | |
| ح | ḥ | | |
| خ | kh | ـَا | ā |
| د | d | ـُو | ū |
| ذ | dh | ـِي | i |
| ر | r | **DIPHTHONGS** | |
| ز | z | | |
| س | s | ـَوْ | aw |
| ش | sh | ـَيْ | ay |
| ص | ṣ | ـِيّ | ivy |
| ض | ḍ | ـُوّ | uww |
| ط | ṭ | | |
| ظ | ẓ | | |
| ع | ' | | |
| غ | gh | | |
| ف | f | | |
| ق | q | | |
| ك | k | | |
| ل | l | | |
| م | m | | |
| ن | n | | |
| و | w | | |
| ه | h | | |
| ة | t | | |
| ي | y | | |

# POPULAR
# MISTAKEN FIRSTS

|  | **FIRST COMMONLY CLAIMED** |
|---|---|
| Aesop | fable 22 |
| *Alkali Act* (U.K.) | pollution legislation 374 |
| Arabs | algebra 187 |
| | place value numbers 182 |
| Archimedes | screw 260 |
| the Ashes | international cricket series 337 |
| Assyrians | sewer 93 |
| Athens 1896 | Olympic gold medal 317 |
| Australia | crawl stroke (swimming) 341 |
| | pavlova 57 |
| | polocrosse 337 |
| | secret ballot 71 |
| Australian rules | derivative of Gaelic football 330 |
| Baekeland, L. H. | plastic 366 |
| Bell, Alexander Graham | telephone 264 |
| Bentham, Jeremy | utilitarianism 131 |
| Bering, Vitus | discovery of Bering Strait and Alaska 298 |
| birth control pill | oral contraceptive 222 |
| Bologna | university 79 |
| Brearly, Harry | stainless steel 239 |

# I

# LANGUAGE AND
# LITERATURE

If there were a way of knowing what was invented first, it might turn out
to be a crudely fashioned tool, a primitive garment for keeping warm, or
something equally simple and ordinary. But the first revolutionary invention was probably language. Many wonderful things have been contrived,
but it is difficult to think of anything done before or since which comes
close to language in power and importance. Speech leaves no trace, and
language came so early in cultural evolution that there is no hope of finding out when it started.

## 1. WRITING AND PRINTING

Writing, on the other hand, has only been invented recently. Because of the
durable traces it leaves in some media, the oldest writings still in existence
are close to the first and it is easy to document landmarks in writing and
printing. Although civilisation came before writing, no civilisation can go for
long without learning to write. This means that historical records were
begun when the memory of the dawning age of civilisation was still being
passed on. The printed word came much later. But at an unknown time and
place in the prehistoric period, two technologies akin to printing were
developed long before writing began. One was the production of seals that
impressed designs in clay; the other, the printing of designs on fabric.

Writing was invented by the Mesopotamians shortly after
4000B.C. The oldest documents have been discovered at the **Writing**
site of Erech, a city of Southern Mesopotamia (in present-day
Iraq). The earliest of them is a small limestone tablet from this
era, inscribed in an ancient and unknown script that was later
superseded by Sumerian cuneiform. The tablet reads from top

to bottom, beginning on the right-hand side. Together with other written fragments from this time, it reveals a written language with a vocabulary of at least 900 distinct characters.

**Cuneiform Script**   The cuneiform system that was later adopted consists of wedge-shaped marks impressed in clay tablets with writing sticks. It came into use after 3500B.C. and for 3000 years was the normal script for the cultures that occupied Mesopotamia.

**Hieroglyphs**   The Egyptians worked out their written characters in the first half of the 4th millennium B.C., probably beginning around 3700. The script was almost complete by the reign of the first pharaoh, Menes, c. 3500B.C. Each character, or hieroglyph, is a stylised picture which originally carried the meaning of the object depicted. At an early stage, shortly before the time of Menes, many of the hieroglyphs took on an additional purely phonetic quality, and came to represent syllables – thus they could be used and combined to make any word not represented pictorially. By Menes's time they were being arranged left to right, right to left and top to bottom.

**Cursive Writing**   Scribes using Egyptian hieroglyphs began developing more fluid ways of writing them almost as soon as they were invented, to serve when speed was more important than formal rigidity. These developments created the hieratic script, which grew and changed much faster than hieroglyphics. Early in the Old Kingdom Period (c. 3500–c. 2500B.C.), by the time of the 2nd Dynasty (c. 3300B.C.) cursive or 'running' writing had developed, and whole words were being written without lifting the hand to start fresh strokes.

**Chinese Characters**   Chinese writing was probably invented in the first half of the 3rd millennium B.C. when ancestors of the Chinese, living in the vicinity of the Yellow River, developed the idea of making symbols to identify words. They were inspired by the footprints of birds and animals, and the knots traditionally made in cords to keep rudimentary records. The diversity of line patterns displayed the possibility of distinguishing things by writing. China's first scribe, Tsarng Jieh, who may have worked around 2500B.C., established Chinese script, which he must have done by bringing together assorted symbols already in existence, and inventing others himself. Although the language has grown and changed a great deal, the scripts of modern Chinese, Japanese and Korean are descendants of Tsarng's system.

**Alphabet**   The Semites of South-west Asia and Sinai, in about 1700B.C., developed an alphabet of thirty letters, borrowed from the hieratic script of Egyptians working at the local turquoise mines. Each letter stood for a single consonant sound. There were no vowels – the reader was left to add them, just as if we had spelt bucket 'bkt'.

The use of this alphabet travelled north and was adopted by the Phoenicians by about 1200B.C. The Phoenicians selected twenty-two letters and introduced the alphabetical order to make them easier to learn. Each letter was named after a word it stood for. The whole list was called the 'aleph beth'.

**Alphabetical Order**

The Greeks were already using writing systems 3000 years ago. However, the scripts of that time did not remain long in use, and the present Greek alphabet was not introduced until about 800B.C. The oldest specimen is an inscription on a wine jug found at Athens, believed to have been made in the 700s B.C. Its characters are the lineal ancestors of the modern letters of Greece and Russia.

**Greek Alphabet**

The oldest existing specimen of the Roman alphabet is an inscription of the 7th century B.C. found not at Rome but at Praeneste in central Italy. This alphabet, which is now used to write Latin, English and all the Western European languages, was first adopted shortly after 700B.C. by the Latin peoples in Italy, amongst whom were the Romans. They obtained it by borrowing the Greek alphabet in use by their southern neighbours – the Greeks of Campania – and modifying it to suit their own language. The Latin peculiarity of using 'C' in place of 'K', which began soon after the new alphabet came in, is probably due to the influence of their northern neighbours, the Etruscans.

**Roman Alphabet**

Runes originated amongst Germanic tribes in Central Europe, before 300B.C., as mystical symbols inscribed on pieces of fruit-tree wood, used for casting lots. Late in the 3rd century B.C., in the present-day Tyrol district of Austria, the runic alphabet was developed by combining Italian letters with the German symbols. The system spread through Central Europe to Britain and Scandinavia.

**Runes**

Shorthand made its first appearance as a heavily abbreviated form of the Chinese script of the Warring States Period (481–221B.C.). It was used by the government of the powerful southern state of Chu on the Yangtze River. Later on, the Chinese adopted a different shorthand system but, as a calligraphic exercise, a poet of the 200s A.D. wrote the passage

**Shorthand**

below in the old system, showing how the first shorthand must have looked. It is written from top to bottom, right to left.

Shorthand

**Cryptography**

The oldest code writing was used to disguise an industrial secret: enciphered instructions on how to make a kind of glaze for ceramics were written on a clay tablet from Mesopotamia, unearthed near present-day Baghdad. The tablet was written around 1500B.C., and three encoding methods were used to make it unintelligible except to initiated readers. One was to respell the words using phonetically similar substitute characters, following the rarest pronunciations of the replacement characters (rather like taking the 'gh' out of 'tough' to use instead of the 'f' in 'fish'). The other methods were to shorten words by dropping endings, and to vary the way words were spelt in different places within the document.

**Alphabet for the Blind**

Valentin Hauy, who founded an institute for blind people in Paris in 1785A.D., was an expert calligrapher. In 1793 he devised simplified letters to be embossed on the page so that blind readers could understand them by touch.

**Braille**

In 1825 Louis Braille was a sixteen-year-old student at the Hauy Institute. He created a new alphabet in which each character is represented by an arrangement of up to twelve dots, which blind people, once trained, could write as well as read. The better known six-dot Braille system is a later refinement.

The catalogue of astronomical works for a library of Sargon I (a Mesopotamian ruler early in the 2nd millennium B.C.) at Agane, carries an interesting instruction to readers. It asks them to write down the numbers of the tablets they require, for the librarian to retrieve. This is the first catalogue with library numbers and the oldest reference to a 'stack service'. **Library Numbers**

People began to make bibliographies of selected works of Sumerian literature, at the opening of the 2nd millennium B.C. in Mesopotamia. The oldest one that has been recovered is remarkable mainly for its tiny size. It is a clay tablet inscribed with cuneiform writing from about 1800B.C. Although it is only 6.3 cm tall and 3.9 cm. wide, it contains the titles of sixty-two literary works, in two columns on each side. Many of them are Sumerian classics, which are quoted elsewhere in this book. **Bibliography**

Stamps made of clay were used by Mesopotamian scribes early in the 2nd millennium B.C. – much in the way people use rubber stamps today. Some of them were equipped with interchangeable parts, making it possible to alter the reading from one impression to another. **Stamp Printing**

Printing began in China at the start of the Tarng Dynasty (618A.D.–906) and was first used for single sheets, with pictures and text. Hsewarn Dsarng (602A.D.–664), who had travelled through India to study Buddhism, had pictures of Samomta Bhadra printed and circulated on his return to China in 645A.D. – the earliest use of printing on record. **Printing**

During the 11th century A.D. barbarians descended on an outlying part of the Chinese empire to retake an area in the northwest that only strong government had been able to keep in Chinese hands. One of the places threatened was Dun Huarng, a centre of Buddhist devotion. Before making a getaway the Buddhist monks walled up the Dun Huarng library, which remained intact for a thousand years until it was raided early this century for the British Museum by adventurer, Sir Aurel Stein. The library contained books in nine languages, amongst them a Chinese edition of the *Diamond Sutra*, printed **Printed Book** in 868A.D. It is the oldest extant printed book, and it and a few other 9th-century publications are the first books to have been printed.

**Moveable Type**

Early in the 1st millennium B.C., in Asia Minor (present-day Turkey), there were stamps used for printing on clay tablets, each of which bore a single character from a pre-alphabetic script – but they could only be used independently, one after another. Typesetting in moveable type was invented by Bi Sheng in the 1040s A.D. during the Sung Dynasty (960A.D.–1279). To make a typefont he inscribed Chinese characters on individual clay blocks and fired them in a kiln. His typesetting was done within an iron frame on an iron plate, and the types were held in position by a cement that set after heating. Moveable type – which is so often represented as printing's great breakthrough – is now of minor importance. It never took over in Chinese printing, and is practically a thing of the past in Western printing. Lithography [see below] is a much more important invention.

**Metal Type**

Metal type was first cast in tin during the 13th century, again in Sung Dynasty China.

**Lithography**

In Munich in 1796A.D., a young Czech playwright, Aloys Senefelder, stumbled on the secret of lithographic printing. He is believed to have begun by writing a laundry account on a piece of stone, which he had on hand for preparing printing ink. Senefelder had been indulging in home printing (with copper plates), for the purpose of making copies of his plays, and consequently possessed stone, ink, and the acidic preparation *aqua fortis*. He found that after leaving aqua fortis on the stone, his laundry account stood out in relief, because the ink had protected the surface from dissolving. He was able to take prints from the stone by inking the raised parts. An almost constant series of improvements since Senefelder's washing day has turned lithography into the dominant method of printing, the one used for this book.

**Colour Printing**

The technique of colour printing was developed in China late in the 11th century A.D. Its first important practical function was in the minting of multicoloured paper money by the Sung Dynasty government from 1107 onwards. Notes were printed with a blue background, a circle design in vermilion and notations in black; this complexity of printing made forgery difficult.

Soon afterwards the first printed colour picture appeared:

In the oldest multicolour printed picture, a legendary hero steals the peaches of immortality from the Queen Mother of the West (early 12th century A.D.).

a woodcut made from multiple plates of an original painted in the 8th century A.D. by Wu Dao Dzu.

**Printed Colour Picture**

## 2. WORLD LITERATURES

What counts as literature is fairly strictly defined for the purposes of this section. It has to be in writing and only includes original works of creative expression. That rules out purely functional composition – like inventories and directories – and translations of foreign works. Many literary languages have started out with translations of religious books like the Bible or Buddhist sutras and only then developed original content.

The literatures are identified by language, not by race or location – except where a number of languages is grouped geographically. Some have been left out because it has not been possible to discover the first: this includes Greek, Jewish, Celtic and Native American literatures.

The oldest literature in the world today is a range of snippets of commonplace songs from the Old Kingdom period (c. 3500–2500B.C.) in Egypt. They are inscribed in hieroglyphs

**Literature**

**Egyptian** on the walls of tomb chapels, dating back to about the 33rd century B.C. Such songs must have been written on the less permanent medium of papyrus a century or two earlier – long before literature appeared in any other land.

**Cuneiform** Southern Mesopotamia was the next country in which literary writing began. Shortly after 3000B.C. scribes began writing verses of Sumerian mythology in cuneiform script on clay tablets. The oldest surviving copies are two legends of the god Enlil, which seem to have been inscribed about 2800B.C.

**Chinese** The first Chinese civilisation left no inscriptions on durable material. The earliest Chinese works, including some extant in the *Book of Documents* (*Shu Jing*) were composed before 2300B.C., but archaeology cannot tell us when they were committed to writing. In those days Chinese script was simple and probably only suited to basic record-keeping, but literature had probably made its beginning by around 2000B.C.

**Phoenician** Early Phoenician literature is the oldest from an alphabetic language. All that remains are some fragmentary translations in Greek of a historical work, the *Annals of Tyre*, and of the religious writings of Sanchuniathon, who lived in Berytus (present-day Beirut, Lebanon). He was a priest, and probably lived in the 11th century B.C.; if so his work predates the *Annals of Tyre*, part of which can be traced back to the 10th century.

**Indian** The original scriptures of Indian religion are the four *Vedas*, the oldest being the *Rigveda*, which includes some hymns that date back to about 1500B.C. No one can tell when the *Rigveda* was first committed to writing; the probable date is slightly earlier than 1000B.C. The classical Sanskrit script which the *Vedas* are now written in is a later development. The script of the first copy of the *Rigveda* is no longer known.

**Latin** For all its endlessly trumpeted splendours Latin literature got away to a very modest start when some anonymous pieces of rustic verse – sacred songs or ballads – were written down, probably in Rome, in the 6th century B.C. Indeed the rustic and modest output set the standard of several centuries to come.

**Persian** In 520B.C. or thereabouts, Darius the Great, Emperor of Persia, wrote a record of his achievements. It is a lengthy declaration of his military successes and moral superiority. The

Persians used other languages more than their own in documents, and Darius's work appeared simultaneously in the more conventional Median and Babylonian as well as in Persian. The three versions are preserved on a contemporary rock-face inscription at Behistun in Western Iran. The author was not a modest man, but he was obviously afraid of readers' doubts:

> There is also much else that has been done by me that is not graven in this inscription . . . lest he who shall read this inscription hereafter should then hold that which has been done by me to be too much and should not believe it, should take it to be lies.

**Armenian** Armenian literature was ushered into being by St. Mesrop Mashtotz, who adapted the Greek alphabet to the Armenian language in 404A.D., so that he could distribute Christian literature to the people. Mesrop and his followers immediately began translating, and writing in their own right. The first batch of original works includes Mesrop's biography of the Patriarch Narses, the histories of Agathangelos and Faustus, and the religious writings of David 'The Invincible' and Eznik.

**Georgian** Early in the 5th century A.D. Christian monks – including the founder of Armenian literature, St. Mesrop – adapted the Greek alphabet to serve as a script for translations of the Bible into Georgian. Later in the century the earliest original works in Georgian utilised this script. They were biographies of saints; St. Shushanik's biography, from about 480, is the earliest in existence.

**German** German language for over a thousand years has existed in two basic forms: the Low German and the High. However the first German literature was in neither, but in the ancient Gothic dialect. This was the tongue used for traditional narrative poetry by the ancestors of the later Germans, as they migrated from Asia to Europe, and settled there. During the 400s A.D. some of this verse was committed to writing in the Latin alphabet, so that the Gothic King, Theodoric (reigned 475A.D.–526), was in a position to give equal support to Gothic and Latin education and literature. None of this early literature survives, although the 4th-century Gothic translation of the Bible by Ulfilas gives us a good idea of the language.

**Arabic** Before Muhammad introduced Islam to Arabia – in the period now known as the Ignorance – there were many talented and imaginative poets composing odes amongst the nomadic Arabs. The crude Arabic script of the 500s A.D. was mainly used in the few towns for functional purposes, not literature. The people as a whole were antipathetic to writing, and poetry was transmitted orally. However a few of the most highly esteemed odes was committed to writing just before Islamic times, probably around 600A.D. The first of these to have been composed was the *Mu'allaqat* of Imru' al-Qays (died c. 540A.D.), foremost of the nomad poets.

**English**

Two important events laid the foundations for English literature: in the 400s A.D. Saxons and Angles came to England from Germany and replaced the old local tongues, Celtic and Latin, with their primaeval English. In 596A.D. St. Augustine and forty monks entered England, and introduced not only Christianity, but the means of writing English in the Roman alphabet. In the following century literary works began to be recorded in this fashion; the earliest as far as we can tell is the poem *Widsith*, a historical survey of prominent people of Europe, mostly from the Germanic race of which the Angles and Saxons were tribes.

**Tibetan**

In 1899 a Chinese monk, restoring cave murals in the frontier town of Dun Huarng, came across a completely forgotten library inside an ancient cave complex. It had been bricked up in the 11th century A.D. to save it from Tibetan marauders. Inside he found over 10,000 books, perfectly preserved for eight and a half centuries, written in nine languages. British marauders led by Sir Aurel Stein stole most of the library in 1907. The French finished his work of plunder the following year. Amongst the treasures carted off to London and Paris were the oldest printed book in the world [I, 1] and the oldest Tibetan book in the world. The library's Tibetan chronicle is a rich collection including native mythology and verse, representative of a tradition going back prior to the first writing of Tibetan. The Tibetan literature began in the 7th century A.D. during the reign of the powerful and visionary King Srong-brt-san-sgam-po, who had a thirty-four character script adapted from India for use in Tibetan about 640. He seems to have been motivated largely by the need to translate Indian Buddhist texts into Tibetan, but the new script was put to use almost immediately for writing down Tibetan works.

**Japanese**

The development of Japanese literature was handicapped by the fact that Chinese writing was the only kind known in Japan. It is suited so much better to writing Chinese than Japanese that the first literary writers in Japan all used Chinese in preference to the local tongue. But during the 7th century A.D., Chinese characters, used phonetically to represent Japanese syllables, or semantically to represent Japanese words, came into literary use. Some of the many Japanese poems composed at this time must have been recorded in writing. The verse anthology, *Manyoshu*, completed in 751A.D., includes a lot of these, as well as earlier works which up till then existed only in oral tradition.

The ancient Turks lived not in present-day Turkey, but thousands of miles away, by the northern border of China. Their **Turkish** language, which in later times has been written in Arabic, Greek and Roman scripts, was first recorded in North Asian Altaic characters. The oldest Turkish documents are inscriptions in stone in present-day Mongolia. In 744A.D., one group of Turks, the Uighurs, established a thriving nation state. An obituary of its second ruler, Maw Yen Chaw, is the earliest Turkish inscription that can be called a work of literature. It appears on a stone monument, dating probably from 759A.D. or 760, at Shine-Usu in Northern Mongolia, and in an autobiographical style it tells of Maw's administration, warfare and diplomacy, and of a city he had established on the Selenga River.

Latin was the literary language of France for some time after the French tongue evolved in the 800s A.D. The variety of **French** French known as Landue d'oil spread through most of Northern France, and the Francien dialect of it used in the Paris region was adopted in the following century for writing vernacular religious works of uncertain dates. Amongst them were sermons, a *Life of St. Ledger* and a *Passion*.

Since before 900A.D., Scandinavian chieftains had court poets or *skalds* in their retinues, composing verses to celebrate the **Scandinavian** deeds of their patrons, and to entertain the courtiers. Wherever the Norse settled, skalds went, but by the later part of the 10th century, the courts were mostly in Norway and the skalds were visiting Icelanders. When their works were first committed to writing is not known. In the 12th century there was a great blossoming of Icelandic writings in verse, prose histories and sagas, but some of the skaldic verse could well have been written down as early as 1000A.D.

**Russian**

The event that set the scene for the birth of Russian literature was the conversion to Christianity of Vladimir I of Kiev and his kingdom, the Kiev Rus, in 988A.D. In the previous century St. Cyril had adapted the Greek alphabet to the 'Old Slavic' dialect, and translated the Bible in it. Within a few decades of its official introduction in Kiev, Russian writers were enthusiastically using the new writing to record original Russian works in the vernacular language of their country: sermons, poetry, lives of saints, treatises and chronicles. They probably began around the 1020s or thirties, and a lot of the earliest material is still recorded in *The Tale of Bygone Years*, a chronology of the period up to 1118. The earliest known sermon and author are the *Sermon on Law and Grace*, by Ilarion, the metropolitan (chief archbishop) of Kiev – a work of considerable ingenuity and literary effect, published in 1050.

**Burmese**

In 1057A.D. the Burmese, under King Anorahta, conquered Thaton, capital city of the Mon people. They carried Mon scholars back to their own capital, Pa-gan, and in the ensuing years, learnt from them how to write, putting Burmese into characters that had originated in Southern India. By the end of the century, Burmese writers were giving vent to a vivacious literary impulse, in religious works and idealistic verse. The usual medium is thought to have been books with palm leaf pages, but all that remains today from this early time are stone inscriptions, many of literary interest.

**Hungarian**

The oldest surviving Hungarian work is the historical narrative written and collected by one of the King's secretaries in the 1100s A.D., during the reign of King Bela. However, in previous centuries, Hungarian bards had composed many ballads and lays extolling the exploits of their rude brothers and forebears, and rather fancifully drawing genealogies of their race back to Attila the Hun. These must have begun as unwritten verses, but in Bela's time, and perhaps in the previous century or two, some were written down; the secretary's compendium undoubtedly includes some of them in paraphrase renditions of the first Hungarian literature.

**Italian**

The idea of using the Italian vernacular for literary writing was delayed till late in the 1100s, by the popularity of Latin amongst educated Italians. Poetry in Italian was written in the Kingdom of Sicily and Naples during the reign of Hohenstaufen dynasty. The poet Pier delle Vigne, friend and secretary of Frederick II early in the 1200s, wrote high quality odes and canzones, and promoted the cause of the new literature. The King, too, was a poet, in his spare time. Their first predecessors in the previous century are anonymous.

Spain was an important home of literature long before a Spanish language existed: Latin, Arabic and Jewish authors there **Spanish** contributed works of international importance. Literature of a more local character arose after the Christian kingdoms of the 11th century gradually seized most of the power from the Islamic authorities. Poems and songs in Spanish dialects celebrated acts of heroism by Christian Spaniards, and retailed patriotic sentiments. It seems likely that poetry in the central dialect of Castille was the first to be committed to writing, in the 1100s. Most of it has been lost but the famous *Poem of the Cid* – a comparatively earthy narrative of the exploits of a noble warrior in the previous century – survives along with several others.

Dutch literature began in the 1100s A.D., in the dialect known as 'middle Dutch'. It was the vernacular tongue of a **Dutch** region north of France, of which Holland was only a part. Fragments alone remain of the Dutch narrative poems of that time, and they furnish so few clues as to dating that putting them in order is not possible. These poems belong to two separate traditions – both in imitation of French literature. 'Heroic poetry' was composed by minstrels for popular entertainment; 'courtly poetry' was the work of poets in the service of aristocratic houses. Heroic poetry is believed to be slightly earlier, but it may well be that courtly poetry was the first to be committed to writing. One of the poets is known by name: Henric van Veldeke, born in the Limburg region. His first known work is the legend of Servatius, in rhyming verse, written in 1170 at the request of the Countess of Loon.

Like many of Europe's modern languages, Portuguese emerged gradually, as new and local influences on a vernacular speech **Portuguese** descended from Latin marked it off from neighbour tongues. By the 1200s A.D., works were being written in an indisputably Portuguese language; the earliest book is *King Diniz's Book of Songs* (*Cancioneiro del Rei Dom Diniz*), a set of love songs and sententious verses by the 13th-century monarch. This book is generally taken as the starting point of literary Portuguese, but since it is a collection it is highly likely that individual poems were being written by Portuguese subjects earlier on, perhaps before 1200.

**Mongolian**

*The Secret History of the Mongols*, composed early in the 13th century, is an anonymous work in prose and verse concerned mainly with the story of Genghis Khan and his associates. It was the first Mongol work to be committed to writing, about 1240A.D. The Mongols use an Altaic script, like that of the Uighur Turks, but the *Secret History* survived to the 20th century only in a Chinese phonetic transcription, and translation.

**Thai**

In 1233A.D. the Thai alphabet, based on a script from Southern India, was officially introduced to the Kingdom of Siam. Vivid literary passages in the Thai language remain in some Sukothai inscriptions from later in the same century. Thai literature might have started very soon after the alphabet was devised, but nothing written on perishable materials is left from those times.

**Polish**

*Bogurodzica*, a poem addressed to the mother of God, is the earliest literary work in Polish. It was written late in the 1200s, but its diction and versification are more refined than those in many later works, suggesting that it draws on a sophisticated oral verse tradition.

**Vietnamese**

For about 1500 years, all the literature in Vietnam was written in Chinese. In the 13th century A.D., *chu nôm*, or southern script, was developed, opening the way for indigenous writing. (Chu nôm was built out of Chinese characters, altered and fitted to Vietnamese words and pronunciation.) The Tran Dynasty poet, Nguyên Thuyên, who lived in North Vietnam in the 14th century, was the first to exploit it in literature.

**Swahili**

Before Swahili literature, literary Swahili was in use in Zanzibar and East Africa for translating Arabic verse and stories, beginning in the 16th century A.D. Early in the 18th century original verse compositions began to appear. *The Lay of Tambuk* (*Utendi wa Tambuku*), an anonymous poem written in 1728, is the earliest known example.

**Illustrated Books**

The oldest play [II, 2] in existence, written in Egypt about the 21st century B.C., contains the earliest extant book illustrations. It has survived in a papyrus manuscript believed to have been copied out several centuries later. The period was an active one in book production; the illustrated papyrus is likely to be just one specimen of a practice that was adopted around then.

Enheduanna of Akkad, priestess, princess and poet, was the first woman to give named literary writings to posterity. She **Lady Writer** lived in Southern Mesopotamia around 2700B.C., during the early days of the flowering of Sumerian literature. From before her time no women and very few men can be identified as writers of literature: writing was used mainly for keeping lists, records and accounts. Fragmentary clay writing tablets recovered by archaeologists testify with tantalising brevity to her existence and work.

## 3. GENRES AND PUBLICATIONS

These entries cover the different types of general books which are published – such as dictionaries and biographies – and the various genres of literature, like epic poetry and ghost stories. Specialist books are entered elsewhere: for instance, medical books [VIII, 6], recipe book [III, I], atlas [V, 3] and so on. Drama is covered in Chapter II.

The earliest dictionaries were for translating one language into another. Proper dictionaries containing a comprehensive account **Dictionary** of the words of one language came much later: the first was *Explaining Words, Analysing Characters* (*Shuaw Wen Jieh Dzu*) compiled by Hsew Shen (in Law Yarng, c. 100A.D.). This Chinese dictionary is a triumph of painstaking linguistic research, and has been in constant use from its publication to the present day. There are entries for 9353 different characters – each one analysed into its constituent parts and given a meaning and pronunciation. The entries are arranged in order of radicals – the parts of characters that give a clue as to their meaning.

The earliest bilingual dictionary was a Sumerian-Akkadian dic- **Language** tionary produced in Mesopotamia on clay tablets in about **Dictionary** 2000B.C. About 500 years later a Sumerian–Babylonian–Hittite **Multilingual** dictionary was probably the world's first trilingual dictionary. **Dictionary**

*Regional Speech* (*Farng Yen*) by Yarng Hsiung, published in 15B.C., was the first dictionary of local dialects. It treated the **Dictionary of** various versions of the Chinese language from all over the **Dialects** country, but unfortunately has now been lost.

*Sounds Classified* (*Sheng Lei*) by Li Deng, published in the 3rd **Rhyming** century A.D. in China, is the first dictionary in which the **Dictionary** words are arranged into rhyming groups. Unlike dictionaries of rhyme in European languages, it was not meant primarily for use in composing rhyming verse. Because Chinese is not an alphabetic language, words are sometimes arranged by rhyme so they can easily be looked up.

**Thesaurus**

The first thesaurus is the *Literary Approximater* (*Erh Ya*), from China, perhaps as early as 800B.C. It is arranged into topic headings and gives the correct use of terms and explains distinctions in their meaning. It was compiled to help students of literature, and new editions were brought out up until the 2nd century B.C. Although only a short work, it contains many illustrations, especially of natural history subjects. It is not known whether the earliest editions were illustrated.

**Dictionary of Quotations**

A *Comprehensive Arrangement of the Grove of Flowers*, written in Chinese by Hsew Mien in 530A.D., was the world's first dictionary of quotations, and included selections from a wide range of Chinese literature and rhetoric up to the author's time. Unfortunately the book has now been lost.

**Dictionary of Biography**

The *Kitāb al Tabaqat al-Kabir* (*The Great Book of Classes*) by the Arabian scholar Ibn Sa'd (died 845A.D.) is the earliest biographical work comprehensive enough to be regarded as a dictionary. Its multiple volumes recount the lives and circumstances of thousands of important figures from all parts of the Islamic world, beginning with a long survey of the life of Muhammad (died 632A.D.). Muhammad's contemporaries and later figures of importance up to Ibn Sa'd's time are included, with details of their writings, occupations, travels, relatives and associates, circumstances and beliefs. Most of the research was done in Arabia and Iraq.

**Encyclopaedia**

Marcus Terentius Varro (116–27B.C.) was the most competent and prolific of Roman scholars. He wrote two whole encyclopaedias in the 1st century B.C. – *Antiquities of Things Human and Divine* (*Antiquitatum Rerum Humanarum et Divinarum*), completed in 47B.C., consisted of forty-one short books. The first was an introduction and guide. The next twenty-four covered a large range of subjects organised into four themes, in six books each: 'Who' (people), 'Where' (places), 'When' (times), and 'What' (affairs). The remaining books dealt with priests, temples, festivals, games, worship and divinity. His other encyclopaedia, *Disciplinarum*, in eleven books, is undated. It treated the main branches of liberal studies under the headings Grammar, Dialectic, Rhetoric,

Geometry, Arithmetic, Astronomy and Astrology, Music, Medicine and Architecture.

Late in the 400s B.C. the Greek sports enthusiast Hippias researched, wrote up and published a compilation of victors in the Olympic Games, from the date of their inception until his own time. His work is lost, and there is no way of knowing whether it included anything other than basic sporting records. It may have done, as some Greeks showed a fondness for listing superlative accomplishments which extended to dramatic performances and tourist attractions as well as feats of athletic prowess. **Book of Records**

*Origins of Ages* (*Shir Ben*), compiled by an unknown author in the 2nd century B.C., is the earliest book of firsts, one of a string of such books published in China up to the 18th century. Most of *Origins of Ages* would induce a state of drowsiness in modern readers, covering as it does the founders of now-obscure ruling houses and famous families. But it has an important section dealing with culture and invention that has been used in compiling this book. Our entry on pan pipes [II, 4], for instance, is translated directly out of it. With only a few hundred entries, *Origins of Ages* is one of the smallest books of firsts. The largest is *Investigating Things – the Mirror of Beginnings*, in ten volumes, published in China in 1735. **Book of Firsts**

The first entry ever to be written for *Whose Bright Idea Was That?* is this one, made at 8.24 p.m. on 27 November 1986. **Whose Bright Idea Was That? Entry**

Not many people these days know about Evagoras, a Greek who died in 374B.C. His main claims to fame are having been a ruler in Cyprus, who maintained his position by skilful diplomacy, fighting a losing war against the Persian Empire, and negotiating a favourable treaty. An admirer of his, the Athenian orator Isocrates (436–338B.C.), chose Evagoras as the subject of the first biographical book known to literature: a little work called *Evagoras*, written soon after his death. **Biography**

Aratus of Sicyon (271–213B.C.) was a politician, soldier and diplomat in Southern Greece who succeeded in writing his autobiography before being fatally poisoned. His memoirs, although perhaps commendable for noting the author's own weaknesses, are insultingly critical of people he disliked. **Autobiography**

China's *Book of Documents* (*Shu Jing*) is the world's first selection of historical documents. It is a compilation of the most important **Book of Historical Documents** speeches, submissions, announcements and proclamations, from the mid-3rd millennium B.C. till the 7th century B.C. The history book as we know it today had not been invented when the *Book of Documents* was put together in Northern China in the 6th century B.C. There were bald chronicles which recorded actual events, but only the *Book of Documents* shed light on causal relationships and historical evolution.

**History Book**

The history book took form at the hands of Herodotus (born c. 485B.C.), a Greek from Halicarnassus in present-day Turkey. His *Histories* is a very readable, skilfully written account of Greece, West Asia and Egypt, tracing the history of the Persian Empire and its wars with Greece. Since his own time, Herodotus has been criticised for uncritically incorporating whatever he was told, a limitation he acknowledges in the book itself:

> For myself, though it be my business to set down that which is told me, to believe it is none at all of my business.
> Let that saying held good for the whole of my history.

**History-writing Bureau**

In 660A.D. China's Tarng Dynasty established a special wing of the bureaucracy in the capital Charng Arn, with the function of writing history. Its ample staff had the task of gathering evidence and records of all kinds; of writing up the past in official histories; and making copious accounts of their own time for the use of future historians. Rulers were not permitted by the officials of this bureau to look at the records of their own time, and this drove some of them mad with curiosity. Previously some individual historians and chroniclers were commissioned by governments on an occasional basis, but there had not been a permanent bureau of historians.

**Book of Jokes**

In Lu, a man with a long pole tried to go in through a city gate. But whether he held the pole upright or side on, he couldn't get through. He was at his wits' end. Then an old man came up and gave him advice which he acted on: 'I may not be a sage, but I have had plenty of experience. Why don't you saw the pole in half and carry it through that way?'

This is not the oldest joke ever published, and there will be some people who don't think it's the funniest. It earns a place here as a specimen from the first joke book, Harn Darn Jun's *Forest of Jokes* (c. 200 A.D.), from China late in the Harn Dynasty.

**Sex Manual**

Once the idea of sex manuals gets around, they seem to blossom in large numbers, as publishing in recent decades shows. But in the past their survival record has been dismal – sooner or later societies go through a wowseristic stage when all such lascivious literature vanishes. A Chinese bibliography of around 100B.C. lists eight different sex manuals then available – not one of which has survived. Two were called *The Way of Yin* (yin is the feminine essence), their authors, Rung Cheng and Wu Cheng. The idea probably came to fruition during the literary flowering of the 300s and 200s B.C., but which one was the first and which expert wrote it, are not known. (The oldest surviving sex manual is India's *Kama Sutra* by Vatsyayana, which may date back to 100A.D. It is a summary of earlier books on the same topic, their dates unspecified. So there is a possibility that India had a sex manual as early as China.)

Perhaps something can be learnt about human nature from what writers have chosen to include amongst the earliest surviving literary works. If so, a doleful conclusion is suggested by the prominence of insults among the ancient literature of Mesopotamia, written in cuneiform script [I, 1] in the Sumerian language. These works, composed probably shortly before 2000B.C., took the form of dialogues in which the characters deliver strings of scathing invective at each other. *The Disputation Between Two School Graduates* and *The Disputation Between Two Ladies* are a couple that have been unearthed, and can supply the modern reader with some good material for vilification.

**Insults**

Epic poetry was a gradual invention in most cultures. Verses grew up haphazardly to form a tradition, based on a popular hero or a body of legend. Usually after that a master poet worked from a selection of this material, rewriting and welding it together into an extended narrative. This occurred in ancient Mesopotamia when the *Epic of Gilgamesh* was written up in complete form; most of the parts were composed before 2400B.C. in the Sumerian language, in cuneiform script. Around 2000B.C. they were brought together in the Babylonian language as a single dramatic narrative.

**Epic**

Shu-Sin, a ruler who lived in Mesopotamia around 2200B.C., must have been a first-rate performer in matters of the heart (and flesh). Two spirited young ladies have committed their immoderate feelings to verse on the subject of marrying him. Writing in Sumerian, one says:

**Love Poetry**

> My precious caress is more savoury than honey,
> In the bedchamber, honey filled,
> Let us enjoy your goodly beauty,

Lion, let me caress you.

and many other things as well. The other has a less direct, more obscure, style:

My god, of the wine maid, sweet is her drink,
Like her drink sweet is her vulva, sweet is her drink,
Like her lips, sweet is her vulva, sweet is her drink,
Sweet is her mixed drink, her drink.

The first poem totals twenty-nine lines, the other, twenty-seven.

**Elegy**  There lived in Mesopotamia, probably around 2200B.C., a very soppy sentimental Sumerian poet named Ludingirra, who has left three verses to posterity. Two of these are elegies – one of 112 lines, lamenting the death of his father, Nanna; the other, sixty-six lines mourning his deceased wife, Nawirtum. The third of his poems is about what a wonderful mother he has, written while she was still alive.

**Satire**  Satirical lines and sentences can be found scattered through some of the very earliest literature. But the oldest sustained piece of pure satire is a witty Babylonian dialogue between master and slave, from some time between 1500 and 1000B.C. It is a scathing commentary on unequal relationships, on people, the divine powers, selfishness, free will, life and death. In each verse, the master explains his intention, then changes his mind. The slave always has a convincing argument for the master's decision. The options considered include:

– washing hands and having dinner
– driving out to the country
– starting a family
– going to court
– leading a revolution
– loving a woman
– sacrificing to God.

The last two verses are as follows:

'Slave, listen to me'. 'Here I am sir, here I am'.
'I will perform a public benefit for my country'. 'So
perform, sir, so perform.'
'The man who performs a public benefit for his country,
His deeds are placed in the ring of the God Marduk.'
'No slave, I will by no means perform a public benefit for
my country'.
'Do not perform, sir, do not perform.
Go on up to the ancient ruin heaps and walk about;

See the skulls of high and low.
Which is the malefactor and which is the benefactor?'

'Slave, listen to me'. 'Here I am sir, here I am'.
'What then is good?'
'To have my neck and your neck broken.
And to be thrown into the river is good.
Who is so tall as to ascend to the heavens?
Who is so broad as to compass the underworld?'
'No slave, I will kill you and send you first'.
'And my master would certainly not outlive me even by
three days'.

**Vers Libre**

Poetry in most early literatures is a regimented mode of expression, with rules governing metre, line length, verse formation and sometimes rhyme. This is a reflection of its origin in music and song. In *vers libre* (free verse), the rules are discarded, or adopted haphazardly where they especially suit the poet's purpose. This approach, so characteristic of the 20th century, was initiated in a variety of Chinese poetry called the *fu*. The first was the *Fu Niao Fu* 'Owl Fu', by Jia Yi (201–169B.C.) of the Harn Dynasty. He wrote it in despair over the ruin of his career, and died of disappointment five years later. There is a certain correspondence between the freedom of the medium and the gist of the poem, which includes the following lines about the true man:

His life is like drifting
And his death like resting
Tranquil as a calm, deep pool,
Untrammelled as a boat adrift;
Instead of prizing his life
He floats in a void.

**Limerick**

The limerick metre has turned up in various languages at times recent and distant. In 18th-century Ireland it was used by some poets writing in a light vein, and that may be why an Irish name was later chosen. However a limerick must have not only the metre, but the rhyme and the characteristic recitation of a personal episode or quality. These yield a product like the following:

There was an Old Woman of Lynn,
Whose Nose very near reached her chin;
You may easy suppose
She had plenty of Beaux
This charming old woman of Lynn.

The old woman of Lynn represents a historic company put before the English public in 1820, by an anonymous poet, author of *The History of Sixteen Wonderful Old Women*. This limerick collection contains the earliest recorded specimens of the new genre, the English language's foremost claim to a literary first.

**Fiction** The first stories of ancient cultures were told in song; thus early literary narratives tend to be in verse, like the narrative poetry [see Epic, above] of Mesopotamia, which dates back to the 3rd millennium B.C. Prose fiction begins later – in 12th Dynasty in Egypt (c. 2100–c. 1950B.C.), when there was a **Short Stories** flowering of short stories. *The Story of Sinuhe*, by an anonymous author, may be the oldest of these. The hero tells how he learnt of a crisis:

> While I was standing there I heard his voice as he was
> speaking and I was a little way off. My heart was distraught,
> my arms spread out, trembling fell upon all my limbs. I
> removed myself by leaps and bounds to seek a hiding place.

Sinuhe flees Egypt and prospers for years in Palestine, longing to return. His homecoming and death complete the narrative.

**Fables** Artificial little stories with simple moralistic messages are fairly common in Sumerian literature, from Mesopotamia late in the 3rd millennium B.C. (or perhaps a little earlier). Like Aesop's fables, they feature a range of stock animal characters, including the dog, fox, donkey, ox, elephant and feral pig.

**Story of Illicit Love** The earliest tale of illicit love in extant prose comes from the oldest known anthology of stories, *King Cheops and the Magicians*, compiled during Egypt's 12th Dynasty (c. 2100–c. 1950B.C.). *The Marvel which Happened in the Time of King Nebkha* is amusing and salutary enough to retell: Webaoner lived out in the country, and his wife fell in love with a man from town. She got Webaoner's caretaker to fix their garden pavilion up and then spent the day there cavorting with the townsman, who capped off his activities with a splash in the pool. The caretaker dobbed them in, so Webaoner made a little crocodile of wax for the caretaker to throw in the pool next time the townsman found it needful to cool off. (Persons planning to read the original work should skip to the next entry at this point, as reading on will spoil it.) After the next 'pleasant day' the caretaker threw the crocodile into the water behind the townsman, where it turned into a real-live 12 foot crocodile that killed him. Webaoner came back from a visit to the Pharaoh, and picked up the crocodile, which again became a wax model. He took his wife to a plot north of the city, and set fire to her there. A later pharaoh was so taken aback by Webaoner's powers that he gave him a big cake, a jug of beer, a joint of meat and a cone of incense. And that was the end of the story.

The fertile prose literature of 12th-Dynasty Egypt also gives us the first fantasy story, *The Castaway* – a peculiar tale **Fantasy** of a man whose ship is wrecked and who washes up on an island ruled by a 15 m. bearded serpent with a deep voice, a genial personality and the gift of telling the future.

Social realism enters literature in a series of short dramatic dialogues, written by Herodas, probably on the Greek island of **Social Realism** Cos, during the 3rd century B.C. Only eight have survived till today, each capturing a few minutes in the unglamorous lives of very ordinary people. His themes include a painful high-pressure salesman (in *The Shoe Shop*), a schoolboy's punishment (*School Master*), a courtroom with a tiresome plaintiff (*Brothel Keeper*), gossip (*A Nice Chat*), a lady chastising her slave for having another lover as well as her (*Jealous Lady*), a lady declining to have an affair (*The Bawd*) and others of the same kind. The colloquial Greek of Herodas's dialogue differs markedly from the literary language of most of his predecessors.

As its name suggests the novel was not an early development. The first was *Cyropaedia*, a historical novel in Greek about the **Novel** life of Cyrus, who founded the Persian Empire, in the 6th century B.C. The author, Xenophon (431–c. 350B.C.), was an expatriate Athenian, who had travelled extensively in Persia, and written many non-fiction books. *Cyropaedia*, written in Corinth about 360 B.C., is an idealised account of Persian society, contrasting with the unsympathetic views of most Greeks.

Novels of romance and adventure did not appear until Hellenistic times, after which many were published in Greek. Those which survive are mostly of uncertain date, so picking the first is difficult. The oldest known is probably *Erotic Tales* **Romance and** *of Chaereas and Callirhoe* by Chariton, if its dating to about **Adventure** 100B.C. is correct. It tells the story of the handsome Chaereas **Novel** and the beautiful Callirhoe. Their love overcomes many obstacles, but when Chaereas's rivals trick him into believing Callirhoe has been unfaithful, he kicks her in a rage and believes her dead. Hoping to be sentenced to death, Chaereas

is acquitted and talked out of suicide. Callirhoe recovers consciousness when her tomb in Sicily is disturbed by a robber,
who sells her as a slave in Asia Minor to an owner who makes
plans to marry her. Action intensifies when Callirhoe finds
out she is pregnant, and Chaereas learns what has happened
to her. To follow their story in various countries and difficult
situations would be rather space consuming, but readers will
be relieved to learn that they lived happily ever after, following their reunion on an island off Lebanon. Like many Greek
novels, it has no villains amongst its characters, and the troubles which befall them are all attributable to normal human
motives and the chances of their circumstances. Chariton
worked as a clerk in Asia Minor (present-day Turkey).

**Science Fiction
Novel**

In his *True Story*, Lucian (c. 115–195A.D.) of Samosata, a city
in Greek-speaking Asia, recorded his adventures in outer space
and in unknown seas, including his seven-day journey to the
Moon. Despite modern indications that English has always
been the lingua franca of the Cosmos, Lucian and his party
were impressed to find that everyone they met spoke Greek.

**Alien
Lifeforms**

The Moon men wore clear plastic clothes or suits of woven
metal. Some were born fully grown out of pods; the rest had
pouches for their children, like a kangaroo's. On death their bodies vaporised and disappeared. They had detachable, interchangeable eyes and prosthetic genitals. Everything taking place
on Earth was televised (with live sound) on their special observation screen. At the time of Lucian's visit they were at war with
the Sun people, whose army included cavalry mounted on
winged ants, 200 feet long, and 'sky dancers' who slung deadly
radishes at long range. Endymion, King of the Moon, had commissioned the local spiders, each bigger than an island, to build
a web from the Moon to a star which he wanted to add to his
empire. Over this a battle was fought; the victorious Sun people
forced the Moon men to sign a treaty by blocking off their light.
Lucian's aim was to ridicule the far-fetched stories told by other
writers, sporting with the counterfeit credulity that science fiction authors have always had to invoke. 'Since out of vanity I
was keen to hand something on to posterity, so that I would not
be the only one excluded from the privilege of poetic licence,
and since I had nothing true to report, never having had any
notable adventures, I have taken to lying.'

**Whodunit**

Although crime literature goes back at least to the Sung
Dynasty (960A.D.–1279), murder mysteries that withhold the

culprits' identity till late in the narrative were not written till about 1700. Probably the first is *Wu Tse Tien Szu Da Chi Arn* by an anonymous Ching Dynasty author. It features three separate crimes solved by ingenious detective work on the part of a district magistrate. It has been translated by Robert van Gulik, under the title *Celebrated Cases of Judge Dee*.

For over 4000 years ghosts have been visiting our literature. Like detectives, lovers and warrior heroes, they have since become so important that a special genre of fiction has grown up around them. The earliest collection of ghost stories was *Tales of Marvels* by Tsao Pi (187A.D.–226) written early in the 3rd century. Today the book survives only in quotations in other works, but these are full enough to give a good idea of the style. Plenty of tried and true themes come up, including a haunted house, and a man who convinces a ghost that he is one too. It is likely that some individual stories in *Tales of Marvels* come from a century or two earlier than Tsao Pi's time, and that the eldest of them is the first of the ghost story genre.

**Book of Ghost Stories**

The first regular newspapers were not like the ones we read today. They were handwritten reports on sheets of papyrus sent out to subscribers, including country residents and travellers who wished to keep up with news from home. They probably began in the Greek language in the cosmopolitan centres of Hellenistic times (after 323B.C.) like Alexandria. By the 1st century B.C. papers of this kind written in Latin were being sent around the Roman Empire.

**Newspaper**

When a daily paper finally came out it was named appropriately, but without much flair, 'The Daily News' (*Acta Diurna*). It was published in Rome by the government from the 1st century B.C. until the 5th A.D. It was more like a modern newspaper and included news, highlights of Senate proceedings and court cases, official proclamations, births and deaths, financial reports, sporting fixtures and results, and stories fictional and miraculous. It was the first paper to have a large permanent staff, including reporters and clerks, and editors who were called *actuarii*. Publication consisted of posting copies up each day on billboards in prominent places.

**Daily Newspaper**

The 'Kai Yewarn Assorted Report' (*Kai Yewarn Tsa Bao*) seems to have the strongest claim to being first in print. It commenced regular publication in Charng Arn in the Kai Yewarn period (713A.D.–741) of the Tarng Dynasty (618A.D.–907), as the official organ of the central government. A surviving copy

**Printed Newspaper**

of an original issue is the oldest remaining printed newspaper. Another Charng Arn paper of those times, the 'Capital Reporter' (*Di Bao*), published by the Bureau of Official Reports, is a rival claimant to the credit for printing first. Papers called *Di Bao* had been issued by various private and official publishers since the 2nd century B.C. (before printing was known), and it is not clear when the Tarng *Di Bao* was first printed.

In later times newspapers reporting government proceedings were consolidated in the 'Metropolitan Reporter' (*Jing Bao*) often known in English as *The Peking Gazette*. This was supplied free of charge to senior officials and government offices throughout the empire and, for a fee, to a limited number of subscribers. It contained general news, law reports, edicts and proclamations, statistics and reports on the imperial family. The most interesting contents were the commentaries and criticisms on government policy and senior ministers, addressed to the emperor by officials. In some periods, such as the Sung Dynasty (960A.D.–1279) these tended to be quite virulent, so the paper scores an unusual precedent for being the first vehicle in which a government published attacks on its own policies and personnel. During the Sung Dynasty the newspaper press experienced a modest flowering and cheap trashy papers proliferated. There was also a more organised and respectable paper purveying gossip and sensation – 'Trivial

**Mass Circulation Newspaper** Reports' (*Hsiao Bao*). Mass circulation throughout the Chinese empire was later achieved by a single newspaper, when regional printers were contracted to publish the popular edition of *Jing Bao* by reproducing master copies sent out from Peking. During the Ming (1368A.D.–1644) and the Ching (1644A.D.–1911) these were produced every second day, by abbreviating, or perhaps we should say censoring, the main daily editions. The same edition could thus be purchased from one end of the empire to the other, for a negligible price.

**Press Agency** In 1835A.D. Charles Havas opened the first press agency, supplying French newspapers with news gathered by agency reporters. In particular Havas enjoyed access to government intelligence, which the agency passed on to the newspapers.

**Magazine** The first issue of the first magazine, *Journal des Sçavans* ('Journal of the Learned'), came out in Paris in January 1665A.D. The *Journal* includes descriptions of new books, reports on developments in the humanities and sciences, news from the court and university, and obituaries.

# II

# ARTS AND MUSIC

Apart from survival, creative expression is the foremost concern of the human race. In one sense every original work of art is a world first in its own right. The topics in this chapter are of course much less individual, being themes which are considered major ones nowadays.

## 1. VISUAL ARTS

This section includes architectural styles. Buildings are in Chapter V, 2.

The strangest enigma in art history is that some of the oldest surviving works of fine art are masterpieces of realism by Stone **Realist Art** Age cavemen. Instead of a gradual development of skill and understanding, there is a great pinnacle of achievement cropping up out of nothingness. In Western Europe during the Ice Age, 13,000 to 16,000 years ago, cavemen adorned cave walls with vigorous lifelike paintings and reliefs depicting wild animals, hunting scenes, and sometimes people. Several sites have been discovered; dating is too approximate to say which was the earliest, but the best collections are at Altamira in Spain and Lascaux in France. In the generations before these very realistic artists, there must have been gradual improvement in skills which made their work possible. It remains remarkable that while they could not even make cloth or build humpies, they painted pictures beyond the abilities of civilised artists in much more sophisticated societies.

When it comes to art which dispenses with peripheral elaboration, and executes only its central object, there is nothing **Minimist Art** simpler, or earlier, than the Pharaoh Seneferu's pyramid at Dahshur, by the Nile River. Time has weathered its smoothness, but when it was built, around 3100B.C., it was a pure and unelaborated compound of square and triangle. Although its size is spectacular (214 feet tall), it is much smaller than the later 'Great Pyramid'. Its main interest to the art historian is the dramatic originality of its outline, which is quite unlike the 'step pyramids', the only other pyramids [see Pyramid V, 2] in existence at the time. It springs from a single stroke of inspiration, not an architectural tradition or gradual evolution. Almost as noteworthy, perhaps, is that the artist was able to convince his government that his stark concept merited the costs involved.

**Hyper-realist Art**

The first hyper-realist painters were Greeks early in the 4th century B.C. – Zeuxis of Heracleia and his younger contemporary, Parrhasios of Ephesus (in present-day Turkey). Early in their careers they won admiration for their draftsmanship and control of depth and colour. However, it was a realism contest that seems to have brought their work to the hyper-realist pitch. Zeuxis entered a painting of grapes so convincing that it attracted birds when he put it on display. Crowing over this success, Zeuxis confidently urged Parrhasios to take away the curtain and reveal his entry. This was not possible, and Parrhasios won the honours, because his was a picture of a curtain, which had deceived Zeuxis. There is no evidence that they could achieve such success except with inanimate objects. When Zeuxis later painted a boy with grapes, he was disappointed because the birds were again attracted to the grapes. Since the birds were not scared to come near the painting, it was clear to him that he could not paint boys as convincingly as grapes.

**Surrealist Art**

Relics from early cultures include many depictions of things that defy possibility and seem to spring from a dreamlike imagination. The earliest specimens are not surreal, because their inspiration is in fantasy or mythology, not a deliberate defiance of observable reality. The surrealist movement began in the Roman Empire in the 1st century B.C. with startling innovations in fresco painting. Images of candlesticks supporting temples, reeds holding up masonry roofs, and plants sprouting human beings are typical of those which received warm acclaim. They are known from the Roman author Vitruvius, who was not an enthusiast:

> When people see these frauds they find no fault with them but on the contrary are delighted, and do not care whether any of them can exist or not. Their understanding is darkened by decadent critical principles.

Some long forgotten artists in the Roman Empire reacted against traditions of conformation and conventional muted colouring to produce vibrant naïve scenes, a few of which survive to this day. The style appears to have begun in the 1st century A.D., but the best surviving examples of this early primitivism are mosaics from the Emperor Hadrian's villa at Tivoli near Rome, c. 130A.D.

**Primitivist Art**

Around 400A.D., some Chinese artists adopted impressionism as their characteristic style. By means of economic and judicious brushwork, they claim to have achieved a striking invocation of light, space and features, without directly mimicking outlines and detail. The approach was called 'arousal of the spirit'. One pioneer was Warng Wei (415A.D.–443), not to be confused with his famous Tarng Dynasty namesake. 'Physical appearances are based upon physical forms', wrote Warng:

**Impressionist Art**

> spirit is invisible, and therefore what it enters does not move. The eye is limited in scope, and therefore what it sees does not cover all. So by using one small brush, I draw the infinite vacuity . . . With a curved line I represent the Sung Mountains . . . A swift stroke will be sufficient for the Tai Hua Mountain, and some irregular dots will show a dragon's nose. Eyebrows, forehead and cheeks all seem to be a serene smile, and the lonely cliff is so luxuriant and sublime that it seems to emit clouds. With changes . . . in all directions, movement is created, and by applying proportions and measure, the spirit is revealed.

(tr. De Barry, Chan, Watson; modif.)

The modern Impressionist School began in Paris in the late 1850s around the works of Edouard Manet (1832–83) and Claude Monet (1840–1926). In Paris in 1874, the school held its first joint exhibition, and adopted the name Impressionist, following the usage of a critic, who derived it from the title of Monet's *Impression: Sunrise*.

**Impressionist School**

The paintings of some prehistoric tribal societies are decidedly abstract. Their artists rendered narratives and landscapes into

**Abstract Art**

dots, lines and washes. In these works, each element stands for a part of the subject matter, just like the symbols on a map. (A group of rings may be a waterhole, a dot may be a person.) When a culture progresses towards civilisation, it loses the gift for abstraction and all its art becomes decorative or representational. In some societies, abstract art is reinvented after long ages of cultural evolution.

*Landscape*, aquatint c. 1785, by Alexander Cozens.

**The Modern Abstract Movement**

In China, such a reinvention occurred in the 7th century A.D. in the field of calligraphy and apparently around 800A.D. in painting. The 'landscape artist' Warng Hsia (c. 740A.D.–804), who used to paint while drunk, pioneered abstract technique. He splattered ink over silk and used his hair and fingers instead of brushes to make unintentional resemblances to nature. Old Chinese painting abounds in semi-abstracts, but not totally abstract works. The modern Western abstract tradition probably doesn't stem from Chinese abstractionism. More likely is that the widespread Chinese and Japanese styles of extreme minimism helped trigger the modern infatuation with abstract art. This is a Western phenomenon, beginning in late 18th-century Britain, with the book *A New Method of Assisting the Invention in Drawing Original Compositions of Landscape*. The author, Alexander Cozens (c. 1717A.D.–1786), repeats the aim of Warng Hsia – to arrive without conscious depiction at a likeness of landscapes. He crumpled paper and smoothed it, then, thinking about landscape but not about what he was doing, he blotted the paper freely with ink. Warng's contemporaries had called him 'Splash Ink'; contemporaries of Cozens dubbed him 'Blot Master' and derided his 'blotscapes'.

Cubism is a technique of abstraction pioneered in Barcelona by Spanish artist Pablo Picasso. It is first identifiable in his *Les Demoiselles d'Avignon* of 1906–7. This depicts a group of five semi-abstract, harshly angular, nude women with fruit (a pear, an apple, some grapes and a slice of rockmelon) in front of them. In the Cubist style, images are broken and distorted into sharp, straight-edged shapes. **Cubist Art**

Although in theory nihilist art need not be abstract, nihilism arose in the 20th century as a manifestation of abstract art. Nihilism can pursue either of two directions: the renunciation of values and culture, or the abnegation of the image and the artist's creative role. In Zurich in 1916, the former motive gave birth to 'Dada' – the earliest nihilist movement, based on the premise that the catastrophe of world war invalidates moral and aesthetic standards. Its foremost exponents were Max Ernst, Hans Arp and the French painter Marcel Duchamp (1887–1968) – who used to make 'works of art' by giving a signature and title to everyday objects, or adding moustaches to the *Mona Lisa*, and so forth. **Nihilist Art**

The Doric order of classical architecture began with a temple said to have been commissioned by Dorus, ruler of Achaea in southern Greece, and constructed at Argolis probably around 800B.C. This early version was rather rustic and did not follow the carefully worked out proportions of the classic Greek temple. **Doric Architecture**

The Ionic order was first employed in constructing a temple to Diana at an unknown location on the coast of Asia Minor (present-day Turkey). It featured columns eight times their diameter in height, as a woman is eight times taller than her foot is long. Volutes were arranged at the capitals, resembling generous curls, and the shafts of the columns were fluted in a manner reminiscent of the folds in long robes. The work was probably completed early in the 7th century B.C. **Ionic Architecture**

The Corinthian order was introduced by the architect Callimachus, at Corinth in mainland Greece, late in the 5th century B.C. For the design of the capital, he was inspired by the sight of an acanthus plant growing up and around a basket near a grave outside the city. These are the three classical orders of ancient architecture, and survive in many public buildings of the 18th, 19th and 20th centuries. **Corinthian Architecture**

**Gothic Architecture**

Gothic architecture owes nothing to the traditional style of the Goths. It appeared almost accidentally from the coincidence of various principles of construction, used by architects to get the best physical results for religious buildings from a limited choice of materials. The transverse arch, the clerestory, the pointed arch, the pointed window, the ribbed vault and the flying buttress all work well with each other for sound engineering reasons. Yet when they were first brought together – in France in the first half of the 12th century A.D. – they produced a striking aesthetic synthesis which promptly became the dominant cultural style in Western architecture. Gothic architecture was the joint invention of many architects in Paris, Beauvais and other parts of Northern France. It was partially implemented in minor buildings and parts of cathedrals, until the Cathedral of St. Denis (1144A.D.) became the first major all Gothic building.

**Functionalism**

Prehistoric societies at their most impoverished or debased used to practise functionalism – because they lacked either the material wherewithal or the spiritual resources to do anything better. However, the congenital resolve of human beings to adorn their works with features which are uplifting or nice-looking everywhere drove it away. Sometimes, there has been a regression to functionalism under the influence of deprivation – as in Dark Age Europe – or boorish ideology. Modern functionalism owes most to the architecture of Charles Edouard Jeanneret-Gris Le Corbusier (1887–1965), a Frenchman of Swiss birth. In 1924 he began designing buildings with regard solely to their material function. The functionalist idea had already been forcibly expressed in Britain by the famous critic John Ruskin (1819–1900), but unlike Le Corbusier, Ruskin did not find a world prepared to implement his vision.

**Vanishing Point Perspective**

The conventional system of perspective utilises the device of a notional vanishing point. Lines which in nature are parallel and receding from the viewer are drawn to converge on this point. This is the basis of what many regard as the 'natural' system of perspective: it projects reality on to a plane surface in the way we believe the eye would apprehend it. (A mirror does likewise.) This system was first practised early in the 5th century B.C. in Athens by Agatharcus of Samos, for making theatre scenery. Agatharcus wrote a treatise explaining his method, and not long afterwards, the philosophers

Democritus and Anaxagoras worked out and explained all the principles of the system.

When people look at buildings, any truly straight edge appears slightly concave – an optical illusion that spoils the perfection **Entasis** of imposing architecture. Skilful architects compensate with bulging distortion to make the line optically correct. Entasis was used on the great ziggurat of Ur in Mesopotamia (present-day Iraq), built about 2300B.C. Varying degrees of entasis were precisely graded to produce the correct effect with various dimensions and positions on the walls facing the building. Such precision and mastery indicate that entasis must have been developed and understood on somewhat earlier ziggurats.

The Dutch inventor Cornelius Drebbel (1572–1634), who worked in England and invented a variety of devices using **Slide** lenses and light, made the first slide projector in 1630. Ini- **Projection** tially, slide projectors were only playthings; Drebbel's purpose was to show pictures of 'people who were not present'. But at Louvain in 1651, the Italian Jesuit, Martin Martini, who had worked in China, gave lectures illustrated with transparencies shown by a slide projector.

*Eikones*, by the Greek author Philostratus Lemnius, is the old-est art catalogue, dating back to the 2nd century A.D. It **Art Catalogue** describes the works in a private gallery in Neapolis (present-day Naples) in Southern Italy. Perhaps the first catalogue of this type is actually now lost, and had been compiled a cen-tury or two before *Eikones*, but this is guesswork. The descrip-tions in Philostratus's book interpret the scenes in each painting and extol their artistry.

The first book on architecture was written in the 5th century B.C. by the Greek author Silenus. It was a work discussing **Architecture** proportion in the Doric order of classical architecture. The **Book** earliest work on a specific building is also from Greece in the 5th century B.C. – Theodorus's, on the Temple of Hera on the **Book about a** island of Samos. **Building**

## 2. DRAMATIC ARTS

Dramatic Arts includes Film. But for the earliest movie film see cinema, VIII, 10.

**Play** We still have a copy of the miracle play performed in the 21st century B.C. for the occasion of the accession to the throne of the Egyptian pharaoh Sesostris I. The script includes the parts of the participants and stage directions. The surviving manuscript copy has the earliest known book illustrations [I, 2].

**Tragedies** In Greece in the 6th century B.C., each year, at the time of the vintage, choruses would chant, dance and sing tragic tales drawn from legend and history. In the village of Icaria near Athens lived Thespis, a promoter of these performances. In the 530s B.C., he had the ingenious idea of having an actor perform parts in the story, in between narrations from the chorus. Thespis wrote lines for the parts, and to begin with, a single actor played all the roles. People who produce plays and perform in them are still called thespians, after their founding father. Vintage time was called *tryge*, from which tragedy takes its name.

At about the same time, comedies were first produced, in the same manner, also at Icaria. Stage comedians had been **Comedies** performing regularly in Greece from about 600B.C., but the parts and the plot development required for a play did not come until the days of Thespis. The earliest comedy writer known by name was Cratinus (519–422B.C.), an Athenian.

**Mime** Bathyllus was an Egyptian dancer from Alexandria, who was brought to Rome in the 1st century B.C. by a great Roman patron of the arts, Maecenas. Working there with a scholar of dance, Pylades, he developed a new style, 'Italian dancing', which though once popular is no longer known. His other invention was the artform of mime, in which things, ideas, emotions and stories can be represented entirely by silent motions of the body. The Romans and Greeks described this art as 'tragic dance' or 'Memphis'. The ancient Greeks had an altogether different set of dramas called 'mimes', which are not like the mimes of today – rather, they are short prose plays unrelated to Bathyllus's 'Memphis'.

**Noh Drama** The old *noh* were musical dramas, popular in Japan in the early 1300s. But these were not the new noh we know now. Noh drama as it is now understood is primarily the work of Seami (1363A.D.–1444), son of a leading actor and presenter, Kwanami. These two worked together, mainly in Kyoto, on developing the new artform. Seami carried on after his father's death in 1384, and added to his practical achievement by writing a detailed analysis of the characteristic qualities of noh. He was the architect of rules governing performance, but more importantly, under the guidance of Zen Buddhists [VIII, 5], he instilled principles of dynamic restraint and implicit mystical meaning in the dozens of plays he composed.

*Li Gieus de Robin et de Marian*, composed in 13th-century France by Adam de la Halle, is the oldest surviving operatic composition. Like the operas of a later era, it is primarily a musical work, with dramatic content playing only a subordinate role. The narrative is rudimentary and comic. De la Halle (died 1297 A.D.) is the only musician of the time whose work survives in significant quantity. His, or the work of one of his contemporaries, is the first opera, but the style did not catch on. No further operas were performed until 1582 in France and 1597 in Italy. **European Opera**

Okami of Izumo, a Japanese dancer, established kabuki dance theatre at the start of the 17th century. She built traditional religious and folk dances into a formal arrangement. Early kabuki dramas had three women actors playing a teahouse girl, her lover and a buffoon. In 1629 the kabuki enacted by women was banned because of its licentiousness. Young men took over the parts, and the form they developed was banned in 1655 because of its erotic character. **Kabuki**

The ballet tradition extends back to the courts of Renaissance Italy. However, the feats of posture and agility that would lead to hospitalisation if attempted by normal persons – of which ballet largely consists – developed later on. If we could see an early dance performed, we would not recognise it as ballet. The stage in evolution at which ballet began is generally said to be during the reign (1643–1715) of Louis XIV in France. Dramatic dance called ballet was promoted in the 1650s in Paris by the King and his minister Mazarin. In 1661 a college of dance was established in the capital, and through the 1660s, dance drama became increasingly skilled and specialised. Its transformation into ballet was essentially a matter of its ceasing to be a participation activity for enthusiasts, and becoming a spectator amusement provided by trained performers. An event that marks, or at least symbolises, the transformation is the decision of Louis, a capable dancer, to give up ballet – because putting on a show for an audience was not consistent **Ballet** with his royal dignity. He so decided in 1670, aged 32, after performing in *Britannicus*, a musical tragedy with dance.

**Ballerinas**
Ballet in France went through a further stage of vigorous evolution in the 1690s, to become more dramatic and to display more feeling. At this time, one of the most important elements was supplied: previously ballet had been an all-male spectacle, but lady performers now began to rectify that terrible shortcoming. Their early roles were modest ones, so unfortunately, we cannot supply the name of any pioneering superstar.

**Peking Opera**
Traditional Chinese opera originated during the Ming Dynasty, later than the advent of opera in Europe [see above]. It includes singing, dancing, mime and acrobatics. Even in Peking itself, from Ming times to the present, many operas are in the styles of other provinces. The Peking style, with its wailing delivery that some might call 'falsetto', and distinctive patterns of performance, emerged about 1830A.D. from the Central Chinese opera, native to cities further south. Since then, it has taken the lead in creative development.

**Feature Film**
*The Story of the Kelly Gang* premiered at Melbourne's Athenaeum Hall on Christmas Eve 1906. In a period when few films ran longer than ten minutes, it went for eighty. It told the story of Ned Kelly and his notorious gang. The film, shot on a budget of £450, was produced by Dan Barry and directed by Charles Tait. It was not only the first full-length feature in the world, but the first of several cinematic retellings of the Kelly story. Ned Kelly's actual armour was borrowed from the Victorian Museum for the filming, which took place in the outer Melbourne suburb of Heidelberg.

**Movie with Sound**
When Thomas Edison patented cinematic movies in 1887, he was allowed to include synchronised sound in the specifications, although it is unlikely he had a workable method for it at the time. Further experiments led to the 'Edison Kinetophone' system developed in 1912–13. Simultaneously with a reel of film, the projectionist played a cylinder record. The records were much larger than the conventional cylinders of the day, so that the sound would not run out before the reel ended. In the U.S.A., screenings using the system began immediately, but it proved difficult to synchronise film with record, and the system was not a great success. The

**Full-length Movie with Sound**
Vitaphone system, devised in America by Edward Craft, was far more successful. The records were sixteen-inch discs played at 33⅓ r.p.m., and screenings began in 1926.

Bill advertising the first feature film.

*Don Juan,* an American feature film of 1926, was the first full-length movie with synchronised sound. Meanwhile, at the University of Illinois, U.S.A., in 1922, Joseph Tykociner had **Film with** shown a demonstrational film with sound recorded on the **Recorded** actual film. The first all-talking feature film on this principle **Sound** to have a public screening was *The Lights of New York*, starring Helene Costello, shown at the Strand Theatre, New York, on 6 July 1928.

**Book on Acting**   Unfortunately, the oldest book on acting no longer survives. Its author was the Greek philosopher Theophrastus (c. 370–286B.C.), who succeeded Aristotle as head of the Peripatetic School in Athens. Theophrastus wrote books on most things, including love, sweating sickness and hair; his book on acting was aptly entitled *On Acting*.

**Millionaire Entertainer**   The first millionaire entertainer was a star of the Roman stage in the 1st century B.C., Roscius (died 62B.C.). His annual income from professional engagements averaged about 500,000 sesterces when his career was in full flight. In spending power, this meant more than half a million dollars each year.

**Screen Nudity**   German director Anton Mester was the first filmmaker to present completely nude actors and actresses on the commercial movie screen. Indeed, some of the scenes in his short films of 1902–3 are little more than nude studies.

# 3. MUSIC

In Music, more than other pursuits, the first steps tend to be lost in obscurity. Most instruments were born into local folk cultures and their origins were already uncertain by the time they began to be widely noticed. In ancient times a lot of people studied and wrote about music, but because their works have been destroyed their enthusiasm did not succeed in preserving the details. For example twenty-three centuries ago, the brilliant Greek scientist and musicologist, Aristoxenus, wrote literally hundreds of books about music. If they still existed, knowledge of musical firsts would be much richer.

Furthermore, because the classifications have not been settled, it is virtually impossible to identify the first examples of various musical styles. Some American folk tunes from around the turn of the century are technically indistinguishable from rock and roll music. Yet rock and roll is always described as a postwar phenomenon. Rock and roll exponents certainly do not accept such old songs as belonging to their genre.

Until rock and roll and the other musical categories have objective definitions they cannot be included here.

**Octave**   The musical octave was worked out by the Greeks in the time of Pythagoras (6th century B.C.) – possibly by Pythagoras himself, after whom it is called the Pythagorean scale. From earlier times, Greek lyre music was based on the interval of the octave, achieved by tuning the two outer strings of the lyre. The breakthrough of the 6th century B.C. was the discovery of the length ratios of the other strings required to produce the intermediate notes.

In the latter part of the 5th century B.C., Philolaus, a follower of Pythagoras, from the Greek city of Tarentum in Southern Italy, discovered the major tone with an interval **Major Tone** between the fourth and fifth. Philolaus seems to have hit on this as a single instance, without analysing the whole system of possible scales. About a century later, however, another **Analysis of** native of Tarentum produced a scientific examination of musi- **Musical Scales** cal intervals as a whole. Aristoxenus (4th century B.C.) was a philosopher and musicologist who had studied at the Lyceum [see University, IV, 3]. He specified the frequency ratios of tones in the various scales, and of their semitones.

Counting the semitones, his calculations produce a range of about fifty notes in the octave. Theoretically, this is ideal, **Well-** and facilitates the most melodious chords. For musicians and **tempered** their instruments, its complexity is impracticable. The well- **Scale** tempered scale – or 'scale of even temperament' – is a deliberate sacrifice of precision that enables musicians to approximate the perfect notes well enough to produce fine quality music. Aristoxenus instituted this by dividing the octave into twelve intervals of tonal ratio, each of the twelfth root of two.

The earliest system of musical notation was adopted in Mesopotamia (present-day Iraq) in the middle of the 2nd mil- **Musical** lennium B.C. Some specimens remain in the form of ancient **Notation** clay tablets with the music signs running parallel to the words of Babylonian songs. Some of the words can be read, and one piece has been identified as a composition for strings. However the notation has not been satisfactorily deciphered: it isn't even possible to be sure how many notes there are in the Babylonian scale, let alone reconstruct the ancient melody.

A conservatorium of music, known as the Education Workshop, was established in 715A.D. in Charng Arn, capital of **Conservatorium** China during the Tarng Dynasty. It was conveniently located beside the Fairyland Palace, and 300 musicians and actors of both sexes were supported and taught there.

**Pitch Pipes**

A general system of regulated musical tones was introduced in China early in the 3rd millennium B.C., during the reign of Huarng Di (the semi-legendary Yellow Emperor). Musicians of the day were ordered to adopt a standardised system. Apertures were made at fixed intervals in specially selected bamboo pipe to create pitch pipes which fixed the national standard.

**Lute**

**Banjo**

The ancestors of most string instruments are lutes, which were separately invented in West and East Asia about 5000 years ago. They had a neck or fingerboard attached to a resonating body, and adjustable strings for plucking, strumming or bowing. Ancient instrument-makers varied the basic features – such as the shape of the resonator – to anticipate most of the now familiar string instruments. In this way, the banjo was invented in Southern Anatolia (present-day Turkey) or perhaps Northern Iraq, in the 3rd millennium B.C. It was a lute with a skin stretched over its circular body, and a narrow fingerboard, usually played with a plectrum.

**Mandolin**

The first mandolin came from much further east. It was a kind of four-string lute made by a barbarian tribe to the west of North China. It is known as the *pi pa*, and is easily distinguished by its pear-shaped resonator. This instrument goes back to about twenty-three centuries ago. The Western European mandolin differs in having paired rather than single strings. It was invented in Spain, by the country people of the region of Navarre or Biscay – probably early in the 16th century A.D.

**Guitar**

Some ancient Egyptian lutes from the Middle Kingdom period (c. 2150–c. 1950 B.C.) had guitar-shaped resonators, but their necks were very long compared to their bodies, so it might be jumping the gun to call them guitars. But there is a picture – over 1900 years old – of a small guitar, near Termez in present-day Uzbekistan. It has a short neck and a resonator in the distinctive guitar shape. Together with later pictures, it makes it clear that guitars were made in Central Asia about 2000 years ago, and spread westwards.

**Fiddle**

The guitar shape was also adopted for early fiddles. These are first known in the Eastern Roman Empire: the vestige of the Roman Empire that survived in Asia Minor and Eastern Europe, with its capital at Constantinople (present-day Istanbul). They must have been introduced around 1000A.D.; the earliest picture shows one that resembles a small guitar, but was clearly a fiddle, as it was played with a bow.

**Violin**

The first violins were made in Northern Italy shortly before 1500A.D. A painting done at Ferrara in 1505–8 shows very plainly a violin of the early type, which looks strikingly similar to those of today, even down to the *f*-shaped slots in the body. However, the violin in 1500 still had some way to go before reaching technical maturity. It had only three strings, and was flatter in cross-section. In some ways, a late-15th-century instrument called the *lira da bracchio* was nearer to today's violin. Some of those had a violin shape, and five strings running down the fingerboard (as well as two 'drone' strings, not meant for fingering). The rapid success of violins **Viola, Cello** in Italy led to early development of the four-string type, and then to violas and cellos by the 1530s at latest.

The zither consists of a long sounding box surmounted by numerous strings arranged on different patterns depending on **Zither** the system of tuning used. As the *se*, it belongs in the Chinese orchestra, and lends to Oriental music the characteristic rapid sequences of notes. As the psaltery, it was once popular in Europe. Its first performances were given in North China, in the days of Fu Hsi, a ruler of the primitive tribal society which preceded Chinese civilisation. Fu Hsi, early in the 3rd millennium B.C., is said to have decreed that it be played at weddings, because he considered that its pure sound encourages spiritual purity and clean behaviour.

The pan pipes which were invented by Shun (ruler of China c. 2200B.C.) were of an irregular shape, resembling the pinions **Pan Pipes** of a phoenix. They had ten tubes and were two feet long.

From these primaeval pipes, Chinese musicians evolved a variety of woodwind instruments. By the early part of the Jo Dynasty, around 1000B.C., they had the first mouth organ. **Mouth Organ** Two rows of outlet pipes were all fed from a single mouthpiece. It was brought to Europe in 1777A.D. The distinctive feature of this invention is the free reed which gives its char- **Free Reed** acteristic quality to the sound, not only of the mouth organ but also to later Western instruments such as the accordion.

In 1821, German instrument maker, Christian Friedrich Ludwig Buschman, added a keyboard and hand bellows and patented a new free reed instrument, which he called the **Accordion** 'Handaeoline'. In Vienna by 1829, Cyrillus Demian (1772–1847) developed it by adding accompanying chords, and christened it the accordion.

The earliest known bassoons were of the single piece type known as the dulcian, first manufactured in the early 16th **Bassoon** century. The invention spread so quickly that it is no longer known where it began. There are several possibilities – one is Northern Italy, another Northwestern Europe, in the area from the north of France to Holland.

**Saxophone** The saxophone was invented by Adolphe Sax (1814–94) in Brussels, shortly before he moved from his native Belgium to Paris in 1842. His work on the bass clarinet inspired saxophone improvements in 1846, which made an instrument much the same as the saxophones of today. Sax, like his father, was a professional instrument maker. He was also a skilled player of the clarinet, which undoubtedly helped him devise the new instrument.

**Organ** The organ used by the ancient Greeks had keys and valves as well as cylinders for compressing air and forcing it into the pipes, and reeds in the pipes – so that it must have sounded quite like the organs of today. It was invented probably in early Hellenistic times (around the 3rd century B.C.).

**Clavichord** There was once an instrument in England and France known as the chekker, from its resemblance to an exchequer – a counting board engraved with lines. A chekker was made in 1360A.D. by Jehan Perrot for £6 13s 4d, to be a gift from King Edward III to his prisoner King John the Good of France. Though the chekker was probably quite new, it is not clear that Perrot was its inventor. The first reference in France, nine years later, recognises its English origins, and later descriptions make it apparent that the chekker was what we now call a clavichord.

**Harpsichord** According to an Italian source in 1397A.D., Hermann Poll claimed at that time to have invented the 'clavicembalum', as the harpsichord was known. His name sounds German, but Poll could easily have migrated to Italy and made the first harpsichord after getting there – or built on the idea of another inventor. Pictures from the 1400s show that the early harpsichord was a short instrument with a thick case and a complicated plucking action.

**Piano** An Italian harpsichord maker from Padua, Bartolemeo Cristofori or Cristofali (1655A.D.–1731) began work on the first piano in 1698A.D. By 1700 there was a piano listed in the musical inventory of the Medici's court in Florence, so at least one must have been finished by then. The earliest pianos resembled harpsichords of the day, but the keys activated buttons which propelled leather-covered hammers. Compared to modern pianos, they were fairly rudimentary, but Cristofori was a visionary inventor whose instrument was hardly improved on till the 19th century.

In 1732, Italian composer Ludovico Giustoni completed **Piano Music** some piano sonatas – the first music specially written for piano.

The didgeridoo originated in what is now Australia's North-ern Territory, hundreds of years ago. It was first manufactured **Didgeridoo** as a musical instrument amongst Aboriginal tribes near the coast, who had access to bamboo growing wild in Arnhem Land. The already hollow stems of mature plants were cut and cleaned out, and it was only later that the hollowed timber version was introduced.

The trombone was developed from the slide trumpet in North-western Europe in the middle of the 15th century. It may have **Trombone** been invented by a Flemish instrument maker supplying the Court of Burgundy, which at that time ruled much of Belgium. One of the musicians performing in Bruges at the Duke of Bur-gundy's wedding to Margaret of York, in 1468, used a trombone to play the accompaniment to a motet for the occasion.

The steel bands of the West Indies have turned the pan into the most popular tuned percussion instrument. It was first **Pan** made in Trinidad in the 1930s, out of the head of an oil drum pounded into a concave shape. Areas marked out on the sur-face are tuned to produce different notes. At first, pans were used like drums and other percussion instruments, to add sounds, but not to play the melody. Winston Spree Simon, a steel band musician, is thought to have been the first to start performing tunes on it.

In the mid-18th century A.D., good techniques for generating and harnessing static electricity were developed in Western **Electric** Europe. Religious orders in France saw different opportunities **Instrument** in the new medium. While the Carthusians [VII, 5] researched electric communications [VIII, 12], the Jesuits [VII, 5] concentrated on electric music. The *clavessin electrique* was the idea of Jesuit priest Jean-Baptiste de la Borde (1730–77). For each note, he had a pair of electrically charged bells, with a clapper in-between. Pressing a key would cut off the charge to one of the pair, causing the clapper to strike it. On striking, the clapper took on a negative charge, attracting it to the other bell. This resulted in very rapid oscillation, simulating sustained tones. Music written for other keyboard instruments, including harpsichords and organs, could be played on the clavessin electrique.

**Electric Guitar**
In the 1920s, experiments were conducted in America with electric methods of amplifying guitars. Early in the 1930s, when satisfactory pick-ups were first introduced, the earliest electric guitars were manufactured. Several pioneers were working on them simultaneously, and the first specimen has not been precisely identified. It may have been the 1930–31 prototype of the 'Rickenbacker' – guitars manufactured in 1931 by the Electro String Instrument Co. They were nicknamed 'frying pans' because of their hollow circular metal bodies.

**Synthesiser**
The RCA Electric Music Synthesizer was invented at the RCA laboratories at Princeton (between New York and Philadelphia) by Harry F. Olsen (1902–82) and Herbert F. Belar. It was constructed in 1951 and 1952 but not demonstrated publicly until 1955. The synthesiser was controlled by a roll of punched paper tape over a foot wide, output from a typewriter-style keyboard. The punched holes in the tape set digital values for the timbre, pitch, envelope and volume of the sounds produced by the synthesiser's analogue sound generators.

**Lullaby**
The earliest lullaby to be written is *U-a a-u-a*, sung in Ur in the 23rd century B.C. by a wife of King Shulgi of Sumer, in Mesopotamia. With over seventy lines, it is long enough to give the infant every reasonable opportunity of dropping off. Modern mothers who wish to test its effectiveness might like to start with the following short extract:

Come Sleep, come Sleep,
Come to where my son is,
Hurry Sleep to where my son is,
Put to sleep his restless eyes,
Put your hand on his painted eyes,
And as for his babbling tongue,
Let not the babbling tongue shut out his sleep.

**Film Music**
The Salvation Army's series *Soldiers of the Cross*, which retold the life of Christ and gruesome stories of the early martyrs, was the first film production with its own music. The music was composed especially by R. M. McNally to accompany this dramatic tour de force of 1900. *Soldiers of the Cross* was probably also the first picture to include real lions in the action – martyrs were tossed to them (in filming at the lions' cage of

Fitzgerald's Circus in Melbourne). It was screened for the first time in September 1900 at Melbourne Town Hall, as several separate films interspersed with Salvation Army lectures.

**Stereo Sound System**

Before inventing his aeroplane [IX, 3], Clément Ader (1841–1925) was France's foremost specialist in telephones. His work on improving and promoting them led him to create the 'Théâtrephone' for relaying live musical performances. His system included two series of microphones, one on the left, the other on the right, side of the performance area. Telephone lines linking each series separately to headphones enabled absent listeners to enjoy the performance in stereo. In 1881 Ader demonstrated the new system to the public: visitors to an electrical exhibition could listen on stereo headphones to performances being given at the Paris Opera.

**Sound Recording**

Thomas A. Edison's phonograph was the first device capable of recording sound for later reproduction. The apparatus was devised by Edison (1847–1931) at his laboratory at Menlo Park, in the Northeastern United States, in 1876. In 1877 the working prototype was built for Edison by John Kreusi. A threaded drum wrapped in heavy tinfoil revolved at a fixed speed, the foil receiving impressions from a recording head activated by a diaphragm that vibrated with the sound to be recorded. The first records were made soon after, in the form of casts taken from the tinfoil wrapper.

**Records**

At a party in 1944, Dr. Peter Goldmark was irritated by a break in the music. Side one of a Brahms recording had run out after the usual four minutes available on a 78 r.p.m. record – right in the middle of the music. For the next four years, the Hungarian-born inventor and his American employer, Columbia Broadcasting System (CBS), worked to eliminate such annoyances, with a long-playing (LP) record. Their invention was made of unbreakable vinylite, so finely grooved that each side could play for 23 min. at 33⅓ r.p.m. The LP was launched in New York in June 1948.

**LP Records**

The first compact disc was a joint project of the Japanese Sony company and the Dutch Philips company. The technology was developed in 1978 but the first commercial release of compact disc music records and playing equipment was in Japan in 1982. The new equipment has all but superseded LP records, but not magnetic musical tapes played by tape recorders [XI, 2].

**Compact Discs**

# III
# FOOD AND DRINK

The French gourmet and politician Anthelme Brillat-Savarin justly points out that there is more advantage in the creation of a dish than in the discovery of a star. Yet for thousands of years, the prestige and fame of astronomers have eclipsed the meagre recognition given to the inventors of food, drink and ways of cooking. Our health and joie de vivre are so much due to their labour and genius that it would be a gross shortcoming not to celebrate the inventors' names and deeds. The pity is that few traces of either have been preserved.

One evil result is the under-representation of women in the records of discovery and innovation. Undoubtedly, legions of brilliant women (and men) have engineered radical progress, in the kitchen and farmyard – the very places where fame and renown are rarely won; while the names of males, who predominate in observatories and laboratories, have become household words for achievements no less inspired and laborious, but less deserving of our acknowledgement.

We pay for this imbalance with our quality of life: food and drink would be better if we promoted improvement by lavishing prestige and renown where they are due. And the countless women nowadays who have forsaken the creative realm of the kitchen for the barren territories of the office could hardly have been persuaded to if domestic achievements were rated at their true worth.

Anyway, the damage is done, and most of the creations recorded here are anonymous, while many wonderful things have to be missed out altogether.

In ancient times, the city of Sybaris was stamped out, along with the records of its heroes. It was the first community to honour its culinary inventors in the way that others have honoured their sportsmen, soldiers and scientists. Some of its effort in that regard is treated under Patent Law [XII, 3].

# 1. COOKING AND EATING

Hippocrates (460–357B.C.), the doctor who founded the most
famous Greek medical school, at Cos, believed that diet plays **Dietetics**
a vital role in preserving health and curing sickness. Many
papers published by his school in the 5th and 4th centuries
B.C. stress the importance of correct diet in patient management, and explain the results of detailed research by their
authors.

> One aims at some criterion as to what constitutes a correct
> diet, but you will find neither number nor weight to deter-
> mine what this is . . . exactness is difficult to achieve and
> small errors are bound to occur. I warmly commend the
> physician who makes small mistakes.

So wrote Hippocrates, or one of his fellows, in *Tradition in
Medicine* (tr. Chadwick and Mann).

The Hippocratic school criticised excessive dieting as a
risky practice. But in *A Regimen for Health* it also published the **Weight Loss**
earliest dietary programme for overweight people – one that **Diet**
endeavours to tackle their undisciplined appetites as well as
their excessive food intakes. For the benefit of fat readers, here
are the main points:

- Before a meal, drink some diluted wine.
- Eat fatty meat, because a small quantity is filling.
- Dish up the meat with sesame seeds or seasoning.
- Do your exercise on an empty stomach, immediately before
  meal time, and begin eating while still out of breath.
- Have only one meal a day.
- Do without showers, wear as little as possible and sleep on a
  hard bed.

Early in the 3rd century B.C. the Greek nutritionist Diphilus, a
doctor from the Aegean island of Siphnos, wrote a book called **Diet Book**
*Food for the Well and the Sick*. He examined a large range of foodstuffs, commenting on their digestive properties, nutritiousness,
benefits and side-effects. His book no longer survives.

The great chefs of ancient Greece began to churn out cookbooks from about 400B.C. First comes Mithaecus, whose book **Recipe Book**
*The Sicilian Cook* was popular in mainland Greece and was
commended by Plato. At the time, Sicily was famous for its
fine food, but none of these early recipe books still exists, so
ancient Sicilian cuisine can only be reconstructed in part,
from fragments. *The Sicilian Cook* had a recipe from Lydia (in

present-day Turkey) for spiced gravy, and a way of cooking ribbon fish (roasted with oil and cheese), but its other contents are unknown.

**Cooking School** Another Greek, Terpsion, was a contemporary of Mithaecus, probably in Sicily. He ran a cooking school and wrote a book called *Gastronomy*, the first cooking textbook, which **Cooking Textbook** included information on the various different foodstuffs, where they came from and how they were to be combined.

**Catering Book** The Roman author Matius was like the Granny Smith [III, 2] of ancient times – he was mainly famous in his own day for developing a new kind of apple. He was a pioneer also in publishing: in the 1st century B.C., he wrote a book on catering, dealing with cooks, waiters, wine waiters and food service. Sadly, the book and the apple are both extinct, and all we now have is a recipe named after him, for pork shoulder and apples.

**Menus** At Greek banquets in classical times (around the 5th century B.C.), it became the custom to hand the diners each a tablet, containing a list of all the dishes available, as they took their seats.

**Chopsticks** Most people ate with spoons and fingers until recent times, despite knives and forks having been around since the Stone Age – so long that their introduction cannot be dated. Chopsticks, though invented thousands of years later, came into general mealtime use long before forks. There may be psychological reasons why the Chinese were reluctant to handle their food – and for why they chose implements that are harder than forks for first-timers. Perhaps the ancestor of the chopstick was used like a fork for stabbing food, and its mate was first picked up as a stabilising aid. The chopsticks technique would have been worked out easily enough after such a marriage. Approximate dating is made possible by three sets of chopsticks discovered near present-day Arn Yarng, in Northwest China, where the Sharng Dynasty had its capital in the period 1300–1100B.C. They represent the first generation of quality chopsticks, but simple wooden chopsticks probably preceded them by a short time.

**Nouvelle Cuisine** Modern cooking, established on the foundations of the old, with less show and fewer encumbrances, although with just as much variety, is simpler, cleaner, more delicate, and perhaps even more accomplished . . . The science of the Cook consists in the breaking down, rendering digestible and quintessentialising of foods; in the extraction of the nutritious but light juices; in blending and so combining them that no single element dominates yet each one makes its presence felt.

This is how French food writer François Marin (in *Les Dons de Comus*, Paris, 1742) describes the new cooking style of the time of Louis XV. He and a number of other French chefs reacted against what they saw as the excessive elaboration and heaviness of traditional French cooking, and began to promote less ample and allegedly more healthy dishes. The most famous of these pioneers is a writer known simply as Menon, who wrote *La Nouvelle Cuisine* (Paris, 1742) and *La Cuisiniere Bourgeoise* (Paris, 1746). Although a reaction against *nouvelle cuisine* subsequently put paid to its separate existence, history repeated itself in the 1970s, with a brand new *nouvelle cuisine* movement.

**Tandoors**

A tandoor is a small earthenware oven required for the tandoori cuisine native to Afghanistan, Pakistan and Northwest India. Tandoors were first used in this region early in the 3rd millennium B.C. Remains have been unearthed from sites belonging to the Indus Valley civilisation, particularly Kalibangan in present-day Pakistan. They were round, mud-lined vessels with large side vents and a place for coals at the bottom.

**Cheese Graters**

Although it is the only instrument which can be said to have revolutionised cooking with cheese in the home, there is almost nothing on record about the origin of the cheese grater. The earliest reference is in a Greek play called *The Harpsinger*, written about 300B.C., which lists it with other everyday articles like meat hooks and skewers. Guessing from this, we might call the cheese grater a Greek invention from an earlier time, perhaps the 5th century B.C., a period when cooking made great progress.

**Canned Food**

Preservation in airtight jars was introduced in ancient times. A later exponent was Paris confectioner Nicolas Appert, who in 1790 went into business selling preserved meat, vegetables, dairy products and fruit. His bottles and jars had airtight seals and their contents had been heated to rid them of bacteria. Early the next century, fellow Frenchman Pierre Durand began manufacturing food containers with an internal tin coating. In 1812, the firm of Donkin and Hall purchased the rights of Appert and Durand for its food business in England. Using Appert's method and Durand's type of container, the English duo started inflicting bulk quantities of canned food on the world.

**Pasteurisation**   It is likely that some early packagers of food and drink in jars and bottles used pasteurisation, but doubtful that they understood its significance or why it worked. French scientist Louis Pasteur (1822–95) established that fermentation results from the multiplication of micro-organisms, and from 1868 to 1870 he worked out the process of pasteurisation. By briefly heating foods to less than boiling point, he was able to arrest fermentation temporarily by bringing the micro-organisms under control.

## 2. FOODSTUFFS AND BEVERAGES

Long before history began, primitive people had used practically every edible natural substance as a food. But the firsts recorded below are all cases of domestication, adoption into a cuisine, or manufacturing processes. Even such firsts as those have often left no trace: sugarcane, for example, was initially farmed at an unknown time and place in Southeast Asia or the Indonesian Archipelago. Some important foods, including potatoes and chocolate, come from America. The Spanish conquistadors so completely exterminated the civilisations of Mexico, Central America and South America that the opportunity to discover their beginnings is lost.

Primary production is dealt with in the section on farming [VIII, 7].

**Cereals**   Before the invention of agriculture [VIII, 7], primitive peoples in many parts of the world used to gather grass seeds and cook them, or grind them into flour. When preparation of cereals in these ways began cannot be known. With domestication, cereals suddenly became the staple foodstuff of agricultural **Domestication** societies, instead of the adjunct they represented to primitive **of Cereals** peoples. This was first achieved with wheat and barley crops in West Asia, perhaps as long as 10,000 years ago. The location is likely to have been in the region between the Mediterranean coast and Persia (Iran).

**Barley**   Archaeologists have discovered clear evidence of domesticated barley at Jericho, in Palestine, and at Ali Kosh, in southern Iran, dating back to around 7000B.C. and possibly up to 500 years earlier. Einkorn, one of the first kinds of wheat to be domesticated, has been detected at both sites, at the same **Wheat** time. At Ali Kosh, emmer, the other early crop wheat, has been identified for the same period. An archaeological site of similar age at Çayönü, in southern Turkey, has also revealed both early wheat types. It is correct to suppose that barley and wheat cultivation began considerably earlier, perhaps even by 8000B.C., since by about 7000B.C. crops were already dispersed around Iran, Palestine and Turkey.

Studies of the distribution of wild rice species and archae- ological remains have traced the origin of rice cultivation to a **Rice** limited area. It must have begun in the 7th millennium B.C., in the region between Northern Thailand and the South China coast. The earliest archaeological remains of domestic rice come from the South China coast near Ningpo, dating back to about 5000B.C., before Chinese times.

Millet, the first staple of Chinese agriculture, appears to have been domesticated in the Yellow River basin (in North **Millet** China) in pre-Chinese times, the 6th millennium B.C.; the earliest archaeological remains are from Shensi, dating to about 5000B.C. The cultivation of maize began in America, the cultivation of sorghum in Africa; in both cases, future archaeology may shed new light on their dates and locales.

Popular breakfast cereals come in two styles: the prehistoric and the modern. The prehistoric style involves cooking the **Cereal with** grain in milk or water and serving it as a pulse. All varieties of **Milk** porridge belong in this group. Puffed rice was the first modern- style cereal – one which is cooked dry so that the milk is added immediately before eating. It was enjoyed this way in Southern India around 500A.D. The cooking process was rather spe- cialised, and involved casting the rice grains onto very hot sand. Sometimes they were given a sugar coating after cooking. By this time, porridge was long established in many countries. Where it began in prehistoric times can never be known.

The Indian jungle fowl, *Gallus gallus*, is thought to be both the progenitor of most or all domesticated fowl and itself the first **Poultry** to have been domesticated. Its husbandry began around 3000B.C. or slightly later, probably on the Gangetic Plain of North India.

A Roman surgeon invented the capon in about 200B.C., as a way to get round the pernicious law against fattening hens for the table. This law was framed in 204B.C. by a wowser **Capons** named Fannius, who wanted to restrict poultry consumption.

Fannius's law would have put chicken out of the reach of law-abiding diners. But then, by castrating male chicks, poulterers found they could raise plump and flavoursome birds – capons – instead of scrawny roosters.

**Granny Smith Apple**  Around 1860 in Eastwood (now a Sydney suburb), Maria Smith (died 1870) tipped out the contents of a wooden packing crate beside a creek that flowed through her small property. Among them was a rotting apple, from a seed of which a new tree grew up on the spot. It produced a new kind of fruit, which was green when ripe, sweet-tasting, good for cooking, and kept for ages without refrigeration. This freak tree, officially documented in 1868, is the ancestor of all other granny smith apple trees throughout the world.

**Olive Oil**  Archaeologists follow the gradual spread of olive oil manufacture around the world by excavating olive oil storage jars. From these finds, it appears that olive cultivation and oil production have been increasing their range steadily but extremely slowly for over 5000 years. Their original home has been traced to Palestine, before 3000B.C. The native olive tree, an oleaster, is believed to have grown wild in Palestine and Syria.

**Tofu**  When the Chinese first domesticated the soybean nearly 3000 years ago, they were not too sure how to take advantage of the obvious nutritional and agricultural advantages of their new crop, because people considered it insufficiently palatable. Soybeans were fed to livestock, and to people in times of food shortage, but they only took a place in cuisine, as a condiment, when soy sauce [III, 3] was invented. With the introduction of tofu (or bean curd), soybeans became a familiar foodstuff, but it was a trickier thing to invent, and probably came in the Harn Dynasty (206B.C.–220A.D.). A passage in the *Huai Narn Dzu*, a book of 139B.C. with many firsts in it, contains the first reference to tofu.

**Margarine**  During the reign of Napoleon III, the French Government became disturbed about the scarcity and high price of butter. In 1866 it announced a reward for those who could devise a good substitute. Hippolyte Mège-Mouriès realised that cows are capable of breaking down their own body fat to make milk, and believed he could make butter artificially by processing beef fat. He failed, and produced margarine instead, which the government conceded was the closest substitute.

Vegemite was created in Melbourne in 1922 by Dr Cyril Callister, of Fred Walker and Company, by blending concentrated **Vegemite** extracts of yeast, malt and vegetables. It was released commercially under its present name in 1923.

The site of the first cultivation of sugarcane is unknown. The extraction of various sugar products began in Northern India, **Sugar** where sugar was well established as a crop by about 1000B.C., if not earlier. Granulated sugar was developed shortly afterwards.

The first jam was quince jam, made to the following recipe:

> Having removed the skin from ripe quinces, cut them into **Jam**
> very small fine shreds and throw away the hard part inside.
> Then cook in honey until the pulp is reduced to half its
> measure, and as it cooks, sprinkle on fine ground pepper.

This is the technique recorded by the Roman writer Palladius in the 2nd century A.D. As recipes usually exist for a while before they get into cookbooks, it is likely that jam was already being made in Roman Italy in the previous century.

Quince was also the flavour of the first fruit jelly, a choice probably owing to its high pectin content. The method was to **Jelly** boil quince juice down with honey and an additive such as wine or vinegar. The pectin reacts with the sugar, and the acids from the vinegar or wine, to gel upon sufficient reduction. Again, the first recipes were recorded in the Roman Empire in the 2nd century A.D., and the invention of jelly was probably similar in time and place to jam.

> The chicken, the pig, the fish and the duck, these are the **Birds' Nests**
> four heroes of the table. Sea slugs and birds' nest have no
> characteristic flavours of their own. They are but usurpers
> in the house.

Thus does a Chinese cookbook by Yewarn Mei (1715A.D.–1797; tr. Giles) condemn some of the most famous delicacies of Chinese cuisine. Yewarn Mei and his sympathisers were outraged at the lengths gone to in order to bring these ostentatious items to Chinese tables. Birds' nests are produced by swifts which regurgitate a glutinous cement to build their boat-shaped nests. The Chinese discovered them in Borneo in the 1400s A.D., and this marks their entry into haute cuisine. However, for the natives of Borneo, their consumption began at an indeterminable date, as an unglamorous protein supplement.

Sea slugs had to come even further to reach China – from the north coast of Australia and the southern parts of the **Sea Slugs**

Indonesian Archipelago. Again, it seems that the Chinese began to devour them in the 1400s, but the Malay natives of the Archipelago must have tried them first, perhaps with less gusto.

**Tea** Tea is native to China and may have been used as a drink there as long ago as 3000B.C. It is probably one of the products referred to in Chinese poems dating back to about 1000B.C., **Writings** and in the *Literary Approximator* (*Erh Ya*), a thesaurus from **on Tea** about 500B.C. *The Tea Classic* (*Cha Jing*), written by Lu Yew (8th century A.D.) in the Tarng Dynasty, is the earliest of several books devoted entirely to tea. It deals lightheartedly with the botany, husbandry, manufacture, brewing, drinking and history of tea, then provides a guide to all the different types available.

**Coffee** Coffee was initially consumed as a medicine, and only caught on as a beverage around 1400A.D., or soon after, when the people of Yemen began to enjoy it. The large number of Chinese ships visiting Yemen from the 1200s to the 1400s must have brought many tea drinkers, who set the example to the locals of infusing a hot drink. At first, coffee was made from the roasted husks of the coffee cherry, which surrounds the **Coffee** bean. By the early 1500s, the beans themselves were being **Grinders** roasted for drinking. From this period come the first coffee-grinders – made in Syria – which could only have worked on roasted beans.

**Cappuccino** In the 1800s, the drink which we know as Vienna coffee was called *kapuziner* in its native Austria. It was introduced to Northern Italy by Austrian soldiers who were stationed there late in that century. The Italians, however, preferred to use hot milk froth rather than whipped cream. Around 1906, when high-pressure nozzle espresso machines had been introduced, they were used to produce a frothy modification of the *kapuziner*, the now ubiquitous cappuccino.

**Instant Coffee** Soluble instant coffee was produced in the late 1800s – probably by a number of separate experimenters. The only one whose identity is recorded is Japan's Sartori Kato, who exhibited his product of 1899 at the Panamerican World Fair. Given the number of people working on coffee-related products in Europe before 1899, he probably cannot claim priority. Commercial success eluded him too. However, instant coffee soon caught on, and was used by both sides in the First World War.

Coffee shops first opened for business around 1500 in Mocha and other towns of Arabia. Further north, coffee shops **Coffee Shops** are known to have been open in Damascus and Aleppo in the 1530s and to have been temporarily banned in Cairo in 1539.

In Northern India, a variety of fruit juices was condensed by boiling down, to make cordial called *yusa*, about 2000 years **Cordial** ago. *Yusa* is first mentioned around 100A.D. by medical writers, who praised its dietary value.

## 3. RECIPES AND INVENTIONS

This section includes dishes, condiments, pastries and desserts. Birthday cake is treated elsewhere [IX, 4], together with birthday parties.

In Italy in the 1st century B.C., Roman gourmets began feeding up their geese to enlarge the livers artificially, and saturat- **Foie Gras** ing the livers in milk and honey. The identity of the goose first treated this way is not known, but it is believed to have belonged either to Scipio Metellus or Marcus Seius.

Lasagne was cooked in Italy in Roman times from about 2000 years ago. There are two lasagne recipes in *Apicius on Cooking* **Lasagne** (*Apicius de re Coquinaria*), a Roman cookbook from the 1st or 2nd century A.D. One, the 'Apician Dish', invented by the master himself, was a lavish composition including sow's belly, figpecker breasts, fish and chicken, minced and combined with nuts, wine and spices, all cooked between layers of pastry. 'An expensive silver platter would enhance the appearance of this dish', says the book. The other recipe is for an 'everyday dish' that is cheaper and simpler to make. Readers who would like to cook lasagne without learning Latin will find the recipes in *Cookery and Dining in Imperial Rome*, J. D. Vehling's translation of Apicius (recipe numbers 141 and 142).

Vichyssoise is a development on the traditional *potage bon femme* (French leek and potato soup). It was invented in 1917 **Vichyssoise** by Louis Diat, chef of New York's Ritz Carlton Hotel, where the new dish was first served. Its distinctive characteristic is that it is served iced.

Mustard seeds were widely known in ancient India and West Asia, and are referred to several times in the Bible. But no one **Mustard** is known to have prepared them into a condiment before the Greeks. From an early time, they were mustard enthusiasts. Pythagoras (6th century B.C.), a great opponent of meat-eating, warmly recommends mustard for its effect on the appetite and the brain.

**Soy Sauce**  Soy sauce was invented in North China, probably after 1000B.C. Soybeans were domesticated around that time, but the sauce-making is a fairly elaborate process, including fermentation, which must have taken time to work out. It had certainly been invented by around 500B.C., when it is first mentioned in literature.

**Black Bean Sauce**  During the Harn Dynasty (206B.C.–220A.D.), black bean sauce is known to have been made commercially; its invention probably goes back prior to Harn times, perhaps even several centuries.

**Fish Sauce**  Pasty sauces made from putrified essence of fish or fish innards are popular with cooks for their flavour, and highly nutritious. These advantages earn fish sauces a place on modern shelves in the form of such revolting preparations as shrimp paste and anchovy sauce. They encouraged ancient shoppers to buy plenty of *garum* – the original fish paste, first made in Mediterranean **Anchovy Paste**  countries from the *garus* (prawn or shrimp). Its first appearance in a recipe book is in *Apicius on Cooking* (Rome, 1st or 2nd century A.D.), but by then it had a long past going back to the Eastern Mediterranean, before 500B.C. The fish, or sometimes just its innards or liver, was spiced, mashed, fermented, exposed to sunlight and bottled. Anchovy paste was one of the ancient types of garum; mackerel was a more popular raw ingredient.

**Mayonnaise**  Mayonnaise appears to have been invented in the Western Mediterranean region, perhaps Sardinia or Spain, about 2000 years ago, as a condiment for salted or pickled seafoods. There is a recipe for it in the ancient Roman cookbook *Apicius on Cooking* (recipe no. 480).

**Vinaigrette**  The oldest recipe for vinaigrette envisages it as the dressing for a cold purée of peas: recipe no. 188 in *Apicius on Cooking* (Rome, 1st or 2nd century A.D.) lists the ingredients as onions, egg whites, egg yolks, salt, vinegar and oil. This dish is either a Roman inspiration, or borrowed from the Greeks, who may have had it for a couple of centuries beforehand.

Bearnaise sauce was concocted in about 1830A.D. by a Parisian chef working at the 'Pavillon Henri IV' in St. Germain, a town on the outskirts of Paris.

**Bearnaise Sauce**

Flavoured ice confectionery must first have been made in snowy mountains, and the most likely locale is modern-day Turkey, where snowy areas were located reasonably close to the main centres of luxury in the 3rd and 2nd millennia B.C. The idea of using snow as a base for flavourings must have occurred there, since mountain people readily eat snow to quench thirst. Flavoured ices served in Rome to the 'Emperor' Nero consisted of snow mixed with fruit juice, probably sweetened with honey.

**Ice Confectionery**

Flavoured water ices were first manufactured in China, perhaps during the Harn Dynasty (206B.C.–220A.D.). Dairy-based ice desserts were developed in the 1500s by the Moguls – descendants of Central Asian nomads who conquered and settled in Afghanistan and North India. They invented the *kulfi*, which is still a popular item of Indian cuisine. One Mogul book, published in Delhi in 1590, describes the method: a mixture containing milk solids, pistachio nuts and saffron is frozen in metal cones sealed with dough. True ice-cream was developed in France in the following century. The earliest ice-cream maker known by name is Jacques, chef to England's Charles I, who served ice-cream to the King in 1640.

**Water Ice**

**Ice-cream**

**Kulfi**

The first ice-cream parlour was in Paris – 'Café Procope', opened in 1660 by the Sicilian Procopio Cultelli.

**Ice-cream Parlour**

Patriotic bon vivants in Australia and New Zealand – casting around for a recipe that puts the world in their debt – have long gloried in the pavlova, each recognising the falseness of the other's claim. In that recognition, they are both right: pavlovas are a Scandinavian invention, said by Danish chefs to be hundreds of years old. In fact, since there is no record of meringue in modern Europe until 1691, it is unlikely that pavlova was invented before the 1700s. The main original contribution of the Australians was to bestow on the venerable dish its modern Russian name, which they did in the 1930s.

**Pavlova**

The French chef George Auguste Escoffier was inspired by the opera *Lohengrin* to make an outlandish new dessert with a swan theme during its 1892–93 season. He carved a pair of

**Peach Melba**

swan's wings out of ice, dusted them with icing sugar and set peaches between them on a bed of ice-cream. This he served to his idol, the star of the show, Dame Nellie Melba. What it lacked, though, was raspberry sauce, which he added in a later version served at London's Carlton Hotel.

**Melba Toast**   Peach Melba was not the only result of the quality in Nellie Melba's voice that enchanted European chefs. In the Savoy, another London hotel, some very thin, dry toast was served (allegedly by accident) during her stay, but turning misfortune to great account, the chef found it could be palmed off successfully on guests who actually liked it, all the more since it began to be offered as 'Melba toast'.

**French Toast**   The French have not been around for nearly as long as the recipe for French toast. It is included in a Roman cookbook, *Apicius on Cooking*, from the 1st or 2nd century B.C., with the recommendation that it be served with honey. Like most of Apicius's recipes, it was probably invented by the Greeks several centuries earlier.

**Pappadams**   Judging from Hindu scriptures, people in Northern India began eating pappadams about 2500 years ago. Their discovery was due to the widespread practices there of frying foods in ghee and of eating spiced pulses. Cooking pulse into biscuits led to the discovery of the expansion and crispiness achievable by deep-frying.

**Baklava**   The westward migration of the Turks from Central Asia, the creation of filo pastry and the invention of the baklava all belong to a single historical phenomenon. Before 1100A.D., the primitive Turks began experimenting with layered doughs while following their herds over the steppes. As time passed and they moved west, the layers got thinner and more numerous. In Azerbaijan, they had the 'baku baklava', with eight pastry layers. Eventually the Turks reached present-day Turkey in Asia Minor and Eastern Europe, and in 1453 they conquered Constantinople. Settled in their present home, they **Filo Pastry** created real filo pastry, and put it to its natural use by making true baklavas. The evolution was probably consummated in Bursa, Constantinople or one of the other opulent cities of their new empire, in the 1400s.

**Croissants**   Having brought the baklava to completion, the Turks might have stopped their westward conquests; instead, they marched into Central Europe, until their arms finally failed them before Vienna in 1683. At the Turkish siege of Vienna, the Austrians took over the initiative, both in military success and in pastry-cooking invention. When the Turks tried to take the city by undermining the city walls, they chose a spot where a bakery was in business just inside. Vigilant bakers heard sounds of digging and tipped off the authorities. For saving their city, the bakers deserved a special reward, and the government granted them a monopoly on cooking *croissants* – rolls in the shape of the Turkish emblem. It is believed the croissants were served at the café of a Polish resident, Kolschitsky, who had daringly purloined some bags of enemy coffee, and thought croissants would be a good way to trumpet his achievement. The Austrian princess, Marie Antoinette – chiefly remembered by French pastrycooks for promoting cake – brioche, to be precise – made a more substantial contribution by introducing the croissant from her native land to France.

**Choux Pastry**

The first published recipe for choux pastry is Lancelot de Casteau's cream puffs, in his cookbook *Ouverture de cuisine*, (Liège, 1604). De Casteau, from Mons in Belgium, was a very international chef whose recipes came from many countries in Europe, so there is nothing to prove a Belgian origin for the cream puff. But his name for it, *pâte à choux*, suggests a French-speaking inventor – if not de Casteau himself, then perhaps a contemporary or immediate predecessor.

**Bread and Butter Pudding**

Bread and butter pudding was invented in England around 1700A.D. The first published recipes, in the 1720s, call for eggs, nutmeg, currants, butter and fresh bread; of these, the last is curious, because now, bread and butter pudding is usually thought of as a way to use up stale bread.

**Chocolate Chip Biscuits**

The chocolate chip biscuit was an accidental discovery by Ruth Wakefield, restaurateur at the Toll House Inn, Whitman, Massachusetts. In 1933 she was too hasty in preparing her batch of chocolate butter drops, which were supposed to be chocolate-flavoured biscuits of regular consistency. Instead of melting the chocolate first and stirring it in with the other ingredients, Mrs Wakefield simply dropped in whole lumps of chocolate, expecting them to melt into the rest of the mixture. Instead, they retained their integrity, but nobody minded because the end result was so pleasing.

**Dog Biscuit**
The *autopyron*, an ancient Roman dog biscuit, is the earliest known purpose-made pet food. It was a hard, dark little biscuit with lots of bran in it, manufactured in Rome probably from about 100B.C. onwards. Although humans could never find them appetising, they were considered to be good for the digestion and were fed to slaves as well as dogs.

## 4. LIQUOR

Alcoholic drinks are produced either by distillation or by being fermented. Both beer and wine are fermented and were invented in prehistoric times. Spirits are all distilled, and the method for producing them was discovered much later. It is possible to locate the beginning of many spirituous drinks by reference to old written records and archaeological artefacts. Not all the many stories concerning the origins of alcoholic drinks are repeated in this section. Sometimes manufacturers put such information on their labels or on little leaflets around the necks of bottles. Readers who require further satisfaction are urged to obtain this material for themselves. It is not all equally trustworthy, but it becomes more plausible the more it is studied.

**Drinking Book**
Cleopatra's lover Mark Antony was the first enthusiast in a longish succession to extol the delights of drink in a book. Antony, famous loser of the Battle of Actium (31B.C.) proclaimed his own drinking prowess in the book, which is not extant. We know of it from the writings of fellow Roman, Pliny, who lamented that 'It was shortly before the Battle of Actium that he vomitted up this volume' (*Natural History* XIV, xxviii).

**Low-alcohol Beverage**
Low-alcohol wine was manufactured in the Roman Empire as a drink for invalids. One of several methods for approximating the flavour of proper wine was to mix water with new white wine and heat the mixture until the quantity was reduced by evaporation to the amount of the wine component. Production was widespread by the first century A.D. and must have begun at least a century or two earlier.

**Spirits**
**Stills**
The manufacture of spirits only became possible with the invention of the still, in which alcohol is evaporated and collected. Consequently, spirits were not drunk until thousands of years after fermented drinks like wine and beer. Distillation was first practised by the Indus Valley people 4500–5000 years ago, in

present-day Pakistan. Each of their stills had a small perforated basin, fitted into the hole in the bottom of a collecting basin. These basins were placed in the top of a large pot, and a basin full of cold water was set on top of them. Vapour from the pot rising through the perforations would condense on the underside of the cold-water basin and drip into the collecting basin. The first drinkable product of these 3rd millennium stills was probably a rough grain spirit, such as a barley spirit. This was the forerunner of whisky, but there is no telling which later distillery first made grain liquor good enough to earn the title 'whisky'. The same obscurity frustrates any attempt to date the first scotch. It's unlikely that the product of Scotch stills 800 years ago would pass for scotch if we had to drink it now; when the quality breakthrough came cannot be ascertained. **Whisky**

The region where distillation was invented and which was the centre of the ancient sugar industry, was naturally enough the first home of rum. In India early in the 1st millennium B.C., rum was distilled from fermented sugarcane juices and from solid cane extract; molasses was also used, although its use may have begun as late as 300B.C. Ancient Indian rum was generally flavoured and coloured with flowers and tannins. **Rum**

The Indian beverage *varuni*, mentioned in literature before 300B.C., appears to be what is now called arrack or raki, the distillate of fermented palm wine. *Varuni* was initially made from *mahua* flowers, but before long, palm juices were introduced for its manufacture. **Arrack**

Faustus's Falernian wine was manufactured in Italy in Roman times by a method of distillation known only on the Faustus estate, in the celebrated Falernian vineyard region. Faustus's was notable for catching fire on exposure to flame. It was in production in the 1st century A.D. and possibly earlier. **Brandy**

Aquavit, also known as schnapps, is a spirit produced in Scandinavia and Germany, variously made out of rye, wheat, potatoes and aromatic seeds. It was first manufactured in Denmark in the 1500s, and may owe much of its distinctive character to King Christian III, who in 1555 bought a set of stills which someone had pawned in Copenhagen. Christian's experiments with his equipment and flavouring materials created a product which became popular well beyond the Danish court. **Aquavit**

**Linie Aquavit**   The greatest esteem attaches to Linie Aquavit (named after the Equator, or 'line'). The method for producing it was discovered by chance after the crew of a Norwegian sailing ship going to Australia failed to consume a cask of aquavit that was stored on board to support morale. The captain was therefore able to celebrate the ship's return to Norway with the fluid in the cask. He was surprised to find it much easier to drink than normal aquavit. The improved properties are attributed to its having crossed the Equator twice. In Oslo in 1927, the Loitens distillery and the Wilhelmsen shipping line began intensive production of linie aquavit, by loading 550 litre oak sherry casks full of ordinary aquavit onto the cargo liner *Tungsha* for a return journey to Australia. The system is

**Sea Finishing**   still in use by the original parties. The idea of improving drinks by taking them on sea voyages had first been exploited by British traders to Portugal in the 1680s. One firm had a tri-angular sea route, linking Britain, Newfoundland and Oporto. The very hard-hitting red wine shipped in Oporto [see Port, below] was sometimes conveyed direct to Britain, and some-times shipped to Britain on a vessel going first to Newfound-land. The wine which travelled via Newfoundland was marketed in England as superior, by virtue of the fact that it had made the return crossing.

**Gin**   Gin production began in Holland in the 1500s A.D., probably as a result of efforts to improve the deplorable taste of rye spirit. The critical additive is juniper – *jineverbes* in Dutch. The earliest known manufacturer, perhaps the first, is Lucas Bols, who made gin at a distillery called the Little Shed, out-side Amsterdam, in 1575.

**Benedictine**   Dom Bernardo Vincelli was a botanist at the Benedictine abbey at Fécamp on France's Normandy coast, in 1510, when he invented Benedictine. He prepared twenty-eight herbs and fruits to mix into a cordial for the abbey's infirmary. Benedic-tine was all but wiped out in the persecution of the French Revolution, but the monks at Fécamp managed to entrust their formula to a friendly lay family, and production resumed in the 19th century after a seventy-year break.

**Chartreuse**   About 1605A.D., François Hannibal d'Estrees, a marshall in the French Artillery, gave the formula for 'an elixir of long life' to Carthusian brothers near Paris. After waiting 130 years, they passed it on to the Abbey of Grand Chartreuse, original headquarters of the Carthusian Order [VII, 5]. There, Brother Jérôme Maubec set to work interpreting its fifty cryptic pages of small script. On his deathbed in 1762, he dictated instructions for making the elixir, known now as Chartreuse. The first sales to the public began in 1765. Because the distinctive ingredients are herbs available in the Chartreuse area, and because d'Estrees had chosen the Carthusians, it is likely that the formula was devised by monks of Chartreuse, before 1600; but when they did so and how they lost it are mysteries that cannot be solved now that the original document is lost.

Drambuie went on sale commercially last century; prior to that, it had been manufactured for a long time in Scotland by **Drambuie** the Mackinnons of Strathaird, in quantities adequate for their own consumption and for annual clan assemblies. After the Battle of Culloden in 1746, Prince Charles Stuart – Bonny Prince Charlie – had fled by boat to the Isle of Skye, where the Mackinnons harboured him until his rescue by the French. The destitute prince expressed his gratitude to Mackinnon by passing on the secret of Drambuie, his own private liqueur. This tradition gives Drambuie a pedigree too noble and romantic for us to consider spoiling it with doubts that have no evidentiary basis.

Tequila is a variety of mezcal, a Mexican spirit deriving peculiar effectiveness from the incorporation of cactus of the **Tequila** maguey family. In 1758 José Maria Guadaloupe de Cuervo acquired a property in the Tequila district near Guadalajara, Mexico. It is not known exactly when he began manufacturing tequila. The authorities in Guadalajara issued him a licence in 1795 to make 'mezcal wine', but often people start doing things before they get permission, so there could have been some illicit tequila around before the 1790s.

The French Revolution was a particularly retrograde development for makers of liqueurs and spirits; apart from halting the **Pernod** production of several drinks, including Benedictine and Chartreuse, in 1790 it caused an exodus of frightened royalist bon vivants. Among them was Dr Pierre Ordinaire, who fled to Neuchatel, Switzerland. There he made an infusion of fifteen flavourings in spirits, among them absinthe. On his death in 1792, he left the formula for this consoling potion to his housekeeper Mme Henriot, who, with her daughters, began producing and selling it in their own shop. In 1797 one of their customers, Henry Louis Pernod, bought the formula and opened a factory to produce it. He unjustly stole the inventor's fame by calling the drink 'Pernod'. This is such an improvement on 'Ordinaire' that we can hardly blame him.

**Angostura Bitters**

Johan Gottlieb Benjamin Siegert (1796–1870) was born in Crosswalditz (in present-day Poland). As an army surgeon, he went to Venezuela to join Simon Bolivar in the fight of the South American republics for independence from Spain. Bolivar put Siegert in charge of the military hospital at Angostura (present-day Ciudad Bolivar), on the Orinoco River. In 1824 Siegert perfected a spirituous tonic for stomach disorders, including in its ingredients the bark of a local native, *Galipea officionalis*. Under the name Angostura Bitters, they are still produced by the Siegert family, though rarely used by hospitals.

**Campari**

Gaspare Campari, a drink waiter from Navara in Italy, wanted to be famous for inventing a new drink. His experiments led to the creation of a strikingly original flavour combining quinine, cochineal, rhubarb, citrus peel and other ingredients. With his wife, he owned and operated a café in Milan, which gave him ready access to an appreciative public. The drink we now know as Campari reached the world by this channel, launched by the Camparis to celebrate the birth of their youngest son, Davide. After Gaspare's death in 1882, the family kept up production and maintained the secrecy of his method.

**Rice Wine**

Rice wine, such as Japanese *sake*, can only be made by a fermentation process in which cultured moulds are used instead of malt and yeast to digest the starch in grain. This process makes rice wine more effective than other fermented drinks. The technique was discovered in China probably late in the Sharng or early in the Jo Dynasty (between 1400 and 1000B.C.).

**Retsina**

Retsina, the distinctive wine of modern Greece, was also manufactured in ancient Italy, at least as early as the 1st century B.C. and probably earlier. One method of manufacture consisted of sprinkling the grape juice with resinous sap at first fermentation stage, which would have given a result very similar to the present-day product.

Vermouth is named after *wermut*, the German word for wormwood or absinthe. Roman vermouth, according to Apicius's **Vermouth**
cookbook, was flavoured with wormwood, mastich and nard.
Apicius's recipe for it comes from the 1st or 2nd century A.D.,
but like most dishes and drinks, vermouth was probably
invented somewhat earlier than the recipe was published.
There may also have been an aromatised wine containing
wormwood produced earlier in other Mediterranean countries, like vermouth, but having a more bitter taste owing to
the use of charcoal in its production.

Punch takes its name from the Hindi word for five: being an
Indian invention and having in all its early recipes five prin- **Punch**
ciple ingredients. The first punch on record – from 1638A.D. –
comprises arrack, spices, sugar, lime juice and water.

In 1688, Dom Pérignon, the Benedictine monk who had the
prize job of looking after the cellar of his abbey in the province **Champagne**
of Champagne in France, was disturbed by the sound of one of
his bottles blowing up. He noticed the minute bubbles rising
in the remaining wine, and tasted the rewards of his hours of
painstaking experimentation. 'I am drinking stars', he
exclaimed. Or so tradition has it. With some further work, he
was able to recreate the conditions which had produced the
freak bottle, and to launch champagne on a grateful world. In
fact, it is unlikely that he had bottles and corks equal to the
task of containing the high effervescence of champagne as we
now have it; his most important contribution was probably in
developing the characteristic champagne taste.

Beginning in the 1670s and going on into the following century, the aggressive policy of the French under Louis XIV led **Port**
the Netherlands, Scotland and England to impose trade
embargos on France. As none of these nations was capable of
producing decent wine, they were suddenly in a quandary
which forced their wine traders to look for supplies in places
they had once disdained. They found some up the Douro
River in the high country behind Oporto. The grapes there
grew in schist rather than soil; the production methods were
rough and unhygienic, and by the time it reached British and
Dutch tables in the 1680s and nineties, the substitute from
Oporto could have natural alcohol levels up to 15 per cent.

    Mark how it smells – methinks a real pain
    Is by its odour thrown upon my brain.

Richard Ames, who wrote these words in 1693, expressed the disenchantment of palates accustomed to fine French table wines. Distaste and headaches prompted the solution, which gave the world port as we now know it. In the first decades of the 18th century, somebody began fortifying the Douro wine with brandy; it ceased to contest the place of French wines at parties and on meal tables, and was enjoyed in smaller glasses and on fuller stomachs, the brandy having neutralised any untoward contents.

# IV

# GOVERNMENT AND SOCIETY

Government originated long before the beginning of history. It is a natural result of there always being some people who are strong and others weak; governmental power falls into the hands either of the strong, or of those who become strong by the support of the weakling majority which relies on their protection. Two distinct kinds of governments – autocracies and republics – also have unknown prehistoric beginnings, as have systems mixing both principles.

The theoretical examination of government and society is dealt with in Social and Political Thought [VII, 3].

## I. SYSTEMS OF GOVERNMENT

Egypt during the Old Kingdom Period (c. 3500–c. 2500B.C.) was ruled by a bureaucracy, wielding in practice the power **Bureaucracy** which, in theory, belonged to the Pharaoh. It came into being almost immediately after unification of Egypt by the 1st Dynasty (in about 3500B.C.). The bureaucracy consisted of two arms: a central administration housed in office complexes in Memphis, and local administrations presiding over official districts or *sepets*. The duties of local officials included trying legal cases, and collecting taxes in their districts. From the 3rd Dynasty onwards (c. 3150B.C.), different parts of the central bureaucracy, acknowledged either of two figures as their bosses: one, the *that* or prime minister, and the other the 'keeper of the seal'. The various departments were staffed by hundreds of scribes. As in a modern bureaucracy, the officials were chosen and promoted, not by election or hereditary title, but on merit, experience and favouritism.

**Feudalism**

The term feudalism was originally applied to the agrarian social system of mediaeval Europe. This mediaeval system is unique in some vital characteristics, such as the precise relationships of villein to lord and vassal to superior; a purist can say there was no feudalism anywhere until Europe in the 800s A.D. However the term is also used for any social structure in which local economic and political power is exercised for the central government by privileged landholders who claim the primary fealty of the people occupying the land. Such privileges and fealty were vested in the *nomarchs* of Old Kingdom Egypt during the 6th Dynasty (c. 2800–c. 2600B.C.). Nomarchs were originally bureaucratic appointees in charge of local administration. The appointments frequently fell to members of the local landed gentry. As time went on they were accompanied by increasing grants of land and the income from lands, so nomarchs gradually became hereditary feudal barons. Eventually it was only by securing their loyalty that the central government maintained its sovereignty over the country and people. From a position of absolute power the pharaohs had descended to be the primates of the first feudal order.

**Bicameral Parliament**

The earliest description of a parliamentary system with an upper and a lower house is in a Sumerian poem from Mesopotamia, written in the 3rd millennium B.C. *Gilgamesh and Agga* describes events of a period, about a thousand years earlier, when Agga, the ruler of Kish, besieged the city of Erech and demanded its submission. Gilgamesh, ruler of Erech, proposed to the Senate that the city refuse to submit, but the senators favoured submission. He put the same proposal to the 'Assembly of Men' or lower house, which took his side, saying 'do not submit to the house of Kish, let us smite it with weapons'. Under the constitution of Erech, the ruler and the lower house in combination must have outranked the Senate, because messengers were then dispatched to the Kish forces, refusing submission. The story ends, after some toing and froing, with the peaceful departure of the Kish forces, leaving Erech in the charge of its disputatious politicians. Many such double assemblies governed early Sumerian cities around 3000B.C., but it is not known how their powers were distributed.

**Federation**

In classical Greece the people of Boeotia were looked down on by the rest for being slow-witted and boring. They had little share in the genius which animated the Greeks to exceptional lives. They also had little share in the absurdly divisive zeal for independence that kept the tiny free cities of Greece fiercely disunited. In 447B.C. ten Boeotian cities voluntarily formed the first federation – a partnership of states equal in political status under a common rule. Their federal government sat in Thebes, Boeotia's most important city. It was presided over by the Archon and a council of four. Executive power was in the hands of 'Boeotarchs', who were elected for one-year terms, from each **Representative** of eleven roughly equal electorates. They were the first politi- **Government** cians to be elected as representatives of local constituencies.

Since civilisation began, socialism has been a principle of organisation in specific branches of government, in states **Socialist State** which were not essentially socialist. A socialist policy as the key to a whole economy is a comparatively late development. The first socialist state was established in ancient Greece by Lycur-gus, king of Sparta (8th century B.C.), whose city ruled over the district of Laconia. He set out to rectify the severe disproportion of wealth between the affluent and poor citizens by imposing an equal apportionment of property. The state repossessed all prop-erty and redistributed it in portions. Gold and silver were replaced by a low-value iron currency to prevent accumulation of private capital. Citizens ate at public tables from communal supplies, which they were bound to contribute from their rural estates. Specific enactments precluded them from trading and manufacturing luxury goods, and permitted them to use each other's horses, carriages and servants. Lycurgus is quoted as say-ing, just after the reform, 'Laconia looks like one family estate just divided among a number of brothers.' However, the numer-ous non-citizens did not share the equal economic and political rights of the citizen body; we will have to wait for a future edi-tion to record the first egalitarian society. Lycurgus's other reforms went well beyond economics, and created the first regime of totalitarianism.

They brought in rigid state control over all aspects of life. Children of citizens were taken young from their parents and **Totalitarianism** reared in state schools. Military service was universal and com-pulsory, and the yields of property were appropriated for com-munal supplies. A variety of measures restricted relations between the sexes within tight bounds, introduced controlled breeding and stabilised the population. A secret police force, the Krypteia, prevented the rise of dissent. The object was to guarantee a stable society that could last permanently without succumbing to internal changes in power structure, economics, morality and culture. Indeed, Sparta retained its regime and remained the most powerful state in Greece until external events overtook it in the 4th century B.C.

**Totalitarian Thought Control**

1984A.D. did not see the advent of the more extreme form of totalitarianism prophesied by George Orwell, which attempts to eliminate independent thought and to prevent individual initiative. But such a system was briefly a reality in China after the Chin Dynasty took over in 221B.C. Implementing the philosophy of Legalism [VII, 2] the Chin state set about eradicating memory of the past and of variant forms of thought by ruthlessly confiscating all books except the official Chin records and those dealing with practical topics. Hundreds of scholars were slaughtered, and the old culture was destroyed. A new script was created with a limited vocabulary, and the old writing perished, so that divergent views became inexpressible. The masses were deliberately kept poor and ignorant, and everyone was trained in a paramount loyalty to the First Emperor, a Big Brother-type figurehead whose interests overrode those of family, friends and country. The state insisted on knowing exactly what its subjects were doing, so the harshest punishments were visited on those who did less or more than the task entrusted to them. The architects of the Chin regime intended it to last forever, by keeping the people destitute and using up surplus resources in warfare. It was overcome in 206B.C. by popular uprisings. So effective was its sixteen-year reign that it then took many decades of painstaking archaeology to recover past traditions and re-establish Chinese civilisation.

**Democracy**

Democracy is a method of government first practised by the ancient Greeks. The word means rule by the people, and anything else that politicians or journalists wish it to mean. With the possible exception of Switzerland, modern countries are not real democracies, because in each government the people's only role is to grant a mandate to a small group at election time. Many ancient states that might pass as democracies in the modern parlance do not merit the title for the same reason. Actual democracy was established by the Greek statesman Cleisthenes in his native Athens in 508–507B.C. Under his constitution, power vested in the assembly in which all male citizens over eighteen were entitled to vote. The assembly met infrequently and could not attend to everything, therefore the Council of 500, which prepared assembly business and attended to many of the lesser items, wielded a lot of real power. Cleisthenes divided the citizen population into ten mixed groups, each sending fifty members to the council. His system retained some undemocratic features – only citizens could vote, and some senior posts, as well as the supreme judicial power, were open only to the wealthiest. Forty-six years later his countryman, Ephialtes, reformed the constitution and made it still more democratic.

Cleisthenes invented a system by which the people could defend their constitution against fellow citizens who attempted **Secret Ballot** to undermine it. Known as ostracism, it came into operation in 487B.C. It worked by a secret ballot in which citizens were entitled to vote for the expulsion from Athens of a person whose **Ostracism** presence they considered threatening. A majority, consisting of at least 6000 voters, meant that the person named was obliged to leave Athenian territory for ten years; the secrecy was intended to ensure that voters would not hesitate to oppose powerful or popular individuals. Votes were cast on shards of pottery – in Greek, *ostraca* – and altogether ten individuals were deported as a result, before ostracism was abandoned in 417B.C.

In Australia in 1851 the Port Phillip District of New South Wales proposed that a secret ballot be held to elect its **Parliamentary** new legislative council in Melbourne. The New South Wales **Election by** Government in Sydney overruled the proposal. When Port **Secret Ballot** Phillip separated from New South Wales to become Victoria, it was ruled at first by an openly elected legislature. However in December 1855 the Legislative Council passed the motion of William Nicholson (1816–65), favouring the secret ballot. The Victorian elections of 1856 were the first in which a parliament was chosen by secret ballot. The vote was taken in the first polling booths, designed for the purpose by a Melbourne **Polling Booth** lawyer, Henry Chapman (1803–81). Voters wrote the names of their chosen candidates on slips of paper. Ballot papers **Ballot Paper** printed with candidates' names adjacent to vacant boxes were invented by W. R. Boothby (1829–1903) for the South Australian Legislative Council elections in 1858.

During the 19th century, elected parliaments increasingly took over the reins of government in many parts of the world. **Female** This process tended to exclude women from political power, **Suffrage** so women's political movements began to press for the extension of voting rights, which were originally enjoyed only by men. New Zealand was the first country whose men caved in. Women there were given the right to vote (but not the right to run for election), in time for the 1893 general elections.

**Parliament Open to Women**

The colony of South Australia followed New Zealand's lead and granted women the right to vote in the following year, 1894. By the same bill South Australia's parliament became the first in the world to be open to women members. Opponents of female suffrage had successfully moved for the bill granting voting rights to women to be amended, by the addition of a section permitting women to stand for parliament. They doubted that parliament would pass a bill including this extra provision, but they misread the prevalent attitude, and their cause suffered doubly as a result.

**Female M.P.s**

In 1907, the year of Finland's first democratic elections, a number of women ran as candidates, some of them successfully. Their country's parliament, the Eduskunta, was thus the world's first to have women members; it continued to lead the way, with a total of twenty-two ladies joining between 1907 and 1920.

**Communist Revolution**

In the 2nd century B.C. Roman power increased steadily throughout Greece and Western Asia. Class conflict there was exacerbated by inequitable division of wealth, and a Roman policy of backing the interests of the wealthy classes to gain local power. From the Greek city of Pergamon, in present-day Turkey, King Attalus III ruled one of the main regional powers. Attalus must have seen that Rome controlled the future: he died in 133B.C., bequeathing his state to Rome. His half brother and heir, Aristonicus, was steeped in the philosophy of communism [VII, 3], and had quite different ideas for the future. Aristonicus and his theorist, the philosopher Blossius, aimed to set up a communist state where all people would be equal in status, work obligations and shared benefits. In 132B.C. they began a revolt against Roman imperialism. It was joined by volunteers, mercenaries and rebelling slaves and it defeated Roman forces over much of Asia Minor. Rome fought back and in 130B.C. captured and executed Aristonicus. His revolutionaries fought on, but this heroic first of the many thwarted efforts to establish an equal society failed completely against Roman opposition in 129B.C.

## 2. INSTITUTIONS OF GOVERNMENT

Of the comparatively few institutions that all governments possess without exception, the two most important are armed force, treated in Chapter VI, and law, which is in Chapter XII, along with finance.

Constantly since history began, the states that rule the world have all been in conflict, vying for shares of resources, territory, population and power. Sometimes they resort to military hostilities; at other times, for expediency, some states cooperate with others. Peaceful cooperation was rare in the early centuries of civilisation, except where strength and weakness established a compelling motive. Around 1270B.C., the two great powers of the Western World – the Hittite Empire (based in present-day Turkey), and the Egyptian Empire – decided to try something new and exciting. After decades of inconclusive fighting they signed a treaty of 'peace and brotherhood forever', which ushered in an age of cooperation between equals. With other problems confronting them, it was expedient for the two powers not to have to fear each other. However both sides were looking for something more sweeping than a common diplomatic advantage. 'We have made brotherhood, peace and goodwill, more than the brotherhood and peace of former times', says the treaty. Cultural exchange, and political and economic cooperation, going beyond the treaty terms began immediately.

**International Goodwill**

Previously heads of state had never paid official international visits to other capitals, except as conquerors, vassals or overlords. But Ramses II, pharaoh of Egypt, invited Hattusilis, emperor of the Hittites, to come on an official tour of Egypt. Instead of taking offence, Hattusilis eagerly made his official tour, twelve years after the treaty date. Egyptian commentators were impressed: 'The people of Kamit [Egyptians] were henceforth one in heart with those of Kheta [Hittites], which had not been the case since the time of the god Ra.'

**State Visit**

About sixty years after the treaty was signed, during the reign of Pharaoh Meneptah, there was a severe drought in large parts of the Hittite Empire; crops failed and food ran out. Egypt donated shipments of wheat to tide the Hittites over their crisis and thus began the long tradition of international disaster relief aid. The genial enlightened regimes that established this new order did not remain the leading powers after the 12th century B.C. Other nations took over pre-eminence, including the super-efficient fascists of Assyria, whose influence plunged Western social morality into darkness.

**Disaster Relief**

A thousand years after the treaty, standards had recovered. In 224B.C. an earthquake on the Greek island of Rhodes (which destroyed the famous Colossus of Rhodes), triggered a historic multinational relief aid campaign, bringing in generous donations from around the Mediterranean Region.

**Multinational Relief Programme**

Egypt shipped large quantities of grain, other goods and money. Sports fans were especially compassionate: much of the Egyptian aid was earmarked for the regular athletic games; two Greek city rulers in Sicily gave a large sum, specifying that three-quarters of it be spent on oil for the gymnasium. One of these two donors was the munificent Hiero (c. 308–216B.C.), former owner of the first luxury liner [IX, 2], which he had donated, fully laden with cargo, to Egypt, at a time of shortages there.

**United Nations**

The United Nations was officially born on 24 October 1945, although most of the founding member states sent delegates to an earlier series of meetings at San Francisco, between 25 April and 26 June 1945, to draft the United Nations Charter and the statute of the International Court of Justice.

**Worldwide League of States**

The first global peacekeeping association of states was the now defunct League of Nations, formed in 1920, in accordance with the Treaty of Versailles (28 June 1919).

**Local Government**

Mesopotamian cities in earliest times (from about 4000B.C.) were administered by local government authorities consisting of a mayor and an assembly of citizens. Each municipality of a large city was identified with the particular city gate that gave access to its district. The local assembly in many cases seems to have consisted of every householder in the municipality and to have been responsible for all matters of local administration.

**Police Force**

The Egyptian Government recruited a specialist police force early in the Old Kingdom Period, before 3000B.C. Policemen were stationed throughout Egypt, attached to the various local administrations. Each administrative district had a police commissioner. He appears to have had a civil bureaucratic staff with some judicial functions, as well as a force of policemen, under his charge.

**Environment Minister**

At about 2200B.C., when Shun took over the rule of the Chinese Commonwealth, he set up the rudiments of a bureaucratic administration. He appointed ministers to be responsible for agriculture, education, works and a number of other areas including the environment. The latter was entrusted to a man named Yi, whose jurisdiction was 'hills, forests, swamps and downs, plants and trees, birds and beasts'. His official title was Guardian (or 'one who takes precautions'), and Shun specifically ordered him to harmonise – an instruction which seems to have related to the balanced pursuit of exploitation and preservation.

In Egypt under the Greek-speaking, socialist regime of the Ptolemaic Dynasty (323–30B.C.) there was a national system of **Socialised** free medical treatment, financed by a levy on the people. It was **Medicine** thus the first compulsory health insurance scheme. For centuries prior to Ptolemaic rule, medical treatment had been **Health** available free of charge in Egypt, from doctors paid by the state. **Insurance**

Official welfare programmes to provide disabled people with employment and sustenance began in China during the War- **Disabled** ring States Period (481–221B.C.). At this early stage disabled **Support** care did not reach all those in need or operate consistently. **Programme** However the Confucian philosopher Hsewn Dzu, who championed the disabled cause at this time, laid down the basis for the national programmes which were subsequently implemented:

> In the case of those who belong to the five incapacitated
> groups, the government should gather them together, look
> after them, and give them whatever work they are able to
> do. Employ them, provide them with food and clothing
> and take care to see that no one is left out.

The earliest official statistic is the height of the Nile River in full flood. Its annual measurement and recording began in the **Statistic** reign of Horus Djer (c. 3400B.C.), a pharaoh of the 1st Dynasty of Egypt. It has probably been kept up-to-date by Egyptian governments every year since then. 1st Dynasty height measurements are given in cubits, palms and fingers. The oldest extant figure is from the fifth year of Horus Djer's reign when the river reached 5 cubits (probably about 3 m.). This is not a measure of the depth to the river bottom, but the water's height above an arbitrary baseline, predetermined for measuring purposes.

Statistics of human phenomena do not begin until the 2nd Dynasty (c. 3300B.C.), when a national count was insti- **Economic** tuted to measure Egypt's resources. The first count was con- **Statistics** ducted during the reign of Horus Ninetjer or possibly one of his two predecessors. From then on the authorities took a count every two years. Some were of 'gold and fields', others of 'oxen and small cattle'.

The first medical statistician was Chun Yu Yi (born 205B.C.). During the Harn Dynasty he worked as a senior official **Medical** at Lin Tzu for the subordinate kingdom of Chi, in present-day **Statistics**

Shantung. He kept statistical records of clinical notes and case histories in order to estimate the success rates of treatments so that future practice would be better informed.

**Uniform Mapping Programme**
In 785A.D. the great cartographer Jia Darn (730–805) was officially ordered to have the entire Chinese empire mapped on a uniform scale. Work began immediately and some areas were completed before others. In 801 the whole project was finished, and the end result was a giant map not only of China, but most of Asia. With a scale of one to one million, the finished map stood 33 feet tall and extended 30 feet across.

**Identity Cards**
The Assyrian Government was the first to issue personal identity cards to its subjects – small thin clay tablets inscribed in cuneiform script. Dating is difficult but the system probably began late in the 2nd millennium B.C. The whole idea is typical of the Assyrians, who were too efficiently organised and not particular about civil liberties.

## 3. THE SOCIAL ORDER

This section includes times and dates, but some of the most important times of year have to be left out because their origins cannot be pinpointed as is generally supposed. Thus Easter is not the anniversary of Christ's resurrection, but a pre-Christian cult festival that originally honoured the fertility goddess, Eostre. Its date is regulated by the phases of the Moon in imitation of the oestrus cycle of women, and it is celebrated with pagan fertility symbols, the egg and the rabbit. Pious Christians nowadays, who clamour for Easter to be decommercialised and to regain its original meaning, are likely to be pretty appalled at some of the goings on when they are taken at their word.

Christmas also poses a difficulty. The First Noel was certainly not intoned on 25 December 1A.D. Jesus was born on an unknown day, and maybe as early as 13B.C., maybe as late as 4B.C.; but B.C. notwithstanding.

It was astute divines in the Northern Hemisphere who first gave the name Christmas to the old midwinter festival, or yuletide, which began in time immemorial as a pagan rite for the solstice. Messiahs, like racehorses and monarchs, have their birthdays assigned at the convenience of common men.

**Civilisation**
Of all the developments that have contributed to making the world what it is today, civilisation was the most sweeping in the permanent changes it brought about. Although some societies have reached a level of great sophistication without

becoming civilised, it is only with civilisation that the fundamental features of our way of life are brought together. The
first civilisation was in Southern Mesopotamia, now Iraq, in
the fertile country around the rivers Tigris and Euphrates, on
the coast of the Persian Gulf. Civilisation arose here amongst
a prosperous farming people of Iranian and Semitic stock,
between 6000 and 6500 years ago, before the great flood or
Deluge. The distinctive feature of their society was that politically, economically and socially it was organised around
cities, which sprang up on many sites throughout the region,
at a time when they did not exist at all anywhere else in the
world.

According to the tradition recounted in the earliest
records, made centuries later in the Sumerian language, the **City**
first city was Eridu, constructed probably around 4200B.C., on
an island at the head of the Persian Gulf. (Its location is now
16 km. inland because silt deposited by the great rivers has
filled in the sea around it.) Although there were towns at an
earlier time, the special features that have to be combined to
make a place a city made Eridu – and soon after, its neighbours
– noticeably different. Each was the headquarters of a government, and belonged to an organised state. In each there was a
complex division of labour so that a household could survive
without producing its own daily needs. Each had monuments
constructed at communal expense and without a functional
end; and each was a political and economic centre for a populous expanse of territory.

The original political organisation was the tribe, which
existed both before and after the invention of agriculture. The **Nation State**
settled agricultural tribes of the Nile River and Nile Delta in
the 5th millennium B.C. were at that time the most prosperous and sophisticated, and their leadership gradually acquired
the trappings of government, exercising control over the military and civil arrangements of society. They gradually progressed from tribes into states. They fought to take over each
other's territory and villages, and shortly before 4000B.C. the
dominant state of the Delta people succeeded in subduing all
the others north of present-day Cairo and establishing the
nation of Lower Egypt. From then on Lower Egypt had a capital, a succession of kings, and common institutions as well as
a common language and racial background. States of similar
antiquity in Mesopotamia did not form nations when they
conquered their neighbours. The conquering state remained
distinct in status from the subdued dependencies which

formed its empire. Egypt's great innovation was to assimilate the victors and the vanquished into a single homogeneous community, the prototype for the nation states that hold sway over much of today's world.

**City State**   In Mesopotamia a more localised concept of statehood gave the world its first city states. These came into existence at the same time as the first cities – about 4200B.C. The subjects of these states were Sumerians, living in the south of present-day Iraq. The earliest of these states was Eridu, the first city. The concept of a city state is quite different from a nation, because it can exist without embracing a whole people in its citizenry or occupying more than a local area, rather than a country. Modern examples are Singapore, Kuwait and Monaco.

**Caste System**   Indian history is in an atrocious state of disarray, making it impossible to tell exactly when anything happened unless it is recent or was recorded by foreign visitors. The establishment of the caste system can only be assigned to an approximate time by reference to ancient Sanskrit literature of uncertain date. The first castes emerged when particular social groups, identified by occupation and lineage, adopted restrictions on intermarriage with outsiders and ritual rules of social purity. In doing this they were imitating the social codes of Brahmin priests, who had segregated themselves from society in the 2nd millennium B.C. Early in the 1st millennium B.C. other groups began to distinguish themselves this way and by the 5th century B.C. dozens of castes would have divided most of the population. They were gathered into four major classes: priests, rulers and warriors, farmers and businessmen, and servile people.

**The Population Problem**   In the 3rd century B.C. Harn Fei Dzu argued that the exponential character of population growth threatened to overrun the world with people within a few generations. Harn was a legalist philosopher [see Amorality, VII, 2] from Central China who worked in the northwestern state of Chin. Anticipating that resources would shortly become inadequate for the growing demand, he believed that the old approaches to economic and political management were becoming obsolete. His answer was a rigid system of legal obligation controlling both people and resources. Exponential growth is the accelerating increase that comes from a given rate of multiplication. In Harn's example, if parents have five children, and each child has five, the two grandparents are succeeded by five descendants in the first generation, twenty-five in the second, and so on upwards.

Lycurgus, the reformer who introduced totalitarianism [IV, 1] in ancient Sparta in the 8th century B.C., was determined to cre- **Population** ate a social order that would remain stable indefinitely. Part of **Control** his method was to introduce measures to reduce the rate of reproduction, so that the population could not increase drastically. Spartiates – the citizens of Sparta – were not to marry until twenty if they were female, thirty if male. Once married they did not live together, and paederasty was encouraged to the disadvantage of heterosexual relations. Babies were inspected soon after birth, and those with physical handicaps were condemned not to be raised. For centuries the system produced remarkable stability, but you will not meet a Spartiate today; decades of warfare beginning in 430B.C. reduced their numbers below a sustainable level and they gradually died out.

The Greek philosopher Plato in *The Laws* (Athens, c. 350B.C.) proposed a model state with 5040 households. The **Zero** population was to be managed by encouraging or discouraging **Population** reproduction so that this number did not vary – 'if too many **Growth** children are born, there are measures to check propagation; on the other hand a high birthrate can be encouraged and stimulated'.

The Lyceum at Athens, converted to a university in 335B.C., was the first tertiary institution to offer a full range of studies **University** in the humanities and sciences. The building complex (a former school) and adjacent walks, were taken over at that time by the Greek philosopher Aristotle, on lease from the state. There were a staff of lecturers, a library and a large collection of natural history specimens. Subjects taught included ethical and political sciences, logic, rhetoric, literature, astronomy, biology, physics, metaphysics, mathematics and meteorology. The curriculum was based on the philosophy of Aristotle and his followers, know as the Peripatetic School [VII, 1]. Aristotle left Athens in 322B.C. but the Lyceum carried on under a succession of other heads.

On the other side of the world, about twenty years after the Lyceum was founded, the first state university opened its **State** many doors. It was established in Northeastern China in the **University** state of Chi. Hsewarn, the king of Chi (reigned 319–301B.C.), was founder and patron. Generous support quickly made it the world's largest academic institution, but it did not last as long as the Lyceum, closing in the next century, when Chi lost its independence. It was called the Hua Mountain Association and had an attendance of thousands, and seventy-six salaried professors who, coincidentally, wore mortar board hats like their 20th-century counterparts. Its greatest claim to fame is the galaxy of eminent philosophers who lectured there, representing all schools of thought. These included Mencius and Hsewn Dzu (the leading classicist philosophers after Confucius), the pacifist Sung Hsing, Dso Yen the dialectician, and probably Juarng Dzu, the most famous Taoist.

**Academic Degree**

A system of academic qualifications was introduced in the early part of China's Harn Dynasty, in 178B.C. The first degree was called 'Worthy and Excellent', and awarded by the state to the most talented students. Further degrees were invented as time passed, so that ultimately equivalents in level to bachelor, master and doctor were available.

**Women in Professions**

In the Old Kingdom Period in Egypt (c. 3500–c. 2500B.C.) women had access to almost all the same career opportunities as men. The only professional role that was not open to them was that of judge.

**Hippocratic Oath**

I will hand on precepts, lectures and all other learning to my sons, to those of my master and to those pupils duly apprenticed and sworn and to none other.

I will use my power to help the sick to the best of my ability and judgement; I will abstain from harming or wronging any man by it.

I will not give a fatal draught to anyone if I am asked, nor will I suggest any such thing. Neither will I give a woman means to procure an abortion.

I will be chaste and religious in my life and in my practice.

I will not cut even for the stone, but I will leave such procedures to the practitioners of that craft.

Whenever I go into a house I will go to help the sick and never with the intention of doing harm or injury. I will not abuse my position to indulge in sexual contacts with the bodies of women or of men, whether they be freemen or slaves.

Whatever I see or hear, professionally or privately, which ought not to be divulged I will keep secret and tell no one.

(*The Oath*, tr. G.E.R. Lloyd)

Traditionally, these are the undertakings framed by the famous Greek medical researcher, Hippocrates (460–357B.C.), for the guidance of doctors. It is actually doubtful whether Hippocrates himself drafted *The Oath*, though highly likely that it was first administered to pupils of his medical school on the Aegean island of Cos in the 5th century B.C. In its tenets can be seen the starting point of many lasting features of Western medical thinking – the restricted eligibility for medical training; the traditional opposition to euthanasia and abortion, and the treatment of surgery as a distinct profession.

**Division of the Medical Profession**

However specialisation of medical practitioners in various fields goes back to the beginning of the Old Kingdom period before 3000B.C. in Egypt. Old Kingdom records still in existence tell of doctors of the stomach and eyes, interpreters of liquids in the bladder and 'guardians of the anus' (whom we would identify more daintily as proctologists).

**Medical Specialists**

To ensure that only qualified doctors could call themselves medical practitioners, a procedure was established in India about 2000 years ago. Candidates were required to demonstrate a thorough mastery of their subject and establish that they had had proper training in making independent observations and in the practical application of their knowledge. As well as satisfying the standards of their professional colleagues on these matters they were obliged to obtain a licence to practise from the state. This procedure is recorded in the *Caraka Saṃhitā*, a medical text extant in an edition from the 1st century A.D; its contents date back probably a century or two earlier at least.

**Licensing of Doctors**

The first dentists practised in ancient Egypt during the Old Kingdom period, prior to 3000B.C. Even in these early times they were subject to regulation, and the 'chief of dentists' is an official position referred to in surviving records. We know one early dentist by name – Hesyre of the 3rd Dynasty (c. 3200– c. 3050B.C.), whose tomb has been excavated, and proclaims him 'Chief of Dentists and Doctors'.

**Dentists**

John Flynn (1880–1951) was a Presbyterian minister born in Victoria. When working in the outback he conceived the idea of a flying doctor to eliminate the medical isolation of homesteads scattered over thousands of miles in out-of-reach locations. In 1926 Flynn's 'Australian Inland Mission' engaged Adelaide radio engineer Alf Traeger, who developed a radio set with its own generator, which could receive as well as transmit. This was christened a 'transceiver', which must have sounded better to them than resmitter. Numerous sets were supplied to outback families, while doctors and pilots were recruited to respond to calls. In May 1928 Dr. Kenyon St. Vincent Welch left Cloncurry, Queensland, in the *Victory*, a

**Flying Doctor**

single-engine plane equipped with a stretcher and soft landing undercarriage, piloted by Arthur Affleck. Their journey to Julia Creek was the first mission of the Flying Doctor.

**Metric System**   Metric measurement has two main characteristics: a decimal structure of units, and more importantly, the use of scientifically ascertainable constants to fix the value of the units. Of these two decimalisation has been around much the longest.

**Decimal Units**   Old Chinese foot rulers are invariably divided into ten inches, and each inch usually into tenths. Such rulers dating back as far as the 6th century B.C. are still in existence, and the ten-inch foot, which lasted until the present century, originated at least as early as the beginning of the Jo Dynasty (c. 1100B.C.). A comprehensive decimal length measurement system was introduced throughout China c. 220B.C.; the smallest unit was the *hao* – ⅟₁₀,₀₀₀ of an inch; largest was the *yin*, one hundred feet. There were Chinese decimal weight and volume units also, but there is no record of when they were introduced.

**Definition by**   The first unit for which a scientifically constant defini-
**Constant**   tion was attempted was the Chinese *li*, defined in 726A.D. as ⅟₃₅₁ of a degree of polar altitude, as measured at the Earth's surface. This was deduced from observations of the Sun's shadow, taken simultaneously at at least eleven stations along a north–south line, from a place near the Great Wall in China's far north, to the neighbourhood of Hué in Vietnam. The programme was superintended by Chief Astronomer, Narn Gung Yeweh, and Yi Hsing, a Buddhist monk; between them they had also masterminded the first expedition to study the southern skies [VIII, 2]. The unit they defined was the shorter li, not the longer one in common use. Their definition was merely an approximation from their results, and the results were wrong because of a flaw in their system. Hence they are not the inventors of a true metric system. This was the inspiration of two men: one an amateur astronomer and mathematician, the Karng Hsi Emperor of China, a Manchu by nationality; the other, Belgian Jesuit physicist, Vice-Director and sometime Acting Director of the Chinese Bureau of Astronomy, Antoine Thomas. At a meeting in December 1698 they decided to reform the length measurement system by correlating it to the Earth's circumference. Between 1702 and 1704, the Bureau took observations at stations in North China, far more detailed and accurate than any before, which fixed one degree of terrestrial latitude at 195 li 6 paces. The standard units of measurement were then revised downwards

so that 200 li equalled one degree, and twenty paces (100 feet) equalled one second of terrestrial circumference.

In 1791 the French Academy recommended a similar reform to its government. It proposed that the basic unit of **The Metre** measurement be the metre, and that this be fixed at ¹⁄₁₀,₀₀₀,₀₀₀ of one-quarter of the Earth's circumference at sea level. This is the metre which has since been adopted throughout the world, although it is now defined more precisely by wavelengths.

In the Old Kingdom period in Egypt the days were divided into twenty-four parts. Twelve of these extended through the **The Twenty-** daytime up to sunset, the other twelve through the night till **four Hours** dawn. The effect was that daytime and night-time divisions were not equal with one another, except at the equinoxes, when they all measured one hour. In the 14th century B.C. the modern twenty-four hour system was invented: a papyrus text containing data from that era clearly indicates hours of fixed length, with a month-by-month hour table allocating progressively fewer hours to the nights as the days lengthen and vice versa. Although this new method of reckoning time has now taken over all around the world, in Egypt the old unequal system remained in use for another 1500 years or so. The division into sixty minutes of sixty seconds is the work of Chaldaean scientists in Mesopotamia.

The seven-day week was officially instituted in the Kingdom of Sumer and Akkad (in present-day Iraq), in the mid-3rd mil- **Weeks** lennium B.C. The idea was taken from the four phases of the Moon, each of a week's duration. The influence of the Mesopotamian astronomers carries through into the names of the days, which were called after the Sun, the Moon, and each of **Sabbath** the five planets. The seventh day of each week was declared a day of rest. The Akkadians made their months twenty-nine or thirty days, but they liked to have four whole weeks each month. The problem of four sevens being only twenty-eight was solved by calling the spare days 'month days' and prudently setting them aside for feasting.

The calendar of the Romans introduced during the reign of their founding king Romulus (8th century B.C.) was initially **Months** a crude 360-day cycle of ten months of varying length:
   March
   April

May
June
Quintilis
Sextilis
September
October
November
December

King Numa Pompilius in the 7th century B.C. invented January and February and put them at the start of the year. After
the death of the dictator Augustus (1st century A.D.), Quintilis was renamed July, after Julius Caesar, and Sextilis, August,
after Augustus, so that the twelve months had their present
names.

**29th of February**

Eudoxus of Cnidos in Greece suggested that every fourth year
should run 366 days instead of 365, during his visit to Egypt
about 380B.C. The idea was taken up by Eratosthenes of
Cyrene (276–195B.C.), who invented what is now called the
Julian Calendar, with a leap year in every four having an extra
day at the end of February. Eratosthenes's calendar was first
used in Egypt where he worked, but was later taken on in
Rome.

**Gregorian Calendar**

The solar year is very slightly less than 365¼ days. This
means that adding an extra day (29 Feb.) to every fourth year
slows the calendar down compared to the Sun. By the year
1582A.D., the Julian Calendar was running ten days behind for
this reason. Pope Gregory XIII decided to cure this by declar-
ing 5 Oct. 1582 to be 15 Oct. 1582, playing havoc with
appointments and party invitations. He also instituted the rule
that from that day forward leap years were to fall on years
whose number is divisible by four, such as 1992. This he qualified by providing that centennial years are not to be leap years
unless divisible by 400, such as 2000. This new calendar which
we use today is still a teensy bit slow, and perhaps another Pope
will have to help out in a few thousand years. The Gregorian
calendar was adopted in 1582 by Catholic countries, in 1700 in
Germany, in 1751 in Britain and 1918 in Russia.

**Islamic Chronology**

The Islamic world numbers its years from the flight from
Mecca of the prophet Muhammad. This it has done since
17A.H. (639A.D.); that is, seventeen years after the Flight
(*Hegira*). In 17A.H. the Arab leader Omar was given a cheque
payable in the month of Sha'ban. Because he could not tell

whether this meant the present Sha'ban or the next one, he decided to establish a convenient chronology. In consultation with leading Arabs and with Persian experts, he selected the Flight as the starting point, because unlike the date of the Prophet's birth, its accuracy was not in doubt. 1997A.D. is 1375A.H.

New Year's Day, the main festival in the Chinese calendar, falls every year on the first full moon after the Sun enters the **Chinese New** eleventh sign of the zodiac (the Dog) – somewhere between **Year** 21 January and 20 February. This system was first adopted in 104B.C., during the Harn Dynasty, when the government of Emperor Wu Di introduced the present calendar. (Well before that the Chinese had ceremonies for the first day of the first lunar month. From the start of the Jo Dynasty, rulers would personally plough fields on this day, a practice that was only abandoned under Western influence in the 20th century.)

It was also during Wu Di's reign that the Moon festival, China's mid-autumn commemoration, was inaugurated. The **Moon Festival** emperor himself instituted three days of banquets and Moon viewings during the eighth month.

In 1621, in what is now the Northeastern United States, William Bradley, governor of the newly settled Plymouth com- **Thanksgiving** munity, invited nearby Indians to join his Puritan colonists in a three-day festival, during which much food would be eaten in grateful recognition of the bounty of the season. The custom of an annual feast for this purpose was taken up all over the New England region; in 1863, during the Civil War, President Abraham Lincoln declared Thanksgiving a national holiday, which has since been celebrated with a big meal on the last or second-last Thursday in November. In Canada it first became an official holiday in November 1879, though the Canadian Thanksgiving is now celebrated on a different day (the second Monday of October).

The Bastille was a fortress in Paris used by the French monarchy as its jail for political prisoners, the culprits and victims of **Bastille Day** court and family intrigues, and offenders against the religious establishment. Bastille Day is 14 July, the date it was stormed by an angry mob, in 1789A.D. At the time, the Bastille held only a handful of prisoners, but it was a hated symbol of royal oppression, and its capture is commemorated as the event that galvanised support for the French Revolution.

**Anzac Day** Australia and New Zealand are the only countries that commemorate a great military failure in their main national holiday. Anzac Day is the anniversary of the landing on Gallipoli of the Australian and New Zealand Army Corps on 25 April 1915: the commencement of a bloody and unsuccessful campaign against the Turkish Empire, which was supposed to knock it out of the First World War. After seven months of carnage the entire force was withdrawn, but the spirited display of courage and the tragic loss were remembered in popular ceremonies on 25 April 1916 and on every anniversary since.

## 4. SOCIAL PHENOMENA

Religious and superstitious practices are dealt with in Chapter VII, section 7.

**Peace Movement** Sumerians in the city states of southern Mesopotamia began agitating for peace around 2500B.C. Although the identities of the people involved are not known, their influence is revealed in literature and documents surviving from the second half of the 3rd millennium B.C. Poems of the day lament the evils of war, and rulers congratulate themselves on fighting for peace. In about 2250B.C. one of the mightiest, Shulgi of Ur, claimed 'that no city was destroyed by me, no walls were breached by me, that like a frail reed no land was crushed by me'. Shulgi brought under his rule the great cultural centre of Nippur, where the peace movement at its strongest had built a special 'Gate of Peace'.

**Strikes** Cases of workmen refusing to complete their tasks go back to distant prehistory, but organised strikes for wages and conditions are an ancient Egyptian innovation. From the early days of the Old Kingdom, (c. 3500–c. 2500B.C.) workers with grievances, usually about pay, would leave work sites and go en masse to temples, where the law protected them from arrest. Such disputes generally ended in a negotiated settlement.

**Student Protest** In the early 160s A.D., students of China's Imperial University at Law Yarng launched a series of protest campaigns against government personnel and policy. Scathing seven-word slogans were chanted in the streets and written on walls. The campaigns were orchestrated by student leaders, including the talented son of a poor family, Guaw Tai, and his comrade Jia

Biao. Many, perhaps most, of the university's 30,000 students were involved, and before long their slogans caught on with the general public. Despite vehement opposition from the students, the palace eunuchs gained predominance in government and from 169 began a stringent crackdown on protest. In 172 a thousand students were placed under arrest and the first great wave of student protest subsided.

Tobacco must have had opponents amongst the American Indians who first used it. But the earliest concerted campaign began in England in 1601. A pamphlet published in London on 'Worke for Chimny Sweepers' denounced the use of tobacco for its harmful effects on the individual and society at large. In 1602 A *Defence of Tobacco* was published in response. Then the government stepped in to combat the 'filthie custome' of smoking. It issued a pamphlet in 1604 entitled *A Counterblaste to Tobacco* under the personal authorship of King James I:

**Anti-smoking Campaign**

> There cannot be a more base, and yet hurtful, corruption in a Countrey, then is the vile use (or rather abuse) of taking Tobacco in this Kingdome, which hath mooved me, shortly to discover the abuse thereof in this following little Pamphlet.

While conceding that tobacco smoke is an 'Antidot to the Pockes' the King denied that this justifies smoking such as was by then common even in dining rooms.

> Surely Smoke becomes a kitchin far better than a Dining chamber, and yet it makes a kitchin also oftentimes in the inward parts of men, soiling and infecting them with an unctuous and oily kind of Soote, as hath bene found in some great Tobacco takers that after their death were opened.

His Majesty had numerous arguments to prove smoking 'a custome lothsome to the eye, hatefull to the Nose, harmfull to the braine, daungerous to the Lungs, and in the black stinking fume thereof, neerest resembling the horrible Stigian smoke of the pit that is bottomlesse.' Since then the lothsome custome has faced an opposition of fluctuating strength. As in the late-20th century, it was clamorous in the early 17th, and kept supporting books. In 1617 one called *Tobacco Tortured* was finished by John Deacon and dedicated to the King. But by then the campaign had manifestly failed.

The learned conferences that attract flocks of experts these days are a much newer idea than diplomatic and political

**Conference**

conferences, which go back to the dawn of history. The first conference for experts was a mammoth affair put on during the Harn Dynasty, by the Chinese government, in Charng Arn in 5A.D. The delegates included specialists in practically everything: lost literature and old writings; astronomy, calendrical science and mathematics; acoustics and music; philology; magical, medical and technical arts; pharmacology; and classics. Several thousand delegates came. To bring them from all corners of the empire, the government laid on official one-horse carriages. This is remarkable: the modern equivalent would be driving each of them to the conference in a government car. The inspiration came from Warng Marng, who usurped the Chinese throne four years later and launched many reform schemes.

**Beauty Contest**

In the 7th century B.C. people from the Greek city of Corinth set up a new town in Southern Greece called Basilis. To commemorate the event, Cypselus, the ruler of Corinth, inaugurated a regular beauty contest, which survived for centuries. The judges at the first contest are not entirely above suspicion as far as integrity goes, because they granted first prize to Herodice (wife of Cypselus), which seems a bit too convenient politically.

**Men's Beauty Contest**

In the 4th century B.C. the city of Athens began its 'Ideal Man' contest, judged on fitness and beauty. Contestants were studied for their bearing, and had to parade mounted and armed as part of the procedure. First prize was a shield.

**Door Knock Appeal**

In the town of Lindus on the Greek island of Rhodes, early in the 6th century B.C., a now forgotten crisis came up, which made it necessary to raise funds. Fortunately Cleobulus, one of the seven sages of ancient Greece, lived in Lindus, and invented a system to solve the problem. He had people go from door to door, appealing for donations. The crisis passed but the technique stuck and in Rhodes, collecting door to door became an annual custom, for individual rather than public good.

**Etiquette Book**

Guidebooks on etiquette were published in China after the foundation of the Jo Dynasty (c. 1100B.C.) and before the time of Confucius (551–479B.C.), who has left comments on them. Owing to later upheavals it has become impossible to tell which book came out first. One contender is the *Summary of the Rules of Propriety (Ju Li)*. This includes a general explanation of the function of etiquette, and details on matters like addressing people, paying visits, going into a room without surprising those inside, naming children, setting the table, eating out, not driving too fast on city streets, and many other things. Another book is *Ceremony and Etiquette* (*Yi Li*), which may be older, and deals with special occasions such as weddings, community drinking sessions, archery contests, state visits, funerals and sacrifices.

The modest achievement of inventing dynamite [VI, 1] would not have been enough to make Alfred Nobel's name a household word outside his native Sweden. But his visionary scheme to recognise the great achievements of others constantly renews in the 20th century the fame which did not attach to his 19th-century life (1833–96). In accordance with Nobel's will, the proceeds of a generous bequest are used to award annual 'Nobel Prizes' for merit in various fields. The winners are chosen by a committee based in Sweden. In 1901, the first prizes in each field were awarded as follows: **Nobel Prizes**

| | |
|---|---|
| **Physics** | Wilhelm Röntgen, Germany, discoverer of X-rays [VIII, 10]. |
| **Chemistry** | Jacobus van't Hoff, Netherlands, pioneer of stereochemistry. |
| **Physiology and Medicine** | Emil von Behring, Germany, bacteriologist and immunologist, who discovered anti-toxins for tetanus and diphtheria. |
| **Literature** | René François Sully-Prudhomme, France, poet – author of *Justice and Welfare*. |
| **Peace** | DUAL WINNERS. Jean Henri Dunant, Switzerland, founder of the International Red Cross [see below] and F. Passy, France. |

Not until 1969 was the Nobel Prize for economic sciences awarded.

| | |
|---|---|
| **Economics** | DUAL WINNERS. J. Tinbergen, Netherlands, and R. Frisch, Norway. |

In Northern Italy in 1859 the Battle of Solferino was fought by the French and Italians against the Austrians. Also present was a Swiss man, Jean Henri Dunant (1828–1910), who distinguished himself by giving emergency aid to wounded soldiers on both sides. In 1862 his *Un Souvenir de Solferino* called on the international community to set up humanitarian relief agencies in all nations. This led to the establishment of the Red Cross in 1864, pursuant to the terms of the Geneva Convention **Red Cross** of that year, binding all signatory governments to care for those wounded in war whether friend or foe. In fact each participating country set up its own Red Cross agency, affiliated to an international secretariat. Dunant was rewarded in 1901 with the first Nobel Peace Prize [see above]. The organisation takes its name from its emblem, a red cross on a white ground, which is the Swiss flag in reverse. Its resemblance to insignia of the crusaders hundreds of years earlier meant that the cross was not an **Red Crescent** emblem that could attract sympathy in the Islamic world, and in 1906, at the insistence of the Ottoman Government of Turkey, the Red Crescent was adopted as the emblem and name of Red Cross agencies operating in Muslim countries.

**Rosicrucianism** The Rosicrucians form a secret society, and it is difficult to discover the details of their commencement. They profess to be followers of a German occultist and chemist, Christian Rosenkreuz, of the 14th or 15th century A.D. Their first manifestation to the outside world comes in 1614 and 1615, with the publication at Kassell, Germany, of certain books including *Fama Fraternitalis* or *Brotherhood of the Illustrious Order of the R.C. (Rosy Cross)* (1614). They interpret mystic signs and work with alchemical formulae.

**Freemasonry** In the countries of mediaeval Europe the guild of masons resembled other craft guilds, and existed for the benefit of stonemasons and sometimes architects. However Freemasonry these days is a brotherhood of initiates from all walks of life, dedicated to the 'practice of moral and social virtue'. In this form it is an English innovation of the 1640s A.D. Its creators were a literary circle centred on Elias Ashmole (1617–92), later the donor of the collection of England's first public museum, the Ashmolean. Imitating the mediaeval guild, they adopted a set of graphic symbols, the compasses and the sun amongst others, and laid down rules of conduct for each other's mutual benefit. The symbols are believed to have been taken from those used by the Knights Templar and the Rosicrucians.

**Cannabis Smoking** The use of cannabis was discovered early in the 1st millennium B.C. by people dwelling near the Caspian Sea in Central Asia. It was thrown onto a fire or hot stones, and party-goers would gather under a canopy to inhale the smoke given off. The use of the same plant as a textile is described under Hemp [XI, 4].

The effects of discipline on the human body can be so great that with a powerful enough motive people are able to make themselves walk over glowing coals without injury. In ancient Italy the motive was evasion of tax. The Roman Senate passed a decree granting immunity from tax (and military service) to a group of families called the Hirpi in recognition of their achievement in firewalking. The Hirpi lived in a district near Rome and began their audacious perambulations almost 2500 years ago. At the sacrifice to Apollo on Mt. Soracte they would walk over a charred pile of logs without hurt or shoes; they repeated this performance every year, just as any of us would in the circumstances.

**Firewalking**

A Mesopotamian collection of moralistic comments written about 2000B.C. includes the oldest reference to transvestite behaviour, of which it takes a dim view. The culprit was 'a low fellow, an Amorite', who told his wife to play the man while he would be the woman. (The Amorites were a race from Northwestern Mesopotamia, generally looked down on by residents of the central part.)

**Transvestism**

The oldest instance on record of two people of the same sex getting married was in Rome at about 100A.D. The bride was a former priest of the war god Mars, son of Jupiter, and the God dearest to the Romans. The story is told by the satirist Juvenal, who criticises Mars in the following terms:

**Homosexual Wedding**

O Father of our City
What brought your simple shepherd people to such a pitch
Of blasphemous perversion? Great lord of war, when came
This prurient itch upon them? A wealthy well-born
Man is betrothed in marriage to another man
And you do nothing! Not a shake of the helmet, no pounding
The ground with your spear, Not even a complaint
To your father. Away with you then, remove yourself
From the broad Roman acres that bear your name, and suffer
Neglect at your hands. This is the kind of talk
We soon shall hear 'I must go down-town tomorrow
First thing a special engagement.'
'What's happening?'
'Need you ask?
I'm going to a wedding. Old so-and-so's got his boyfriend
To the altar at last – just a few close friends are invited.'

(tr. P. Green)

# V

# TOWN AND COUNTRY

The first people, the ancestors of all human beings, were born an immeasurably long time ago: in Africa, according to palaeontologists; in one of a variety of other places, according to the Bible and various mythologies. The first great achievement of the human race was to multiply and spread. Most islands and all continents except Antarctica were populated aeons ago by primitive peoples. The Ice Age [VIII, 3] restricted the range of habitation, but afterwards, a new way of life developed, which led to a big population increase. This was the raising of livestock – a more productive way of subsistence than the hunting it replaced. Nomad communities followed cattle and sheep as they ate pastures and moved on; human action began transforming the countryside, wherever grasslands could be made to support large herds.

The biggest of all man's changes to the environment – from the beginning of time until now – was caused in late prehistoric times by the introduction of agriculture [VIII, 7], which converted the wilderness to farm land. Hardly had agriculture begun than people started to live in villages, the first settled communities. In Western Asia, the most prosperous villages grew large and some tradespeople started to find a livelihood in them, without doing their share of the farming. These were the first towns.

With the beginning of civilisation [IV, 1] came cities, and soon afterwards, with the invention of writing, people began recording new developments so that later they could be written up in books of firsts.

Since then increasingly intensive settlement and burgeoning demands on resources have led to recognition of the population problem [IV, 3], to conservationist philosophies [VII, 3] and to environmental protection laws [XII, 1].

## 1. COMMUNITIES AND AMENITIES

Ancient Babylon had a million or more residents. The million mark was probably achieved soon after establishment of the **City of a** very prosperous Neo-Babylonian Empire (612–538B.C.) But **Million People** since no census figures are extant, its population has to be estimated on the basis of its area, using the measurements given by Greek and Latin writers from the 5th century B.C. onwards. Figures for the perimeter of Babylon's square city wall range from 360 stadia to 480; 368 seems the most likely. This means a city area of well over 250 sq. km. Several million people could have lived within the walls – but a lot of the space was taken up by parks, boulevards, public buildings and fortifications.

In 375A.D., when its heyday was past, the urban area of Rome had 46,602 large blocks of flats. Even making only a **Multi-million** small allowance for soldiers and slaves in barracks and domes- **City** tic service, the total population could not have been much less than four million, and might have been a lot more. It was probably greater still in happier times two centuries earlier. Unless Babylon had two million people earlier on, Rome must have been the first multi-million city. The likely date for passing two million is in the boom years late in the 1st century B.C.

Town sewerage systems were introduced in Southern Mesopotamia around 2700B.C. They superseded the old methods of **Sewerage** running sewage into nearby pits and trenches, or carting it away in containers. Instead, sewers from buildings were led into large sewer mains that carried away the output of entire town areas. Archaeologists have dug out the sewerage system of the city of Eshnunna. It is made of baked brick, and the mains are vaulted channels two to three metres deep. This is the oldest system discovered, but other towns in the region may well have been similarly equipped.

The Egyptians began to install plumbing nearly 5000 years ago – not that they had it in ordinary houses at that time. It was, **Plumbing** however, an important feature of some of their public buildings. A temple from about the 30th century B.C., beside the pyramids near Gizeh, included a remarkable 1300 feet of water piping, all made of copper, like much modern plumbing.

Around 400B.C., well before the introduction of true pedestrian **Pedestrian** zones, there were restrictions on driving passenger vehicles in **Zone** some city areas in Italy. In the city of Rome, a curious system developed whereby male citizens were prohibited from travelling through the city in carriages, but their wives were free to do so. This discrimination against the male sex was instituted as a perpetual reward to the Roman ladies for their zealous fundraising activities during the invasion of the Gauls in 390B.C. Eventually, a man rose to such power that he was almost able to put the women in their place. Their town-driving privileges were taken away, with a few exceptions, in 45B.C. by Julius Caesar. Caesar also had a law passed to stop goods vehicles using the streets between sunrise and 4 p.m. By these two measures, he turned the whole city area of Rome into a pedestrian zone – the first of many throughout the Roman Empire.

**Roundabouts** Fifteen hundred years ago it was the policy of town planners in India to round off the corners of building blocks at major intersections, and widen the roadway into a circuit or *pradakshina*. In the middles of the intersections they placed a variety of features – sometimes a tree, sometimes a lamp post or shrine. The effect of traffic keeping to the left was to create a clockwise circulation around the central feature, avoiding congestion and accidents. In towns and villages, the spreading tree and the raised ground around it provided the venue for the local elders to confer on civic matters – a rare sight on the roundabouts of modern cities. The Indian books that refer to these features are of uncertain age; roundabouts could have been introduced longer than 2000 years ago, but that will need archaeological confirmation.

**Traffic Light** The first traffic light – in London in 1868 – was inspired by railway signals. It had signal arms which were raised and lowered, and red and green gas lamps for night use. Pedestrians needing to cross could activate the system manually. It was not an unqualified success, and soon after its installation it triggered a general panic in a troop of cavalry. After a brief existence, its gas supply blew up, killing a policeman.

**Traffic Noise** In the days before noisy engines were invented, there could
**Complaint** only be traffic noise complaints in a particularly busy, badly planned city with irritable residents. This takes us straight to ancient Rome, whose residents probably whinged all the time about traffic noise. The first to record a grievance in literature is the satirist Juvenal, about 110A.D.:

> Insomnia causes more deaths amongst Roman invalids
> Than any other factor (the most common *complaints*,
>   of course,

# POLICE NOTICE.

## STREET CROSSING SIGNALS.
### BRIDGE STREET, NEW PALACE YARD.

| CAUTION. | STOP. |
|---|---|
| The Semaphore Arms lowered, and by Night with a Green Light. | The Semaphore Arms extended, and by Night with a Red Light. |

By the Signal "**CAUTION**," all persons in charge of Vehicles and Horses are warned to pass over the Crossing with care, and due regard to the safety of Foot Passengers.

The Signal "**STOP**," will only be displayed when it is necessary that Vehicles and Horses shall be actually stopped on each side of the Crossing, to allow the passage of Persons on Foot; notice being thus given to all persons in charge of Vehicles and Horses to stop clear of the Crossing.

**RICHARD MAYNE,**
Commissioner of Police of the M——

What to do at the traffic lights, 1868.

Are heartburn and ulcers, brought on by over-eating).
How much sleep I ask you can one get in lodgings here?
Unbroken nights – and this is the root of the trouble –
Are a rich man's privilege. The waggons thundering past
Through those narrow twisting streets, the oaths of draymen
Caught in a traffic jam – these alone would suffice
To jolt the doziest sea-cow of an Emperor into
Permanent wakefulness.          (tr. P. Green)

The Emperor Asoka, who ruled India from 273 to 232 B.C., was a zealous humanitarian who presided over a public-spirited Buddhist regime. In order to make sure that all his subjects, no matter how poor, could have medical treatment and nursing care, his government opened up publicly funded hospitals in cities throughout the Empire – extending from Afghanistan to Bangladesh. Prior to this, medical treatment in the ancient world – even surgical operations – was normally provided in doctors' rooms, medical schools, clinics and temples. Asoka also established veterinary hospitals throughout India, care for animals being a high priority of his regime.

**Public Hospitals**

**Animal Hospitals**

**Old People's Home**

Homes for the care of old people without families to look after them are amongst the earliest institutions of Chinese civilisation. According to most authorities, they were established in the time of the early ruler Shun (c. 2200B.C.), although the dating is uncertain. Originally, the same premises served as both the local school and the old people's home.

**Hotel**

Hotels that provide accommodation and serve food and drink are not quite as ancient as civilisation itself. The call for them only arose with the advent of active commercial contact between cities, which takes us to Mesopotamia no later than the 4th millennium B.C. If we had actually been taken there, we might find hotels in cities such as Lagash, Kish, Ur or Akkad, but would be unlikely to get a room to ourselves, or even much in the way of bedclothes. They probably differed little in size or design from ordinary houses. Later, hotels opened on the main routes leading to the major Mesopotamian cities.

**Hotel Chain**

A great step forward in travel conditions was made in the 23rd century B.C. during the reign of King Shulgi of Ur, whose government introduced a chain of purpose-designed hotels open to the public and operated by specialist staff. His efforts were set down posthumously in 'Shulgi's Hymn':

> I enlarged the footpaths, straightened the highways of the land,
> I made travel secure, built there big houses,
> Planted gardens alongside them, established resting places,
> Settled there friendly folk;
> Who came from below, who came from above,
> Might refresh themselves in their cool,
> The wayfarer who travels the highway at night,
> Might find refuge there, as in a well built city.

**Motel**

The Roman Empire had two kinds of motel: the *mansio*, located by main roads in country areas, and the *stabulum*, a more compact design for towns and cities. Remains of a stabulum found in Pompeii (destroyed 79A.D.) have made it possible to reconstruct a typical urban motel of Roman times. Facing the street was a lobby off which ran the reception area, the restaurant and a public toilet. Behind them was a courtyard for carriages and wagons, with a driveway from the street and stables at the back. Guest rooms opened onto a colonnade alongside and all along the upper storey. Country mansiones provided vets and mechanics, spare horses, baths, central heating, porters and room service. Rooms were ranged along the first floor with stables underneath, or around a courtyard with stables forming one side. These ancient motels did not offer electric blankets, video machines or vibrating mattresses, but they bravely attempted to substitute all three by providing girls for their guests. The Romans probably learnt the mansio design from Greece, where lodgings on a similar plan date back to the 5th century B.C., without, however, the motel comforts and conveniences.

Archaeologists have unearthed a remarkable establishment on the site of ancient Corinth, Greece. It was a two-storey build- **Luxury Hotel** ing about 150 m. long behind an intricate portico. The first floor comprised a large number of elegant split-level suites, all entered off a single indoor corridor. On the ground floor there were no less than thirty-one separate bars, each equipped with a storeroom, a rear toilet, and an indoor well descending to a common tunnel filled with chilly spring water, into which containers were hung on ropes from floor level, guaranteeing each bar a constant supply of refrigerated food and drink. It was put up in the 4th century B.C.

The public swimming pool at Mohenjo-Daro, on the Indus River in present-day Pakistan, was built as part of a bath com- **Swimming** plex at an uncertain date, probably shortly after 2500B.C. It **Pool** was 12 m. long, 7 m. wide and had a maximum depth of about 8 feet. The complex to which it belonged was also equipped with the earliest known central heating and sauna [see XI, 1].

The ancient Greeks considered physical education to be as vital as intellectual education, and gymnasia for that reason **Gymnasium** were amongst the principal secular buildings in their cities and towns, from the 500s B.C. onwards. They were large insti- tutions that served as high schools where all subjects were taught. However, complexes of buildings and courtyards known as *palaestrai* formed part of the gymnasia and also existed independently; they were dedicated to athletic train- ing, the same as modern gymnasia, but were more lavish.

The first zoo was a logical development from the menageries of strange animals collected by kings in ancient times. The **Zoo** difference was that the collection was gathered for its scien- tific interest rather than amusement value. This zoo was estab- lished in Alexandria, the capital of Egypt under the Ptolemaic Dynasty during the reign of Ptolemy II (called Philadelphus

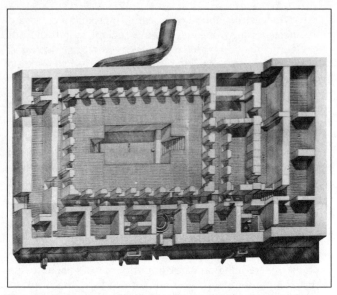

The pool complex excavated at Mohenjo-Daro included central heating, flush toilets, changerooms, saunas and a well. (Cutaway reconstruction by Sir John Marshall)

because he married his sister), 285–246B.C. A serious effort was made to represent a wide cross-section of animal types from many parts of the world; it had a collection which many zoos would envy. In particular, there was a 45-foot python, and a range of cats, including the lynx and the leopard; there was the wild ass of the Moab, the giraffe, rhino and polar bear; buffaloes from India and Africa; and many birds, including peacocks and parrots. The zoo was located near the city centre in the gardens surrounding Alexandria's famous Museum.

**National Park**  Ancient rulers used to set aside wild areas as private pleasure parks, and imposed heavy punishments on any intruders hunting wildlife there. This had a conservationist value, but it was more often interpreted as royal self-indulgence and harshness. In the gloomy last days of China's Sharng Dynasty, around in the 12th century B.C., King Wen, rebel ruler of the subservient territory of Jo in western Central China, had the inspiration of opening his park to the general public, and thus created the first national park. It covered an area of about 80 or 90 sq. km., and was appreciatively referred to as the Spirit Park in a poem written in Wen's time or soon after.

The king stood in his 'Spirit Park'
deer and doe lay there so fine,
so fine so sleek; birds of the air
flashed a white ring while fishes splashed
on wing-like fin in the spirit pool. (tr. Ezra Pound, modif.)

In 695B.C. in Ninevah, capital of Assyria, a park was established, which was said to have included specimens of every **Botanic**
plant species which grew in the Assyrian Empire. It was not a **Gardens**
small empire, and in the strict sense, it would have been practically impossible to grow every species in one park. However,
the effort was serious and it must have been a very noteworthy
botanic garden. Ninevah stood on the banks of the Tigris River
in the northern part of present-day Iraq. The empire that supplied the plants included present-day Jordan, Israel, Lebanon,
Syria, Iraq, Northern Arabia, Kuwait, Southern Turkey and
Western Iran. Another audacious venture in botanic gardening
occurred almost a hundred years later in the Southern
Mesopotamian city of Babylon. King Nebuchadnezzar, whose
Neo-Babylonian Empire had ousted the Assyrians, decided to
build the celebrated Hanging Gardens of Babylon, one of the
Seven Wonders of the World. It seems that the gardens, built **Imitation**
around 600B.C., occupied a large roofless building on more **Environment**
than one floor. Nebuchadnezzar's intention was to replicate
exactly the environment of a mountain area, and there must
have been means of regulating the temperature and moisture
levels, as well as plants brought in from a great distance.

Even though enthusiastic references to gardens are found
amongst ancient literature, there is no record of any book **Gardening**
devoted to the topic until quite late. The first was *Wei Warng's* **Book**
*Flower and Tree Book* of about 500A.D. Although it was in Chinese, the author, Taw Ba Hsin, was one of a powerful family of
Toba barbarians that conquered part of North China.

Sergius Orata, the man who equipped Roman houses with
showers [XI, 1], made another important contribution to the **Oyster Farm**
easy life with his invention of oyster farms. He introduced
them in the Gulf of Baiae, offshore from Italy's foremost resort
towns, near present-day Naples, in about 90B.C.

In 1953 the Danish vessel *Kista Dan* sailed from Melbourne
under charter to the Australian National Antarctic Research **Settlement in**
Expeditions. Its destination was Horseshoe Harbour, on the **Antarctica**

northwest coast of the Australian Antarctic Territory. On the basis of previous aerial surveys, this place had been chosen by expedition leader, Dr. Phillip Law, as the site for a government research station. On 11 February 1954 *Kista Dan* broke through surrounding sea ice and became the first ship to enter Horseshoe Harbour. Twelve days later, the ship sailed away, leaving an assortment of prefabricated huts and ten men prepared to stay for winter. Their base, Mawson, has been continuously occupied ever since, although the personnel are constantly being changed to save them going out of their minds.

## 2. BUILDINGS AND WORKS

Bridges are included in this section but other transport facilities are treated in Chapter IX, sections 1 and 2. For artistic styles in architecture see II, 1.

**Architecture**

In contrast to the ancient and simple art of building, architecture did not arise until about 3200 B.C., or just before, when simultaneously in Egypt and Mesopotamia elaborate buildings began to be designed and constructed out of stone. The first official state architect was an Egyptian, Imhotep, who worked for the Pharaoh Xoser about the 32nd century B.C. His principle achievements were in funeral architecture, and much of his work remains in a tomb complex at Sakkara near the Nile River. His most notable innovation was the pyramid, which he chose for the pharaoh's personal tomb. This first of all pyramids is known as the Step Pyramid, because it is constructed as a series of stepped stone platforms, reaching a height of about 200 feet. Imhotep's achievement is remarkable because before his time, Egypt's largest buildings were single-storey structures built mainly of mud brick. The technology that developed under his tutelage enabled the Egyptians to build, a generation after his death, the largest stone building of all time (the Great Pyramid), even though only a century before his birth they had not built in stone at all [see Stone Building, below].

**Official Architect**

**Pyramid**

**Arch**

The Sumerian architecture of Southern Mesopotamia (in present-day Iraq) was beneficially influenced by the traditional reed buildings still familiar on the swamplands of the Tigris–Euphrates Valley. These have tall, pliable corner posts made out of reed bundles. Sometimes the tops of the posts were drawn together and joined to form an arch, which architects

Some of Imhotep's architecture has that mid-20th century feel. Tomb chapel, reconstructed by Lauer.

began to imitate in masonry probably around 3200B.C. Initially, such masonry arches would have been purely ornamental, but early in the following millennium the weight-bearing arch came into regular use.

When four bundled reed corner posts are tied together at their tops they can support a dome-shaped roof. This too was **Dome** imitated by the architects. The oldest known example is a dome covering one of the royal tombs of Ur, probably built shortly before 3000B.C. out of limestone rubble set in mud and mortar. This was constructed over a dome-shaped timber framework, which was removed once the mortar set.

The dome was soon followed by the barrel vault, which quickly became the most popular construction for Sumerian **Vault** royal tombs, and eventually, one of the most generally used architectural features all over the world. Rather than resting on a temporary timber framework, vaults were originally constructed as long successions of brick archways, sloping diagonally so that each rests on the one before.

The lofty Sumerian temples popularised in schoolbooks and in the Tower of Babel story began to be built before 3000B.C. in **Ziggurat** Southern Mesopotamia. The oldest ziggurat was in Erech, probably constructed for the worship of the sky god An. It consisted of an oblong temple 60 feet by 80 feet on top of a platform of levelled earth, 40 feet above the surrounding land.

About 280B.C. the 'Pharos Tower' – or Lighthouse of Alexandria – was built on the little island of Pharos, part of Alexandria **Skyscraper** in Egypt. Height estimates range from less than 100 to about

200 metres. 125 m. to 150 m. seems most plausible. If so, it may only have been the third or fourth-tallest building in Egypt – lower than the best pyramids, and about the same as a modern forty-storey office block. Unlike the pyramids, it is called a sky-scraper because of its slender form, and its partition into floor after floor of rooms. These were set around the external faces of the building. In its core there was, it is believed, a lift and a steep spiral roadway. The limestone structure was faced with marble and decorated with statues. On top was a powerful light pro-jected far out to sea by convex reflectors. Its beam out-distanced safety requirements; it was mainly a navigation aid, guiding ships directly into port. A huge notice on the exterior of the building credited the Greek architect – Sostratos of Cnidos.

**Pagoda** The pagoda came into existence as a result of Indian archi-tectural influence on Northern China. Shrines known as *stu-pas* had been built in India 2000 years ago for Buddhist worship. Chinese Buddhists, probably late in the Harn Dynasty (2nd century A.D.), adopted the same practice, but their designs abandoned the stocky outlines of the Indian stupa and resembled in many respects the tall slender towers of brick and timber which were already popular in China. By adorning the resulting hybrid with ornamental balconies and awnings, the Chinese created the pagoda.

**High-rise** In the city of Rome, blocks of flats called *insulae* began to grow
**Housing** very tall in the 2nd century B.C. These buildings are described by Vitruvius in his *Ten Books on Architecture* (1st century B.C.):

> As the ground floors could not admit of so great a number living in the city, the nature of the case has made it neces-sary to find relief by making the buildings high. In these tall piles reared with piers of stone, walls of burnt brick and partitions of rubble work and provided with floor after floor, the upper storeys can be partitioned off into rooms to very great advantage. The accommodations within the walls being thus multiplied as a result of the many floors high in the air, the Roman people easily find excellent places in which to live.                     (tr. Morgan)

The Phoenician city of Tyre, on an island off present-day Lebanon, had high-rise housing at the same time – a need imposed by the island's limited building space.

**Clerestory** The clerestory roof, with two levels separated by rows of win-
**Roof** dows, was invented by ancient Egyptian architects as a way of

bringing light into tall buildings. The earliest example is the Valley Temple of Pharaoh Khafre (about the 31st century B.C.), next to the Sphinx at Gizeh. The central roof was supported on massive square granite columns and the clerestory windows were fairly narrow, oblique slots.

The concave curve so characteristic of roofs in China was not invented until after the end of the Harn Dynasty (220A.D.), **Chinese Roof** possibly as late as the 4th century A.D. Before that, Chinese buildings resembled those of the West, with a straight sloping roofline. Instead of having beams that run from the ridge to the eave, the weight-bearing members in the Chinese construction are horizontals and verticals; the corners where they meet are the support points for the roof itself, which is curved to suit the structural configuration of its supports.

The door that opens automatically was first invented not as a convenience to shoppers, but to demonstrate the opposing prin- **Automatic** ciples of religion and science. The priest who operated it did so **Doors** by kindling a fire on his altar. This traditional rite for honouring the god caused the temple door to open without further instigation by mortals – a fitting display of the efficacy of worship. The scientist who designed it used the altar to hide an expansion chamber, with the fire as his source of heat energy. Hot air passing under pressure into a cistern propelled water into a suspended container, which pulled the draw cords of the door down by its increased weight – a convincing demonstration of the principle of pneumatic expansion. The inventor is Heron of Alexandria, who probably lived in Hellenistic Egypt around 100B.C. His theory that the space between molecules of fluid substances increases when heat is applied led him to a multitude of pneumatic inventions, including a steam engine [VIII, 9].

For a long time, bricks were the most substantial building material available. Stone came into limited use during Egypt's **Stone Building** 1st Dynasty, when some tombs after about 3400B.C. were floored or lined with limestone or granite, sometimes quarried far afield. Between tomb interiors and large stone buildings, a great deal of development is required. The Egyptians developed very rapidly, and after a hundred years they had the largest of all stone buildings: the Great Pyramid. Between the tombs and the pyramid came the world's first stone buildings: modest experiments in stone construction made during the 2nd Dynasty, just after 3300B.C.

**Glass Building** A movable 'glass palace' was constructed in the capital city of Northern Wei, in what is now Shansi province, during the reign (424A.D.–452) of Tai Wu. It was built to take advantage of Western mass-production glass technology newly introduced by foreign technicians from Central Asia. The novel structure held over a hundred people – such a trifling accomplishment that it must have been quite modestly sized compared to kindred follies of the 19th century such as London's Crystal Palace.

**Metal Building** The earliest known permanent metal building was a Chinese cast-iron temple constructed in 688A.D. It was a tall, thin structure in three storeys, towering to a height of 294 feet. It was less than one-third the height of the Eiffel Tower, but still very ambitious for a new concept. It is no longer standing, but it began a tradition of iron and bronze tower construction, which lasted for centuries in China.

**Great Wall** The Great Wall was built on China's northern frontier from about 220 to 210B.C. during the shortlived and authoritarian rule of the Chin Dynasty. It was constructed under the direction of General Meng Tien – the foremost commander in the service of Chin Shir Huarng Di, China's First Emperor – by myriads of convicts and conscript labourers, many of whom died in the process. In 210B.C., when Meng Tien received a forged imperial order to commit suicide, he was unrepentant:

> What crime have I before Heaven? . . . Beginning at Lin Dao and extending to Liao Dung I have made ramparts and ditches over more than 10,000 *li*, and in this distance it is impossible that I have not cut through the veins of the Earth. This is my crime.

But a century later, Szu Ma Chien – the historian who wrote Meng's biography – looked unsympathetically on the manner of his death:

> He did not alleviate the distress of the common people, support the aged, care for the orphaned, or busy himself with restoring harmony to the masses. On the contrary, he gave in to the Emperor's ideas and conscripted forced labour. Isn't it fitting that he should meet death like this? What did his crime have to do with the veins of the Earth?
>
> (tr. D. Bodde, modif.)

**Bridges** Bridges go back to prehistoric times, probably first constructed in West Asia. Originally they consisted of horizontal beams connecting stone piers. Pier and beam construction has survived to the present day – given a new impetus by the invention of pre-stressed concrete [VIII, 8], although sometimes with disastrous results. The first refinement in design principle was the arch span, initially semi-circular, which is stronger and more durable than beams.

Arches probably began to be used about the same time in the Roman Empire and Harn Dynasty China, for constructing **Arch Bridge** culverts and bridging gullies. The first substantial arch bridge, however, is the 'Senatorial Bridge', built in 127B.C. in Roman Italy by Caius Flavius, with multiple arches spanning about 40 feet each. The 'elliptical' arch bridge, which dispenses with **'Elliptical' Arch** the full semi-circle, was a much later development. **Bridge**

The first elliptical arch bridge.

So successfully does its segmental arch design combine economy, beauty and strength that the first example, though cheaply built, continues even now to carry traffic and delight the eye. The Arn Ji Bridge, built in 610A.D. in China's Hopei Province by Li Chun, has a span of 123 feet. It appears also to **Secondary** be the earliest bridge to carry the roadway on secondary arches **Arches** placed above the spanning arch.

A different approach is the cantilever bridge, with its roadway carried on beams that project unsupported at their **Cantilever** outer end. By setting one cantilever above another, bridge **Bridge** engineers can span 170 feet with timber beams. A cantilever bridge over the Danube River in Central Europe was constructed in 104A.D. by Roman engineers. It was depicted in 113A.D. on Trajan's Column, still standing in Rome today.

**Multi-angle Cantilever Bridge**

Arch and cantilever are married in the multi-angle cantilever bridge, which uses material so efficiently that the entire structure consists only of the roadway and the beams on which it rests. Instead of running parallel to each other, the superimposed cantilevers are angled into the approximation of a curve. The Rainbow Bridge at Kaifeng was built on this system during the 11th century A.D. (the Sung Dynasty), when Kaifeng, in Northeastern China, was the imperial capital. It crossed the river in the suburbs of the city in one span, estimated at about 150 feet in length.

Few bridges could be more economical of materials than the multi-angle cantilever bridge in 11th century Kaifeng. The span was supported solely by timber beams, clearly shown, along with suburban restaurants and takeaways, in Jarng Dse Duarn's 13th-century reconstruction.

**Suspension Bridge**

The earliest suspension bridges on record are described in a Chinese book discussing the mountainous Hindu Kush, in present-day Afghanistan. *The History of the Former Harn Dynasty* (c. 90A.D.) refers to the bridges in its chapter on Central Asia. Suspension bridges at this time were simply narrow walkways held aloft by rope cables across ravines and narrow valleys. The Chinese book is the oldest written record of a type of structure which may have been in use several centuries earlier.

**Flat-deck Bridge**

A bridge built across the Brahmaputra River in Tibet in about 1420A.D. may have been the first flat-deck suspension bridge. It had a flat roadway hanging from the weight-bearing rope cables. Earlier suspension bridges had roadways that followed the curves of the spanning cables.

**Concrete Bridge**

Early bridges were made of stone, timber, rope and brick. The Romans built the first concrete bridges in Italy in the 1st century B.C. These were semi-circular arch bridges with stone facings. Metal was first used during the Harn Dynasty, on the Larn Jin suspension bridge across the Mekong River, constructed in Southwestern China in the 1st century A.D. The only metal, however, was in the cables, which were iron chains.

The first true metal bridge was built during the Sung **Metal Bridge** Dynasty, in the Chinese industrial centre of Jing De Jen, then called Fo Liarng Hsien. It was constructed on twelve cast-iron columns by an engineer from Chiangsi Province, Dsarng Hung, in the 11th century A.D.

In 1779 Thomas Pritchard designed the first metal arch **Metal Arch** bridge across England's Severn River at Coalbrookdale. The **Bridge** roadway was supported on five parallel cast-iron arches, spanning 100 feet and weighing almost 400 tons. A pre-stressed **Pre-stressed** concrete arch bridge was first constructed in 1936 over a 19 m. **Concrete** span in Algeria. The designer was Eugene Freyssinet, pioneer of **Bridge** pre-stressed concrete construction [VIII, 8].

Late in the 3rd millennium B.C., at least one artificial harbour was built, by the eastern shore of the Arabian Sea (in present- **Artificial** day India and Pakistan). Archaeologists have discovered a **Harbour** large oblong basin with entry channels and a spillway at Lothal, India, not far from Pakistan's Indus Valley, one of the ancient homes of civilisation. This harbour, built of fired bricks, was 250 m. long, and lay adjacent to a small riverside port that must have handled traffic to the Gulf of Cambay. It has two entry channels, one apparently built (around 1970B.C.) because the other silted up.

In about 210B.C. the navy of the Hellenistic empire of the Ptolemies in Egypt launched a huge new ship, that was 420 feet **Dry Dock** long, 72 feet high and 57 feet wide. By modern standards this is large, but nothing exceptional. In those days it was extraordinary, and facilities for looking after it were inadequate. Some time after the launch, a Phoenician who worked in Egypt's main port, Alexandria, devised the dry dock to handle this, and other large ships. Alexandria's dry dock was an excavation which must have been about 500 feet long. Its stone foundations were 7 feet thick, and 6 feet above them was a series of crosswise stone skids, continuing for the length of the dock. It could be filled with water to admit ships, then pumped dry to leave them standing on the skids, ready for maintenance work.

According to archaeological evidence, the massive system of underground canals (*qanats*) in Persia and neighbouring **Qanat** countries was begun in the 8th century B.C. Qanats were built to bring fresh water across dry plains and deserts to agricultural areas to the south. The oldest known were constructed near Urarta in Armenia.

**Underground Pipelines**  Long-distance underground pipelines for the same purpose were begun in Iraq during the 8th century A.D. The first 500 km. were completed during the reign of the Caliph al-Mutawakkil.

## 3. MAPS, PLANS AND SURVEYS

Projections are in Chapter VIII, section 3.

**Map**  In ancient Mesopotamia (present-day Iraq), proper maps drawn on clay tablets date back to the middle of the 3rd millennium B.C. One map found near Kirkuk shows a 127 ha. plot of land, some hills on each side and a river or canal. Compass directions are marked on the edges, with east on top. Another map of similar age marks the location of nine towns or villages and the roads and canals between them.

**Scale Bar**  Often, very early maps are not drawn to a consistent scale, so it is hard to tell what area is covered. The use of a scale bar overcomes this difficulty, and dates back to around 2100B.C. Even in those days it was a bit unusual to bother including a scale bar on a work of art or on someone's clothes. But the oldest specimen is carved, for some reason, on the robe worn by King Gudea of Lagash in a statue of him in the Louvre, Paris, which is more than 4000 years old. It shows the scale for the plan of a building that appears on his lap.

**Town Plan**  The earliest town plan is a diagrammatic painting from the second half of the 7th millennium B.C., discovered at the site of the prehistoric town at Çatal Hüyük in present-day Central Turkey. It comprises a plan representation of the houses in one part of the town, and a profile view of the volcano behind it.

**Town Map**  The earliest city shown on a contemporary town map is Nippur in Mesopotamia. Nippur was the home of the first peace movement [IV, 4] and the point of origin of the oldest case report [XII, 1] and the first marathon run [X, 1]. The map showing it was inscribed on a clay tablet during the 2nd millennium B.C., probably before 1500. For such an early map, it is quite accurately to scale, and distances between certain points are marked in. The tablet is broken, but about 4 sq. km. of the city centre remains, showing city walls, gates, major buildings, 'City Centre Park', canals and the Euphrates River. Though no actual city maps can be traced to an earlier time than Nippur's, Mesopotamian cartographers must have worked previously on maps of some kind, to reach the level of skill exercised on this one.

An Egyptian map on papyrus from approximately 1300 B.C. identifies gold and silver-bearing areas in a mountainous region inland from the Red Sea. Labels designate features, including roads, with their destinations, and a mining settlement, as well as the distribution of gold and silver. Red shading is used to identify the gold-bearing mountains.

**Geological Map**

The great Chinese scientist Shen Gua began to make relief maps in the late-11th century when he worked as an official inspecting frontier areas. His method was to map a region on a wooden base, and add the mountains and valleys by modelling in a mixture of sawdust and glue. He went personally on the field work, but changed over to a melted wax technique after a bout of cold weather froze up his modelling paste. When he got back to his office in Kaifeng, he had the wax original copied in carved timber. Soon afterwards, orders were issued for the production of similar timber maps for all of China's frontier areas.

**Relief Map**

In the 3rd century B.C., the Greek scientist Eratosthenes of Cyrene, who measured the size of the Earth [VIII, 3] and divided it into seven climatic zones [VIII, 3], also made a map of the world. Although it was far more accurate and comprehensive than any small-scale maps from earlier times, it was very deficient by today's standards and even those of the following centuries. Eratosthenes confined himself to the known world, Europe, Africa, Asia, and outer islands like Iceland and Ceylon (called Thule and Taprobane). He used his study of longitude and latitude to assign positions for places in all continents, although the accuracy of the map decreased with distance away from the Mediterranean.

**World Map**

Knowledge grew in the wake of his work, and in the 2nd century A.D., Marinus of Tyre was able to produce a world atlas in which the known world was divided into small map areas. Ptolemy, who later in the same century produced a more comprehensive world map, commented that there were few areas where he had information to add to that of Marinus: the African coasts, India and East Africa, China, the East Asian port of Cattigara, and the silk routes. It seems that the atlas

**World Atlas**

only covered known lands, and left out America and Australia, believed or suspected to exist, but not known. Marinus used a simple square projection, which made no proper allowance for the Earth's curvature.

**Terrestrial Globe** The world was mapped on a globe by Crates of Mallos, a Greek scholar working at Pergamon (in present-day Turkey) during the 2nd century B.C. He divided the globe into Northern and Southern and 'Eastern' and 'Western' hemispheres, including continents in the approximate places of Australia and America on the basis of conjecture.

**Quantity Survey** In the ancient Greek city of Ephesus, in present-day Turkey, architects were required to furnish an exact statement of the costs applicable to the building projects they were engaged to complete. This was more than a price quotation or a cost estimate: it formed the basis of an insurance scheme funded by the architect, and no public project could go ahead without it. If actual costs overran the statement figure by more than twenty-five per cent, the architect was obliged to cover any further expense. The exact date when the system came into operation is unknown, but it was hundreds of years old by the 1st century B.C. It is said to have stimulated a great improvement in estimating practices.

**Archaeology** When the hated fascist empire of the Assyrians collapsed, the new Chaldaean dynasty ruling in Babylon (612–538B.C.) set about reconstructing the traditions and authority of the extinct, 1500-year-old Old Babylonian Empire. The archaeological investigations put in train by King Nabopolassar and his son, Nebuchadnezzar, at the end of the 7th century B.C., were therefore not just a quest for knowledge of the past. As an instrument of imperial policy, they aimed to enable society to mimic the style of old times, and to replace Assyrian religious and cultural influence with Babylonian. Ruined temples were excavated to discover their designs, and to find the minute inauguration inscriptions concealed by their founders in the foundations. The first archaeologist whose personal work is still known is the last Chaldaean ruler, Nabonidus (reigned 555–538B.C.). He was passionate about archaeology and a stern critic of the inadequate methods used by his predecessors in the field. Nabonidus's work on recording ancient inscriptions, and dating early buildings and rulers, still proves useful to archaeologists today; if he had given as much attention to more important issues, perhaps he would not have lost his kingdom.

# VI

# WARFARE AND DESTRUCTION

The human race invests more initiative and resources in the cause of defeating enemies than in anything else. In one way, the progress achieved completely outstrips progress in other fields. Comparisons of early societies with later ones often show them on a par in important assets like artistic creativity, intellectual sophistication and material prosperity. Not in military effectiveness though: the best equipped armed forces of early times would be swiftly annihilated in any combat with their latter-day counterparts. History often demonstrates this: for example, when tiny European forces quickly seized control of the whole American continent from militarily backward defenders.

Looked at another way, this field shows no progress at all. Military improvements always spread amongst potential combatants and cancel each other out; if all there were to fight with were sticks and firebrands, there would still be a balance of power. When powerful modern weapons are blamed for massive slaughter and destruction, the real issue is avoided. Since the dawn of history armed forces have been capable of exterminating civilian populations. Nowadays, bomber aircraft can obliterate cities overnight, but so could horsemen with torches 5000 years ago. So in the 1940s – when cities were destroyed as never before, and civilian slaughter reached a newfound intensity – the world first which made it all possible was not a new height of sophistication in weapons, but a new depth of depravity in morals.

## 1. DESTRUCTIVE CONCEPTS AND AGENTS

Nefer-Rohu was an Egyptian priest of the cat goddess Bastet, in the 4th Dynasty (c. 3050–2850B.C.), during the Old King- **Prophet of** dom period. He is first in the long series of sages who have left **Doom** claims that man will bring destruction and calamity on himself by carrying on in his established manner. The version of his forecast that survives today was written up in the Middle Kingdom Period, after a series of disasters had indeed wiped out the Old Kingdom. It is impossible now to know how much the Middle Kingdom scribe embellished Nefer-Rohu's views with the benefit of hindsight. However, even if it only dates from the Middle Kingdom (c. 2150–c. 1950B.C.), the prophecy is the oldest of its kind. The disasters predicted are mainly ecological: the land is topsy-turvy, clouds obscure the sun, rivers dry out, foreign birds breed in Egypt and the good things are damaged, such as ponds which had been crowded with life. These setbacks were not due to random workings of fate but to human misconduct: among other things, rapacious administration, high taxes and Asian immigration. Nefer-Rohu is the father of an important Western tradition. The art of foretelling disaster was learnt by the Jews in Egypt and practised repeatedly by the prophets of the Old Testament. From them it passed to European Christians such as Nostradamus, to the American evangelists, and to the Australian oracles who warn of Asian immigration in modern times.

**Famine**

> Grain was scant, fruits were dried up and everything was deficient. Every man robbed his companion. They moved without going. The infant was wailing, the youth was waiting; the heart of the old men was in sorrow, their legs were bent, crouching on the ground, their arms were folded . . .
> The sanctuaries held air. Everything was found empty.

This depressing appraisal might describe the most recent famine as accurately as the first. In fact it refers to Egypt in the 32nd century B.C., during the 3rd Dynasty. Undoubtedly, before this and back into prehistoric times, local famines had afflicted agricultural societies, but the 'Seven Lean Years' of the 3rd Dynasty is the earliest nationwide famine on record. For seven years the crops failed because the Nile River did not rise enough to irrigate them properly. Eventually gifts were offered to Khnum, god of the river's source, and the land recovered. The record we still have was written much later, and perhaps seven is an exaggeration. But the account of suffering is based on the real misery of ancient Egypt's darkest days.

**Genocide**

Genocide took place in prehistoric times as the natural result of the competition between one people and another for territory and the limited resources for survival which the land could offer to Stone Age technology. In many parts of the early world, the law of survival of the fittest was undoubtedly assisted by campaigns of slaughter carried out by folk of superior strength, culture or numbers, against their weaker competitors. There is a fossil record of this in areas where archaeological sites reveal two different skull types from human communities of overlapping eras. Typically, one skull type reveals that the earlier inhabitants perished, and the other that a new race took over during their last days. This phenomenon must go back earlier than the fossils now available, practically to the first days of human tribal organisation. However, the motive was merely to grasp control of resources.

A deliberate intention to exterminate all members of a particular race did not arise until civilised times, when it was first developed amongst the Jews: **Call for Genocide**

> But of the cities of these peoples, which the LORD thy God giveth thee for an inheritance, thou shalt save alive nothing that breatheth:
>
> But thou shalt utterly destroy them; the Hittite, and the Amorite, the Canaanite, and the Perizzite, the Hivite, and the Jebusite; as the LORD thy God hath commanded thee . . .

These embarrassing words from the Bible (*Deuteronomy*, 20, 16 and 17) command the destruction of the ancient inhabitants of Palestine, Lebanon and parts of Jordan, Syria and Turkey. *Deuteronomy* was probably written about 500B.C. but going by the races selected for annihilation, the teaching dates from about 1200B.C. Fortunately the people knew better than to take the Scripture literally, and the Jewish nation outlived the others only by a greater determination to keep its separate identity.

*Deuteronomy* and other books of the *Pentateuch* contain a message apparently tailored to encourage and justify Jewish invasion of Palestine (Canaan). They instruct the people of Moses to fight wars on the Lord's behalf, to gain possession of Canaan, and to suppress foreigners. Only the six races named were scheduled for extermination; in the event of conquests elsewhere, the ancient Jews were instructed merely to massacre all the grown males and to carry off the women, children and livestock as plunder. The Bible thus records the first doctrine of holy war, formulated perhaps around 1200B.C. **Holy War**

The long and illustrious career of the Chinese doctor Sun Szu Miao (581A.D.–682) gave the world the urinary catheter and the modern procedure for mending dislocated jaws. But Sun's work as a pharmacologist led to the invention of a less genial **Gunpowder** novelty. In order to render sulphur less volatile, and safe for medicinal use, he heated it with potassium nitrate (saltpetre). Sulphur, potassium nitrate and carbon together make gunpowder, and Sun's method led, probably by accident, to a mixture which must have been potentially explosive. During the Tarng Dynasty (618A.D.–906), gunpowder's incendiary powers were recognised, and it was also listed officially as a medicine (it is effective against certain skin conditions).

**Nitro-glycerine**

Ascanio Sobrero, an Italian student in Paris, first produced the diabolical explosive nitro-glycerine in 1847A.D. Commercial manufacture was begun in 1864, by the Swede Alfred Nobel (1833–96), famous now for his Nobel Prizes [IV, 4]. Nobel was troubled by the accidents which nitro-glycerine caused, and invented dynamite in 1866 or 1867, by soaking inert material such as silica in nitro-glycerine.

**Dynamite**

## 2. SOLDIERS AND WEAPONS

Military methods keep improving, but often by evolutionary development which doesn't present clear-cut firsts. Inventions of new weaponry and equipment that can be assigned to particular times and places mostly belong to three specially innovative eras. The earliest was the Warring States Period (481–221B.C.) when China, like Europe later on, was divided into powerful independent kingdoms. It was an age of inventiveness and of warfare; even avowed pacifists worked on weapons development, thinking that by improving defences they would discourage aggression. In one memorable instance they put on a laboratory demonstration. Leaders watched as defensive devices neutralised the would-be aggressor's new weapons – all in miniature – and the war was called off. The same period saw many innovations in the West also.

The second age of inventions was the time of the Sung Dynasty (960A.D.–1279). Highly organised northern barbarians were making vigorous assaults on civilised countries. The Chinese, reluctant fighters, tried to save their necks with new weapons. But the barbarians, especially the Mongols, were fast learners and China was overrun. Mongol forces advanced as far as Japan and Java and deep into India, West Asia and Europe; by 1300 most of the world had been introduced to modern firearms. Warlike Muslim and Christian powers took over the initiative, and from then on the West led in military development.

The third age of inventions is still underway after over 200 years. Its greatest achievements are the work of European and American inventors, but as in the 1300s, their international spread has been very rapid.

In the 2nd millennium B.C., soldiers in the Egyptian army who fought with exceptional bravery were decorated by the **Military Medal** pharaoh with an award called the 'Gold of Valour'. The earliest mention is from the 18th Dynasty (c. 1600–c. 1350B.C.).

A military academy for training officers was opened by the Chinese armed forces in 1044A.D., during the Sung Dynasty. **Military** It was run along the lines of a university, and occupied the site **Academy** of a former temple in Wu Cheng.

'Greek fire' was the secret weapon used by the defenders of the Greek-speaking eastern remnant of the Roman Empire to pro- **Firearms** tect their capital, Constantinople, against the Arab campaign launched in 668A.D. Syrian chemist Callinicus of Heliopolis introduced them to a formula believed to have combined petroleum, sulphur and pitch. It is easily kindled, unquenchable with water and long burning; it became the ammunition for the first arsenal of firearms. The Greeks flung it at the Arabs from catapults, poured it on them from cauldrons and set it among their fleets in fire ships. Their favourite dis- **Flame** pensers were long copper flame throwers. **Thrower**

What is always overlooked is that eleven centuries earlier the Greeks had already employed a similar preparation in the first flame thrower. In 423B.C. during the Peloponnesian War, the Athenians invaded Boeotia and hastily occupied the holy site of Delium. Boeotian forces attacked the Athenian fortifications there with a new device comprising a long, thick, metal-plated wooden pipe, connected to a cauldron of sulphur, pitch and burning coals. Driving air through this with bellows, they destroyed the temporary fortifications by throwing flames on them, and had no difficulty overcoming the Athenian position.

In 970A.D., the newly established Sung Dynasty in China **Gunpowder** tested a new kind of 'fire arrow' with successful results, and **Weapon** gave rewards to the inventors (Yaw Yi Farng, Feng Ji Sheng and others). This is believed to be the first weapon based on gunpowder [VI, 1], which was attached in packets to the fire arrows. (Previously, fire arrows had been treated with flammable substances other than gunpowder.) Even equipped with gunpowder, fire arrows were incendiary weapons rather than explosives. Soon afterwards, arrows of this type were the first **Gunpowder in** gunpowder weapons used in combat. In 975 Sung forces used **Combat** them to drive off defenders of the kingdom of Narn Tarng.

**Bomb**

Simple bombs – containers full of gunpowder which must have been ignited by fuses – were developed in China in the late 900s. One kind, named the 'fire ball', was presented to the throne in 1000A.D. by its inventor, Tarng Fu. The first bombs were designed to be flung at the enemy by the same kind of catapult as had long been used for launching heavy stones.

**Scatter Bomb**

Tarng Fu was a lieutenant in the Imperial Guard during the Sung Dynasty's war against the Liao Tartars in the North. At the same time as presenting his bomb to the emperor – 1000A.D. – he presented another invention: the first scatter bomb – his 'barbed fire package' containing gunpowder mixed with small pieces of flammable material, which sprayed around to make the enemy's path impassable.

萬 人 敵

Early shells were very disconcerting to attacking forces.

These early bombs were cased in leather, bamboo, wood and ceramic. By 1221A.D., the forces of the foreign Jin **Shell** Dynasty, running North China, had a new weapon which came to be known as the 'heaven shaking thunder crash'. In an important way it ushered in the modern style of warfare. High-explosive powder was encased in a 2 inch-thick cast-iron shell. The result was greater explosive force; 'when it went off', says an account from the 1230s:

> it made a report like sky-rending thunder. An area more than half a *mu* [⅙ acre] was scorched, on which men, horses and leather armour were shattered. Even iron coats of mail were riddled.

*The Military Compendium of Essentials*, written in 1040A.D., includes the first description of a smoke bomb, a **Smoke Bomb** canister packed with gunpowder and smoke-generating materials. Its inclusion means it was probably an invention of the previous decades; like other bombs of the time, it was designed to be launched at the enemy by catapult.

The *Compendium* was written by a number of Chinese authors in 1040A.D. but not published until 1044. It describes **Grenade** many Sung Dynasty innovations. Grenades, it reports, are hollow pieces of bamboo, 1.5 inches in diameter, filled with gunpowder and fitted with iron fragments and pot shards. These were to be ignited with a red hot iron, and made a noise like thunder on exploding.

The book refers to mines as 'bursting fire balls', to be buried at places where the enemy was expected. They con- **Land Mine** tained gunpowder, ceramic shards and ingredients that produced thick smoke on explosion. These mines were probably set off manually by observers concealed at the end of long fuses.

Mines that went off automatically when the enemy tripped a detonating mechanism came considerably later. The **Self-** first descriptions are in a Chinese weaponry book of the mid- **detonating** 1300s. Self-detonating mines must have been around earlier **Mine** than that, judging by the complete range of systems which had developed. Perhaps the first came about 1200A.D. One of the detonating mechanisms consisted of steel wheels resting on flints, which began turning – and sparking – when the tread of an unwary enemy released a pin. Another relied on an incandescent preparation which would smoulder for days or weeks. [See also Ship Mine, VI, 3.]

On 6 August 1945 a United States bomber aircraft over Hiroshima, Japan, dropped an atom bomb named 'Little Boy' **Atom Bomb** onto the city below. This first combat use of nuclear weaponry was an unqualified success, destroying the city and immediately claiming 80,000 lives – mostly civilians. Little Boy was the first uranium bomb to be exploded. It had a gun-type detonator which worked by driving one piece of enriched uranium into another, to produce the supercritical mass required for explosion. However, the first atom bomb ever exploded was of the plutonium type, and had been detonated in a test at Alamagordo in New Mexico, U.S.A., on 16 July that year. Both kinds were invented by the Manhattan Project – an operation established in 1942 by the U.S. Government, with the express object of developing nuclear weapons. It was staffed by a team of American and foreign scientists based at Los Alamos, New Mexico, and led by Prof. J. Robert Oppenheimer (1904–67).

**Rocket** The first rockets were probably developed from the Chinese fire arrow [see above]. An unknown Chinese inventor – either in the 12th century A.D. or around 1000A.D. – used a cylinder full of gunpowder mounted on the arrow shaft for high-speed propulsion. Such rockets proved highly effective in warfare, especially when shot in numbers out of purpose-built rocket launchers. But soon after their invention, a more advantageous use was found for them in firework displays.

These rockets of the Sung Dynasty are only distantly related to the amazing Russian and American space rockets of the 20th century. Two new technologies in particular were required to **Stage Rocket** make space rocketry possible. One of these, the stage rocket system, was developed in China by the 14th century, for an ingenious anti-ship missile. The 'fire dragon issuing from the water' consisted of a canister loaded with small rockets, with four large slanting rocket cylinders fitted to its exterior. The external rockets could carry it a few feet above water level for a mile or so. Shortly before they burnt out, the second-stage rockets inside would ignite and launch out of the mouth of the canister.

The other vital improvement, the liquid fuel rocket, was **Liquid Fuel** first successfully launched in the United States in 1926 by an **Rocket** American professor, Robert H. Goddard (1882–1945), who had been working since 1907 to find a suitable fuel and a rocket design. Goddard saw liquid fuel as the key to reaching outer space, but being human, people applied it to military uses first. [For civil uses, see Spacecraft etc., IX, 3.]

The 'magic fire flying crow' was invented in China at **Flying Bomb** about the same time as the stage rocket, probably around 1300A.D. It consisted of a bomb in a basket-weave casing, with fixed wings, a head and a tail attached. It looked like a model bird, but two rockets under each wing propelled it through the sky like a jet aircraft. The bomb blew up as it landed.

Wernher von Braun (1912–77) was an amateur rocket enthusiast when he was discovered by Walter Dornberger, the German Army's recently appointed chief of rocket research. Dornberger recruited him and a team of supporters to develop military rockets, and shortly before the Second World War, established them at Peenemünde on the North Coast. In October 1942 they launched the first successful long-range rocket missile, which cleared the atmosphere and soared to an altitude of 96 km. before landing on target in the Baltic Sea, 192 km. from Peenemünde. This test model was propelled by a fuel of liquid oxygen and ethyl alcohol, ignited in a combustion chamber. The same system was immediately adopted for the notorious 'V-weapons', which carried one-tonne warheads for distances up to 300 km. The path of these missiles was pre-programmed, and achieved in flight by movable carbon vanes in the exhaust. They reached their maximum speed of 5500 km/h in about a minute. Von Braun's work was largely based on the theories of Hermann Oberth, a Hungarian–German promoter of space flight.

**Long-range Ballistic Missile**

While this new terror weapon was striking British cities from great heights, the Japanese were working on a low-trajectory liquid fuel war rocket for use against Allied fleets in the Pacific. The Ohka ('cherry blossom') kamikaze aircraft built in 1945 was both a rocket and an aeroplane. It carried 1200 kg. of high explosive in the nose, and had three rocket motors in the tail. Like today's space shuttle, it was borne aloft by a conventional aircraft, the twin-engine Mitsubishi bomber. When the target came into view, the rockets were started up, and the expendable pilot guided it to the target ship at over 800 km/h – with precision that the unmanned V-weapons lacked.

**Manned Rocket**

The first weapons which could discharge multiple projectiles at once were manufactured over 1500 years before the invention of the gun, on which magazines now have their main use. In North China, giant crossbows were used as defensive artillery pieces during the Warring States Period (481–221 B.C.). One description of the time mentions a model which was manned by a team of artillerymen, and loaded with innumerable small arrows and sixty large ones, 10 feet long. The large arrows could be hauled back for reuse by windlasses. Very similar weapons made later (in the Tarng Dynasty) used iron arrowheads 7 inches long and 5 inches in circumference, and had a

**Magazine Weapon**

range of more than a kilometre. The likely date of the invention is in the 4th century B.C.

**Trigger**

Before guns, triggers were mass produced in China for use on
portable crossbows, the standard weapons of Chinese soldiers.
Their bronze mechanisms were finely balanced works of considerable precision, with toothed wheels and cams. They were
invented around 200B.C. and first became standard issue for
the Harn Dynasty forces of the 2nd century B.C. The trigger
was instrumental in enabling Harn forces to drive away the
Huns. The exact timing of the Chinese crossbow shots made
the Hun horsemen vulnerable targets for the first time. This
revolution in weaponry triggered the slow westward movement of barbarians from Asia towards the Roman Empire.

**Repeater Mechanism**

The repeating crossbow was invented in China during the
Sung Dynasty, probably in the 1100s. It could fire eleven bolts in
less than 15 seconds. A magazine above the stock held ten bolts,
which dropped into place one at a time, as a firing lever re-
engaged the bow and reset the loading mechanism. By moving
the lever fully forward, the bowman tightened the string. As the
lever came back, the next bolt moved into place. Further progress
of the lever raised a pin to release the string and shoot.

Semi-automatic crossbow.

The first weapon for discharging projectiles under the force of compressed air was invented by the Greek scientist Ctesibius, **Air Gun** who worked in Egypt at Alexandria, early in the 3rd century B.C. Compressed air and liquid intrigued Ctesibius, who used the compression principle in some of his other inventions, like the piston pump [VIII, 11].

The creation of the 'abrupt fire lance' in Southern China in 1259A.D., during the Sung Dynasty, is the first confirmed inven- **Handgun** tion of a gun, although it is possible that similar weapons were known several years earlier, and in the North around the same time. Its thick bamboo barrel was packed with gunpowder and a bundle of pellets: on firing, it spat out pellets and flames. Bamboo is not a strong enough material for a lethal shot except at close range. Very soon after this time, metal barrel guns were being used in North China – perhaps by the 1260s or 1270s. Such a gun – from 1290 or before – is now in the Heilungchiang Provincial Museum. It is 34 cm. long, with a muzzle bore of 1 inch. It seems to have been made to shoot bullets of almost the same diameter as its bore, like a modern gun.

Its design could not be called a hard one to improve on, but most of the countless improvements over following cen- **Rifle** turies did less to make the gun better than to disguise its ineffectiveness. The invention and development of the musket were the main result. One poor valuation of the musket was made in Britain in the 19th century. In an episode during the 'Kaffir Wars', British soldiers firing 80,000 cartridges at their African enemies scored twenty-five hits. The gun's inaccuracy at a distance is overcome in the rifle, because it puts spin on the bullet, but military armourers learnt the lesson awfully slowly. Augustin Kutter (or Koster) of Nuremberg had already made the first rifles in 1520. He made his barrels grooved, so they were rose or star-shaped in cross-section. Inside, the grooves ran in spirals to impart the rifle motion.

Ideas for machine guns abounded from the 16th to the 19th centuries, but until a satisfactory way was found to harness the **Automatic** force of the recoil, there was no workable means of automatic **Machine Gun** firing. In Britain from 1882 to 1884, the American-born inventor Hiram Maxim (1840–1916) made a series of machine guns which successfully utilised recoil to keep on firing unassisted. In 1883 he created a semi-automatic, by con- **Semi-** necting a moving grip to the cocking lever of a Winchester **automatic Gun** carbine. It had a crank engaging the gun's bolt action, as well as a firing button which, if pressed, caused the action to repeat automatically without cranking. The following year Maxim completed his famous fully automatic Maxim gun, on which he dispensed with the crank.

**Bayonet** Until the middle of the 17th century, the musketeers in European armies relied on pikemen to defend them while they reloaded. The bayonet was developed in Bayonne, France, at about 1650A.D. It was simply a pike point on a stock with nearly the same diameter as the musket bore. The first design was less than ideal because after firing, the musketeer had to jam it into his musket barrel to be able to wield it in self-defence, then, after reloading, take it out again to be able to fire. A ring clamp on later bayonets meant they could be mounted on the outside of the barrel and left there.

**Cannon** The westward spread of gunpowder in the 12th and 13th centuries meant that cannons were developed separately in East and West. The first recorded use was in the West, by Muslim armies. According to one report, the Almohads used a cannon as early as 1204A.D., in North Africa. If there is room for doubt about this, at least in the middle of the 13th century the defenders of Islam were using cannons. They are reported in use against the Christians at Seville in Spain (1248) and in Central Asia against the Tartars at 'Ayn Jalut (1260). These early cannons are described in an Arabic book *Collection Combining the Various Arts*, written around 1300. They were rather primitive weapons, which fired out multiple balls or arrows, embedded in the gunpowder. Similar crude cannons were probably made in China before 1300A.D., though there is no proof. It may seem strange that Islamic peoples – who only learnt how to make gunpowder centuries after the Chinese – could have been the first to use it in big guns. But it could be they were so familiar with large-bore flame throwers [see above] that they instantly adapted the design to gunpowder and solid projectiles. By about 1300, the proper cannon, firing projectiles of almost the same width as the bore, had been invented; but there is no way of telling whether the Christians, Muslims or Chinese came on it first.

**Automatic Weapons System** The people of the Greek city of Syracuse in Sicily used to prefer parties to warfare. Recognising this, King Hiero made his reign (270–216B.C.) a time of peace and revelry. Hiero prevailed on his relative Archimedes (287–212B.C.) to put his science into practical use – a very unusual thing for a Greek scientist to do. Archimedes responded by equipping Syracuse with automatic weaponry to spare his people the business of combat: machinery worked by levers, pulleys, springs and counterweights. He perforated the city walls with apertures which could open up and discharge well-aimed volleys of darts and missiles. Contraptions emerging from the parapets would crush enemies at a distance under masses of rock, while all along the foreshore, his largest machines stood by to disable hostile ships. Hiero died, peace ended and in 212B.C. the Roman fleet sailed proudly in to sweep away Syracusan resistance. But huge beams started coming out of the walls, from which great weights dropped onto doomed ships. Giant cranes lifted ships on high and rolled them over so the men fell out, before smashing them on the rocks. Others hooked up the prows of ships till they were almost vertical, then let them go to the bottom. Meanwhile, every approach on land by the Roman Army left heaps of pulverised legionaries, while the Syracusans worked their equipment, safely inside the walls. One night, though, while a party was on in the city, the Romans got stealthily into a weak part of the wall. They overran the city and killed Archimedes while he was working out a scientific problem with diagrams. His weapons system died with him, because thinking it a sordid work, Archimedes had not deigned to explain its operation in writing.

**Tank**

Credit for introducing tanks during the First World War belongs to Britain; nevertheless, British authorities had been very slow to warm to the idea. They rejected a French design in 1903, an English one in 1908, and an Australian one in 1912. By 1915, when the War Office again turned down the Australian design of Lance De Mole, work was already underway on a new concept. This was the design of Tritton and Wilson. It was not as good as De Mole's in some respects, but it shared the basic advantages which all these designs had over ancient contraptions that are sometimes called tanks: the use of endless tracks instead of wheels. The new vehicle was manufactured by the British engineering firm William Foster of Lincoln. A small prototype model was working by the end of 1915, and in February 1916 a test tank named *Mother* – which had caterpillar tracks running right around the top of her hull – performed successfully over a mock trench system in England.

**Tanks in Combat**

The British army planned for a hundred tanks to go into action on the Somme in July; instead, thirty-two were available to take the field on 15 September 1916. The commanders, unpractised in their new weapon, scattered the tanks uselessly along a wide front, instead of concentrating them as an assault force, so the first combat use of tanks made no impact on the war.

**Chemical Weaponry** Chemical warfare was initially the product of China's Warring States Period. About the 4th century B.C., the original method was described in the *Maw Jing*, the book in which the Mohist philosophical school recorded the pacifist views of its master, Maw Dzu. The chemical warfare mechanism it described was for use in defending towns against attacking armies. The gas released by combustion of dried mustard and other plants was directed at enemy forces or into enemy sap tunnels, by double-acting piston bellows operated with a lever. The active ingredient was not in fact mustard gas, but the highly irritating allyl iso-sulpho-cyanide.

**Poison Gas Projectile** Missiles which release poison gas after striking their target are a much later development than fixed apparatus for dispensing toxic substances. They were developed for the armed forces of China's Sung Dynasty, early in the 11th century A.D. *The Military Compendium of Essentials* (Kaifeng 1044A.D.) describes them in detail as bombs containing arsenic and toxic plant materials, together with flammable oil and fibres, and gunpowder for dispersion. Their victims suffered debilitating symptoms, including bleeding from nose and mouth. For a long time they were stockpiled but not used; eventually in the 1120s, they were fired at besieging Jin barbarians in North China. They must have been around for about 100 years by then.

## 3. SEA AND AIR WARFARE

Rockets, including flying bombs and rocket aircraft, have been treated in the previous section.

**Naval Battle** Very early in Egyptian history, perhaps around 3000B.C., people from West Asia sailed against Egypt in a fleet of vessels with distinctive upright prows and sterns. We know of a major naval battle which ensued, from a drawing inscribed on an old knife handle now kept in the Louvre (Paris). It shows the battle line of 'sickle-shaped' Egyptian ships confronting the square-ended craft of the attackers.

The first battle between fleets of purpose-built warships was fought in Greek waters by the navy of Corinth against that of Corcyra, in about 600B.C. The Corinthians, inventors of the Greek warship, had earlier colonised Corcyra and given it full independence. That was not a successful move, and the hostility of the colony to the mother city was expressed in naval battles over three centuries.

**Warships in Combat**

After the war galley was invented, the next development in warship design was the introduction of larger galleys with multiple banks of oars. These originated on the coasts of the Indian Ocean and Red Sea, where early in the 1st millennium B.C., ships were built with oarsmen on an upper and a lower level. Around the beginning of the 7th century B.C., the Greek shipwright Aminocles of Corinth built the first trireme – a galley with three tiers of oarsmen and a strong ram; this became the standard vessel of classical Greek navies. Later, increasingly complex and expensive ships, named after the number of oar banks, were invented by the following peoples, at the times given:

**Multi-tiered Galley**

**Trireme**

Quadrireme (four oar banks): the Carthaginians, 5th century B.C.

Quinquireme (five oar banks), the most common vessel in Carthaginian and Roman navies): the Salaminians, 4th century B.C.

Sexireme (six banks): the Syracusans, 4th century B.C.

Many varieties were larger still, built from the 4th century B.C. onwards, but not individually of sufficient importance to receive our attention. The largest of all ancient war galleys was a ship with forty rows of oars; its arrangement is a mystery, but it is known first to have served in the navy of Ptolemy Philopator Tryphon, ruler of Egypt (221–205B.C.).

**Large War Galleys**

The first warships to be completely encased in metal armour were two Sea Hawk-class paddlewheelers built at Chir Jo shipyards in 1203A.D., for the navy of China's Sung Dynasty. The ingenious designer, Chin Shir Fu, built one ship of about 100 tonnes with two treadmill-driven paddlewheels, and the other of about 250 tonnes with four wheels. He provided armour made of iron plates, protecting all sides, the paddlewheels, and possibly also the roofed-in top of the ships. The ships were equipped with a variety of devices for launching missiles and bombs, and with rams for holing less formidable enemies.

**Ironclad**

Armoured ships driven by engines were pioneered by the British Navy early last century. The first to take part in battle

**Ironclad in Combat**

was the *Nemesis* (Commander W. H. Hall). In 1842, during the Opium War, in which Britain fought for the right to import opium to China, *Nemesis* was one of a squadron of fourteen steam paddlewheelers moored in the Yangtze River estuary. In the Battle of Wu Sung, five wooden Chinese tread-mill paddlewheelers advanced with greater bravado than prudence on the British ships. The encounter finished with all the Chinese ships either captured or destroyed.

**Ship Mine**   Ship mines were probably invented in the 13th or early 14th century, well after land mines. Technically, they posed greater problems when it came to controlling their depth and achieving ignition. The first sea mine was the 'submarine dragon king' in Chinese waters. It was placed on a weighted platform and enclosed in animal entrails, which provided a waterproof tube for the fuse. The fuse connected the mine to a buoyant container, with a burning joss stick in it.

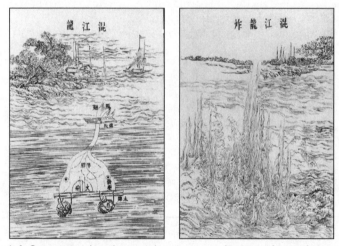

Left: Cross-section through an anti-ship mine, wrapped in watertight entrails.
Right: What happens when it goes off.

**Torpedoes**   Torpedoes are described in detail in Arabic in *The Book of Horsemanship and Stratagems of War* (1280s A.D.), by Najm al-Dīn Ayyub al-Ahdab al-Rammah, a military technician living in Syria, who died in 1294. From his description and illustration we know that in the 13th century the first torpedoes were made out of sheet iron and filled with gunpowder and incendiary materials. Two or three long rods projecting backwards from the pear-shaped body ended in burning jets. They acted as propulsion rockets, and gave the torpedo directional stability as it travelled on the surface of the water.

In the 1570s A.D. the English mathematician William Bourne produced a workable design for a craft that might 'goe under **Submarine** water unto the bottome and . . . come up againe at your pleasure'. It included flexible air chambers for use in regulating the displacement, so that the submarine would sink or rise: in essence, the ballast tank principle that has been used ever since for this lamentable invention. Brilliant Dutch inventor and scientist, Cornelius Drebell (1572–1633), built the first submarine, employing Bourne's principles, in 1620. It travelled at a depth of several metres below the surface of the River Thames in England, propelled by twelve rowers whose oars emerged through tightly fitting flaps of greased leather.

The military use of submarines began in 1776 when two Americans, Robert Fulton and David Bushnell, tried to navi- **Military** gate their wooden sub, *Turtle*, up to a British ship in New York **Submarine** Harbour, so they could sink the ship with a time bomb. It is not altogether surprising that they were carried away by the current instead; their only motive power was a crank, turned by hand from inside the little craft.

The submarine *Hunley*, belonging to the American Con- federate forces, scored the first 'kill' during the American **Successful** Civil War, when it sank the Union ship *Housatonic* in Febru- **Submarine** ary 1864. *Hunley* was similar to *Turtle*, but eight men turned **Engagement** the crank. The crew could not free it from *Housatonic*'s hull, so the first successful submarine went down with its victim.

The earliest nuclear submarine, USS *Nautilus*, was the achievement of a special operation directed for the U.S. Navy **Nuclear** by Hyman Rickover (1900–86), a Polish-born American **Submarine** naval captain. Rickover's team began work on atomic energy-powered submarines in 1946. *Nautilus*, launched in 1955, used a nuclear reactor to generate steam without consuming oxygen, and soon demonstrated her novel capability of staying under water indefinitely. In 1958 she travelled from the Pacific Ocean to the Atlantic underneath the Arctic icecap.

The duck is a vehicle that becomes a boat on water and a truck on land, named in the Second World War after its mil- **Duck** itary acronym, DUKW. A hundred and forty years earlier it was called 'Oructor Amphibolis' by American inventor Oliver Evans, a boatbuilder and blacksmith of Philadelphia. To make the first duck, Evans built a flat-bottomed craft and fitted it with a stern paddlewheel, and four large iron wheels for land use. An inboard steam engine could be made to drive either the paddlewheel or the axles. In 1804 he drove this contraption along Walnut Street, and on into the Schuylkill River.

**Battleship** The features incorporated by the British Navy in HMS *Dreadnought*, launched in 1905, revolutionised warship construction. All had been applied in the 19th century but never combined with such effectiveness. *Dreadnought's* ten 12-inch breech loading guns were mounted on five armoured rotating turrets, whilst the hull itself was built of steel armour up to 11 inches thick. The huge ship was driven by turbine engines. Initially, ships conforming to the lines and layout favoured by *Dreadnought's* designers were called dreadnoughts; as design changed, the battleship retained the appearance and basic technology of this prototype.

**Shipboard Take Off** In 1910 the warship USS *Birmingham* was fitted with a sloping timber launching ramp, 83 feet long. In November that year, while the *Birmingham* was off the coast of Virginia, pilot Eugene B. Ely took off from it in a Curtiss biplane, for the first flight launched from a ship.

**Ship-launched Air Assault** In 1915 a Short 184 seaplane took off from the British warship *Ben-My-Chree*, which had been modified to include a take-off deck. The plane sank a Turkish supply vessel in the Sea of Marmara in the first torpedo strike by a carrier-launched aircraft.

**Aircraft Carrier** In 1918 a former passenger liner was converted by the British Navy into the earliest true aircraft carrier, HMS *Argus*, with a flat deck extending from bow to stern, and hydraulic lifts to raise aircraft from hangars below deck. The deck was 550 feet long, and a squadron of twenty aircraft could be housed on board. *Argus* was completed too late to see action in the First World War.

**Bomber** In November 1911 the Italian Army Aviation Service used a 'Taube' aircraft manufactured by the German firm Rumpler to drop bombs on North African towns in the possession of Turkey, during the Italian–Turkish War.

**Heavy Bomber** In 1913 the Russo–Baltic Railcar Works in St. Petersburg constructed the first of many Ilya Muromets bombers, designed by Igor Sikorsky. They were 60 feet long, with a span of 102 feet, and could carry a tonne of bombs. The fully enclosed fuselage included a glazed, armour-plated and heated cockpit, and a number of other rooms. Each plane had four 220 horsepower engines and seven guns. Most belonged to Russia's 'Squadron of Flying Ships', which flew hundreds of devastating missions over German positions. Only two of the eighty built were ever shot down.

In 1938 an interesting race began between Germany's two leading aircraft manufacturers, Heinkel and Messerschmidt. **Jet Plane** The Nazi Government had ordered both to develop a jet fighter design for the Luftwaffe (Germany's airforce). At the same time, various engineering firms were commissioned to design and build engines for the new aircraft. Both Heinkel and Messerschmidt were delayed by the inability of the engine-makers to deliver a suitable product. However, Heinkel had a head start with the jet engines [VIII, 9], developed in house by Hans von Ohain. In August 1939 a Heinkel He 178 became the first jet plane to take to the air and make a flight. The prodigious fuel consumption of the Ohain engine meant that it could only stay airborne about 10 minutes, although it could reach a speed of about 700 km/h.

In April 1941, near Rostok on the Baltic Sea-coast, a new Heinkel He 280 took off, to become the first jet fighter in **Jet Fighter** flight. It was able to reach 785 km/h and a ceiling of 37,000 feet. Another brilliant new invention was incorporated in the design: an ejector seat that could throw the pilot clear in the **Ejector Seat** event of a disaster. It worked by unleashing a blast of compressed air.

In 1941 work began in Germany on the design and testing of the Arado 234, a jet-powered bomber. A variety of experi- **Jet Bomber** mental models made test flights in 1942 and 1943; in mid-1944 a twin-engine version, the Arado 234B, went into production. It had a 1.5 tonne bomb load and a speed of 740 km/h. Its power came from two Junkers Jumo turbo-jet engines.

The earliest form of radar was a simple system devised in 1903 and 1904 by German engineer, Christian Hülsmeyer. His sys- **Radar** tem involved a spark transmitter on a ship, accompanied by a receiver that would detect a signal reflected from a nearby ship, without indicating its distance. In the 1930s technicians working with the German navy, following the guidance of Dr. Rudolf Kuhnhold, developed radar that could determine the location of distant objects. In 1933 they recorded the presence of a small vessel at a distance of approximately 13 km.

# VII
# PHILOSOPHY AND
# RELIGION

This chapter pinpoints the permanent expressions of the most important general ideas and beliefs. But the first statement of an idea in isolation often has no bearing on philosophy or religion. It's easy to imagine one Stone Age person saying to another in prehistoric times: 'I don't believe in gods, you know'. But their conversation would not be mentioned in the entry on atheism [VII, 6], even if we knew about it. The full meaning and the permanent significance of an idea are realised when it is set forth as part of a system of belief or a pattern of thinking.

Of course the meaning and significance of ideas cannot be discovered just by reading here about their first exposition. That is for the texts and masters to impart.

## I. PHILOSOPHIC SCHOOLS

**Taoism**  Taoism (pronounced daoism) is the school of philosophy that regards the order of nature (the *tao*) as of supreme importance, and considers human efforts, progress and development a troublesome waste of time. The school was founded by Lao Dzu, who came from China's southern state of Chu in the 6th century B.C. Although little is known of the circumstances, it seems that Lao Dzu first worked as an official historian in central China, but became famous for his rejection of conventional values, and his retirement from public life. It is said that as an old man he decided to leave China and travel, without a destination. On the road out he met an admirer who persuaded him to write down his thoughts; the result, the *Dao De Jing*, was China's first philosophy book. It has now been published in all major languages, dozens of times in English.

Pythagoras was a Greek philosopher born on the Aegean island of Samos about 570B.C. Aged about thirty he moved to the Greek city of Croton in Southern Italy, where the Pythagorean school was born. Its mysterious tenets were revealed in full only to believers. They included the beliefs that the world is organised by numbers, that everything which has happened will repeat itself exactly, that the soul is endlessly reborn in other living creatures, and that all living beings are related.

**Pythagoreanism**

Classicism is the system of philosophy that teaches self-cultivation and the study of classical literature as keys to developing one's innate capacity for humanity, and the understanding of universal truth. Its founder was Confucius – called Kung Fu by the Chinese – born in 551B.C. in the town of Dso, in the northeastern state of Lu. The Kung family was poor, and Confucius began his career as a granary keeper. His renown quickly spread and he attracted thousands of disciples as he travelled, until his death in 479B.C. One of his famous sayings is 'I am a transmitter, not a creator'. But although his moral principles were transmitted from classical sources, the system for establishing their veracity and for cultivating humanity is his own creation; Chinese Classicism is known in European languages as 'Confucianism' in recognition of this. It is the first ethical system to demonstrate that right conduct is the fulfilment of the inner nature, rather than obedience to external standards or authority.

**Classicism**

Utilitarianism was first taught by the Chinese philosopher Maw Dzu, founder of the Mohist school, in the 5th century B.C. His only objective was to advance the material wellbeing of others, and in this cause he wished to stamp out warfare, luxury and even music, all of which he denounced as wasteful of resources and effort. Although he considered it appropriate for a country to defend itself against an invader, he was completely opposed to aggressive warfare.

**Utilitarianism**

**Mohism**

Maw's main opponents were the Classicists [see above], who followed Confucius and believed that human nature calls on them to care more for their family, rulers, fellows and selves than for strangers. In contrast, the utilitarian position was taught as 'universal love' – equal solicitude for all people, including strangers. This embodies a selfless commitment to work for others, and the first philosophy of altruism [VII, 2]. The Mohists studied military technology in order to try and

**Universal Love**

convince aggressors to desist. Amongst other things, they threatened them with the consequences of chemical weaponry [VI, 2]. They also studied science and framed one of Newton's Laws [VIII, 1].

**Utilitarian School**   The modern Utilitarian School was founded late in the 18th century by the English philosopher Jeremy Bentham (1748–1832), whose catchcry was 'the greatest happiness for the greatest number'. The modern school differs from Mohism mainly in recognising a wider range of benefits that can legitimately be conferred on others, and is therefore less opposed to luxury, music and warfare.

**Cynicism**   Antisthenes was an Athenian philosopher who taught that the things most people take seriously, including pleasure, are rubbish. He claimed to value only virtue, but his virtue consisted chiefly in abstinence, and disdain for honours, wealth and learning. He developed his ideas late in the 5th century B.C., but lived well into the 4th century, dying in Athens at the age of eighty. Although Antisthenes was an admirer of Socrates, he thought all Plato's speculations are a waste of time. He wore shabby clothes to proclaim his indifference and frugality, but Socrates is said to have told him: 'I see your pride through the holes in your cloak.'

**The Academy**   The Athenian philosopher Plato (429–347B.C.) studied under Socrates in his youth, but when Socrates died in 399B.C. he began travelling and developing a new approach to philosophy. When he came home in 389B.C. he started teaching his philosophy at the Academeia, a garden in suburban Athens, which was instantly popular with students. His school became known as the Academy, distinguished primarily by Plato's theory that knowledge lies in understanding ideal truths in their higher reality of universal forms [VII, 4], of which the actual world is merely an inaccurate copy.

**Old Academy**   Plato's immediate followers are called the Old Academy, which identified itself soon after his death. In 224B.C. Arcesilaus modified Plato's system, and thereby founded the Middle **Middle Academy** Academy. In 160B.C. Carneades took a more sceptical view of **New Academy** philosophy and established the 'New Academy'.

**Peripatetic Philosophy**   The Peripatetic School was founded by Aristotle (384–322B.C.), from the Greek city of Stagira, on the coast of Macedonia. Aristotle studied in Athens under Plato at the Academy, but when Plato died in 347B.C. he left Athens, and from this time forward

developed his own philosophy, which differs distinctly from
Plato's by seeking true knowledge through close observation of
the actual world, rather than abstract contemplation of ideals.
After twelve years Aristotle returned to Athens and established
the Lyceum, the first university [IV, 3]. Here peripatetic philosophy took root, and probably took its name from the walking
paths (*peripatos*) in the Lyceum grounds. In ancient times its
influence was significant but limited; in mediaeval Europe it
became dominant; but today it is only heeded in the fields of
logic and politics.

The Athenian philosopher Epicurus (341–271B.C.) founded a
school which taught that the only end worth pursuing is plea- **Epicureanism**
sure for oneself, but that it is obtained by moderation, justice
and decent conduct to others. Epicurus considered pleasure to
be merely the absence of pain. He advised his followers to **Pleasure is**
avoid troublesome affairs and heated passion, so as not to risk **Absence of**
their personal tranquility. He believed the world to be entirely **Pain**
material, governed only by the natural properties of atoms,
and hence that mental tranquility is safeguarded by studying
science. Epicurus wished to eradicate religion for putting fear **Opposition to**
in people's minds, and to teach instead Democritus's scientific **Religion**
system [see atoms and molecules, VII, 4] with certain curious
amendments. He believed free will and necessity [VII, 4] to be
inconsistent with each other; to preserve free will he claimed
that atoms sometimes act independent of external cause. His
devotion to this doctrine was like the religious faith he
denounced; it is also linked to quantum mechanics [VIII, 1].

According to the Stoics, a single intelligence pervades the
Universe, manifest in the brightness of heaven and in indi- **Stoicism**
vidual minds. This divine intelligence looks after everything
in the world by its providence, and lays down an inexorable
fate which can be read by divination. The proper course is to
cultivate one's mind by acting according to nature, in the constant practice of virtue. In this way, mental stability can be
preserved at all times; the wise man is self sufficiently happy
even if isolated, and maintains his integrity in any situation.
By being true to his nature, anyone can attain complete virtue
and unite his mind with the divine Universe.

Zeno of Citium (335–263B.C.), a Phoenician from
Cyprus, began teaching this doctrine in late middle-age in the **The Stoic**
Stoa, a public portico in Athens. The school of thought he **School**
established there took its name from the building. However,

by a remarkable coincidence, all the ideas recited in the previous paragraph had first been published together in China in the 5th century B.C. They are contained in *The Doctrine of the Mean*, by Confucius's grandson, Dzu Szu (483–402B.C.). However, Dzu Szu did not establish a school of doctrine, and it is unrealistic to propose that his ideas could have been conveyed to Athens in time to influence Zeno.

**Feminism**   So few books written by women in ancient times have survived that we can only speculate about ancient feminism by reference to the writings of men and to historical phenomena. In Greece the Athenian dramatist Aristophanes wrote comedies about women organising to withdraw their conjugal services and force their men to end the war (the *Lysistrata*, 411B.C.), and taking over political power (the *Ecclesiazuzae* or 'Assembly Women', 392B.C.). Soon afterwards, Plato urged equal roles for the sexes [VII, 3] in education, government and war, despite his conviction that the sexes are unequal. Perhaps like men today who write with feminist sympathies, they were influenced by feminist contemporaries. There was a vigorous women's movement in ancient Greece, which organised orgiastic revels on a mind-boggling scale, but jealously guarded its secrecy, so there is no knowing whether its principles ever included feminism. In ancient history there are periods when women had high status and ready access to learning, the arts, the professions and economic power, such as Old Kingdom Egypt, and Roman societies in the 1st centuries B.C. and A.D. But there is nothing to confirm that feminist agitation had a part in bringing those circumstances about. The rise of feminism is not likely to have begun in those times, but when the restricted status and opportunities of women were particularly apparent. Thus modern feminism began in the late-18th century after generations of shrinkage in women's prospects. The first in those times to declare the feminist position in its complete form was Mary Wollstonecraft (1759–97) in Britain. Her book *A Vindication of the Rights of Woman* (1792) is a radical affirmation of the equality of the sexes in mental and moral aptitudes; a denunciation of the ignorance and uselessness of the kept women of the prosperous classes; and a demand for equal access to education and employment.

**Existentialism**   The Danish philosopher Sören Kierkegaard (1813A.D.–1855) examined existing religious and philosophical systems in light of his own crisis over how to use his personal freedom. He

found them unsatisfactory because of their purported objec-
tivity. Rejecting rationalism and idealism, he formed the view
that, as an individual, he was responsible for finding and pursuing his own purpose in life. This is how existentialism
began, and why existentialists decided to turn their backs on
philosophical speculations and simply enter the fray, to
resolve all with their life experiences. Kierkegaard's first published account of the idea is *Either Or* (Copenhagen, 1843).

Marxism is a communist doctrine developed by German **Marxism**
scholar Karl Marx (1818A.D.–1883), and his offsider, Friedrich
Engels. Marx's political ideals were published in his *Communist Manifesto* (1848), but the most original part of his work,
which distinguishes Marxism from other forms of communism
[VII, 3], was completed after he moved to Britain in 1849.
Pursuing the method of dialectical materialism [VII, 3], Marx
claimed to prove his theories by a historical analysis. He
divided history into five stages, each of which, except the last,
contains the seeds of its own violent destruction. The stages
are: primitive communism, slave-owning society, feudalism,
capitalism and communism. Marx identified his own society
as capitalist, and urged the proletariat to overthrow it in a
revolution which would institute socialism, followed by his
own form of worldwide communism. The full statement of his
philosophy, *Capital (Das Kapital)* was first published in 1867.

The Anthroposophical Society was founded in 1912 by Aus-
trian scholar Rudolf Steiner (1861A.D.–1925), to inculcate his **Anthroposophy**
new 'spiritual science'. This is based on his conviction that
the human intellect, suitably developed, can make contact
with spiritual worlds. In the following year, at Dornach in
Switzerland, he founded the first Goetheanum, his school for
teaching spiritual science.

## 2. FURTHER IDEAS OF MORAL PHILOSOPHY

Most of the philosophic schools can be differentiated by their contrasting
ethical positions. There are also other moral issues, dealt with in this section, not so clearly identified with famous schools.

The first philosopher to renounce morality completely was a
Chinese politician. Sharng Yarng (died c. 335B.C.), who was **Amorality**
born in the central Chinese state of Wei, moved to Chin in

the Northwest, where as prime minister he directed the government in a range of new totalitarian policies. He founded **Legalism** the Legalist School, and set out his views in the *Book of Lord Sharng*. Campaigning against morals, he denounced the ten evils: rites, music, poetry, history, virtue, moral culture, filial piety, brotherly duty, integrity and sophistry. Elsewhere he added intelligence and humanity to his black list, and predicted doom for any country governed by these principles.

In their place he advocated a strict code of laws governing all aspects of life, and enforced with harsh punishments. This is the cornerstone of the philosophy of Legalism **Rejection of** which he founded. He was also the first to argue for the **Tradition** overthrow of political and cultural tradition on the ground that the experience of the past cannot be relevant in modern times.

By means of laws, taxes and the discouragement of education, Sharng Yarng intended to turn people away from commerce and luxury, and keep them ignorant and hard at work in the most basic occupations. He was conscious that this would produce a superfluity of basic requirements, and advocated a policy of fighting wars to use up resources and keep the **Bellacity** state in balance. 'If the country is strong and war is not waged, the poison will be carried into its territories.' Although many societies have habitually waged war since primitive times, Sharng Yarng was the first philosopher to develop a political theory which argues that war is essential for the wellbeing of the state. Sharng Yarng was so convincing that his entire reform programme was put into practice in Chin, which he turned into a police state. Consistent with his aim of discouraging luxury and trade, he legislated against accommodation for travellers, prohibiting hotels to take in guests without official permits. At the end of his political career, he was accused of treason by a rival faction, and had to flee the Chin capital. When he was almost at the border he tried to book in to a hotel, but having no permit, was not allowed. With nowhere else to go, he went home, and died soon after leading an unsuccessful rebellion against the Chin ruler. After his death, Chin thrived on his principles – a later ruler became the first emperor of China.

Humanity, as a measure of what is morally right, is specified in **Humanity** a Mesopotamian tablet from about 2000–1700B.C. It occurs in a passage by an angry scribe, chastising his son for appalling behaviour. 'Because you do not look to your humanity, my heart was carried off as if by an evil wind.' The word translated as humanity is *namlulu*. 'May your humanity exalt you' is the irate author's conclusion – an aspiration consistent with the foremost ethical philosophies of later and more sophisticated cultures.

The Greek philosopher Protagoras (485–415B.C.) of Abdera, the first agnostic, is most famous for his dictum 'Man is the measure of all things', catchcry of the first explicitly anthropocentrist philosophy. Prior to his time, humanity had been taken as a moral authority, and human standards formed the basis of the classicism [VII, 1] of Confucius. Protagoras went further, denying that there is any valid standard or plausible authority beyond the assessment made by a human being. **Humanism**

The diametrically opposite view was expressed in China around 500B.C. by Lao Dzu, founder of Taoism [VII, 1]. He advocated that man suspend all his assessments and the discussion of issues that people regard as important. According to the Taoists, to be a human being is merely to possess one of many forms of existence, with no prime importance to creation as a whole or even to mankind. His alternative is to dwell in the *tao*, the way of nature. **Anti-humanism**

Hedonist philosophy teaches that the pursuit of pleasure is the proper activity of life. This teaching began with Aristippus of Cyrene (c. 435–350B.C.), a philosopher from North Africa, a pupil of Socrates in Athens. His main doctrines are that particular pleasures are the end in life, that happiness is the sum of these, and that all pleasure is good, even if it proceeds from unseemly conduct, although bodily pleasure is best. **Hedonism**

Aristippus founded the Cyrenaic School, and set an example by living in strict accordance with his teaching. He was challenged for delighting in women, and consorting with a lady of easy virtue. 'Is there any difference', he replied, 'between taking a house in which many people have lived before and taking one in which nobody has ever lived? . . . It makes no difference whether the woman you live with has lived with many or with nobody.' When he asked his rich friend Dionysius for money, Dionysius replied 'No, you told me the wise man would never be in want.' 'Pay! Pay!' said Aristippus, 'then we will discuss the question.' Dionysius paid; Aristippus said, 'Now you see, do you not, that I am not found wanting?' **Cyrenaic School**

The debate between those who claim that the code of behaviour that individuals follow is learnt, or socially conditioned, and those who consider that it is bred into us is sometimes identified as the debate of 'nature versus nurture' or 'heredity versus environment'. In East and West it began early in the Classical period of philosophy. The Chinese philosopher Mencius (or Meng Dzu, 372–289B.C.) argued strenuously that the understanding of right conduct is inherent in our nature, and lost in those who do not possess it, only by want of proper nourishment. He supported his argument with a variety of psychological examples, for instance, the distress we automatically feel on seeing a baby about to fall into a well:

**Moral Disposition is Innate**

> not as a ground on which we may gain the favour of the child's parents, nor as a ground on which we may seek the praise of neighbours and friends, nor from hating to be ill thought of about it . . . The sense of compassion is the germ of humanity; the sense of shame is the germ of public morality; the sense of modesty is the germ of propriety; the sense of acceptance and rejection is the germ of knowledge. People have these four germs just as they have four limbs.

The first statement of the opposite position was put with equal vehemence in Greece in the 5th century B.C. by Protagoras, who was notorious for always charging money to instruct his followers; this he justified by claiming that he could teach *arete*, the Greek name for the capability of living well with oneself and within the community. He claimed that aptitude for this learning, which we all receive from our society, varies from pupil to pupil, and that arete is more effectively imparted in advanced societies than in primitive ones. Hence, although he believed that our principles of conduct are learnt from others, he also believed in the moral superiority of the best principles, which he himself taught.

**Moral Disposition is Learnt**

But the belief in a learnt rather than an innate morality led others to deny that one brand can be superior to another. According to Archelaus, an Athenian contemporary of Protagoras: 'things are just or ignoble not by nature but by convention'. He was thus the first to argue that right and wrong are not grounded in a true morality or the ordinance of God but are purely matters of custom.

**Right and Wrong Questions of Convention**

It is one thing to use power to force obedience from others, another to add that having power justifies your domineering ways. During the time of Pericles (died 429B.C.), the city of Athens compelled many other Greek cities to pay tribute and

**'Might is Right'**

obey her. She eventually dominated more than half of Greece. Many Greeks were passionate devotees of political freedom, so this was controversial behaviour. To defend it, the Athenians developed the 'might is right' principle. In 432B.C. cities opposed to Athens sent representatives to Sparta, urging Sparta to act against Athenian bullying. Athenian representatives also addressed the Spartans, as follows:

> It has always been the law that the weaker should be subject to the stronger. Besides, we believed ourselves to be worthy of our position, and so you thought us till now, when calculations of interest have made you take up the cry of justice – a consideration which no one ever yet brought forward to hinder his ambition when he had a chance of gaining anything by might.

Consistent with this principle, Athens was sometimes brutally cruel to weak opponents who did not surrender quickly enough. For arrogance of this kind, history normally has retribution in store ('nemesis' is the Greek word). Certainly in 404B.C. the Athenians looked awfully weak and wrong when they had to surrender to Sparta, counting on the kind of mercy they had denied to so many.

Although many schools of thought urge their followers to act from selfless motives, the tenet of unqualified altruism is rare. It was first taught by China's Mohist school [VII, 1], founded by Maw Dzu in the 5th century B.C. The Mohist doctrine of 'universal love' means an equal love for all, without distinctions in favour of one's self or people in special relationships to one's self. The Mohists were taught to be willing to make any sacrifice for the benefit of the community at large. **Altruism**

On the other hand, Maw Dzu's countryman Yarng Chew (c. 440–c. 360B.C.) declared that he would not sacrifice a hair off his shin to save the world, and would never act except in self-interest. He taught the first philosophy of pure selfishness. (In the West the same doctrine was soon afterwards adopted, in Epicureanism [VII, 1].) **Selfishness**

Since history began, almost everyone has taken a position between these two extremes. The first philosopher to explain it was Confucius (551–479B.C.), who advocated love for all creatures, but who differentiated this to make preferential allowance for one's self and those who stand in certain close or significant relationships to oneself. **Qualified Altruism**

**Evil Generates Corresponding Good**

Saint Augustine of North Africa (354A.D.–430) wrote in his book *The City of God* (426A.D.) that God puts evil and suffering in the world to test His people and bring out good in them. This concept was developed in Germany by Gottfried Wilhelm von Leibniz (1646A.D.–1716), who is notorious for saying that everything which happens in life is for the best, and that ours is the best of all possible worlds. This creed is known to philosophers as 'optimism'. According to Leibniz, every evil produces, in proportion, a greater countervailing good. God has had to supply suffering so that we could have fortitude and compassion; poverty so there can be charity; hangovers to encourage moderation; and so on. In the *Theodicy*, he claimed that we have been dealt exactly the right quantity of evil to guarantee the best conceivable result. There is something about this philosophy that stops most people from accepting it. But in 18th-century Europe, it was an important answer to those who said that if God were all good and all powerful, He would not allow evil in the world.

**Good Generates Corresponding Evil**

The reciprocal view, that good things produce a countervailing evil, was advanced much earlier for an entirely different purpose. The Taoist philosopher Juarng Dzu (c. 300B.C.) was opposed to progress – moral, social and technical. He claimed that the more the world improves in these respects, the worse are the evils which befall it. Juarng noted, for instance, that technology causes environmental chaos, that valuables promote theft, and that moral conduct invites exploitation.

**Femininity of Truth**

While feminists insist on the equality of women in terms of traditionally male values, there have been other thinkers who saw in traditionally female qualities, such as yieldingness and emotionalism, the guidance to what is of most value for men as well as women.

> In the union of the world,
> The female always gets the better of the male by stillness.
> Being still she takes the lower position.

The author of these lines is the first Chinese philosopher, Lao Dzu, of the 6th century B.C. In the *Dao De Jing* he commended the way of the 'mysterious female'. This was a general and external concept; but the Japanese philosopher and literary critic Motoori Norinaga (1730A.D.–1801) described a feminine principle in the minds of all individuals that represents their true feelings and the key to beneficial self-expression. Norinaga advocated an uninhibited reliance on this feminine part of our natures, which for him represented tenderness, sensitivity, emotionalism and profound sadness. Possibly this line of thought originated in Japan because of the strong tendency there to disdain these qualities as effeminate. Norinaga in middle-age changed his mind, and abandoned his campaign for effeminacy in favour of faith in ancient religious concepts.

In China, however, another literary critic had decided that genuine morality and feeling can come only from the mind of childhood. Li Chir (1527A.D.–1602) complains that nearly all people have irreparably lost their true minds by letting conventional education and morality block their minds out with phoney nonsense. Only people who have kept their childhood minds intact are not lost and can understand something that is not fake. **Childlikeness of Truth**

Pythagoras (6th century B.C.), the Greek philosopher from the Aegean island of Samos, who taught in Southern Italy, was the first to preach a vegetarian diet on grounds of morality rather than health or religious taboo [VII, 1]. The attitude of Pythagoras and his followers is described by the later Greek writer Porphyry, in *Abstinence*: **Moral Vegetarianism**

> Pythagoras and Empedocles and the rest of the Italians say that we have a fellowship not only with one another and with the gods but also with the irrational animals. For there is a single spirit which pervades the whole world as a sort of mind and unites us with them. That is why if we kill them and eat their flesh, we commit injustice and impiety.

The earliest moves to protect animals from man are connected with wildlife conservation [see Wildlife Sanctuary and Listing of Protected Species, XII, 1] and vegetarianism [see above]. Although these are very ancient, no general animal liberationist can be identified before the Roman encyclopaedia writer, Pliny (Caius Plinius Secundus, 23A.D.–79), railed against human exploitation in his *Natural History*. Pliny thought using animals for subsistence is consistent with the natural order, but he also believed that in nature animals are supposed to be free, and that man has proved himself morally inferior to other creatures. He was particularly irritated that animals should suffer to support luxuries, and amongst other things denounced the hunting of elephants for ivory and the caging of birds. **Animal Liberationist**

According to the *Arthasastra*, an ancient Indian manual of government, there are three pursuits in life: wealth, charity **'Money is Everything'** and desire. 'Wealth alone is important', says its author, Kautilya, because it is the way to satisfy the other two. This book is about 2000 years old.

**Dismissal of Worry**

Do not let evil sleep afflict your heart;
Banish misery and suffering from your side;
Misery and suffering produce a dream
Though the dream makes bad . . . your heart
Let your heart be quit of . . .
Your countenance . . . may your face smile.

Such is the author's sound advice in *Counsels of a Pessimist*, a Babylonian essay of the 2nd millennium B.C. The breaks in the last three lines represent damage suffered by the clay tablet – the only record of the pessimist's opposition to worry and misery.

## 3. SOCIAL AND POLITICAL THOUGHT

This section covers the main ideas about the organisation of society. All the entries deal with the theoretical side of this issue. The application of political and social thinking is dealt with elsewhere. Chapter IV includes government and social institutions, systems of government, and social phenomena. Chapter XII deals with social and political legislation.

**The Social Contract**

Social contract theorists all identify an age of chaos when people suffered because there was no central authority to govern and prevent them abusing each other. The remedy is said to have been the social contract: people surrendered – to a sovereign and government – the power of ruling and enforcing standards, in exchange for the benefits of order and protection. It was a parting with freedom in consideration of being promised a better life. The idea was expounded in China in the 5th century B.C. by Maw Dzu, founder of utilitarianism [VII, 1]. He envisaged a contract formulated in two stages: the first when the multitude agreed to abide by the sovereign's interpretation of what was right, and the second when this sovereign righteousness was brought into line with the righteousness ordained by heaven. The reader will observe that we are still having some trouble with this second stage.

**Psychology of Ritual**

The Classicist school of philosophy established in the 500s B.C. by Confucius was the first to examine and promote ritual behaviour and traditional ceremony for secular reasons. Its exponents claim that whether there is life after death and whether or not deities exist are irrelevant to how human beings should observe ritual. They point out that individuals need ritualistic behaviour to manage their emotions and desires, and that society can use it to maintain order, and respect for the values it depends on. The theory is manifest in the laconic teachings of Confucius (551–479B.C.), but treated most fully in the writings of Hsewn Dzu (c. 312–c. 230B.C.), for example in his *Funerals*.

Dialectic is the resolution of philosophical issues by persuasive argument. In the 19th century, German thinkers, including Hegel and Marx, used the term 'dialectical materialism' to denote the operation of the dialectical process on actual historical developments, rather than just on concepts and ideas. In his *Republic* (Athens, c. 380B.C.), the Greek philosopher Plato is the first to pursue such an analysis, when he traces the evolution of political psychology. In Plato's analysis of the state the evolution begins with an aristocratic constitution and frame of mind and thence descends to the timocratic, the oligarchic, the democratic and the tyrannical. Each stage, except the first and last, contains in itself the elements which resolve themselves in its overthrow and replacement by the next.

**Dialectical Materialism**

The basic anarchist principle, that in a correctly ordered world no person is subject to the authority of the state, is inherent in the ancient philosophies of Taoism [VII, 1] and Stoicism [VII, 1], particularly in the teachings of their founders Lao Dzu and Zeno. The British philosopher William Godwin is the first to build a whole system of political philosophy around anarchism, in his book *Inquiry Concerning Political Justice* (1793A.D.).

**Anarchism**

The doctrine that advocates violent overthrow of a condemned government, and proclaims the legitimacy of the regime taking over, was espoused in China in the mid-2nd millennium B.C. (perhaps the 17th century). It appears in the *Book of Documents*, concerning the destruction of the oppressive Hsia regime by Tarng the Completer, first ruler of the new Yin (or Sharng) Dynasty. According to the documents, Tarng adopted the theory at the start to justify defying the authority of a corrupt and inhumane government, and killing its leader. It is possible, however, that having seized power, his faction

**Revolutionary Theory**

invented revolutionary doctrine to legitimise its own authority. Thereafter, Chinese political theorists maintained that a new regime which ousts the old and wins the allegiance of the people has been awarded the 'mandate of heaven'.

**Utopia** An imaginary society, which operates according to ideal principles, for the maximum welfare of its members, was first proposed by the Greek philosopher Plato of Athens (c. 380B.C.). In Plato's utopia, power is to be wielded by men and women with an education in philosophy, for the benefit of all. Advantageous though this sounds, his system also includes controlled breeding, the extinction of the family unit, and censorship restrictions that make free expression impossible. His ideal state is primarily drawn up as an exercise in demonstrating how his social theories apply in relation to human capabilities and psychology. Afterwards, many utopias arose in Greek literature: Plato, in *The Laws*, constructs a state operating under strict legal regulation. Other authors propose a world commonwealth and a paradise of communism [see below].

**World Commonwealth** Zeno of Citium (335–263B.C.), the Phoenician philosopher from Cyprus who founded the Stoic school [VII, 1] in Greece, dreamt of an ideal world where people of all cities and nations unite in a single state, of which everyone will be a citizen. Its only law will be divine law, it will have no enemies, and its citizens will act correctly not under legal obligation but out of love for each other and the whole world.

**Communism** The earliest communist was the Greek political philosopher Iambulus, who worked around 300B.C. He explains his principles by portraying a fictional communist utopia, 'Sun State', located on an island in the Indian Ocean. The people of Sun State are divided into communes, or 'systems', each responsible for the social and economic wellbeing of its members. The society he dreamt of is totally classless and based on the novel **Equalitarianism** concept of absolute equality. Each member contributes work, draws equal benefits, and performs in turn all responsibilities from the servant's to the governor's. Wealth, ambition, academic learning and class war are banished, replaced by harmony. In 132B.C. Aristonicus of Pergamon tried to establish such a regime, and mounted the first communist revolution [IV, 1].

**Separation of Powers** Charles de Secondat, Baron de la Brède et de Montesquieu, set forth the doctrine of the separation of powers in his book

*Spirit of the Laws* (Paris, 1748). Montesquieu divided the functions of government into three classes: judicial, legislative and executive (to do with judging, law-making, and policy and administration, respectively). He believed that by dividing these responsibilities into separate hands, abuse of power can be prevented, and stability preserved by a system of checks and balances. This principle was widely accepted, and is fundamental to the constitutions of a number of countries, including America and Japan.

The belief that all living things belong to a delicate balance and that people have to allow for this in their actions – even with regard to minutiae – was adopted in China during the Warring States Period (481–221B.C.). A contemporary description of good environmental management relates, for instance, that ponds and dams were not fished until the otters had had a chance to feed. Hunting did not commence until the wolf had captured its prey. Bird nets were not set until the dove had changed into a hawk (sic). Burning off did not begin until the insects had all withdrawn into their burrows, and so on.

**The Ecological Balance**

    The view that the environment is vulnerable to imbalance and damage if misused by human beings had already been expressed in Egypt, in the prophecies of Nefer-Rohu, the first prophet of doom [VI, 1]. Nefer-Rohu was a sage of the 4th Dynasty (c. 3050–2850B.C.), whose opinions are known only from records of the early Middle Kingdom period (c. 2150–c. 1950B.C.). The calamity of a 'topsy-turvy land' will ultimately be rectified, according to the prophecy, by a ruler who brings peace, mends the administration, lowers taxes and excludes Asiatics. The relationship envisaged between human action and environmental disturbance in this early document is fairly unscientific and at least partly mystical. Purely naturalistic analyses of the human cause of environmental degradation came later, in China's Warring States Period. These relate to specific instances. Generalised environmental disruption was first put down to human action in the 2nd century B.C. in Liu Arn's *Huai Nam Dzu*, by the contributor who is also recorded for his condemnation of industry [see below]. He held man responsible for everything: 'The harmonious cooperation of Heaven and Earth, the evolution of creation by the yin and yang depend on the spirit of man.'

**Environmental Degradation Noticed**

    All conservationists make the claim that human welfare depends on the healthy operation of the natural order, which can be disrupted by human action. But the most primitive

**Conservationist Perspectives**

thinking on environmental protection always included a numinous link (a divine or magical influence) by which human misconduct triggers disarray in nature. This is why Nefer-Rohu ascribed climatic upheavals to the growth in Egypt's Asiatic population.

**I. Material Antropocentrism**

Some thinkers in later times relied on a purely material link between environmental neglect and material resources under threat. So they argued for conservation on the grounds that it is in mankind's interest to defend its resources. Their point of view was first explained by the Chinese philosopher Mencius (372–289 B.C.).

**2. Anti-anthropocentrism**

The opposite rationale to anthropocentrism insists that human beings have no entitlements beyond those of any other creatures, and must neither make ways of their own in the world nor appropriate for themselves any more resources than originally ordained by nature. This view also comes from China, advanced by Taoist [VII, 1] philosophers, beginning with Juarng Dzu (c. 300 B.C.). He used it, in general, to oppose moral, social and material 'progress'. It takes a specifically conservationist character in the *Huai Narn Dzu*, Liu Arn's Taoist book compiled in the 2nd century B.C. One of the dissertations in that work bitterly laments the development of agriculture and industry at the expense of wilderness: 'Thus, the world of life partially failed and things miscarried so that the larger half of creation failed of fruition.'

**3. Spiritual Anthropocentrism**

To defy economic utility and conserve something as 'part of our heritage', 'so that everyone will be able to enjoy it' or 'so that our grandchildren can see it' is an anthropocentric policy based on the value in human estimation of a spiritual resource. The first case on record is the 'Spirit Park' established in China about 1100 B.C. (the first national park [V, 1]) by King Wen of the Jo Dynasty. According to Mencius in the 4th century B.C., the first to teach in favour of spiritual anthropocentrism, wildlife in it was protected and its purpose was to provide enjoyment for Wen and his people.

**4. Natural Place of Industry and Civilisation**

Somewhere in all these points of view can be found a 'man-made versus natural' concept and an effort to accommodate human development and preservation of nature as two worthwhile but opposing aims. But there is one approach which is distinct from all these: it counts human agriculture, industry and civilisation as parts of nature in the same way as wildlife, sea, sky and wilderness. Man's responsibility is to discover the natural role and level of everything, and conserve that. Hsewn Dzu (c. 312–c. 230B.C.), a classical philosopher from Northern China, was the first to expound this analysis:

> When society is properly organised, then all things will find their proper place, the six domestic animals will breed and flourish, and all living beings will fulfil their allotted span of life.

The idea that women should be educated and selected for exactly the same activities as men has its earliest lasting exposition in the *Republic* by Plato (Athens, c. 380B.C.). For his proposed ideal state, Plato requires that women be involved in every activity open to males, even combat roles in war and exercising naked with the men, no matter how old and ugly they might be. While Plato was convinced that there is nothing a man can do that a woman can't, his comparison of their abilities will not win the favour of the average feminist:

**Equal Roles for the Sexes**

> Can you mention any pursuit of mankind in which the male sex has not all these gifts and qualities in a higher degree than the female? Need I waste time in speaking of the art of weaving, and the management of pancakes and preserves, in which womankind does really appear to be great, and in which for her to be beaten by a man is of all things the most absurd?

Eugenics is a system of mating people like farm animals – under controlled conditions to produce the best stock. The Athenian philosopher Plato (429–347B.C.) proposes it in his *Republic*. He envisaged a state run by guardians – selected for physical and intellectual prowess, and courage. The supreme rulers were to select the best guardians of breeding age, and pair them off from time to time. This system was to be disguised either as the drawing of lots, so that inferior guardians who missed out would only blame bad luck, or as rewards for courageous behaviour. The babies were to be whisked away at birth, to a nursery, and only the undeformed offspring of the better guardians were to be raised.

**Eugenics**

The first case of eugenics in practice was the scheme of Germany's Nazi regime in the 1930s A.D., when selected women were mated with model officers, in special houses run by the state.

**Eugenics in Practice**

> There is no glory in victory, and to glorify it despite this is to exult in the killing of men. One who exults in the killing of men will never have his way in the empire.

**Pacifism**

These are the words of Lao Dzu, founder of Taoism [VII, 1], author of the *Dao De Jing* and the first pacifist philosopher. He taught his views in Central China in the 6th century B.C.

**Condemnation of Industry**

Radical opposition to industrial development is one of the themes of the *Huai Narn Dzu*, a collection of philosophical views compiled by Liu Arn in the 2nd century B.C. in Huai Narn, in Central China. Some of the contributors were strongly influenced by the Taoist preference for a return to the primitive lifestyle [see Taoism, VII, 1]. Looking back on the industrial development that had gone hand in hand with civilisation, and supplied mankind with luxuries superfluous to survival, one of them had only regret.

> No tall trees were left on the mountains and the silkworm oaks and lindera trees disappeared from the groves. Untold wood was burnt for charcoal and masses of plants turned to white ash, so that the jasmine and anise could never reach perfection. Above, smoke obscured the very light of heaven and below the riches of the Earth were totally exhausted.

Although his opposition to industry is here expressed on ecological grounds, his school of thought equally deplored the personal consequences of the social and economic complexity spawned by development.

**Laissez-faire Policy**

> The best of all rulers is but a shadowy presence to his subjects.
> Next comes the ruler they love and praise;
> Next comes one they fear.
> Next comes one with whom they take liberties.
> When there is not enough faith there is a lack of good faith.
> Hesitant, he does not utter words lightly.
> When his talk is accomplished and his work done
> The people all say, 'It happened to us naturally'.

> The sage ruler says ... 'I prefer stillness, and the people are rectified of themselves'.                    (tr. D.C. Lau)

Since its establishment in China in the 6th century B.C., the advocates of Taoism [VII, 1] have vehemently opposed government intrusion in economic and social affairs, and urged rulers to refrain from large-scale actions. Lao Dzu, author of the *Dao De Jing* quoted above, believed that the natural order of the Universe (the *tao*) provides for the livelihood of all beings and should not be interfered with, by either government or private initiative.

## 4. PHILOSOPHY OF NATURE AND KNOWLEDGE

There is no clear boundary between Philosophy and Science. For example, cosmology – a branch of philosophy treated in this section – deals with issues that are essential to scientific understanding; physics [VIII, I] is a science with direct implications for Philosophy. In fact, up until last century physics was called natural philosophy. Mathematics is dealt with in Chapter VIII, even though it is a product of purely mental labours and, unlike other sciences, is true or false independently of any tests or observations in the material world.

The realisation that the natural order of our world follows universal laws is the first scientific breakthrough in the field of natural philosophy. Subsequently, Science has been striving endlessly to identify these laws (or principles as they are sometimes called); the quest has given us Archimedes's Principle [VIII, 1], Newton's Laws [VIII, 1], the Periodic Table of Elements [VIII, 4] and a multitude of other findings. The ancient Sumerians of Mesopotamia, who first described them, called the laws *mes* and believed they govern every aspect of the universal order. Like later scientific writings, Sumerian records surviving from the 3rd millennium B.C. have very little to say on where the laws come from. Belief in them probably developed around 3000B.C. and formed part of Sumerian religion. One tradition relates that the laws are written on tablets kept by the gods.

**Laws of Nature**

According to a Sumerian poem from the 3rd millennium B.C., human affairs, just like natural phenomena, are governed by universal laws. It relates a myth of the goddess Inanna, who wishes to make her city, Erech, into the centre of civilisation. She visits Enki, god of wisdom, with the aim of purloining all the tablets on which the laws of human society are recorded. The poet lists over a hundred topics covered by this divine legislation, including: kingship, truth, sexual intercourse, prostitution, law, art, music, power, falsehood, goodness, justice, terror, strife, peace and judgement. As well as abstract qualities, the other headings include technological crafts, religious concepts and offices, emotions and musical instruments.

**Universal Laws in the Humanities**

The concept of two equal and opposite forces jointly regulating the Universe – one associated with darkness, Earth and the female (*yin*) and one with brightness, Heaven and the male (*yang*) – was first expressed in the eight trigrams of

**Yin and Yang**

ancient Chinese cultures. Each trigram consists of three parallel lines which can differ only in being either broken or continuous. The continuous line (—) signifies yang; the broken
line, yin. The resulting trigrams are:

☰ ☱ ☲ ☳ ☴ ☵ ☶ ☷

Of these the first signifies Heaven, and pure yang; the last,
Earth, and pure yin. Collectively they symbolise the ways the
two principles combine to engender all phenomena. They
were invented in the mid-3rd millennium B.C. by the primitive Chinese of the Yellow River Basin, and are traditionally
ascribed to the legendary ruler Fu Hsi.

**Atoms**

Around about 450B.C., Leucippus, from the Greek city of Elea
in Southern Italy, decided that the Universe is made of minuscule indivisible particles which he called atoms. According to
his book, *The Great World Order*, the Universe is infinite in
extent, but consists only of void and a partial filling of atoms
in constant motion. These atoms he recognised as elements,
which can combine in various ways to form new substances.

Leucippus had a follower, Democritus (460–357B.C.), who
came from Abdera in Northern Greece. The people of Abdera
were chided for their unusual stupidity; but Democritus was
one of the smartest men of all time. He is called the laughing
philosopher because he advocated constant cheerfulness; but
his main contribution to Science was to develop atomic theory
by explaining the nature of compounds. He claimed that the
properties observed in materials, such as heat or taste or hard-
ness, do not belong to the individual atoms, but derive from
their arrangement and agitation, and particularly the way they
**Molecules** join up. The shape and exterior of different types of atoms
enable them to link up in a variety of ways to constitute material substances. He likened atoms to alphabetic letters that
form words, and thus illustrated the concept of the molecule.
Although Democritus maintained that the bonds between
atoms can be broken by the action of stronger forces in their
environment, he did not envisage the splitting of the atom
[VIII, 1] itself.

**Atomic Theory
of Time**

We tend to think of Time as a continuous sequence, but just
as a movie film is made up of thousands of static frames, some
people think time is a string of countless atoms and that
movement takes place in tiny steps that can only be recognised as continuous motion. This analysis was first adopted by

philosophers of the Jain [VII, 5] sect in Northern India, around 200A.D. In the Jain conception, an atom of time is a point without length, but it occupies a temporal space which is the minimum unit of duration – just as a single movie frame contains no lapse of time, but represents a given duration when projected.

The atomic conception of Time was later employed to undermine the present notion of cause and effect, which is **Denial of** based on motion in a continuous sequence. According to Abū **Causation** Isḥāq al-Naẓẓām – an Arab theologian of Islam in the 800s A.D. – the Universe is reassembled every instant by God, with its atoms in minutely different positions. To him, and his successors in the Sunni school [VII, 5], the laws of nature, detected by Science, are God's habits, followed in the reconstruction. Miracles occur when God departs from habit to produce phenomena not in correspondence with those 'scientific laws'. The atomisation of Time and the abnegation of Cause and Effect are intimately linked with quantum physics [VIII, 1].

According to Anaximander (c. 610–540B.C.), a Greek philosopher from Miletus (in present-day Turkey), the Cosmos is **Infinity of the** infinite and includes our own universe and an infinite number **Cosmos** of other worlds. He described the Infinite as the cause of the **Infinity of** generation and destruction of the Universe, believing in the **Time** unlimited duration of Time.

Our own universe was first thought to be of limited extent, with the Earth in the centre or at the bottom, and the stars in **Infinity of** circular motions within its outer boundaries. But Anaxagoras **Matter** of Clazomenae (c. 500–429B.C.), a Greek philosopher working in Athens, introduced a theory that the quantity of things is infinite, implying that the Universe has no end.

The principle that matter cannot be created or destroyed was first expounded by the Greek philosopher Empedocles, of **Conservation** Acragas in Sicily. His poem *On Nature* (5th century B.C.), **of Matter** which introduces natural selection and the 'Big Bang Theory' [see below], also states that all the contents of the Universe are eternal and that birth and death are expressions we use to describe transformations of indestructible matter. The principle was immediately adopted by pioneers of atomic physics, including Democritus. They realised that everything perceived as tangible matter (such as rocks and lakes) is in fact an assemblage of inconceivably small particles, travelling at speed to give the illusion of bulk and substantiality. So they put forth a more refined version of the principle of conservation of matter, stipulating that it is these material particles (rather than the continuous sequence which they simulate for us) that have no birth or death. In more recent times, subscribers to the Big Bang Theory have expounded the principle of the conservation of matter in combating the rival 'Steady State Theory', which argues that new matter is constantly being supplied.

**Conservation of Energy**

**E = mc²**

The parallel observation – that *energy* cannot be created or destroyed – has only been accepted since the time of Sir Isaac Newton (1642A.D.–1727), who gave it to the world in his *Philosophiae Naturalis Principia Mathematica* (1687). In the hands of Newton's successors the principle has been one of the cornerstones of physics. The resolution of these two principles is in the equation $E = mc^2$ (energy equals mass times the velocity of light squared), discovered in 1907 by Albert Einstein, father of the Theory of Relativity [VIII, 1].

**Big Bang Theory**

The philosopher Empedocles (c. 495–c. 435B.C.), from the Greek city of Acragas in Sicily, described what he called the cosmic whirl, in his poem *On Nature*. All the contents of the Universe are at one time congregated in a homogenous sphere. Subsequently they fly apart, whirling outwards from a vortex and gradually assuming the forms of the universe we live in. Ultimately everything is again drawn back into the great sphere, to be dispersed in a process that eternally repeats itself.

**The World as a Living Being**

In his dialogue *Timaeus*, Plato (429–347B.C.) gives us the earliest picture of the World as a living organism, host to countless other organisms, including us. His world includes the Earth, all the celestial bodies and the heavens. These make up its body, but he also gives it a mind, and declares it the perfect creature, to which all others can be compared, falling short in greater or lesser degree. Its perfection is expressed partly in its exactly spherical shape, which is constantly rotating.

**Evolution**

**Artificial Selection**

Before the advent of civilisation [IV, 3] primitive herdsmen realised that animals can inherit particular traits from their parents, and that over a number of generations, preferable characteristics can be strengthened. Using this knowledge they modified their livestock by culling less suitable individuals and breeding from selected stock. This evolutionary process of artificial selection has given us sheep (descended from wild goats), cows (descended from bison) and pigs (descended from boars).

The idea that a comparable process of natural selection is responsible for the development of the well adapted lifeforms **Natural** which populate the world today was first advanced in the 5th **Selection** century B.C. in a poem, *On Nature*, by Empedocles of Acragas, originator of the Big Bang Theory [see above]. His concept of evolution is rather crude: he suggested that amongst the ill-adapted early species screened out by natural selection, there might have been such misfits as neckless heads and shoulderless arms. Later Greek thinkers developed a more sophisticated theory. Natural selection supported their view that well-adapted organisms exist because amongst the random products of the natural creative process, they were the best qualified to survive and multiply. To exponents of the theory, it displaced the belief that individual creatures are the design and handiwork of God. In the 1st century B.C., natural selection again found its way into poetry, in *The Nature of Things*, by Lucretius of Rome:

> Before a species can survive – it needs
> Food first of all, and reproductive parts
> Whereby the seeds of life can find their way
> From male to female, and their bodies join
> In mutual delight.
> In those old days
> Many attempts were failures; many a kind
> Could not survive; whatever we see today
> Enjoying the breath of life must from the first
> Have found protection in its character,
> Its cunning, its courage, or its quickness.   (tr. Humphrey)

The ideas in this poem come from the Greek philosopher Epicurus. Epicurus's scientific views are mostly taken directly from Democritus and Leucippus, inaugurators of the theory of atoms and molecules [see above]. So it was probably one of these two Greeks in the 5th century B.C. who first gave a cogent account of natural selection. Since their works are lost, we will never be sure.

It was the great Islamic scientist Abū Rayḥān Muḥammad ibn Aḥmad al-Bīrūnī of Khwarizm (973A.D.–1048) who con- **Descent from** cluded that humankind is ancestrally related to other primate **the 'Apes'** species. In his book *Kitāb al-jamāhir*, he says that the human species is descended from a chain of increasingly advanced mammals, of which primates are the nearest. The view that human beings themselves have evolved genealogically, from **Evolution of** the earliest men to the modern kind (which we know as *homo* **Modern Man** *sapiens sapiens*), had previously been put forward in China in a collection of scientific and philosophical papers published by Liu Arn in Huai Narn, the *Huai Narn Dzu* (2nd century B.C.), during the Harn Dynasty. According to this work, humankind has evolved through five species, beginning with the cryptically named 'chimney man' and descending to today's 'common man'.

**Common Ancestry of Life**

Another important idea found in the *Huai Narn Dzu* is the realisation that all life on Earth springs from a common ancestry. This was the view of one of the contributors, who compared creation to a tree – having one trunk and countless offshoots. Implicit in this concept is the belief that the differences between species developed progressively in the generations which separate us from the first ancestor of all lifeforms.

**Degeneration**

Knowledge of the evolutionary process led to the development of specific views abut the future of the human race. One of these was the policy of eugenics [VII, 3] advocated by Plato; another was the idea that repetitive breeding from a limited stock leads to degeneration and unfitness. That notion appeared in England in 1813 in a work titled *Lectures on Physiology, Zoology and the Natural History of Man*, which argued that for this reason, Europe's ruling classes were degenerate, and in need of replacement. England's Lord Chancellor disapproved, and declared the book contrary to Scripture; its author, the surgeon William Lawrence, protected his own prestige by disowning his scurrilous book. However, in Lawrence's maturer years, the establishment rewarded him with a baronetcy and the post of sergeant surgeon to the Queen, and Charles Darwin reiterated Lawrence's many ideas on natural selection in *The Origin of Species* (1859). Darwin never gave the credit due to Lawrence and his other British predecessors, but he acknowledges the antiquity of evolutionary theory in *The Origin of Species*: 'it is very far from true that the principle is a modern discovery . . . The principle of selection I find distinctly in an ancient Chinese encyclopaedia'.

**The Food Chain**

It is natural that the philosopher Juarng Dzu (c. 300B.C.), who stressed the organic cycle [VIII, 5] and decomposition, should also have commented perceptively about the food chain, Nature's endless sequence of nourishment for living creatures. The *Book of Juarng Dzu* tells how he saw a large unusual bird, which he chased with his bow ready, to the tree on which it perched:

> he noticed a solitary cicada so intent on having found a fine spot of shade that it forgot to protect its body, so a mantis, its forelegs already poised, seized it. But, intent on the capture the mantis forgot to look after its own form.

The strange bird then took advantage of this situation, and noticing only the gain it was making, forgot about itself. Instead of shooting it, Juarng Dzu said 'Alas, living things invariably enmesh each other; each species will both call on and be called on.'

There are three fundamental ideas on the question of whether everything that happens is predestined. The earliest is that all lives are governed by the dictates of a fate laid down at the whim or discretion of supernatural powers. This is a religious belief dating back to prehistoric times. It is often accompanied by the conviction that individuals can do nothing to vary the destinies appointed for them. **Destiny** **Fate**

A second view holds that all events are inevitable because they are results necessarily proceeding from causes already present in the constitution of the Universe. So the way things are now will lead with absolute certainty to the way they will be in a thousand years. This theory was first stated by the Greek philosopher Leucippus of Elea, in his book *On Mind* (c. 450B.C.). Subscribers to this view acknowledge that we can influence our own futures by actions and decisions, but consider that the way we make our minds up is like everything else, determined by existing causes. Leucippus was the inventor of the atomic theory of matter [see above] and believed that atoms invariably follow fixed laws in their behaviour. **Necessity**

The third view is that atomic behaviour does not obey fixed laws, but includes actions independent of external cause; that consequently, events are not predestined. This was introduced by another Greek philosopher, Epicurus of Athens (341–271B.C.) [see Epicureanism: VII, 1], who described the causeless behaviour as the 'atomic swerve'. Some modern theories of quantum physics [VIII, 1] similarly hold that atoms behave in defiance of fixed laws. **Anti-determinism**

Did Sigmund Freud, the great student of the psyche in 19th-century Vienna, copy Plato's *Republic*, published in Athens in the 4th century B.C., and then pretend to have a new system? Or was he ignorant of Plato's work and thus genuinely creative? It must have been one or the other, as the essence of Freud's theory is to be found in Plato. **Freudian Psychology**

Freud pointed out that an individual's behaviour is the product of the three motivational sources in the mind: the ego, the superego and the id. Plato's terminology, as set out in Book IV of the *Republic*, is different: he found a reasoning **Three Elements of the Mind** principle which he likened to a man; a principle responsible for indignation, shame and courage, which he likened to a lion; and a principle concerned with appetites and desires, which he likened to a many-headed beast. These three principles – the rational, the spirited and the appetitive – determine our character by their inter-relations and relative strengths. In the harmonious individual, the rational principle rules, controlling the appetitive with the assistance of the spirited.

**Desires Revealed in Dreams**

Freud's theory claims that in dreams, our desires, which are largely restrained and confined to the subconscious, shake off their restraints and manifest themselves. Plato calls them 'banished desires':

> which are awake when the reasoning, human, ruling power is asleep; then the wild beast within us . . . starts up and having shaken off sleep goes forth to satisfy his desires; and there is no conceivable folly or crime – not excepting fornication with a mother, man, god or brute, or patricide, or eating of forbidden food – which at such a time when he is not constrained by the shame and the reason, a man may not be ready to commit.                    (tr. Jowett)

**Control of Depraved Appetites**

Freud echoes the advice given by Plato on controlling depraved dreams: ensure that the appetites are adequately catered to, but not over indulged; and hone the reasoning principle with fine thoughts, enquiry and meditation, before going to sleep. What Freud said of Plato in *The Interpretation of Dreams* is interesting: 'As everyone knows, the ancients before Aristotle did not consider the dream a product of the dreaming mind, but a divine inspiration.' It is a poor reflection on Freud's knowledge of the classics, but at least this clears him of the charge of copying.

**Scepticism**

The leading religious authority in ancient Greece was the Oracle at Delphi. Here the priestess of Apollo passed on the god's answer to any difficult question put by an enquirer. Chaeroephos, an admirer of Socrates (469–399B.C.), asked the Oracle whether anyone was as wise as the Athenian philosopher. On learning that the priestess had answered 'no one', Socrates raised his eyebrows and denied that he possessed any wisdom at all. So he embarked on a quest to make sense of the oracle, by rigorously interrogating people who might be wiser, including leading politicians and educators, poets, artists and workers. He found not only that their professed wisdom was a mere sham, but that there was no way to make them realise they were ignorant. Socrates concluded that the oracle pronounced him wisest because he alone recognised his own ignorance. Throughout the second half of his life he laboured to demonstrate his sceptical approach to the world, and to reject opinions that were not based on rigorously tested grounds. In the process he laid the main foundations for the subsequent development of all Western philosophy, by obliging every significant thinker to make it clear where his knowledge comes from.

The Sceptic School of philosophy was established later, by Pyrrhon of Elis (c. 360–270B.C.), after he returned to Greece from travels in Persia and India. He claimed that as all knowledge is uncertain, one should follow good sense and practicality in choosing how to think and behave. **Sceptic School**

The Greek medical writer Alcmaeon (c. 500B.C.), of Croton in Sicily, observed that it is not possible to know anything for certain. He admitted that there is true knowledge regarding both everyday matters and the mysterious questions of existence. But this is something we can only hope to approximate by interpreting from our own experience. He was not trying to undermine the wisdom which man imperfectly possesses, but to draw attention to the way our reliance on our minds and senses leaves us open to being entirely misled about reality. (For instance you might be dreaming that the world around you is real.) Alcmaeon's solution was to assume he was on the right track, and believe things according to inference based on the evidence available. Alcmaeon was a student of Pythagoras, and performed the first eye operation in Greece. **Impossibility of Knowledge**

The French philosopher René Descartes (1596A.D.–1650) shared Alcmaeon's view, but qualified it by emphasising that there is one fact of which he could be utterly certain: the fact of his existence. 'I think therefore I am' he said (in Latin, 'cogito ergo sum'). This he explained by denying that he could have certain knowledge of anything else – but that his own existence was proved by his conscious experiences, including thought. His theory was published in 1637 in his book *Discourse on the Method of Rightly Directing One's Reason and of Seeking the Truth in the Sciences.* **'Cogito Ergo Sum'**

The fears expressed by Alcmaeon and Descartes, that the world around us might be imaginary, became an article of belief to Chinese Buddhists from about 600A.D. An example of their thinking arose when two monks were debating whether a flag they saw was itself moving or was being moved by the wind. The Buddhist Patriarch Hui Neng (638A.D.–713) settled the question by saying 'neither the flag nor the wind is **The World is Illusory** moving, there is only movement within your minds'. For Buddhists generally and Zen Buddhists [VII, 5] especially, the notion that the world is an illusion became a tenet of faith.

**Inapplicability of Words to Reality**

Before the time of Zeno of Elea, people resolved arguments, and expressed ideas, in words, confident that the language they were using was an adequate medium to convey truth and the arguments by which they pursued it. In Greece in the mid-5th century B.C., this faith was undermined by Zeno's book, which included forty arguments proving it impossible for more than one thing to exist. Zeno constructed a proof that everything has infinite magnitude and a proof that everything has no magnitude. In many other ways he claimed to be making a rigorous use of language to reach conclusions that contradict the reality we all recognise. From then on philosophers began to attack the validity of words, on the grounds that they are based on illusory distinctions, that their meanings are relative or arbitrary, or that they are purely subjective.

**Applicability of Words to Reality**

A similar trend blossomed in China soon afterwards; one philosopher, for example, claimed to demonstrate that a white horse is not a horse. One of China's classicists – who followed Confucius – answered it with the first analysis establishing words as true vehicles for expounding ideas. Hsewn Dzu (c. 312–c. 230B.C.), who taught in the northeastern state of Jao, wrote that distinctions apprehended by the senses, and species and distinctions discovered analytically by the mind, form the basis of dependable terminology. Dilemmas raised by gimmicks of dialectical manipulation – like 'a white horse is not a horse' or 'mountains and chasms are on the same level' – are all to be resolved by testing them against the considered understanding which acts on data received by the senses or in thought.

**Higher Reality of Universal Forms**

Plato of Athens (429–347B.C.) is the first philosopher to deny that our world is the realest thing that can be known to us. In his view it is a collection of defective copies of a higher truer reality, which the mind can know by exploring the universal form of each thing. He took geometry as a logical starting point for his teaching. The best circle that can be drawn in this world is an imperfect imitation of the idea of the Circle discovered by the human mind. Obviously one cannot know what a circle is just by seeing drawings of circles. One has to envisage the concept mentally if one is to come at truth in the matter of circles. Plato extends this idea to cover everything –

from mundane articles like doors to general qualities such as justice and beauty. In the *Republic* and some of his other philosophical dialogues, he repeatedly advocates the quest for wisdom carried out by contemplation of the forms. He asks us to imagine people who through their whole lives are forced to watch nothing but images moving on a screen. They believe what they see on the screen is reality. Taken out into the daylight of our three-dimensional world, they are dazzled and do not understand. They do not appreciate it as the real world, nor their motion pictures as copies from it. In the same way, he claims, our common fellows do not realise that the world is a copy, nor grasp the truth of the forms in the world that is explored by philosophers.

Aristotle (384–322B.C.), founder of the Peripatetic School [VII, 1] of philosophy, was the first to make a scientific study of logic, **Science of** and to analyse the process of argumentation. His results are pre- **Logic** sented in a body of publications now known as the *Organon*, each of uncertain date. In two of these – now entitled *Prior Analytics* and *De Interpretatione* – he introduces and examines the concept of the syllogism, a 'propositional expression, in which, certain things having been laid down, something other than what is laid down follows of necessity from their being so'. **Syllogism** This is the familiar structure of premises and a conclusion which follows from them. Distinguished into its different types, the syllogism is the centrepiece of the study of logic.

The Chinese Taoist philosopher Juarng Dzu (c. 300B.C.) had a belief in the theoretical capabilities of science which went **Natural Limit** well beyond the scientific achievements of his own time. He **of Scientific** said that the entities and processes observable in our universe **Knowledge**

> can be examined and however minute can be recorded. The principles determining the order in which they follow one another, their mutual influences now acting directly, now revolving . . . these are the properties of things. Words can describe them and knowledge can reach them.
>
> (tr. Needham)

This is the foundation of his more important point: that there is an immobile limit beyond which scientific inquiry cannot go, questions it cannot answer – such as where the Universe, its laws, and the properties of things, ultimately come from. 'Those who study the Tao know they cannot follow these changes to the ultimate end, nor search out their first beginnings.'

**Subjectivity of Truth**

The Greek philosopher Protagoras of Abdera (485–415B.C.), who invented agnosticism [VII, 6], was the first to teach the idea that truth is not objective. According to conventional thinking, if a statement be true, then a statement disagreeing with it must be false. But Protagoras said: 'What seems to be true to you is true for you, what seems to be true to me is true for me.'

**Extra-terrestrial Life**

Anaxagoras of Clazomenae (500–428B.C.), a Greek philosopher living in Athens, wrote the first European book to be illustrated with diagrams. He recognised that moonlight [VIII, 2] is reflected sunlight; and he claimed that the Universe contains an infinite quantity of things, amongst them, living beings on the Moon. What form he supposed they might take is no longer recorded, but later Greek writers, including Aristotle and Plutarch, stressed that they are not likely to resemble any life known to us, especially considering the different system of nutrition that would apply. The Greek satirist Lucian, in a novel about space travel, described fictional alien lifeforms [I, 3] in detail.

**Music of the Spheres**

The early Greek poet Homer (c. 900B.C.) speaks of 'those invested with the seven melodies', remarking that they 'speak and give answer to each other in a pleasant tone'. The melodies in question belong to the Sun and Moon, Mercury, Venus, Mars, Jupiter and Saturn. Homer's reference is the first statement of the popular Greek belief that the celestial bodies make a kind of perfect sound as they travel through the heavens – the 'music of the spheres'.

## 5. RELIGIONS

Religion exists amongst the most primitive people who have ever been observed, so it obviously began an enormous length of time ago. Its origin is so lost that it isn't possible to say where it came in the order or things – before or after the beginning of art, for example.

With the exception of Shinto, the religions dealt with here are all of the advanced kind – which developed in recent millennia – that marry original encompassing theologies with popular faith. The older-style religions – with their multiple independent deities who resemble people or animate nature, have generally been supplanted in developed societies.

Judaism is omitted because of the difficulty in telling when it started. Confucianism is omitted because Confucius's school of thought is entirely secular, and is dealt with under Classicism [VII, 1].

Hinduism was not the religion of the earliest Indian civilisations; it was developed by descendants of the white-skinned Aryan invaders who immigrated from the northwest. Late in the 2nd millennium B.C. they wrote a large collection of religious verse called the *Vedas*, after which their religion is named. Vedic religion believed that the forces of nature are in the hands of divinities with personalities, to whom their holy men, the Brahmans, sacrificed. They were convinced of the soul's immortality, but had not developed a system of belief in cyclical return, nor of social castes.

**Hinduism**

**Vedic Religion**

Hinduism evolved gradually from this background, first in Northwest India, then in the Ganges Basin. Probably by about 600 B.C. the general belief in Brahma as a divine spirit permeating all things, the theory of the transmigration of souls [VII, 7], and the rigidity of the caste system [IV, 3] with its accompanying rituals, had come together to form Brahmanical Hinduism, the ancient form of the Hindu religion.

**Brahminical Hinduism**

The Hare Krishna sect is the brand of Hinduism that has penetrated most successfully into the Western world. It was founded in the U.S.A. in 1966 by His Divine Grace A. C. Bhaktivedanta (1896–1977). However, it honours Caitanya, who lived in India in the 16th century A.D., as its original master, believing him to be an incarnation of Krishna the Warrior God and Krishna the Lover God. Believers seek to reestablish their relationship with Krishna, or 'Krishna Consciousness'.

**Hare Krishna**

Yoga began in Northern India, as a Hindu religious system for disconnecting the spirit from the entanglements of the senses and experience. According to the first textbook about it, Patanjali's *Yoga Sutra*, the practice of Yoga is an eight-stage procedure involving correct thought and behaviour, postures and breathing control, and intense meditation. In the ultimate stage, the *yogin*'s soul unites with the object of his meditations. Patanjali recommends God as a suitable object. Like many other Indian institutions, Yoga cannot be given a reliable date – it probably emerged around 400 B.C. from the various brands of Hindu asceticism. *Yoga Sutra* seems to be a summary of Yoga as practised in Patanjali's time, but it does not pretend to teach Yoga without the instructions of a master.

**Yoga**

**Yoga Textbook**

The prophet Zarathustra (or Zoroaster) established the Zoroastrian religion in Northern Persia (present-day Iran) and Bactria (in part of present-day Afghanistan and Turkmenistan),

**Zoroastrianism**

in about 700 B.C., and composed the *Zend Avesta*, its sacred book. It quickly attracted a vast following and became the official religion of the Persian Empire, although nowadays its only important adherents are the 'Parsees' (Persians) of India. Zarathustra's main teaching was that Mazda (Ormazd), the god **Goodness in** of goodness and light, is locked in a struggle with Ahriman, the **Human** power of darkness and evil. Worship and good behaviour **Nature** increase the power of Mazda, and evil-doers are punished in the after-life. Zoroastrianism was the first religion to teach that there is in all people a right nature that can animate them to good ends.

The Jain religion was founded in the 6th century B.C. by a **Jainism** contemporary and countryman of Buddha, Vardhamana Mahavira Tirthankara, from Magadha in Northeast India. He taught that every person, animal, plant and even rock is endowed with an individual soul. He denied the existence of **God the** a supreme deity or creator. Mahavira's most remarkable tenet **Manifestation** is that God is only the ultimate and perfect manifestation of **of Humanity** the powers inherent in the soul of man.

Buddhism was invented in the 6th century B.C. by Siddhartha **Buddhism** Gautama (c. 563–c. 483 B.C.), son of the Rajah of Kapilavastu, in Northeast India near Nepal. Gautama took the name Buddha from *bodhi* – the spiritual realm – after enlightenment came to him, in middle-age, while sitting under a bo tree. He taught the Hindu doctrine that the soul is trapped in a cycle of rebirth, but he rejected the caste system in favour of an egalitarian position. Buddha looked on birth as a great misfortune, and offered his followers release from the cycle of rebirth if they could accumulate sufficient good *karma*. This is to be achieved by purity of thought and action, by celibacy, by not destroying life, by abstaining from theft, deceit, slander, intoxicants, dancing, singing, and spectating at amusements, by not eating in the afternoon, not sleeping in a bed, eschewing ornaments and luxuries, money and valuables.

Buddha's teaching is a moral system aimed at achieving **Theravada** personal tranquility. However, his followers, organised in a **Buddhism** monastic system, were already creating a religion out of it before his death. Theravada Buddhism was the original religion of these followers, who established a veritable church with a hierarchy of teachers.

**Mahayana** In the century following Buddha's death, the idea devel- **Buddhism** oped that Buddha himself is a divinity, and that the release sought by Buddhists is union after death with Buddha in eternity. To assist other souls to salvation some souls are released from the cycle of rebirth to remain on the scene as bodhisattvas. Because this version of Buddhism magnified Buddha into a divine principle which could carry all to salvation, it is known as the Great Vehicle, or Mahayana Buddhism, and its followers describe Theravada Buddhism as the Little Vehicle – Hinayana.

From the 2nd century A.D., Buddhism declined in India while spreading and evolving in China. The Chinese schools are notable for their intricate variety and massive book learning. Vast libraries were filled with Buddhist texts, especially Indian books and translations. Some Buddhists frowned on the growing intellectualism and superstition. Those who emphasised *charn* (meditation) broke from the mainstream in the 7th century A.D., and taught that Buddhism can only be conveyed from mind to mind, not learnt from books. Charn as a distinct sect is the work of three contemporaries: Hui Neng (638A.D.–713), Shen Hsiu (605–706) and Shen Hui (670–762). Of these, Hui Neng, China's sixth Buddhist Patriarch, was the most vigorous and influential. His teaching spread to Japan and thence to America and Europe. It is now called Zen, from the Japanese pronunciation of charn; ironically many of its modern adherents have 'learnt' Zen from the hundreds of Zen books now available. **Zen**

Lamaism was the state religion of Tibet, with many adherents in neighbouring countries and in Mongolia, under the leadership of the Dalai Lama. Buddhism first caught on in Tibet under the encouragement of the Tibetan king Srong-brtsan-sgam-po (reigned 629A.D.–650), who is also responsible for introducing the alphabet from India, and founding the capital, Lhasa. The Lamaist version did not develop until the 11th century. In 1038A.D. the monk Atísa from Magadha (in Northeast India, near Buddha's birthplace) and a group of his colleagues visited Tibet. They had been invited by the king, and they introduced sweeping religious reforms. By spreading Mahayana beliefs amongst the Tibetan masses, they established a national church in which elements of Tibet's ancient religion – such as demons and complex ritual – persisted alongside Mahayana Buddhism. **Lamaism**

Shinto developed during Japan's prehistoric period, before the coming of writing and civilisation. It is an indigenous animistic cult of nature worship – typical of primitive societies – **Shinto** which has tenaciously survived the progress of civilisation and the importation of sophisticated religions like Buddhism and Christianity. The first account of it is in a Chinese description of Japan published around 297A.D., which describes Shinto divination and ritual bathing. It also tells of the avoidance of ritual pollution – by appointing 'fortune keepers', who abstain from washing, meat and women on behalf of believers going on trips and ventures; and by community merry-making and singing during the period of lamentation after a funeral. These and other Shinto observances had developed gradually in the 1st millennium B.C. as mainland immigrant races settled down on the island of Kyushu and the western part of Honshu – the areas where Japanese culture was born.

**Christianity**  Jesus Christ (c. 10B.C.–30A.D.), born in Bethlehem, established Christianity in the Roman province of Judea. His teaching was based on His ancient native religion of Judaism, but Christ made an important original contribution as a moralist, enjoining habits of charity and self-abnegation on His followers, and developing the concepts of eternal damnation and bliss for those who did not or did welcome God into their lives. Christianity as practised today is largely based on the elaborations of His early teachings at the hands of churchmen; to them we owe the various sects identified below.

Two existing denominations have substantial claims to a direct origin in the Christian Church established by Christ's
**Roman** immediate successors, in the 1st century A.D. Both the East-
**Catholic** ern Orthodox Church and the Roman Catholic Church are branches of the orthodox catholic church, which, before
**Eastern** 1054A.D., was a single entity commanding the adherence of
**Orthodox** all Christians except those whose beliefs it condemned as heretical. In the Schism of 1054, it split into a western church, with headquarters in Rome, known as Roman Catholic, and an eastern church, with headquarters in Constantinople (present-day Istanbul), the Orthodox Church. Although there are significant differences in the doctrines and calendars of the two faiths, their separation was mainly due to conflicting claims to authority by their spiritual heads, the Pope at Rome and the Patriarch of Constantinople.

The identity of the first Pope is a matter of sensitive reli-
**Pope** gious controversy, which we will not resolve here. According to widespread belief and official church chronology the office was first held by Christ's disciple St. Peter in the middle of the 1st

century A.D. Leo I, who was Pope from 440A.D. to 461, was the first to adopt the title *pontifex maximus* (the supreme religious position in the Roman Empire, and previously a pagan priesthood). During Leo's term the supremacy of the See of Rome was first generally acknowledged, and to some this is the beginning of Roman Catholicism. The first Pope to hold office after the Schism of 1054 was Leo IX, whose envoy Humbert had proclaimed his supremacy to the Patriarch of Constantinople. The reaction in Constantinople was to deny the Papal authority, and the Patriarch, Michael Cerulanios, became the first to reign after the Schism. Since the 4th century Constantinople had had a patriarch, initially junior to the Bishop of Rome.

**Patriarch of Constantinople**

In the second half of the 1st century A.D., as Christianity spread well beyond Judea, some Christians, especially in Syria and Egypt, renounced for the first time the Judaic part of their religion and heaped derision on the Old Testament and the God of the Jews. They lauded Christ as the Earthly manifestation of the true God, and splitting into innumerable schools, borrowed various doctrines from Zoroastrianism [see above], Pythagoreanism [VII, 1] and Greek philosophy. Corinthus, in the mid-1st century was one of the founders of their movement. They were vehemently opposed by the orthodox church, and gradually died out after the 3rd century A.D., but not before developing a more enduring offshoot, Manichaeism [see below], from which in turn grew the Albigensian sect of Christianity, which spread widely in Europe in the 12th century.

**Gnostic**

**Albigensian**

Arius (280A.D.–336), a Libyan presbyter living in Alexandria, outraged fellow Christian clergymen by claiming that God the Father is the senior member of the Trinity and had by Himself created *Logos* (the word), which was the author of our world. Although this belief met widespread opposition, Arius quickly attracted a numerous following, including: two bishops, seven presbyters, twelve deacons and 700 virgins. Disturbed by the strength of the Arian party, the church referred the matter to an ecumenical council convened at Nicaea in 325A.D. There the Arians admitted their rejection of the theory of consubstantiation of God the Father and God the Son, and were accordingly denounced as heretics.

**Arian**

Nestorius was a monk in Antioch in Western Asia, who became Patriarch of Constantinople. In the late 420s A.D. he began preaching the distinction between the divinity of Jesus and the humanity of Christ. This led him to deny that the

**Nestorian**

virgin Mary was the mother of God, and to deny that the infant Christ (as distinguished from the divine nature with which he was invested) is a suitable object of worship. These tenets outraged one Cyril, Patriarch of Alexandria, who worked up devout opposition from all the right thinking Christians of Egypt and Italy. An ecumenical council was convened at Ephesus in 431A.D. Cyril was able to secure the condemnation of the Nestorian heresy by arranging for the vote to be taken before most of Nestorius's supporters turned up.

**Coptic** A fresh distortion of the orthodox creed was cooked up in the late 440s by the monk Eutyches, who preached that Jesus Christ possesses only a single nature and had not derived a separate bodily nature from the virgin Mary. The Monophysite sect was founded by those who shared Eutyches's view; it was condemned in 451A.D. by the Council of Chalcedon, but took root in Egypt, where it survives in the form of Coptic or Egyptian Christianity.

**Protestant** In previous paragraphs are catalogued some of the denominations of Christianity formed in ancient times; most have been pronounced heretical, but more recent offshoots of the Church are normally called Protestant. Initially this was because they were based on a protest against the decree of the 2nd Diet of Speier, passed in 1529, banning any new religious development. The first Protestant religious leader was Martin Luther (1483–1546), who published his denunciation of the papal system of granting indulgences to sinners, in 1511, at Wittenberg in his native Germany. Luther denied the supremacy of the Pope and the rulings of the church councils, claiming that the Scriptures are the sole authority on Christian doctrine. He renounced the principle of priestly celibacy as a late invention of the Church, and he **Lutheran** himself married a nun. On most subjects he shared the views of the Christian Reformation of the 16th century, but in 1529 he took issue strongly with other reformers on the significance of the Lord's Supper. His followers on this issue were called Lutherans, and it is from this time that a distinct Lutheran Church is identifiable.

**Reformed Churches** Luther's opponents in the debate of 1529 were the founders of the branch of Protestantism subsequently known as the Reformed Churches. They were led by the Swiss theologian Ulrich Zwingli (1484–1531). They claimed that the body of Christ is not actually present in the bread and wine of the Sacrament, and consequently they had insufficient common ground with their Lutheran rivals to remain in the same church.

In 1533 the French scholar Jean Calvin (or Cauvin, 1509–64) dressed up as a vine dresser to escape Paris, where **Calvinist** his Protestant views were about to call the ire of the establishment upon him. He began a career of writings and wanderings that resulted in the foundation of Calvinism. The first Calvinist church was the Reformed congregation of Geneva, of which he took up the management in 1537. However, Calvinist doctrine is actually that of St. Augustine, the Roman theologian from North Africa (354A.D.–430), author of *The City of God*. In addition Calvin imposed a wowseristic code of conduct as part of his dedicated campaign against sin.

There were many English Christians who challenged the authority of the Roman Catholic Church after the time of radi- **Anglican** cal theologian John Wyckliffe (1320A.D.–1384). However, until King Henry VIII came to the throne (1509) they were routinely got rid of by being burnt. In 1533 Henry married a second wife, Anne Boleyn, and the church in England declared his previous marriage, to Catherine, to have been void. But soon after, the Pope in Rome pronounced the first marriage valid, leaving Henry in a pretty kettle of fish. Henry's solution was effective and simple: he cancelled the authority of Rome in England, disinherited Catherine's daughter, Mary, and launched the Anglican Church as a separate organisation with himself as its head. Those who did not recognise the new arrangements were put to death; for the rest, official doctrines were promulgated, the old faith was persecuted, and Anglicanism was born.

In Europe early in the 16th century, a sect called the Anabaptists became powerful, and preached that baptism of **Baptist** infants, who have no intelligent participation in the ceremony, is of no effect. They also believed that all goods are held in common and that women are to be enjoyed in common. The Anabaptists had to be bloodily suppressed, and in 1535 conformist Protestants attacked and overthrew their headquarters at Münster in Germany. But in the 1530s and 1540s, milder members of the sect in the Netherlands built a more socially acceptable church, which maintained its opposition to infant baptism, but in other respects adopted the doctrines of the Reformed Churches. Their Dutch founders were glass painter David Joris (1501–56) and priest Menno Simons (1496–1561). They were known in Holland as Mennonites or

Doopsgezinden, in Germany as Taufgessinte, and in English-speaking countries as Baptists.

**Presbyterian** The Presbyterian denomination dates from 1581, when the Reformed Church of Scotland, in a general assembly, adopted a scheme of organisation devised by Andrew Melville. Its crucial feature was the authority vested in the presbyters – elders of the congregation – to superintend church affairs.

**Quaker** George Fox (1624–91) was an apprentice shoemaker in rural England at the age of nineteen when his spiritual urges prompted him to forsake his awl and take up the life of a wandering mystic. In 1648 in Manchester he began the work of making converts to his personal brand of Christianity. He preached the presence of Christ in everyone's heart, as an inner light superseding all the external sources of religious belief, including the Scriptures. Fox was jailed because of the disturbance caused by his behaviour at Manchester, the first of several visits to prison for his preachings. The name Quakers was given to his followers in 1650 because Fox bade them tremble at the word of God; their proper name is The Society of Friends.

**Methodist** The Methodist sect was founded in England by John Wesley (1703–91), one of nineteen children of the Anglican clergyman Samuel Wesley. However, of Methodism, John Wesley expressed the wish that the 'very name might never be mentioned more, but buried in eternal oblivion'. It had not been his intention to start a new church, but rather to preach his message to the masses whose faith was being overlooked by the established church. So successful were he and his followers in Britain, Asia, America and the Pacific that a new church sprang up under the momentum of their following.

**Mormon** Many are the wonderful religions which have originated in the United States of America, though few have beginnings as miraculous as those of the Church of Jesus Christ of the Latter Day Saints, named Mormons. In 1823 an American angel named Moroni visited Joseph Smith (1805–44) of New York state, and told him about the book of Mormon, which Moroni allowed him to dig up in 1827. Smith was able to read its hieroglyphic characters with the aid of special glasses that came with the book. To make an English translation he used an egg-shaped stone with chocolate on it. Smith and his followers set up the Church in Manchester, New York in 1830. The faith included a number of peculiar tenets, notably that the destruction of the world was nigh and that the Church was to establish a new Jerusalem in America, as it has done at Salt Lake City.

In 1831 the American preacher William Miller began the Seventh Day Adventist movement. Miller taught his followers to abstain from alcohol and drugs, to make Saturday their holy day and that the world would end in 1843. The movement took its name in 1860 and was constituted into a formal church in 1863.

**Seventh Day Adventist**

The Tai Ping religion, whose adherents rampaged through China in tens of millions in the 1850s, had a beginning at Canton in 1838. Twenty-three-year-old student Hung Hsiu Chuarn, having just failed his examinations for the last of many times, got sick and retired to bed. There he was visited by a dream that told him that he was Jesus Christ's younger brother, and that he had a mission to stamp out evil and false religion. In 1843, when the meaning of the dream became clear to him, he set up the Society of God Worshippers, and began to expound a brand of Christianity which denounced religious images, alcohol and drugs, and extolled communism and the equality of all men and women. God had given his younger son a destiny to overthrow the false creeds of Buddhism and Taoism and the evil secular philosophy of Confucius. (In 1863 Hung failed in this commission and the Tai Ping rebels were crushed by an army under the leadership of a Confucian scholar.)

**Tai Ping**

The next militaristic sect to form was rather more peaceable. In 1865 former Methodist minister William Booth established his 'Christian Mission' in London, with the aims of spreading the word of Christianity and rendering charitable service to the poor. In 1878 the movement took the name Salvation Army, and Booth styled himself its General.

**Salvation Army**

In 1872 Charles Taze Russell began a religious movement in Philadelphia, which combined vigorous proselytising activity with the belief that Jesus Christ was a mere mortal, a perfect man but not divine. His 'International Bible Students' did not celebrate birthdays, including Christmas, nor acknowledge allegiance to temporal authority. They took the name Jehovah's Witnesses in 1931.

**Jehovah's Witnesses**

In 1875 Mary Baker Eddy (1821–1910), the American founder of Christian Science, published her book, *Science and Health with Key to the Scriptures*, explaining that only God is real and that matter, evil and disease are the imaginary products of wrong thinking. The sect grew rapidly

**Christian Science**

around this theory, and adopted its practical extension, spiritual healing, which does away with doctors, hospitals and medical treatment.

**Unification Church**

In 1936 Jesus Christ appeared to Sun Myung Moon – a sixteen-year-old in Northwest Korea – and asked him to complete His work on Earth. Circumstances hampered young Moon until he escaped from prison in North Korea and gathered a small following in the south in 1950. In 1954 he formed the Holy Spirit Association for the Clarification of World Christianity, known as the 'Unification Church' or 'Moonies'. Its programme is to unite the Christians of the world under Moon's doctrines and leadership. Significant followings have so far been enrolled in Korea, Japan and America.

**Religious Orders**

The Catholic Church has mothered so many monastic and missionary orders that here we can only itemise the most important – which means in this case those that have given the world very significant firsts. The Augustinian order was

**Augustinians**

begun in North Africa, before the death of St. Augustine (354A.D.–430). Pious hermits there chose to live by St. Augustine's rule, which requires the renunciation of private property and imposes a strict way of life. The order began its northward spread when the Vandals invaded North Africa in 428. Refugee Augustinian friars set up monasteries in Northern Italy. An Augustinian monk of the 19th century, Gregor Mendel, discovered the laws of heredity [VIII, 5].

**Benedictines**

Benedict of Nursia (480A.D.–543) was the principal founder of monasticism in Catholic countries. The abbey at Monte Cassino in Italy, which he founded in 529, is normally identified as the first Benedictine monastery, every though Benedict had begun founding monasteries elsewhere in Italy as early as the 490s. Monte Cassino is given primacy because it was Benedict's headquarters when he brought out his 'monastic rule' – the Benedictines' famous set of instructions by which Western monks were to live for centuries to come. The rule included a daily allowance of alcohol – a softness that Benedict regretted having to countenance. This provision is responsible for the order's most original legacies to the modern world – it led to the invention of Benedictine liqueur [III, 4] and champagne [III, 4].

**Carthusians**

The Carthusian order was established in 1086A.D. at Chartreuse (Carthusia in Latin), near Grenoble in France, by the German monk Bruno (c. 1057A.D.–1101). Its most notable austerity is the obligatory solitude of the monks, who see each other only on Sundays and special occasions. It was through 200 Carthusians in a circuit that the first long-distance electric transmission [VIII, 12] passed; but the order's fame does not rest only on that distinction. It also developed a liqueur, Chartreuse [III, 4], to raise money with.

The Jesuit order was founded in 1534 by Ignatius of Loyola (1491–1556), a former soldier, with three fellow **Society of** Spaniards, a Frenchman and a Portuguese man. Their aim was **Jesus** to promote a pilgrimage to the holy land and conversion of the heathens in those parts. Because their plan was frustrated by war between the Christians and the Turks, they extended their aims to include permanent educational, monastic and proselytising institutions. Their new charter was approved by the Pope in 1540. The Society of Jesus rapidly distinguished itself for its ambition, superior learning and far-flung missionary activity. Its members attract our notice for constructive use of the slide projector [II, 1], invention of the model car [IX, 2] and the steamboat [IX, 1] and the application of a constant to a metric system [see Definition by Constant, IV, 3].

Like the Zoroastrians, the Manichaeans believed that the world is in the hands of competing powers of light and dark-  **Manichaeism** ness, which they said had neither beginning nor end. Manichaeans were urged to be charitable and to refrain from injuring plants, fire, water and especially animals. Their religion was founded by Mani, born in Persia in 204A.D., who began his teaching about the year 240. Mani described himself as God's next messenger of light after Buddha, Zarathustra and Jesus, and his faith blended Persian, Mediterranean and Indian religious concepts.

In 609A.D. the prophet Muhammad, his wife Kadijah, a servant, one of his cousins, and his friend, Abū Bakr, constituted **Islam** the congregation of a new religion, forming in a desert backwater, Arabia, in the isolated little city of Mecca. The religious organisation that was destined to hold sway by 740A.D. from the beaches of Spain to India and the frontiers of China, had added fourteen members by the year 613, when Muhammad declared his prophet status to his fellow townsmen. Over the next ten years scores of them joined his cause, but the rest were not impressed, and their wrath forced him to flee Mecca in 622, the first year of 'the Flight' (*Hegira*), when Islamic **Hegira** chronology begins. Muhammad returned to Mecca as a conqueror in 630, and died there in 632.

**Sunnis**

Just as the two greatest Christian churches trace their foundation back to the church originally established by Christ, the two principal sects of Islam claim to have originated with the prophet Muhammad himself. The schism that split the Sunni from the Shiites, and first gave them their identity as sects, began in 632A.D., within weeks of the Prophet's death, before their theological differences were worked out. The Sunni, or 'traditionalists', base their faith on the *Koran* and the traditional accounts of Muhammad's life and teachings, and have always constituted the mainstream of Islamic belief. They recognised and supported the caliph Abū Bakr, first successor to Muhammad's political office as head of the Islamic state.

**Shiites**

The Shiites supported Muhammad's cousin and son-in-law, 'Ali ibn Abi Talib, who claimed that as the Prophet's nearest male relative he was the only legitimate successor, and that Muhammad had confirmed this by especially distinguishing Ali throughout his prophetic career. In 655, Ali became the fourth man to be elected to the position of caliph, but according to the Shiites he is the first caliph, his predecessors being mere usurpers of Ali's office. Shiism is primarily the work of Ali's supporters rather than of Ali himself, and its founding beliefs were in the merit of the family, and the divine right to rule that is conferred on one family. Developing separately, Sunni and Shiite theology later came to differ in a variety of other matters.

**Ismailites**

The Ismailis are an unorthodox offshoot of Shiism, presided over nowadays by the Aga Khan. They began as a group of separate underground movements in Syria, Iraq and Arabia late in the 8th century A.D. These were loosely united about 800A.D. by accepting Ismā'īl, son of Ja'far al-Ṣādiq, as the seventh Shiite *imam* (spiritual chief), a tenet they share with no other Shiite. However, their most distinctive feature is the eight grades of teaching propagated by their missionaries. The first grade is conventional religion for ordinary believers, not far removed from Sunni dogma. The higher grades inculcate the rejection of religion and adopt an allegorical reading of the *Koran*. In these grades the Ismailis adopt free thinking, secular philosophy and a material analysis of the Universe.

**Sufism**

The mystic savants of the Islamic world are known as *Sufis*, from the meditational significance of the sounds S, U and F. They regard ancient figures such as Pythagoras and Christ as Sufi teachers, but the Sufi movement actually grew from the teachings of the great mystics of the 9th century A.D. in Iraq and Egypt. In particular, al-Muḥāsibī, Abū-Yazīd al-Bisṭāmī, al-Hallāj and Dhu'l-Nūn al-Masrī laid the bases of Sufi wisdom, renouncing intellectual learning and attempting to guide their followers to real truth.

The Sufis laid down various practical pathways to the knowledge they extolled, mostly involving forms of self- **Dervishes** discipline and renunciation of worldly advantages. Beginning in the 9th century, followers of these disciplines, known as dervishes, formed dervish orders. The oldest major order is that of the *Bistami* dervishes, formed in 874A.D. to follow the **Bistami** teaching of Abū-Yazīd al-Bisṭāmī, who died the following **Dervishes** year.

The most famous of all orders is the Mevlevi, founded by Jalāl al-Dīn Rūmī (1207–73), a famous poet from Balkh in Central Asia. Rumi met and learnt from a dervish, Shams al- **Whirling** Dīn of Tabriz, while both were living at Konya in Turkey. **Dervishes** Shortly after the latter's death in 1244, Rumi founded the order famous as the whirling dervishes. In the ceremony of the *sema* they turned rapidly on their left heels, with arms extended. The Turkish Government banned them in 1925, but at the Mevlana Museum in Konya one can still see electric model dervishes turning around.

In 15th-century India, tension between the egalitarian monotheist religion of the conquering Muslims, and the caste **Sikhism** system and pantheon of the Hindu majority, encouraged some teachers to try and break down religious barriers. One of them was Nanak (1469A.D.–1539), a Hindu by birth. He toured India, teaching that the differing ceremonies and books of the various religions are of negligible importance compared to the goodness of the individual. He denied the validity of the caste system and proclaimed the supreme God as the proper object of worship by believers in all religions. His poems, while disparaging the particular usages of Islam, Hinduism and Buddhism, constantly marvel at God.

> If as many people as lived in all the past
> Were now to describe Him each in his own way
> Even then He would not be adequately described.

Nanak's ideas offer believers a humane and workable road out of the morass of conflicting religions. But posterity has turned his campaign into an ironic failure. Instead of overcoming religious dissension, it created a new religion that has usually been violently at odds with Hinduism. The Sikhs

**Guru**    saw themselves as a distinct community under the leadership
of their 'Guru' (teacher) and recognised Nanak as the first
guru.

## 6. FURTHER IDEAS OF DIVINITY

**Agnosticism**
Concerning the gods I cannot say whether they exist or
not, or what they are like in form; for there are many hin-
drances to knowledge: the obscurity of the subject and the
brevity of human life.

This is the judgement of the Greek philosopher Protagoras of
Abdera (485–415B.C.), who is best known for his doctrine
'Man is the measure of all things'. Protagoras was the first
'sophist' – one of a group of teachers who made a point of
charging fees, and thereby incurred the scorn of Socrates and
his followers. This is the only reason Protagoras is not famous
any more.

**Atheism**
The first philosopher whose theory incorporates an outright
denial of the existence of any god is the Greek Diagoras of
Melos. He was a student of the great Democritus of Abdera.
Democritus's atomic theory of the Universe and his scientific
appreciation of destiny may have encouraged Diagoras to
develop atheism. He taught it in Athens, where he was
accused of impiety, and so left, in 411B.C., continuing his
career at Pallene and Corinth.

**Monotheism**
The modern Christian who finishes his prayer with 'amen' is
using the oldest word in our vocabulary to invoke the assent
of the one true God. Amen is the term used by Egyptians in
the mid-4th millennium B.C., the first monotheists, to denote
the one God. The word and the religion were adopted by the
Jews during their residence in Egypt. The Egyptians professed
not to know God's true name, and worshipped him under a
variety of headings.

> Thy beauties seize and carry away all hearts,
> the love of thee maketh the arms to drop,
> thy beautiful deeds make the hands to tremble,
> all hearts melt at the sight of Thee, O Form,
> One, creator of all things, O One, Only, maker of things
> which are.

These are the words of a monotheistic hymn of the 2nd millennium B.C., but less well preserved writings from the 4th

millennium make it clear that the belief in one supreme god had already arisen. The hosts of minor Egyptian gods and goddesses were regarded by these believers merely as creations of the supreme deity, with delegated powers.

Plato (429–347B.C.), the famous Athenian philosopher, was convinced that God is perfectly good – or at least he said he was convinced. But he also observed that most things which happen in our universe are not perfectly good, and therefore it cannot be God who is responsible for what befalls us. In Book II of his *Republic* he makes Socrates argue that it is essential that God be upheld as an example of perfection to man, and this is more important than defending the claim of his omnipotence. Plato did not believe that God could be morally perfect if accountable for all the evil in the world; later thinkers developed the doctrine of Optimism [VII, 4] to urge that He is not only all good but all powerful. Zoroastrianism [VII, 5] is an earlier religion which maintains that God's control exists only insofar as He succeeds in the battle against evil.

**God Not in Control**

> Not even for God are all things possible – for he cannot, even if he wishes, commit suicide . . . nor bestow eternity on mortals or recall the deceased nor cause a man who has lived not to have lived . . . he has no power over what is past save to forget it, and . . . he cannot cause twice ten not to be twenty or do many things on similar lines: which facts undoubtedly demonstrate the power of Nature.

**God Subject to Laws**

These words, from *Natural History* are the views of the Roman scholar Pliny (23A.D.–79), describing the God worshipped by most religions and proclaimed by most philosophers. Pliny's conclusion is that not He, but the power of Nature, is the true God. This true God is not, in his view, a person, so the religious mind would regard Pliny's view as false.

# 7. ARTICLES AND TRAPPINGS OF FAITH

Strange to relate, some of the austerities by which the faithful manifest their devotion to one exacting deity or another have been taken up voluntarily by others for far more secular reasons, and are thus treated in other chapters – including fire walking [IV, 4], pole sitting [X, 4] and gladiatorial combat [X, 4].

**Angels**

Angels entered the cosmic stage as the *devas* of Hinduism in its late Vedic period, in Northern India. They date back probably to the early 1st millennium B.C. They are referred to in Hindu texts of the period, including the *Gita*, *Samkhya* and Patanjali's *Yoga Sutra*.

**The Ten Commandments**

In the 13th century B.C. and three months after their getaway from Egypt, the Jews of the Sinai Peninsula congregated at the foot of Mount Sinai. Moses, their leader, instructed them to stay put while he made excursions up the mountain, alone or with his brother, to receive, in dictation from God, the laws of the Hebrew people. Moses explained that they must not follow, because the thunderous voice and dazzling sight of God would be the death of them. Modern sceptics imagine that Moses was actually hiding away on the mountain while he worked out for himself the contents of the Ten Commandments, and the corpus of laws now recorded in the Bible. If the Commandments are merely the product of a human mind, it must have been an almost divinely gifted mind. To distil the fundamentals of the moral and religious culture of a nation into ten concise commands was an unprecedented breakthrough, requiring inspiration and courage. Moses's natural intelligence seems to have been aided by an Egyptian education, which must have helped him either to compose the Commandments and other laws, or at least to understand what God was imparting.

The first four commandments deal with religion, the remaining six with morality. The Second Commandment is of particular interest:

**Ban on Idolatory**

> Thou shalt not make unto thee a graven image, the likeness of any form that is in heaven above, or that is in earth beneath, or that is in the water under the earth:
> Thou shalt not bow down thyself unto them, nor serve them . . .

This ruling was a nasty setback for the visual arts, but an important development in the history of religion. It is the first prohibition of the worship of idols, and has become a fundamental part of some major modern religions.

**Resurrection**

The first account of anyone coming back to life after death is from a Sumerian myth originating in the 3rd millennium B.C., called by scholars *Inanna's Descent to the Nether World*. Inanna, queen of Heaven in ancient Mesopotamian religion, went to the Underworld in an attempt to enlarge her domains.

Understandably enough, the queen of the Underworld opposed Inanna's plans, and had her killed. Enki, the god of Wisdom, sent helpers from Earth who brought her corpse back to life, but Inanna could only return to Earth under the obligation to provide a substitute to the Underworld. Certain deities approached to fill this role grovelled in the dirt before her, wearing sackcloth, so she let them off. When she reached her husband's town, he was, not unreasonably, on his throne wearing a noble gown. Inanna was not impressed by this failure to grovel, and dispatched him to hell in her place. Not unnaturally, his face turned green, but his demise completes Inanna's successful repatriation.

According to the doctrine of transmigration of souls ('metempsychosis') after death the soul is reborn for another lifetime on Earth – a repetition that may continue through countless lives or end in release from the cycle of rebirth. In ancient India it was incorporated into the beliefs of Hinduism and Buddhism [VII, 5]. However, before that, Indian religion early in the 1st millennium B.C. had no concept of metempsychosis. The idea was probably imported from Greece, where it was invented very early, perhaps the 7th or 8th century B.C. Plato mentions it in a number of his philosophical dialogues, and says that the idea comes from 'tales of the ancients'. **Transmigration of Souls**

The fields of Osiris amongst the stars were the destination of the souls of pious Egyptians after death. There they expected to live with the gods, to eat, drink, plough, reap, be strong and make love. In the 4th millennium B.C. Egyptian priests of Osiris developed the concept of Heaven as the place of reward for eternity for the souls of good men. Others who did not qualify for admission were expected to die a second death after suffering in the land of Tuat. **Heaven**

Tuat was not a hell of eternal damnation underneath the world, merely an inhospitable territory for souls to traverse. The inhabitants of Northern India who practised the Vedic religion [VII, 5] were the first to grasp, around 1500 B.C., the full horror of what Hell is all about: a site of eternal punishment for the souls of bad people, outside the world and underneath it. Their descendants abandoned this belief and replaced it with the Hindu theory that the soul suffers after death by being born into the world again – but the Vedic concept of Hell spread westward, and was ultimately incorporated into Christianity. **Hell**

**The Deluge**

All the windstorms, exceedingly powerful, attacked as one,
At the same time, the flood sweeps over the cult centres.
Afterwards, for seven days and seven nights,
The flood had swept over the land,
And the huge boat had been tossed about by the wind-
storms on the great waters,
Utu came forth, [sun god] who sheds light on Heaven and
Earth,
Ziusudra opened a window on the huge boat,
The hero Utu brought his rays into the giant boat.

(tr. Kramer, modif.)

These lines are part of the earliest story of the deluge, the
same legend that is told in the Bible, where Noah features
instead of Ziusudra. The version quoted here comes from the
Sumerians of Southern Mesopotamia, dating probably from
the 3rd millennium B.C. It is translated from a tablet excavated from the remains of the ancient city of Nippur, probably
written about 2000B.C. Though Noah's flood lasted forty days,
this one was a disappointing seven. The part of the poem
relating to animal passengers has been destroyed, but elsewhere Ziusudra is called 'the preserver of the name of vegetation and of the seed of mankind'.

**Astrology**

Astrology seems to have its beginnings in prehistoric times –
probably in Egypt or Mesopotamia – when people began
watching the heavens as an aid to foretelling events and as a
source of warnings. But modern astrology is more concerned
with discovering a person's fate, fortunes and character from
the position of the celestial bodies at the time of his birth.

**Horoscopes**

This is the working out of horoscopes, which began in Egypt,
seemingly during the Old Kingdom period (c. 3500–c.
2500B.C.). In the Egyptian system every day and month was
sacred to a particular star god; a person's whole life was lived
under the influence of the god in whose times he or she was
born.

**Feng Shui**

In the feng shui ('wind and water') conception, the Earth is the
body of a living spirit, or spirits, who can be pleased, displeased
or wounded by the way people use it. This idea arose early in
China's Warring States Period (481–221B.C.) and is first mentioned in a mystical-political manual from Northeast China,
the *Guarn Dzu* (c. 400B.C.), which speaks of water as the blood
and breath of the Earth. From this conception, a superstitious
belief developed that specialist feng shui geomancers can

divine advantageous and disadvantageous arrangements of works and buildings by reference to their compass points. It is not clear when such divination began to be practised, but it was familiar by the 2nd century B.C.

The first people to discover the baleful gaze of the Evil Eye were the ancient Sumerians of Mesopotamia. Mentions appear amongst their oldest surviving religious documents, and it probably goes back earlier, to the 4th millennium B.C. Ordinary people cannot see the evil eye, but unfortunately for some individuals it can watch them and, in doing so, condemn them to misfortune.

**The Evil Eye**

The problem of house haunting first reared its ugly head in Mesopotamia amongst the ancient Sumerians. It is first referred to in records drawn from the 3rd millennium B.C., but may go back earlier, to the undocumented 4th millennium. According to the Sumerian analysis, spirits on this Earth find dwellings of various kinds, but they like houses best of all. They prefer to haunt unoccupied houses, because there are no residents to put up amulets and charms or call in exorcists.

**Haunted House**

One of the religious duties of members of the Islamic faith is to make the pilgrimage to Mecca, in present-day Saudi Arabia. In the 7th century A.D., Muhammad, the founder of Islam [VII, 5], tried to wipe out the primitive star and idol-worshipping religion of ancient Arabia. Although he was successful in most respects, the pilgrimage was too popular to stop, and he simply made it into part of the new religion. The pilgrimage to Mecca began about twenty-one centuries ago, 700 years before the time of Muhammad, when Mecca, the cultural and religious centre of Arabia, was under the control of the Homerites, a division of the Arabs. At that time, the Homerite ruler began to present, each year, a drape for the holy shrine of Mecca, and worshippers converged on it at a set time from all over the Arabian Peninsula. To this day the temporal ruler donates a new drape every year, and the devout from all over the world meet at the Ka'bah, a small building containing the meteorite that has been venerated since the days of star worship, and which all Muslims face in prayer.

**Pilgrimage to Mecca**

The Ka'bah was nominated as the *kibla*, the principal object of veneration, by the prophet Muhammad, in about 630 A.D.; previously the devout had oriented themselves towards Jerusalem when praying.

**Prayer Facing Mecca**

**Rosary Beads**

Rosary beads are Buddhism's most tangible contribution to Roman Catholic devotion. The *japu mala* (muttering chaplet) was a string of beads used by Indian Buddhists from the 1st century A.D. They proved so successful that Muslims later adopted them, and spread the invention to the bounds of Christendom and the enthusiastic attention of the Roman Church.

# VIII
# SCIENCE AND
# TECHNOLOGY

Most human activity involves technology one way or another. As a result, information about technology in various applications is distributed through all chapters except Chapter VII. Even in prehistoric times there was a lot of technological development, though most of it left too little evidence to be pinpointed now.

Wherever there are people there is technology; Science on the other hand is rare. Most people do not participate, and large, sometimes complex societies can get by with none at all. Although it still had science education, the ancient Western World after the Roman takeover was nearly devoid of creative Science. Russia was without sciences until the late 1600s, but it didn't prevent the Russians constructing a large durable empire and spreading civilisation. To become established in a society, Science depends on the far-sightedness of people who control resources and lead public opinion. Such people are true visionaries; a few, like Peter the Great, are recent and known by name, but the most remarkable are the first sponsors of Science in very ancient societies, who had no foreign examples for inspiration.

Where and when Science started are controversial questions. Many careful scholars would deny the view taken here, that it began in Egypt about 5000 years ago. In Mesopotamia, mathematics and astronomy became far more scientific than the Egyptians ever made them, which promotes doubts about Egypt's priority. However, well before the Mesopotamians produced any extant evidence of scientific work, Egypt supported an institution called the House of Life, where knowledge was cultivated for its own sake. Egyptians recorded data, wrote now lost works on subjects that called for scientific treatment and had a highly specialised medical profession. Medicine in Egypt was probably the world's first fully fledged science, seconded most likely by biology, or botany at least. The powerful aristocrat, Imhotep, who was also a doctor and architect, and his pharaoh, Khufu, who reigned about 5000 years ago, may well be two of Science's first visionary patrons.

## 1. MATHEMATICS AND PHYSICS

Physics overlaps with philosophy and theology, and some firsts have been recorded in Chapter VII, section 4.

**Place Value Notation**   Place value numbers in which each digit stands for units, tens, hundreds and so on – depending where it is placed in the sequence – now seem completely natural. It is surprising to consider that number systems – such as Roman numerals – which operate independently of place value, were once the norm. Place value numbering began in Mesopotamia early in the 2nd millennium B.C. In the cuneiform numerals of that time, the last digit represents units, indicated by vertical impressions of the writing stylus. The digit next to it, rendered in horizontal impressions, enumerates the tens. But instead of using the next position for hundreds, Mesopotamian scribes reserved it for sixties, again shown with vertical impressions.

**Sexagesimal Numeration**   Their numeration combined the decimal system with the base sixty system – a Mesopotamian invention that has numbers going up by the power of sixty instead of the power of ten. It is still in wide use as degrees, minutes and seconds. Chaldaean scientists favoured sixty as a base because it is divisible by eleven smaller numbers.

**Decimal Notation**   The first evidence of a fully decimal place value system is on bone inscriptions from the Sharng Dynasty in North China, around the 14th century B.C. In contrast to the Mesopotamians, the Chinese made their third digit from the end the enumerator of hundreds, as we do in the Arabic system. However, like the Mesopotamians, who alternated between vertical and horizontal, the Chinese modified their characters to show which position they belong in. For example, in the number four hundred, four has a triangle in a loop attached, indicating hundreds. Such methods countered the ambiguity resulting from not having any nought symbol to occupy the vacant positions.

**Nought Symbol**   A nought was devised early in the 1st millennium B.C. by Chaldaean scientists. They used a solid circle • until about 300 B.C. when a vacant circle, O, was adopted. However they only used it in the sexagesimal system.

The nought symbol for decimal numeration was developed

much later, in Cambodia and Sumatra. Stone inscriptions in both locations mark the year 683A.D. as year 605 in the Indian Saka era. In each case ௧•౿ means 605, the circle in the middle being nought. A hollow nought like the one used now was inscribed three years later on nearby Banka Island to mark the 608th year (686A.D.). **Decimal Nought**

Unlike the base ten system which has ten number characters, or the Mesopotamian sexagesimal numeration, binary numeration employs only nought and the number one. 1, 10, 11, 100 and 101 equal one, two, three, four and five. Binary numbers have been widely used in recent times with computers, but the Chinese philosopher Shao Yung developed them first, in support of his belief that everything is organised numerically. In *The Book of the Supreme Principle Controlling the World* (c. 1060A.D.) he included the sixty-four famous hexagrams of the *I Ching*. They are made up of all the combinations of the eight trigrams: see the illustration with yin and yang [VIII, 4]. The hexagrams are popular nowadays for telling the future, but Shao changed their order around so that hexagram two came first, followed by twenty-three, eight, twenty, sixteen and so on. **Binary Numeration**

| 2 | 23 | 8 | 20 | 16 |

Reading a broken line as nought and a continuous line as one, this makes 000001, 000010, 000011, 000100 and 000101 – one to five in binary notation. The remaining hexagrams are then listed in binary numerical order. Leibniz, the German philosopher who introduced binary numeration to Europe in 1673, believed the system had been worked out by Fu Hsi, a Chinese leader of the 3rd millennium B.C. But although Fu Hsi has been credited with inventing the eight trigrams it is unlikely he understood binary numeration.

Pi, represented by the Greek letter of the same name, $\pi$, is a number defined as the ratio of the circumference (or perimeter) of a circle to one diameter of the circle: in other words, the number of times the diameter goes into the circumference. It is essential to mathematicians and draftsmen for calculating the circumference and area of circles and the volume of spheres, amongst other things. It is also impossible to state **Value of Pi**

correctly. Books ancient and modern give many different figures. Three and a half thousand years ago, Babylonian mathematicians estimated it at 3⅛, which is close but wrong.

**3⅐ for Pi**  An important positive step was taken when Archimedes
of Syracuse – more famous for his screw and his principle [see
below and VIII, 11] – adopted the method of devising
straight-sided polygons inside and outside a circle to approximate the value of pi. In the 3rd century B.C. he went up to a
96-side polygon as the basis for his famous approximation, 3⅐,
which is now used most often.

**3.14159 for Pi**  3.14159, the figure normally used by geometricians, was
first reached by China's Liu Hsia in the 3rd century A.D. His
biggest polygon had 3072 equal sides.

**Accurate**  But the first to get really close was Dsu Chung Jir in the 5th
**Range**  century. To begin with he offered two values – 3⅐ for inaccurate
work and ³⁵⁵/₁₁₃ for accurate computations. Later he established
that pi lies somewhere between 3.1415926 and 3.1415927. The
reader will see that new decimal places were not won quickly or
easily. Perhaps then he will spare a sympathetic thought for the
dedicated mathematician William Shanks who in 1835 produced a valuation to 707 decimal positions, unaware that his
last one hundred were wrong. (20th-century computations have
subsequently engendered myriads of decimal places.)

**Proof of Pi's**  For a long time no one could tell whether it was ulti-
**Transcendency**  mately possible to nail $\pi$ down with precision. It was James
Gregory, a Scottish professor working in Italy at the Univer-
sity of Padua who proved the transcendence of $\pi$ in 1668
(proved, in other words that the quadrature of a circle cannot
be exactly and finitely performed with the aid of $\pi$).

**Decimal**  The decimal place value system pioneered by the Chinese,
**Fractions**  and which is used everywhere today, extends naturally to represent numbers less than one, or with parts less than one, by
the decimal point system. The units enumerator in the number is followed by another digit enumerating tenths, another,
hundreds, and so on. It was introduced by Yarng Huei with his
maths book, *Yarng Huei's Computing Methods*, published
around 1275A.D.

**Square Roots**  A Chinese maths book from the Harn Dynasty (206B.C.–
220A.D.) contains the first description of a dependable
method for extracting square roots. The book is *Nine Chapters
on Mathematics*, by a forgotten author, published in the 2nd
century B.C.

Early Chinese works are silent on the question of square roots of negative numbers, which were first recognised by Indian mathematicians of the Gupta Period (320A.D.–647). Babylonian maths tables [see below] dating from about 1800B.C. include square roots, but these may have been discovered by multiplying up trial roots rather than by extraction.

**Roots of Negatives**

Hsew Yaw's book, the *Account of Some Traditions of Mathematical Practice* of 190A.D., describes the 'great unity' system of plotting numbers graphically, taught to the author by Tien Mu Hsien Seng, who had also described the abacus [VIII, 10] to him. The great unity is a graph on which the X axis (the horizontal one) is graded in powers of ten, that is, units, tens, hundreds, thousands, myriads etc. The Y or vertical axis is graded in units from one to nine. Thus in this precursor of Cartesian arithmetic, every number can be represented graphically by moving counters along the nine horizontal lines running from the Y axis.

**Plotting on Coordinates**

The oldest maths tables come from Nippur in Mesopotamia, on clay tablets dating from about 1800B.C., in the time of the Old Babylonian Empire. The tables, recovered by archaeologists, are specimens of what must in their time have been a very recent development. They were produced for use in schools, and cover multiplication, division, squares, cubes and square and cube roots.

**Maths Tables**

The *Orbit and Gnomon Mathematical Text* compiled during China's Jo Dynasty (11th to 3rd centuries B.C.) is the oldest maths textbook, dating back probably to around the 6th century B.C. Because there is now only a later version, the Harn Dynasty (206B.C.–220A.D.) edition, the age of the contents is unknown. It contains a lot of astronomical material, some division and multiplication of fractions, and a chapter on Pythagoras's Theorem, and correctly identifies moonlight [VIII, 2] as reflected sunlight.

**Maths Book**

The first book of maths problems is *Nine Chapters on Mathematics*, written anonymously early in the Harn Dynasty. This book contains the first statement of the theory of percentages and also of negative numbers. Algebra and quadratic equations are also found in it. The use of negative numbers in Chinese mathematics probably goes back to a time shortly before the Harn Dynasty. Counting rod sets of uncertain antiquity included red rods to signify positive numbers and black rods for negatives.

**Maths Problem Book**

**Percentages**

**Negative Numbers**

**Definitions:**
**Point**
**Line**
**Plane**

**Three-**
**dimensional**
**Universe**

The *Maw Jing* ('Maw's Classic'), a Chinese book of philosophy and analytics was written in the 5th century B.C. by followers of Maw Dzu and extended in the following century by members of his school. From these people comes the earliest definition of *point*, in the geometric or scientific sense: 'part of a line not having any length'. The same book also furnishes definitions of *line* and *plane*, in each case the oldest known. In doing so it gives the first analysis of the three dimensions of which the universe is built.

**Pythagoras's**
**Theorem**

Mesopotamian mathematical texts dating back to the Old Babylonian Period (c. 2050–c. 1650B.C.) contain material relating to the solution of problems that make it clear that Pythagoras's Theorem was by then understood. There is no express statement of the theorem – that the square on the hypotenuse equals the sum of the squares on the other two sides – until over a thousand years later, but this is probably due to the incomplete state of the records.

**Trigonometry**

Trigonometry was developed by Greek scientists in the 2nd century B.C. Foremost amongst these is Hipparchus (195–125B.C.), who worked at the Museum in Alexandria, and at Rhodes. Hipparchus was primarily an astronomer, and he drew up a table of chords to assist in plotting stars. Trigonometry as we have it today is the work of Islamic scientists in the 9th century A.D. Abū 'Abdallāh al-Battānī and Ḥabash al-Ḥāsib knew the tangent, sine, cotangent and cosine. The secant was introduced by Abu'l-Wafā' al-Buzjānī.

**Logarithms**

Before logarithms were given any general application, there were mathematicians who examined or understood the principle behind them, including Archimedes in the 3rd century B.C., and Ibn Ḥamzah al-Maghrībī of North Africa, in the 16th century A.D. However the first limited use of a logarithm is earlier revealed in Mesopotamian cuneiform texts which probably record mathematical practice of the early 2nd millennium B.C. In dealing with the exponents of given numbers the Mesopotamians had logarithms of special cases. From their time to the 16th century A.D., mathematicians occasionally touched on logarithms without building them into a general system of calculation. The Scottish scholar, John Napier of Merchistoun (1550A.D.–1617), was the first to do that, in his book *Mirifica Logarithmorum Canonis Descriptio* (*Description of the Marvellous Canon of Logarithms*, Edinburgh, 1614).

In the 10th century A.D. (Sung Dynasty), Ma Huai De of Su Jo made an instrument described as a set of ebony rulers, with one ivory one which were positioned in relation to one another to aid calculation. The method of operation and the result to be calculated are unknown. **Slide Rule**

The earliest logarithmic slide rules were made in England, probably just before 1650 by William Oughtred. Oughtred made circular as well as straight slide rules. **Logarithmic Slide Rule**

The earliest magic square puzzle is called *haw tu* in Chinese and is three numbers deep by three numbers across. By adding any three numbers in a row, up, down, back, forth or diagonally, an answer of fifteen is obtained, and every number from one to nine is contained in the square. **Magic Square**

| 4 | 9 | 2 |
|---|---|---|
| 3 | 5 | 7 |
| 8 | 1 | 6 |

The oldest specifications for this puzzle date from about 80 B.C., but its invention goes back much earlier. One legend says that a dragon horse came out of the Yellow River and gave the haw tu to Yew, ruler of China in about 2100 B.C. Yew is a historical figure, the dragon horse perhaps not. Also it isn't certain that Yew's haw tu was the one shown here, since mathematics must have been rather primitive in his time.

Algebra was developed by the Babylonians and appears to date back to the days of the Old Babylonian Empire (c. 2050–c. 1650 B.C.). They used it in linear equations and in quadratic equations, which they invented at about the same time. However the use of algebra together with quadratic equations may have arisen later than the invention of either. In the algebraic quadratic equations which have been recovered from after 300 B.C., the unknown quantities are what we would call $x$ and its reciprocal $1/x$. However, for all their mathematical ingenuity, the Babylonians never developed such a convenient notation, and always used words to stand for the unknown numbers. **Algebra**

**Quadratic Equations**

Adversaries have never fought with more tenacity and acrimony, for the honour of a first, than Sir Isaac Newton and **Calculus**

Gottfried Wilhelm von Leibniz. The Englishman and the German contested each other's invention of calculus – their revolutionary method for squaring the area under a curve – the main mathematical breakthrough of modern times. The glory that the discovery shines on their divine intellects is matched by the disgrace that the ugly dispute smears over their human characters. Beginning in the 1690s – with Newton's private carping about the theft of his invention – the squabble surfaced in 1711 and raged till Leibniz died in 1716. Newton (1642–1727) and his disciples went on campaigning after that, wasting more effort condemning Leibniz than both had spent developing calculus in the first place. In 1684 Leibniz had published *Calculus Differentialis*, intimating that his method was otherwise unknown, even though in 1676 he had read papers by Newton that proved Newton's awareness. Newton's party publicised Leibniz's acquaintance with these documents and accused Leibniz of theft. Leibniz then deceitfully maintained that in 1684 he had been unaware of Newton's knowledge. He wrote and circulated anonymous reviews and papers implying that Newton had copied his work. Newton used his disciples to denounce Leibniz, especially the venomous mathematician John Keill. Like Keill, Leibniz belonged to Britain's Royal Society, and in 1711 he asked the Society to investigate Keill's allegations and determine the truth. Newton, the Society's president, ran its rigged enquiry and prepared a dishonest official report repudiating Leibniz. Newton had invented calculus, which he called the method of fluxions, in 1665–66. He kept the discovery to himself, leaving written evidence that proves he knew it, without explaining how it works. Leibniz did not work it out until ten years later, but already knew it before he examined Newton's papers in 1676, which clears him of Newton's accusation of theft. The world owes its knowledge of calculus to Leibniz, whose publication in 1684 explained the method in full. Leibniz's system was also somewhat more polished than Newton's. However that does not concern *Whose Bright Idea Was That?*, which must record Newton as the first inventor of calculus. Leibniz still has a place in the book as the philosophical exponent of optimism, [VII, 2].

**Archimedes's Principle**

Some people say that Archimedes (287–212B.C.), the famous Greek scientist, was getting into the bath at the same time as his mind was busy with the problem of weight and displacement. As he watched the water rise in the tub, the solution dawned on him. Thrilled with his new discovery, he ran down the streets of Syracuse, yelling 'eureka' and dripping water and soap [XI, 3]. One difficulty with this version is that the Greeks normally washed with oil rather than soap. Also, specific gravity is a fairly prosaic thing to make such a performance over. Whatever the circumstances, credit is undoubtedly due to Archimedes for what is now called Archimedes's Principle. It was first published as 'proposition no. 7' in his book *Floating Bodies* (Syracuse, 3rd century B.C.): 'Solids heavier than the fluid will if placed in the fluid . . . be lighter in the fluid by the weight of the amount of fluid that has the same volume as the solid.'

Sir Isaac Newton (1642A.D.–1727) brought together all three of the laws named after him, and established them as the scientific basis for the study of motion, at the beginning of his book *Philosophiae Naturalis Principia Mathematica* (1687). This is the most famous of many contributions by the great British scientist to the field of physics. **Newton's Laws of Motion**

Each law had previously been stated separately by others. Newton's first law is: 'Every body continues in its state of rest or of uniform motion in a right line unless compelled to change that state by forces impressed upon it.' Its oldest recitation is in a Chinese book completed about 300B.C., called the *Maw Jing*. This work is an account of the views of the philosopher Maw Dzu, together with philosophical and scientific definitions, and propositions worked out by Maw's anonymous followers, of which this law is part. **First Law**

Between the time of Maw and Newton's immediate predecessors, the first law was recognisably stated a number of times. However the first scientists to adopt the second and third laws did not propound them explicitly in the same language as Newton. The great Italian physicist, Galileo Galilei (1564A.D.–1642) used the second law: that the change of motion is proportional to the impressed force and takes place in the direction of the straight line in which the force acts. **Second Law**

In the 1660s the Dutch scientist Christiaan Huygens Van Zuylichem (1629–93) knew the third law: 'to every action there is an equal and contrary reaction', as did Englishman Sir Christopher Wren (1632–1723), who incorporated it in a paper read in 1668. **Third Law**

That something makes heavy objects drop is a principle which any caveman could confidently assert. The first major step in a more scientific understanding of gravity was the realisation **Concept of Gravity** that it is a force drawing everything towards the centre of the Earth, so that the paths followed by falling bodies are not parallel, but convergent. Aristotle stated it explicitly in the 4th **Gravity Draws** century B.C. in his book *The Heavens*, and included it **to the Centre** amongst his proofs of the Earth's roundness [VIII, 2]. In the 6th century B.C., Pythagoras, who believed in life on the opposite side of the Earth, was well aware of the principle, as the Chaldaean scientists may have been before 600.

Second, light objects and dense ones drop at the same **Gravity Draws** speed except in so far as the medium in which they travel **Objects at** buoys them up or resists their motion. 'All things, though **Equal Speed** their weights may differ, drive through unresisting void... with the same speed', writes the Roman poet Lucretius (born 94B.C.). It is not clear whether the proposition was first advanced by Epicurus in the 4th century B.C., or Democritus and Leucippus in the 5th.

Sir Isaac Newton concluded that two bodies attract each **Law of** other with a force proportional to the product of their masses **Universal** and inversely proportional to the square of the distance **Gravitation** between them. He set out the principle fully in his book *Philosophiae Naturalis Principia Mathematica* (1687), but it is said to have struck him first in 1665 at his garden in Woolsthorpe, England, when an apple fell out of a tree on to his head. (The less precise conclusion that the attraction between two bodies increases, as their mass increases and the distance between them decreases, had been drawn by Islamic physicists around 1000A.D.)

Ancient Greek physicists envisaged that atoms have compo- **Discovery of** nents without dimensions, but said nothing of their behaviour **Atomic** and position. The modern understanding of atoms – as small **Structure** positively charged nuclei orbited by small numbers of electrons – was made possible by the work of a number of scientists in the 1890s and the present century. Of these, the first to arrive at this description of the atom was Ernest Rutherford (1871–1937), a New Zealander working in England. Rutherford and his colleagues began working towards his analysis in 1908; he announced it in May 1911 to the Manchester Literary and Philosophical Society.

Much earlier, the founders of the theory of atoms [VII, 4] **Splitting of the** had conceived of them as indivisible. The Greek philosopher **Atom** Carneades (213–128B.C.), working in Athens, was the first to assert the contrary view. Carneades considered that in theory at least there is no atom which cannot be split. In 1917

Rutherford became the first to split atoms deliberately and artificially. He bombarded nitrogen atoms with alpha particles, knocking protons out of the nuclei. He revealed his results to the scientific community in 1919. Although he had indeed split atoms, many people do not consider his experiment to have been the splitting of the atom, because by that term they mean nuclear fission, with a net release of energy, and the potential to sustain a chain reaction. This is possible with uranium atoms, but not nitrogen.

In Italy in the 1930s Italian physicist Enrico Fermi (1901–54) experimented with bombarding atoms of uranium and other heavy elements with neutrons in an endeavour to create new, heavier elements. This must have caused atomic fission, though Professor Fermi's team was apparently unaware of it when it first occurred. First to make a sure identification of the phenomenon were Austrian-born physicists, Lise Meitner and Otto Frisch, in Sweden in 1939. Otto Hahn had split uranium atoms in 1938 in Germany but cautiously refrained from concluding that he had achieved nuclear fission. Meitner had been working under Hahn at the time, but only after she fled Germany and teamed up with Frisch was she able to confirm that fission had taken place.

**Nuclear Fission**

Quantum physics is based on the notion that certain phenomena at the minutest levels cannot occur in an even progression – the way observable phenomena appear to – but only in whole increments known as 'quanta'. In the 4th century B.C. the Greek philosopher Epicurus described a type of motion at atomic level unlike familiar kinetic motion. He called it the 'atomic swerve': the sporadic instantaneous hopping of a particle from its course by a minimum fixed interval, the *elachiston*. He contrasted his swerve with motion that occurs directly in response to gravitation or collision: what modern commentators call billiard ball motion or Newtonian mechanics.

**Quantum Mechanics**

The swerve is the only case of quantum physics in the Epicurean system. But about 600 years later the Indian Jain philosophers reduced all material phenomena to quantum phenomena. This was the necessary result of their atomic theory of time [VII, 4] which conceives of time as a series of quanta. Modern Western investigators – because they did not explain quantum leaps by reference to atomised time – erected quantum physics plank by plank, as each one

**General Theory of Quantum Physics**

accounted for certain manifestations. In the 1890s German physicist Max Karl Ernst Ludwig Planck (1858–1947) observed that the intensity of radiation doesn't go on rising with shorter wavelengths, as traditional theory had forecast. In 1900 he advanced the explanation that energy in radiation is emitted in fixed quanta, the quantum value depending on the frequency of oscillation. First to extend the analysis to the structure of atoms was Danish scientist, Niels Bohr, in 1913. Bohr proposed that electron motion can only hop instantaneously from one level to another, rather than responding progressively to an influence.

**Uncertainty Principle** The all-or-nothing character of quantum phenomena means the behaviour of individual components cannot be forecast by reference to known laws. It is like trying to pick the result of a soccer game by weighing minute differences in competence between the teams, when all along the outcome can only be expressed in entire goals. In 1927 the German physicist, Werner Heisenberg (1901–76), introduced the Uncertainty Principle, defining this unpredictability. He pointed out that in relation to a sub-atomic component, the more precisely one measures one pair of physical quantities – position/momentum – the more uncertain becomes the other pair – energy/time – and vice versa. The small scale and vast number of quantised phenomena mean that the workings of probability cause large-scale phenomena to appear to comply rigorously with the laws of traditional physics. However, uncertainty at the minutest levels has led some to deny the rigorous link between cause and effect and to postulate that chance or some foreign factor is involved in material phenomena. In modern science this is a 20th-century innovation, but Epicurus had already envisaged the atomic swerve as an unpredictable phenomenon, because it occurs independently of external physical cause. Epicurus accepted the view of the atomists, Leucippus and Democritus, that all phenomena are material – even will and imagination. But he also believed in free will, and did not accept that it can operate if all phenomena are preordained by their compliance with the laws of mechanistic physics. Because the swerve occurs independent of external cause, it provides the physical explanation for Epicurus's antideterminism [VII, 4]. 'Epicurus thinks that the necessity of fate is avoided by the swerve of the atom', wrote the Roman commentator Cicero, but 'Democritus preferred to accept the view that all events are caused by necessity rather than to deprive the atoms of their natural motions.' The controversy described by Cicero was reincarnated after twenty-three centuries, in the disagreement between Albert Einstein and the quantum physicists. 'He does not play at dice', Einstein protested.

In 1905, Albert Einstein (1879–1955) was an obscure German-born Jew living in Switzerland. Obscurity suddenly **Relativity** ended that year when he published five important scientific papers. Amongst these was one expounding what is now known as the Special Theory of Relativity, encapsulating two fundamental assumptions: that the laws followed by observable phenomena are the same in all systems irrespective of their velocity, and that the observable velocity of light is constant, irrespective of the motion of its source and its observer. The theory led him in 1907 to his famous conclusion that energy equals mass times the velocity of light, squared: $E = mc^2$.

The Special Theory of Relativity is not equal to the task of analysing phenomena produced by accelerated motion, including those on which gravity operates. To encompass **General** these Einstein developed the General Theory of Relativity, **Theory of** completed in 1915 and published in 1916 in his *Die Grundlage* **Relativity** *der Allgemeinen Relativitätstheorie*.

The basic propositions of optics were developed almost simultaneously in the East and West. The original Chinese exposition **Optics** is in the *Maw Jing*, a collection of scientific and philosophical writings put together by members of the Mohist school in North China in the 400s and 300s B.C. Amongst other optical properties they knew about the motion of light in straight lines, focal points and the reason for inversion of images, reflection as the essence of visibility, angles of reflection and the conic shape of light-generated forms. Most of this knowledge is also presented in *Optics* by the Greek scientist Euclid of Alexandria, who lived mainly in the 200s B.C. By the time *Optics* was written, the *Maw Jing* was probably complete, so the Chinese take first place.

Euclid's *Optics*, however, includes the first scientific explan- **Analysis of** ation of perspective – a phenomenon already taken into account **Perspective** by artists who used vanishing point perspective [II, 1].

When these early studies were conducted the only lenses were simple bi-convex types used as burning and magnifying **Analysis of** glasses [XI, 2]; consequently ancient optics left out the proper **Lenses** analysis of lenses. That first came around 940A.D. when *The Book of Transformations* (*Hua Shir*), attributed to Tarn Chiao, was published, explaining the optical phenomena of the four types of lenses – bi-convex, bi-concave, plano-convex and plano-concave. The next important development was the use of lenses in combination, the practical step behind the invention of the telescope [VIII, 10].

## 2. ASTRONOMY

From its early days astronomy was used to improve the measurement of time [IV, 3] and to support astrology [VII, 7].

**Astronomy**

The science of astronomy began in China before it began in the West. This is surprising because in most other respects Chinese culture that long ago was more primitive than the leading Western cultures (in Mesopotamia and Egypt). Around 2700B.C., Chinese astronomers began to take and record specific observations of the heavens. They divided the firmament into twenty-eight sections, observing the constellations in each; they recorded the culminations of stars for each, at the equinoxes and solstices; established a Pole Star, and looked for regular patterns in the movement of Sun, Moon and stars. According to tradition, which cannot be verified, the founding work was done by 'star officials' during the reign of the ruler Huarng Di.

**Year Measurement**

Mesopotamian astronomer Kidinnu of Sippar, who worked around 300B.C., measured the year as 365 days, five hours, forty one minutes and 4.16 seconds. Modern astronomers think he must have been out by a few minutes, but his accuracy cannot be precisely measured because we no longer know what year the calculation was made in (despite our personal experiences, scientists believe that as time goes on the years are getting longer). Previous calculations had been out by over an hour.

**Month Measurement**

Hipparchus (195–125B.C.), the Greek astronomer who pioneered trigonometry [VIII, 1], was also the first to determine the precise length of a lunar month. He worked at Rhodes and Alexandria in the 2nd century B.C. His computation of the length of a month was accurate to within one second.

**Speed Measurement of Celestial Bodies**

In the 1st millennium B.C. the Babylonians worked out, from their observations of the Sun and Moon, the varying speed of these two bodies relative to the Earth. The oldest extant tables recording these speed variations are on cuneiform tablets of about 250B.C. – but the first observations probably go back well before that, to the early centuries of the 1st millennium.

It seems that Mesopotamian astronomers began predicting eclipses during the days of the Assyrian Empire – around 800B.C. Their efforts were important in the battle of science against superstition, because to the superstitious, eclipses are a sign from Heaven of dissatisfaction or disaster. If the astronomers could show that they occur only due to pre-dictable motions of the Sun and Moon, they would undermine the basis of the superstition. It is not known when their fore-casts were first successful. They kept complete eclipse records from at least as early as the mid-8th century B.C. and by 300B.C., long after the demise of Assyria, they were predicting eclipses of the Moon with confidence and accuracy. They were not so good with the Sun – there is, for instance, a report from the Assyrian State Astronomer in the 7th century B.C., that a watch was kept for three days for a solar eclipse that was meant to take place, but that nothing happened.

**Eclipse Predictions**

The Greek explorer, Pytheas of Massilia in Gaul (present-day Marseilles), whose great voyage of c. 300B.C. took him north towards the Arctic pack ice [see Discovery of Iceland, IX, 4], took observations of the Sun in latitudes of the mid-60s° North, which led to the conclusion that in high lati-tudes the sun shines twenty-four hours a day during summer, and never during winter. The result, as the Greeks described it, is nights and days each six months long, at the North and South Poles.

**Polar Night and Day**

Kidinnu, the Mesopotamian astronomer who measured the length of the year [see above] was also the first to detect the phenomenon of the precession of equinoxes. Kidinnu worked at Sippar, one of Mesopotamia's three pre-eminent astronomi-cal schools, around 300B.C. Before his discovery the equinox was assumed to be fixed from year to year.

**Precession of Equinoxes**

The Greek philosopher Pythagoras of Samos (6th century B.C.), founder of the Pythagorean School, was the first to claim that the Earth is a globe. He even believed that there were people living at the *antipodes* – opposite his feet – and that his up was down for them. Previously Mesopotamian sci-entists had discovered that the Earth's surface is globally curved, but for unknown reasons they assumed it was cut off at the bottom so as to resemble an upturned brandy balloon or an egg with the end chopped off.

**Round Earth Theory**

The Mesopotamian astronomers were the first to realise

**Round Moon Theory** that the Moon is like a ball rather than a disc. Their view probably goes back to early in the 1st millennium B.C. It was explained to the Greek world by the Babylonian scientist Berossus (about 300B.C.), who passed on many of the achievements of Mesopotamian science. He conceived of the Moon as being half illuminated, and half dark, except during eclipses.

**Moonlight** Early in the 5th century B.C. several Greek cosmologists pointed out that the Moon has no light of her own, but shines with light reflected from the Sun – they include Anaxagoras of Clazomenae (500–428B.C.), Empedocles of Acragas (c. 495–c. 435B.C.) and their older contemporary, Parmenides of Elea. The earliest Chinese explanation of this fact is in the first maths book [VIII, 1], the *Orbit and Gnomon Mathematical Text*, which is thought to be more recent than the Greek exponents. In fact, though, it could have been written as early as 600B.C., which would make it the world's oldest exposition of the idea.

**Rotation of the Earth** After the Earth's sphericity was accepted, people still thought that it remains fixed, with the Universe whirling around it. But, in Syracuse (Sicily) in the 5th century B.C., some Greek followers of Pythagoras, including Hicetas and Ecphantus, developed the idea that the Earth rotates on its own axis once every twenty-four hours. In the 3rd century B.C., Aristarchus, a Greek from Samos, went further and

**Heliocentrism** claimed that the Earth, and other bodies, revolve around the Sun. Aristarchus believed that what we call the fixed stars are incomparably more distant than our sun; that all the bodies in our solar system are relatively close to the Sun, and make oblique annular revolutions. According to one Greek com-

**The Solar System** mentator, Plutarch, Aristarchus proposed the concept, but it was not proved till the next century, by the astronomer Seleucus. In fact it is only true in a subjective way and can never be proved, but Seleucus must have reconciled it with various observable phenomena.

**Galactic Shape and Rotation** The Milky Way galaxy – the huge group of stars of which the Earth is part – is believed to consist of spirally curved arms radiating from a core. The discovery of its shape and rotational motion was made progressively in the first three years of the 1950s by a joint programme of radio astronomy in the Netherlands and Australia. In 1951 the Dutch astronomer Jan Hendrik Oort and his collaborators constructed the first map of the Milky Way from detailed observations compiled in both countries.

The celestial globe, used in Astronomy to identify the posi- **Celestial** tion of stars, was invented by the Greek philosopher, Anax- **Globe** imander (610–c. 530B.C.) of Miletus in present-day Turkey.

In the 4th century B.C. a group of scientists in Northern China began to determine the exact position of stars by plot- **Stars Plotted** ting them on coordinates parallel to and at right angles to **on Equatorial** the Equator. Shir Shen, Garn De and Wu Hsien used degrees **Coordinates** and fractions of degrees to specify the positions of 283 constellations and a total of 1565 individual stars. To ascertain the positions with such exactitude they made the first use of the armillary sphere, a sophisticated instrument of astro- **Armillary** nomical observation, which enables positions to be taken in **Sphere** degrees.

Early in the 8th century A.D. China's government astronomer was an energetic official named Narn Gung Yueh who spent **The Southern** lavishly to widen astronomical knowledge. He established **Skies** observation stations in a north–south line 4000 km. long, to measure the length of a degree at the Earth's surface. In 724A.D. with the astronomer Yi Hsing (maker of the first clock [VIII, 10]), Narn Gung Yueh organised a nautical scientific mission that travelled to the waters north of Australia to take detailed observations of the Southern skies. The expedition discovered hundreds of previously unknown stars, especially in the region 20° North of the South Pole.

The only planets known to ancient astronomers were the six which are visible to the naked eye: the Earth, Mercury, Venus, **The Planets** Mars, Saturn and Jupiter.

In February 1656, the Dutch scientist Christiaan Huygens van Zuylichem (1629–93) hypothesised that there are rings **Saturn's Rings** around Saturn. He wanted to have credit for working it out first, without giving the clues to anyone else or committing himself prematurely. So in his *De Saturni Luna Observatio Nova*, published in The Hague that March, he included an anagram stating his findings, which seems to have escaped notice completely at the time.

In 1780 a German organist and music teacher, carrying out observations by telescope at Bath, England, identified **Uranus** what he first thought was a previously unknown comet. This discoverer, William Herschel (1738–1822), later established that what he had seen was the hitherto unknown planet Uranus. Herschel, helped by another outstanding astronomer, his sister Caroline, went on to discover six moons of Uranus, and a string of other celestial phenomena.

**Neptune**  The planet Neptune is so very far away, and so pale viewed through powerful telescopes, that few astrologers concede it any important influence. Its discovery, although it may not have affected anyone much, is a remarkable achievement for which credit is due to the English mathematician, John Couch Adams. He discovered Neptune by following the clue of irregularities in the motion of Uranus, the next most distant planet. In 1841 he rightly surmised that these can only be explained by the presence of a more distant planet. In October 1844 he deposited with the Astronomer Royal, at Greenwich Observatory, his computations on the location of Neptune; but he took no steps to publish them. (The French astronomer, Leverrier, published similar findings in November 1845, based on his own work that year.)

**Pluto**  Pluto – most distant of our known planets – was discovered as a result of observations of Uranus by American astronomer, Percival Lowell (1855–1916). Lowell established an observatory at Flagstaff, Arizona, and between 1893 and 1897 detected perturbations in Uranus's orbit, which he did not believe are adequately explained by the presence of Neptune. From these results he calculated the position of the ninth planet – 'Planet X' – but he never succeeded in sighting it. After Lowell's death, and on the eve of his seventy-fifth birthday, Pluto, as it is now known, was first observed by Clyde Tombaugh, an astronomer working at Flagstaff. Because it is very dim, Tombaugh, like Lowell, could not spot it through telescopes. He implemented an alternative method of minute comparisons of photos taken on succeeding days, and found Pluto that way in March 1930.

**Comet**  The earliest sighting of a comet on record was in Mesopotamia in about 1140B.C. The oldest sighting which can be clearly identified with Halley's Comet is an observation of 240B.C.
**Halley's**  taken in China. The British astronomer, Edmond Halley
**Comet**  (1656–1742), who saw the comet in 1682, was the first to recognise that it would keep returning at seventy-six-year inter-
**Periodicity of**  vals. His prediction was published in 1705 in his *Synopsis*
**Comets**  *Astronomiae Cometicae*. Over 2000 years earlier, Chaldaean scientists in Mesopotamia had come to the view that, like planets, comets have annular revolutions and fixed periods. The Roman philosopher, Seneca (died 65A.D.), accepted this and accounted for their behaviour by the great eccentricity of their orbits.

On 23 January 1995, two amateur astronomers in the United States were separately studying the sky at the same time. Almost simultaneously Alan Hale and Thomas Bopp reported an unknown comet, since christened the Hale-Bopp Comet. It became visible to the naked eye in 1996 and very conspicuous in 1997. It then disappeared for 2300 years, allegedly taking passengers to another dimension; members of America's Heaven's Gate cult killed themselves in order to join it. The same comet probably visited in about 2000B.C., but no identification from records of that time has been ascertained.

**Hale-Bopp Comet**

A guest star does not belong to the regular cast, but makes a temporary appearance in a prominent role. These days the term is mainly used on television, but the scientists who coined it in 1054A.D. were only watching the sky – over the Sung Dynasty capital Kaifeng. They identified there a guest star, bright enough to shine by day like Venus. This was the supernova which later formed the 'Crab Nebula' as it broke up and spread. Its colour was variously described as iridescent yellow or red–white. The same star was observed and recorded in Peking, which at that time was capital of the Khitan dominions, and in Japan.

**Supernova**

These dusky blemishes obscure the face of the Sun quite frequently, but thousands of years went past without any astronomers noticing. Sun watching is an uncomfortable activity, and most of the spots are too tiny (100,000 km. across, or less) to be identified without concerted scrutiny. The record eventually begins with a sun spot observed in China in May, 28B.C. From then on frequent observations were made. Chinese astronomers viewed the Sun through translucent sheets of jade and described sun spots as black vapours.

**Sun Spot**

The idea that cosmic radiation is continually bombarding the Earth was proposed in 1901 by the British physicist Charles Wilson (1869–1959). He was unable to prove his theory. But in 1911 and 1912, Victor Hess (1883–1964), a lecturer from the University of Vienna, made nine balloon flights to great altitudes, with an electrometer capable of measuring radiation. He found that radiation increases sharply as one gets further from the Earth's surface, thus establishing that its source must be in space. One of his flights, in August 1912, reached 5350 m.

**Cosmic Rays**

**Quasar**  The first quasar to be discovered – 3C273 – was located in 1963 by radio astronomers attached to Australia's CSIRO, using the huge radio telescope at Parkes, New South Wales. Its radio image resembled that of an ordinary star, but after they referred its location to astronomers operating the powerful optical telescope at Mt. Palomar, California, the unique properties of quasars could be identified. 3C273 was found to be about 2000 million light years away and retreating at 47,400 km/sec. The strength of its radio image from such a distance indicates a very intense source of radiation and supports speculation that quasars are collapsed galaxies. By analysing the colour range of its optical image, Maarten Schmidt (born 1929), a Dutch astronomer working in the United States, was able to ascertain 3C273's speed and distance in 1963.

**Pulsar**  In England in 1967 observer Jocelyn Bell (born 1943) discovered radio signals reaching Earth from a mysterious source in outer space. The peculiar feature of the signals was that they come in regular pulses at intervals of just over one second. Working from this and follow-up observations, astronomers Franco Pacini and Thomas Gold developed the concept of pulsars: small, rapidly rotating stars, made of the neutrons remaining after the collapse of much larger stars. In 1938 the existence of stars very like pulsars had been predicted by J. R. Oppenheimer (father of the atom bomb [VI, 2]) and George Volkoff.

## 3. THE EARTH AND ATMOSPHERE

**Climatic Zones**  In the 6th century B.C. Pythagoras, the Greek philosopher from Samos, divided the heavens into five celestial zones and nominated five corresponding zones on the Earth's surface. But another Greek, Parmenides of Elea in Sicily (born 513B.C.), was the first to plot climatic zones based on terrestrial conditions. He instituted the five-zone system, with Northern and Southern Frigid Zones beyond each arctic circle, Temperate Zones between the tropics and the arctic circles, and the Torrid Zone between the two tropics. Amongst later refinements the most important was the discovery by Eratosthenes (who worked in Alexandria in the 3rd century B.C.), that there is an equatorial temperate zone lying between the Northern and Southern Torrid Zones. This brought the seven-zone system into being.

**Five Zones**

**Seven Zones**

The Italian physicists Evangelista Torricelli (1608–47) and Vincenzo Viviani happened across the barometer as a result of an experiment they were performing in 1644. They stood a glass pipe containing mercury in a bowl full of mercury to observe the natural level found by the mercury in the pipe. They noticed slight variations in the level in the pipe from day to day, which they correctly surmised were due to changes in atmospheric pressure. They then made the connection between the level variations and weather patterns, and realised that low air pressure is a sign of impending bad weather. This understanding is the basis of modern weather-forecasting technique.

**Barometer**

After atmospheric pressure, the most important indicator used in weather forecasting is the humidity of the air. In China this began to be measured in the 2nd century B.C. by balances containing hygroscopic materials (which absorb moisture from the air). The materials used included elm charcoal and feathers; their weight increases as they absorb moisture, and can be used to measure humidity. The first references are in Liu Arn's *Huai Narn Dzu*, a 2nd century B.C. book containing many firsts.

**Hygrometry**

Eratosthenes was born in the Greek city of Cyrene in North Africa, and worked at the Museum of Alexandria – home of more firsts than any other research establishment. He was nicknamed 'Beta' (the letter B), unfairly implying that because he dabbled in all fields, he came first in none. Because the hundreds of books that he wrote have all been destroyed, he can only be credited with firsts reported by other people: amongst them, the measurement of the obliquity of the ecliptic and division of the Earth into seven climates [see Seven Zones, above]. By the time he was eighty-one (194B.C.), he had investigated everything and was bored, so he starved himself to death. In the 3rd century B.C., in order to measure the Earth, he had gnomons set up in Egypt – at Alexandria and at Syene on the Tropic of Cancer. Calculations based on observation of the shadows they cast led him to measure the Earth's circumference at 252,000 stades (about 39,700 km.), which is roughly 300 km. less than 20th-century estimates.

**Measurement of the Earth**

Eratosthenes (276–194B.C.) – who first worked out the measurement of the Earth [see above] – devised a system of latitude and longitude in order to indicate relative positions of

**Longitude and Latitude**

various places, and lay the world out on maps. North–south location was indicated by parallels of latitude – notional lines running parallel to the Equator. Three-hundred-and-sixty meridians of longitude, each marking out one degree on the Earth's circumference, were drawn to cross each other at the North and South Poles, and gave the east–west location. His work was done in Alexandria in the 220s B.C.

**Conic Projection**

The conic projection for mapping the Earth renders meridians of longitude as straight lines that converge on the Pole. The parallels of latitude are shown as regular curves each on a radius from the Pole. In a representation of a hemisphere two parallels can be of the exact scale length; the others are inevitably distorted, but all the meridians are equal. This system was adopted by the Greek-speaking Egyptian geographer Claudius Ptolemy of Alexandria, about 150A.D.

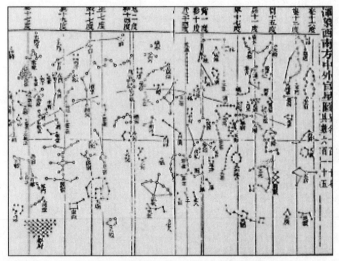

Su Sung's star map on Mercator's projection. The horizontal mid-line is the Equator. Curving above it is the ecliptic – the Sun's path between the Equator and the Tropic of Cancer. The map is an illustration in Su's book (1094A.D.) about his clock (see p. 251).

**Mercator's Projection**

Mercator's projection is a system for mapping a spherical surface in an oblong shape that fits on a wall chart or tea towel. The meridians of longitude are parallel and the parallels of latitude are all the same length, so that on a world map, Greenland comes out bigger than Africa. Before it was used for a map of the Earth Mercator's projection served for the heavens, showing the position of stars and planets. Su Sung's book, *New Design for an Armillary Clock* (Kaifeng, 1094A.D.), includes a star atlas, which uses Mercator's projection for the first time.

Empedocles (c. 495–435B.C.), from the Greek city of Acragas in Sicily, maintained that the Earth is hot within: full of streams of fire, as he put it. Empedocles – who is also founder of the Big Bang Theory and the principle of Conservation of Matter, both in VII, 4 – was probably encouraged in his conviction by observing Mt. Aetna, the notorious volcano on his native island. **Hot Earth**

That the Earth's heat is sustained by atomic reactions was claimed first by New Zealand physicist Ernest Rutherford (1871–1937) in lectures given in Britain in 1904. **Atomic Reactions in the Earth**

Comparison of flood levels of the Nile River, taken over a period of centuries, convinced ancient Egyptians observers that their land had gradually been laid down from silt carried North by the river. Every year the Nile brings huge quantities of sediment from the high country of inland Africa and deposits it on the flood plains of Egypt and in its delta, protruding into the Mediterranean Sea. In distant prehistoric times sea waters covered the area where the lowlands of Egypt now lie. **Alluvial Land Formation**

This insight was passed on by the priests of Memphis and Heliopolis to the Greek historian Herodotus in the 5th century B.C., and the earliest record of it is in his *Histories*. The Chinese scientist Shen Gua (1031A.D.–1095), who made three-dimensional relief maps [V, 3], was the first to explain the converse process by which erosion creates mountainous terrain from country which was originally level or gently sloping. Around 1070A.D., studying formations produced in this way, especially around Wen Jo, he noticed numerous peaks almost on a level, separated by deep steep rifts. He became convinced that erosion, especially by water, had removed the soft earth and left the hard rocky parts standing. **Formation of Terrain by Erosion**

Greek scientists two thousand years ago considered that some land masses, including the island of Rhodes, had originally been thrust upward by forces inside the Earth. **Uplift of Land Masses**

Anyone who inspects a world map can see that some widely separate land masses look as if they would fit together. This led to suggestions that lands which had once been united were **Continental Drift** torn asunder and moved apart in prehistoric times. No one can tell who first raised this idea; it may not have been until the 1500s, when South America was mapped and it was possible to see how its Eastern coast matched the West Coast of Africa. For centuries it was merely a popular notion with no place in scientific theory. However some scientists compared coasts of separate lands, such as Australian geologist Louis Bernacchi, who was struck in 1899 by the resemblance of geological formations in Antarctica and Australia. The founder of the continental drift theory is German geophysicist, Alfred Wegener (1880–1930) who began to lecture on it in 1912 and in 1915 published *The Origin of Continents and Oceans* (*Die Enstehung der Kontinente und Ozeane*). He maintained that continents are rafts of comparatively light rock, which slide on top of the Earth's crust. He postulated the primaeval supercontinent, Pangaea, in which the continents of today had once all been joined.

**Plate Tectonics**    Laymen seemed ready to accept Wegener's ideas, but few scientists of the time agreed, chiefly because Wegener had no mechanical cause with which to explain the drift motion. The explanation was supplied in the 1960s by geophysicists who observed that the rock of the sea floor is not very old, unlike the continents. In the 1930s, Harry Hess (1906–69) of the United States had begun to consider that some sea floor characteristics might be due to convection currents in the crust. As commander of a naval vessel in the subsequent war against Japan, he used his ship's sonar equipment to survey the floor of the Pacific. In the 1950s he proposed that new crust material constantly emerges at mid-ocean ridges and travels outwards, eventually to disappear under the Earth again; and that the continents being too light to be drawn down remain on top, their motion subject to shifting of the crust. In 1965 the Canadian geophysicist J. Tuzo Wilson observed that the Earth's surface comprises a number of sections or plates, each belonging to a convection cell within the Earth, and bounded by active zones where crust material emerges or is drawn down by the currents of the cell.

**Seismograph**    The first seismograph was more interesting to look at than present-day models:

> It had a domed cover, and the outer surface was ornamented with antique seal characters, and designs of mountains, tortoises, birds and animals . . . Outside the vessel there were eight dragon heads each one holding a bronze

ball in its mouth, while round the base there sat eight toads
with their mouths open, ready to receive any ball which
the dragons might drop.

The inventor was Jarng Heng (78A.D.–139), in 132A.D. in
Law Yarng, capital of China. (His was also the genius that
made a model propeller aircraft and differential gearing [IX, 3
and VIII, 2].) Inside the seismograph was a delicately balanced
column which rocked during a quake and operated a mechanism along one of eight directional tracks. One dragon then
vomited a ball into the mouth of the toad facing it, and the
machine made a loud noise to alert the observers. The earthquake direction was known by which toad had received a ball.
'By following the direction one knew where the earthquake
was', says the *History of the Later Harn Dynasty*.

> When this was verified by the facts there was an almost
> miraculous agreement . . . On one occasion one of the drag-
> ons let fall a ball from its mouth though no perceptible shock
> could be felt . . . But several days later a messenger arrived
> bringing news of an earthquake in Lung Hsi [700 km. away].

The first fossils observed in ancient times were remains of sea
creatures and seaweed, which had been petrified, and owing to **Recognition of**
changes on the Earth's surface, left on dry land. Xenophanes, **Fossils**
a Greek philosopher who lived in Asia Minor and Italy, correctly explained them as impressions left in mud in prehistoric
times – evidence that areas which are now land must have
been under the water. Xenophanes was definitely living in
500B.C., but as he was over a hundred when he died – perhaps
around 480 – it is not possible to date his realisation with precision. In China, when fossil bones of dinosaurs and other prehistoric animals were recovered, they were identified as
dragon fossils. The Chinese idea of dragons springs largely
from these remains and dinosaurs are still called dragons in
Chinese. A fossil skull at Cheng Cheng in North China was
revealed in 120B.C. during excavation of the subterranean **Fossil Proof of**
'Dragon Head Canal'. Warng Chung (27A.D.–c. 100) in his **Evolution**
*Balanced Discussions* (*Lun Heng*, Law Yarng, 83A.D.) is the first
to claim expressly that these fossil finds are evidence that
unfamiliar creatures lived earlier in the same areas which are
now inhabited by the quite different lifeforms of today.

Last century the Swiss natural historian, Jean Louis Agassiz
(1807–73), realised that there had been a prehistoric Ice Age, **Recognition of**
by examining glaciers in mountainous areas. He recognised **the Ice Age**

landforms widely distributed in temperate regions that must have been sculpted by glacial action long ago; and he saw that transport by glaciers could explain why isolated bodies of rock are found long distances from their parent material. In 1837 he began to expound his view that most of the now inhabited world had been ice and snow-bound during the Ice Age – a theory which he published in *Glaciers* (1840). His previous studies of fossils had confronted him with a dilemma that plagued Christian naturalists: the clear fossil record of life before the biblical Creation. The Ice Age offered a solution to Agassiz, who said it had killed off all life, leaving the Earth vacant for God's new work of creation.

**Explanation of Tides**

In about 300B.C. the Greek explorer Pytheas from Massilia (present-day Marseilles) sailed to Britain and Ireland, and made detailed observations of the huge tides of the North Atlantic (he measured a tide in the north of Britain at 120 feet). At the same time, he and his team were collecting data on the Sun, Moon and stars, and on the basis of all these observations, Pytheas concluded that the Moon controls the rise and fall of the tides (which is also the modern view). Seleucus, a Greek scientist in Seleucia, on the shores of the Persian Gulf, worked out the details of the lunar influence on tides around 180B.C., establishing that their height depends on the Moon's position relative to the Sun.

## 4. CHEMISTRY

Chemistry is unique among theoretical sciences, because nearly all the current fundamentals have been worked out since the 18th century. (This is not true of applied chemistry: much ancient medical and industrial chemistry [VIII, 6 and 8] remains valid.) Earlier theoretical findings are mostly out of date and only of interest to enthusiasts, which is why they are not included here. Biochemistry is also an entirely modern field, covered in the next section.

**Periodic Table**

The Periodic Table of Elements, which is the cornerstone of modern chemistry, was drawn up at the same time by two men working independently. One was the Russian chemist Dmitri Mendeleev (1834–1907), at the University of St. Petersburg. His table began as a fixed scheme for arranging the elements in accordance with regular increments in atomic weight. According to Mendeleev's 'periodic law' the elements demonstrate a periodic change in properties when arranged this way, so that elements of similar weight have similar characteristics. Mendeleev started in 1869, with only sixty-three known elements. By filling in the gaps in the table he was able to identify as yet undetected elements and to describe their characteristics by reference to their atomic weight. These included gallium, scandium and germanium. His contemporary was Julius Lothar Meyer, in Germany.

The Swedish chemist Jöns Jakob Berzelius (1779–1848) drew up the first table of elements in which each is ranked according to the strength of its positive or negative electric charge. He found that the amount of affinity between two elements is proportional to the extent of their separation on his table.

**Affinity of Elements**

Hydrogen was discovered in 1766 by the wealthy scholar Henry Cavendish (1731–1810), in his private laboratory in London. He christened it 'inflammable air' because of what happens when you set fire to it. In 1781 Cavendish found that he could produce water artificially by exploding hydrogen and common air together. Repeating the experiment later with hydrogen and oxygen, he was able to work out that water is a compound of these two, and determine the proportions of each in its composition.

**Discovery of Hydrogen**

**Composition of Water**

    Cavendish also studied common air to determine the composition of the atmosphere. Karl Scheele (1742–86), one of the discoverers of oxygen and nitrogen, had already established that air is a mixture of the two. Cavendish ascertained the proportions, which he quoted at 20.83% oxygen and 79.17% nitrogen, all else being counted as impurities.

**Composition of Air**

In the 1810 *Memoirs* of the Academy of Sciences of St. Petersburg, the distinguished historian of science, Julius Klaproth (1783–1835) partially translates Mao Hua's *Confessions of the Peaceful Dragon* – a book lately brought from China by a French traveller. This book – dated 756A.D. (during the Tarng Dynasty) – calls oxygen *chi yin*, and explains that although it occurs nowhere in its pure form, it is mixed into the air and combines during combustion with various elements, including metals, to form new substances. The book adds that oxygen is one of the constituents of water. If Mao Hua discovered oxygen in the 700s it is a breakthrough that merits great renown. Unfortunately there is no trace of him or his book except in Klaproth's paper. If Klaproth got his dating badly wrong it is

**Discovery of Oxygen**

conceivable that the Peaceful Dragon confessed these revelations after the English theologian Joseph Priestley (1733–1804) discovered oxygen. In 1774 Priestley had published a fuller account of oxygen than Mao Hua's. If the parties involved had moved quickly, Priestley's knowledge could have been taken to China and explained to Mao Hua, written up in one, or very few copies, one of which was stumbled across by a visiting Frenchman, who left it in Russia in time for Klaproth to prepare his 1810 publication. Such a chain of events, though remotely possible, doesn't explain Klaproth's 756 date. Mao Hua, or whoever taught him about oxygen, thus remains one of the greatest mystery men in the history of science. If he turns out false, then credit for the first discovery will have to be transferred not to Priestley, but to the Swede, Karl Scheele who identified oxygen in 1772 or 1773, and only published his findings in 1777.

**Radioactive Element**

**Radium**

Polonium, the first radioactive element to be identified, was named by its Polish discoverer, Marie Curie (1867–1934), after her native land. She and her French husband Pierre (1859–1906) extracted Polonium from the mineral pitchblende in Paris in 1898. Later the same year she discovered the more radioactive element, radium.

**DNA**

**DNA Molecular Structure**

Deoxyribonucleic acid – 'DNA' – was first discovered in 1929 by Phoebus Aaron Theodor Levene (1869–1940), a Russian scientist working in America. The unique double helical structure of DNA molecules was first worked out in 1953 as a result of the joint efforts of two pairs of researchers working in England. In that year Francis Crick (born 1918) and James Watson (from America, born 1928), working in Cambridge, completed the first model of DNA's molecular structure that answers to all the observed characteristics of the substance. Their work was made possible by the findings and ideas of Rosalind Franklin (1920–58) and Maurice Wilkins (from New Zealand, born 1916), who worked together in nearby London, studying the DNA molecule. The three who were still alive shared a Nobel Prize for their discovery in 1962. Before its structure was worked out the hereditary function of DNA [see Genes, VIII, 5] had already been discovered.

**Carbon Dating**

Willard F. Libby (1908–80) was an American chemist on the team that produced the atom bomb [VI, 2]. His other famous contribution is the radio-carbon method of establishing the antiquity of archaeological remains. Carbon fourteen exists in living tissue in a fixed ratio, and is lost at a steady rate. While an organism remains alive its carbon-fourteen ratio is maintained by its metabolism; on death diminution of the quantity begins. Libby worked out how to determine the time that had elapsed since death, by assessing the quantity of carbon fourteen still held in remains. In 1960 he was awarded the Nobel Prize for Chemistry.

## 5. BIOLOGY

Whale biology is dealt with together with whaling [VIII, 8].

**Cells** The idea of living organisms being composed of distinct, microscopic, living cells was initially put forward by the Indian botanist Parasara, whose work on 'Plant Science', the *Vrksayurveda*, came out in the 1st century B.C. or A.D. According to Parasara, each invisible cell in leaves is covered by a wall of fine membrane, and stores a sap containing the elemental properties and pigment. He believed that their substance is brought from the earth by various transport systems supplying the plant's organs. The first observer to see plant cells was English scientist, Robert Hooke (1635–1703), in the 1660s, when he examined cork tissue under a microscope.

**Animal Cells** Parasara had confined his remarks on cells to leaf tissue. German philosopher Lorenz Oken was the first to postulate that animals are all composed of individual microscopic cells: in 1805, in his book *Generation* (*Die Zeugung*), published in Bamberg.

**The Organic Cycle** Penetrating discoveries of Classical philosophers sometimes go unnoticed because the modern experts who translate their ideas are not fully conscious of the power of Classical thought. Lieh Dzu's identification of the organic cycle (of decomposition and nutrification), is repeatedly labelled a theory of evolution, even though that would make it the silliest theory of evolution ever published. Lieh Dzu's actual point, made in the 300s B.C., is that living beings are composed from elementary constituents, and they eventually decompose; the constituents are later reassembled in other beings by the operation of an endless organic process. It is a theme which Lieh Dzu shares with other Taoist philosophers, including Juarng Dzu (c. 369–c. 287 B.C.), whose book is the oldest which quotes Lieh

Dzu's explanation of integration and disintegration. 'In seeds there are the elements', Lieh writes, 'they receive water, then start integrating.' He goes on to give an example of a course taken by some nutrient material through the natural process – from soil through a variety of plants, insects, birds, microorganisms, mammals and a human being. 'The human again returns to go into the conversion process. The multitudinous life forms all come out of the conversion process and all go into the conversion process.' (*Lieh Dzu*, ch. I; *Juarng Dzu*, ch. 18) Few modern theorists would disagree with his analysis. Some, however, might be less ready to accept the moral which the Taoists drew from it: that death is not a matter for regret because it is nothing other than the return of one's constituents for reuse. 'The coming to life of a human being is the integration of matter-and-energy . . . it disintegrates, then there is death . . . Stinking putrefaction again changes to make splendid wonders.' (*Juarng Dzu*, ch. XXII)

**Micro-organisms**   Micro-organisms were first conceived of much earlier in a primitive Mesopotamian conjecture of germs [VIII, 6]. There is no proof that they were thought of in China before the 4th century B.C., but they are referred to by a number of Taoists, including writers of the *Juarng Dzu* book – based, of course, solely on surmise as there were no microscopes. By way of illustration one species was said to land in huge numbers on an eyelash of a mosquito, 'without jostling each other'. More

**Microbial Decomposition**   importantly, Lieh Dzu referred to micro-organisms which carry out the decomposition process: his examples include those that work on saliva and those that cause pickling.

**Plant Nutrition**   The Taoists wanted their findings to affect the way people think about life and death; they were happy to leave the biological mechanics of nature's system to be worked out by others. The Islamic scientist, Abū Rayḥān Muḥammad Ibn Aḥmad al-Bīrūnī of Khwarizm (973A.D.–1051) described the mechanics of plant nutrition in his book on geology and nature, *Kitāb al-jamāhir*. His observations cover the transporting of nutrients from the soil to the extremities through capillary vessels; the storing of liquefied nutrients and the system of evaporative transpiration.

**Atmospheric Nutrients**   Photosynthesis, which is the chemical system plants use to produce food from sunlight, carbon dioxide and mineral nutrients, was discovered in stages. In 1727 British biologist Stephen Hayles published *Vegetable Staticks*, in which he demonstrated that plants draw material nutriment from the air. In 1779, working in a country house near London, Dutch

scientist Jan Ingen-Housz (1730–99) discovered that plant **Photosynthesis**
respiration, taking place night and day, has what was called a
'putrefying' effect on the surrounding air, but that in sunlight
a process takes place by which plants have the opposite –
'restorative' – effect on the air. He had thus observed photosynthesis – the process in which plants absorb atmospheric
carbon dioxide, and give out oxygen. He published his findings that year in *Experiments upon Vegetables*. Henri Dutrochet
in 1837 showed that this process occurs only in the parts of
plants which contain chlorophyll, and only in the presence of
light. Biochemists are still pursuing an entire knowledge of
photosynthesis but the basic recognition was completed in
1865 when Polish-born German botanist Julius von Sachs
(1832–97) ascertained that in chloroplasts chlorophyll turns
carbon dioxide and water into starch, giving off oxygen.

Theophrastus (370–285 B.C.), the Greek scholar from Lesbos,
explained his plan to classify the plant kingdom in his book **Scientific**
*Enquiry into Plants*: 'One must take into account their parts, **Classification**
their qualities, the ways in which their life originates and the **of Plants**
course which it follows in each case.' (I. 1. vi) His system has
four major classes to cover 'nearly all' plants, but no provision
for microscopic plants which were unknown to him.
Theophrastus's system was a combination approach giving
weight to many different sorts of facts; now it has been completely displaced by the system based on genealogical relationships of plants. However, many of the distinctions which
Theophrastus considered important – such as between dicotyle-
donous and monocotyledonous plants – are still drawn.

The idea of discussing plant species by using fabricated
binomial terms unrelated to the common name began in
China, in the 4th or 5th century B.C., and some of the terms
survive in the *Literary Approximater*, a thesaurus [I, 3] of the
time. Of the two words for each variety, one denoted the category to which it belonged, and the other identified the
species. This system of terminology never led to a uniform
classification of living things, which is what European science, **Binomial**
with a similar system, has given the world. **Nomenclature**

Binomial nomenclature was introduced to Europe by the
Swiss anatomist, Gaspard Bauhin (1560–1624) in his *Pinax
Theatri Botanici*, published in 1623. His terms identified genus
and species. The system used in modern biology for classifying
organisms came into being with Pierre Magnol's book, *Prodro-
mus Historiae Generalis Plantarum in quo Familiae Plantarum per*

**Classification in Families** *Tabulas Disponuntur.* It was published, title and all, in France in 1689. Magnol's work introduced 'families' – genealogically related groups of genuses. Amongst others he christened the compositae, gramineae, cruciferae and leguminosae, families which are very familiar to botanists.

**Sex of Plants** The Roman philosopher Pliny (Caius Plinius, 23A.D.–79) included in his *Natural History* the earliest surviving affirmation that, like animals, all plant species have male and female sexes. This was first detected in relation to palm trees, for which, according to Pliny, it is particularly obvious. Mesopotamian farmers, cultivating date palms since early in the 2nd millennium B.C., used to tie male and female trees together to facilitate fertilisation. Pliny's information about plant sex in other species probably comes from the work of botanists of the Hellenistic world during the 2nd or 3rd century B.C., which is now lost.

**Laws of Heredity** Gregor Mendel (1822–84), born in Silesia (present-day Poland) was an Austrian monk of the Augustinian Order in the monastery at Brünn (present-day Brno, Czech Republic). In 1857 he began experiments with garden peas to work out the system by which genetic characters are inherited. Observing clear-cut traits such as tallness and dwarfing, smooth seeds and wrinkled, he worked out the fundamental laws of heredity, the statistical predictability of traits and the operation of dominant and recessive strains over generations. Coming at the time when Darwin's *Origin of Species* was triggering renewed clerical opposition to the concept of natural selection [VII, 4], Mendel's findings were central to the evolutionary controversy. Mendel's work was almost completely ignored, and published only in the *Transactions* of the Brünn Natural History Society in 1865 and 1869. There it slept unnoticed till 1900, when de Vries of the Netherlands, Correns of Germany, and von Seysenegg of Austria each separately rediscovered Mendel's laws. In that year a remarkable thing occurred, without parallel in the recording of firsts. Instead of squabbling with each other over priority, the rediscoverers each independently combed the records for previous work on the subject, stumbled each on Mendel's forgotten papers, and voluntarily acknowledged Mendel as the discoverer. Self-effacing honesty – rare enough in the annals of western science – coming from three at once, really is a world first.

Chromosomes were detected first in Germany by Walter
Flemming (1843–1905) – during his studies of cell division in **Genes**
the 1870s and 1880s. But he was not aware of their central
function in reproduction. An American biologist, Thomas
Hunt Morgan (1866–1945) became the first to understand
heredity at cellular level, as a result of his intensive experiments with *drosophila* fruit flies between 1907 and 1911. His
results demonstrate that genes borne on the chromosomes are
the carriers of hereditary characteristics. In 1944, Oswald
Avery (1877–1955), a Canadian doctor heading a research
team in the United States, discovered that deoxyribonucleic
acid – DNA [VIII, 4] – is the substance responsible for genetic
transmission.

Stanley H. Cohen and Herbert W. Boyer in the United States
in 1972 were the first people to take genetic material from one **Genetic**
organism and implant it in another living organism. They used **Engineering**
bacterial enzymes to cut a piece out of a plasmid of bacterium,
and inserted it into an opening in a gene of another bacterium.
Cohen's and Boyer's operation used individuals of the same
species, *Escherichia coli*. Over the following year a number of
geneticists began mixing the DNA of different species; fruit fly
and frog genes, for instance, were implanted in bacteria.

While the existence of microbes was deduced in ancient
times, none was actually seen until the Dutch naturalist, **Protozoa**
Anton van Leeuwenhoek (1632–1723) developed high-
powered single-lens microscopes and put them into intensive
use. This led to his discovery in 1654 of single-celled animals,
protozoa. Leeuwenhoek discovered bacteria – single-cell **Bacteria**
plants – by putting matter collected from his teeth under the
microscope. He wrote of these in 1683 but had been examining them for many years prior to that.

Beatrix Potter (1866–1943) did her most valued work as an
author and illustrator of children's stories – the creator of **Lichen**
Peter Rabbit. She was also the first observer to describe accurately the nature of lichen. A lichen is not a single plant, but
a colony of algae and fungi symbiotically supporting each
other. Beatrix Potter wrote a paper on this discovery but the
director of London's Royal Botanical Gardens, observing that
she was a woman and worse, an artist, declined to investigate
her ideas. They were eventually read with approval to the Lin-
naean Society in 1897.

**Coral** The first scientist to describe coral accurately was al-Bīrūnī, the man from Khwarizm who claimed that humans are descended from apes. In his book on geology, *Kitāb al-jamāhir fi ma'rifat al-jawāhir*, he classifies corals as animals, distinguishes between the alcyonarian and zoantherian types, and identifies the mesenteries, the gullet, and the vessels running into it.

## 6. MEDICINE

Entries on the medical profession are in Chapter IV, section 3. For hospitals see V, I.

**Germs** Just how scientific the first thesis on germs, and their disease-causing effects was, can be judged by reading it:

> The Earth created the rivers
> The rivers created the canals
> The canals created the marshes
> The marshes created the 'Worm'.
> Came the Worm and wept before Shamash,
> Before Ea came her tears: –
> 'What will you give me for my food
> What will you give me to devour?
> . . .
> Let me drink among the teeth
> And set me in the gums
> That I may devour the blood of the teeth
> And of their gums destroy their strength'.

> (tr. Thompson, modif.)

Shamash and Ea are gods; the Worm is the micro-organism that causes dental infections; the verse is in Sumerian, *The Legend of the Worm*, from Mesopotamia in the 3rd millennium B.C. Sumerian thought envisaged the operation of germs in certain cases; whether anyone of that time believed in a general pattern of infection by germs is impossible to say. To cure the tooth worm, *The Legend* recommends a rub-on prescription and the services of a magician to repeat an incantation three times. (In the 1600s when bacteria [VIII, 5] were first discovered, it was in scrapings from the teeth that they were found by Anton van Leeuwenhoek.)

**Anatomy of the Heart** *The Heart*, a book by an anonymous Greek author in the 4th century B.C. correctly describes the heart as a muscle with left and right ventricles (chambers), the openings to which are covered by left and right auricles (smaller chambers) and closed by the valves. He also describes the roughness of the inside of the ventricles, and the vascular connections of the heart to the lungs.

This anatomy is so good that it is disappointing that the book's treatment of the heart's function is so hopeless. The author says the auricles draw air from the lungs to the heart, and that water from the lungs is filtered in the heart, to supply the pericardial fluid. Over a thousand years earlier Egyptian scientists had discovered the heart's function of pumping blood through vessels to all parts of the body. They were aware that pulses of the vessels are synchronised with the heartbeat, but it is not clear that they recognised the circular character of the bloodstream. Their knowledge is proved by papyrus books over 3500 years old, recording medical knowledge of the Middle Kingdom period, perhaps dating back to 2000B.C. **Function of the Heart**

In the 200s B.C., Greek researchers Herophilus and Erasistratus studied the anatomy and function of the heart, but too little is left of their work to know if they understood how its multiple chambers and valves achieved the pumping action. The mechanics of the pumping action were correctly described by the Greek doctor Galen (129A.D.–200) who came from Pergamon and worked in Rome. **Pumping Action**

Herophilus and Erasistratus also described the capillary blood vessels – minuscule tubes connecting the arterial system with the veins. Since they did not have microscopes they must have deduced the existence of capillaries – perhaps by observing that they are essential to circulation of the blood. **Capillary Vessels**

'Blood flow is constant and circulative.' This simple-sounding statement represents a revolution in medical understanding. It comes from the Chinese *Canon of Internal Medicine* – compiled in about 300B.C. from researches completed during the previous two or three centuries. It is a sparse source of detail on blood circulation, and contains errors as well as truth. However, it does state (correctly) that the heart is the chief organ of circulation, that the peripheral pulses are synchronised with the heartbeat and that the blood flows first to the lungs and throughout the body, distributing nutrients even to the skin and hair. It also points out a qualitative difference between venous and arterial blood. **Circulation**

An important fact not recognised by the authors of this work is that blood from the heart is pumped through the pulmonary artery, to the lungs, and comes back to the heart again **Pulmonary Circulation**

before circulating to the rest of the body. This was first identified in the 13th century A.D. by the Arab researcher 'Alā'-
al-Dīn ibn Nafīs (d. 1288), working in Cairo and Damascus.
He was following the lead of ancient Western researchers into
the respiratory system [see below], and of Ibn Sīnā (known in
Europe as Avicenna), author of *The Canon*, the most famous
work of Islamic medicine. Unlike his predecessors, ibn Nafīs
gave an accurate description of the pulmonary circulation,
which he included in two works. One of these was *A Commentary on the Anatomy of the Canon*, the other, *A Commentary on the Canon*.

**Respiratory System Explained**

Physiologists amongst the ancient Greeks realised at an early
stage that we draw substance out of the air we breathe, which
has to be circulated throughout the body to support life.
Chemists had not then identified oxygen so medical
researchers called it 'vital pneuma'. Its path was plotted by
Erasistratus, in the 3rd century B.C., who states that it is
drawn into the lungs through the windpipe, then passes
through membranes into the pulmonary vein, on to the left
ventricle of the heart, and thence via the arteries to the entire
body, but not into the veins. This broad outline is correct, but
his finer details were either omitted or wrong. In particular it
took Galen in the 2nd century A.D. to make it clear that,
rather than a direct exchange of air between the lungs and the
vessels, respiration involves the incorporation of the pneuma
into the circulatory system by a transformation made possible
by the special nature of the membranes of the lungs.

**Subdivisions of the Brain**

**Cerebrum Cerebellum Ventricles**

One of the many pioneering medical works produced by Hippocrates and his school, *The Sacred Disease* (Cos, 5th century
B.C.), is best known as the first scientific treatise on epilepsy.
It identifies epilepsy as a condition of the central nervous system. The work is also the earliest to describe the right and left
halves of the brain and the membrane that separates them.
In Athens in the 4th century, Aristotle was the first to identify
the cerebrum, cerebellum and meninges, while Herophilus,
working in Alexandria around 300B.C., added a complete
anatomical knowledge of the ventricles. Galen in the 2nd century A.D. established the cerebellum as the source of most
motor nerves and the seat of muscular organisation, and the
cerebrum as the source of the sensory nerves and the seat of the
intellect.

The notion that there is an exact relation between the size of the brain and the level of intelligence has never attracted educated credence, because so many stupid people and beasts seem to have big heads. A more popular view is that intelligence is determined by the degree of convolution and complexity in the brain's structure. This was proposed by the Greek Erasistratus in Alexandria in the 3rd century B.C. His view remains popular, but unproven. Galen points out in *The Usefulness of the Parts* that 'even donkeys have an exceedingly complex brain whereas judging by their stupidity it ought to be perfectly simple.'

**Relationship of Cleverness to Brain Structure**

Acupuncture began in the Yellow River valley in North China in the legendary age of the early 3rd millennium B.C. It originated as a primitive and superstitious practice of perforating the skin with needles of bone and stone. Later, as its medical effectiveness was observed, and it became possible to manufacture fine metal needles, it developed into a secular art with a scientific basis. By the early Jo Dynasty (c. 1000B.C.) acupuncture began to be used on such a footing although still at that stage little was known about it.

**Acupuncture**

Beginning in the Jo Dynasty, pulse-feeling developed hand in hand with acupuncture, and gradually attracted an increasingly scientific and detailed interpretation. Chinese practitioners used the pulse as a diagnostic guide then treated patients with acupuncture, moxibustion (heating of acupuncture points) and drugs. But pulse diagnosis was first practised in ancient Egypt, beginning around 2000B.C., during the Middle Kingdom Period. Priests of Sekhmet and all doctors were trained in pulse feeling.

**Pulse Diagnosis**

Diagnosis by sounds began with the percussion technique – tapping the patient's chest – invented by ancient Egyptian doctors. The oldest description is in a medical text written in the 16th century B.C., which is thought to describe medical practice that may date back more than a thousand years earlier. A wide range of illnesses seated in the chest is diagnosed by listening to the sounds made by the tapping.

**Diagnosis by Sounds**

A major improvement was introduced by René Théophile-René-Hyacinthe Laennec (1781A.D.–1826), chief physician of France's Necker Hospital, who, between 1816 and 1819, invented the stethoscope and mastered its use. Not long after the publication (in 1819) of his book explaining the new device, a stethoscope applied to Laennec's own chest

**Stethoscope**

successfully conveyed the sounds of a consumptive patient. Thanks to Laennec, diagnostic methods were well ahead of treatment, and the dependability of his stethoscope was borne out by his own death from consumption in 1826.

**CAT Scanner** The computerised axial tomographic scanner was conceived by Godfrey Hounsfield (born 1919), a research scientist with Britain's EMI corporation, in 1968, while taking long walks in the country. It was a device for measuring the differing densities of tissues penetrated by an X-ray beam rotated around a patient's head – which has since dramatically improved diagnostic practice. CAT scan images, as they are generally known, were first used medically in Britain in 1972. In 1979 Hounsfield shared a Nobel Prize for his invention with Allan Macleod Cormack, a South African American who did much to develop it.

**In-vitro Fertilisation** The first human pregnancy due to in-vitro fertilisation was the work of the Monash University Medical Centre in Melbourne in 1973. However the operation was only a success in the experimental sense, because the embryo died in the early stages of gestation. The formidable course an ovum has to run to become a 'test tube baby' begins with extraction from the mother or donor, followed by fertilisation with sperm in a laboratory, initial cell multiplication in its laboratory vessel, placement in the mother's uterus so it attaches to the wall, and finally successful completion of an ordinary old pregnancy. Louise Brown, born in July 1978 at Oldham in Lancashire, was the first child of this new method. Her conception was the work of a British team under physiologist Robert Edwards and gynaecologist Patrick Steptoe.

**Donor Embryo** In November 1983 the first baby was born to a mother who was the recipient of an embryo from another woman. The woman who gave birth was herself infertile but the donor's embryo was fertilised in vitro by a team from Monash University, including Alan Trounson, Carl Wood and John Leeton. **In-vitro Multiple Births** This research team is also responsible for the first in-vitro fertilised twins (June 1981), triplets (June 1983), quadruplets (January 1984), and deep-freezing of a human embryo later **Frozen Embryo** born (the birth in April 1984).

**Caesarean** Julius Caesar, the Roman politician, is the earliest recorded survivor of a caesarean operation on a live mother. By this means he was born on 12 July 102B.C. but his mother did not survive the birth. Caesareans were performed on dead mothers in Mesopotamia during the Old Babylonian Period (c. 2050–c. 1650B.C.) to save living foetuses. It is not known whether the operation was performed on live mothers anywhere before Caesar's time.

The first heart pacemaker was installed in Sydney in 1926. The inventor, a doctor at Crown Street Women's Hospital, **Pacemaker** chose to stay anonymous, because of the questionable morality of prolonging life beyond its natural span. In this he succeeded so well that even now we cannot give his name, and of course he missed out on patenting the new device.

The first human heart transplant was performed on Louis Washkansky in December 1967 by South African surgeon **Heart** Christiaan Barnard (born 1922), supported by dozens of doc- **Transplant** tors and nurses at Groote Schuur Hospital in Cape Town. The patient died after eighteen days, but his death was due to postoperative pneumonia, his new heart having been successfully implanted.

In China the Ming Dynasty surgeon, Warng Ken Tarng **Reattachment** (1549A.D.–1613), operated to reattach a severed ear, success- **of Severed** fully restoring enough blood circulation to the rejoined mem- **Parts** ber to ensure its healthy survival.

Taxation plays a role in many parts of life, from firewalking to pyramid construction [IV, 4 and V, 2]. Here it concerns us as **General** the first recorded purpose for the administration of a general **Anaesthetic** anaesthetic. The anaesthetic, prepared in Northern India a little over 2000 years ago, could render a person unconscious by being given as a drink or sprinkled over his face. In his manual of politics, the author Kautilya (c. 1st century B.C.) recommends it to governments in the throes of fiscal emergency. In such a case the state is to send spies amongst the people to swindle money out of them by playing on their credulity. People who are not sufficiently gullible are to be anaesthetised and have their insensibility attributed to the curse of the gods.

The first surgeon to perform operations under general anaesthetic was Hua Tuaw of China (died 208A.D.). He **Operation** administered an effervescing powder called *ma fei sarn*, dis- **under** solved in wine, to knock out the patient. Its composition is **Anaesthetic** unrecorded but speculation is that it included the narcotic drug datura which is also effective in retarding infection and physical shock. Hua Tuaw opened the abdominal cavities and intestinal tracts of his somnolent patients to extract tumours and growths, then sutured the incisions. A plaster was applied and patients were expected to return to normal life after one month.

**Cosmetic Surgery**

The Chinese philosopher Mencius (372–289B.C.) observed that people are quite prepared to travel from one country to another to find a surgeon who can rectify an unsightly deformity in one finger, but lamented that they go to no such lengths to rectify their minds. Although this shows that some kind of plastic surgery was performed in China in the 300s B.C., Mencius's example is deliberately insignificant and does not reveal whether advanced techniques – such as grafting from elsewhere on the body to remodel conspicuous features – were by then practised.

**Tissue Grafting**

It is therefore possible that cosmetic surgery practised in India was the first to undertake such sophisticated procedures. The Sanskrit medical text, *Susruta Samhita*, discusses the repair of facial malformations by grafting of skin and muscle tissue, and remedial procedures in the case of lost ears and noses. The edition of this text that now exists is from around 300A.D., though its contents date back perhaps a couple of centuries earlier. India's earlier lead in the art seems to be due in part to the widespread use there of nose and ear lopping as punishments.

**Homoeopathy**

The Greek doctor Hippocrates of Cos (460–357B.C.) advocates homoeopathic remedies – treating a condition with a small dose of a remedy that produces similar symptoms – but only in specific instances. His general theory is quite the opposite. The homoeopathic principle was first advanced as the correct basis of all medical practice in an article in *Hufeland's Journal* in 1797 by Samuel Hahnemann, a German physician from Saxony. Hahnemann and his colleagues proceeded to test thousands of drugs on themselves to discover which diseases their effects resembled. Early in the 19th century they had successfully promoted homoeopathy throughout Western Europe and North America.

**Blood Transfusion**

References to blood transfusion by Roman poets of the 1st century B.C. lead us to believe that the operation had been invented in that century or perhaps the previous one. It is more likely to have been an innovation of Greek-speaking researchers than of Romans, who were not creative scientists. It seems to have been inspired by the simplistic notion that the blood of a young person can be injected into the veins of an infirm patient to restore health and prolong life. In 1492A.D. Pope Innocent VIII's doctors, aware of this notion, decided to try out the operation for the purposes of enlivening their decrepit pontiff. They hooked him up to a succession of young boys in such a way that the donors got his blood as he got theirs. Unfortunately the patient remained as inert as ever, but the bizarre procedure did produce the result of dispatching three boys to their maker in the double cause of piety and medical research. If the Greeks and Romans had a less lethal system of transfusion, it might have been because they did not require the donor to take blood back from the patient.

But any success in an individual case would have required the good fortune of the donor's blood being compatible with the recipient's. This was a matter of chance until 1901, when blood groups were discovered by the American pathologist, Karl Landsteiner. Landsteiner's discovery enables relatively safe blood transfusion by making compatible matches detectable.

**Blood Groups**

The first doctors treated infants in the same way as adults, and although they used reduced doses and milder treatment, there was no paediatric medicine with a scientific basis of its own. This branch of study first arose in China with the idea that children of five years and under are biologically different from other people. The reputed founder of the theory is a Dr. Wu of the 10th century B.C. Wu is the purported author of a book on children's medicine called *The Fontanel Canon*, named after the gap in the top of the craniums of infants, which in adults is closed by bone. However information about Wu is suspiciously scant and the view that *The Fontanel Canon* was written centuries later may be correct.

**Paediatrics**

Instead of leaving suicides peacefully dead, the Harn Dynasty doctor, Jarng Jung Jing, gave detailed instructions on how to revive them in his *Discussion of Febrile and Other Diseases* (China, c. 200A.D.). His method requires lying them down under a warm quilt, drawing back the head and shoulders and administering cardiac massage. This method is indeed likely to succeed for patients who are clinically dead but not past the point of no return. Present-day practice also calls for blowing air into the patient's mouth, but Jarng's book, in its present

**Resuscitation**

form, recommends the curious procedure of blowing into the ear. It is possible that he originally wrote mouth and that later it was mistakenly transcribed as ear. Coincidentally, in the late-20th century mouth to mouth resuscitation has been officially renamed 'EAR'.

**Contraceptive** According to an early Egyptian medical text, now known as the 'Kahun Papyrus', ladies who insert, in the appropriate place, a plug made out of crocodile dung and *auyt* paste, can copulate without risking the bane of pregnancy. This formula, written in about 2000B.C., is the oldest known contraceptive which would actually have worked (on the same principle as a modern diaphragm), instead of just representing wishful thinking. It is one of several Egyptian recipes for barriers to fertilisation, some of which may have been invented during the 3rd millennium B.C.

**Spermicide** Also from Egypt comes a more sophisticated variant on the same idea, in the 'Ebers Papyrus' (c. 1600B.C.), which calls for a lint pad to be soaked in a mixture of honey and acacia tips. Acacia tips yield lactic acid, the active ingredient of most spermicidal preparations to this day.

**Oral Contraceptive** The ancients trusted oral contraceptives extracted from a range of improbable sounding plants: not just ordinary folk avoiding parentage, but leading medical scientists. The gynaecologist Soranus – working around 100A.D. in Egypt and Italy – wrote that sylphion and other fennel plants are ideal. Like the eminent researcher Galen he also believed in rue as contraceptive. The pharmacist Dioscorides (1st century A.D.) recommends pennyroyal. Widespread reliance on birth control drugs is evident from well known writers outside the medical field – beginning with casual mentions in Greek comedies by Aristophanes in the 400s B.C. It is unlikely that most of the drugs recommended can do much to retard ovulation. Unlike the modern contraceptive pill, they mainly operated by preventing implantation of the embryo on the uterus.

**Abortifacients** Other popular birth control drugs were meant to cause abortion very early in pregnancy. Around 400B.C., a Greek gynaecological work by Hippocrates, or one of his school, advised that nothing is better for an abortifacient suppository than the squirting cucumber. Soranus prescribes pomegranate; Dioscorides, Galen and others mention a variety of drugs including juniper and Queen Anne's lace, to be taken orally or vaginally. Many modern experts scorn the notion that any of these drugs could be relied on to produce such a powerful response as shedding an embryo – and similarly reject the efficacy of anti-implantation drugs. However, ancient observers confidently attributed low birthrates to their widespread use. Certainly some areas in classical times, including Greece and Italy, had birthrates very low in proportion to the propensity of their people for coitus. Modern tests on rats and mice strongly support the ancient claims. Juniper was found only sixty per cent effective against embryo implantation, but Queen Anne's lace and rue have been tested to one hundred per cent effectiveness. Fennels tested nearly a hundred per cent effective as abortifacients for rats. Squirting cucumber prevents ovulation, and pomegranate is an effective source of steroid oestrogen.

Although oral contraceptives and abortifacients are not mentioned in medical texts before the time of Hippocrates (460–357B.C.), they were in popular use well before that in the Eastern Mediterranean region, and endured for centuries. Peter of Spain (1226A.D.–1277) in his *Thesaurus Pauperum* ('Drugs for the Poor') included not only thirty-four aphrodisiacs, but twenty-six contraceptives. The advance of Catholicism should not too readily be blamed for the extinction of this knowledge. Peter's promotion of birth control did not prevent him becoming Pope John XXI. Ancient contraceptives did not have to be **Pill** taken daily for a month like the contraceptive pill invented in 1961. A suitable dose shortly before or after copulating sufficed. However, if any reader is induced by this to discard more involving products and head for the garden with secateurs, we must urge her to refrain. The extraction of effective compounds from plant materials and the neutralising of toxicities often require special techniques; she will seek sylphion in vain, as it is now extinct, and might kill herself with the poison in at least one of the other plants. In due course, however, a commercial contraceptive is likely to become available based on research into the anti-implantation drugs.

The operation of hormones was partially revealed in very ancient times to herdsmen who castrated livestock, and could **Hormonal** observe the influence of the testicles on growth and behaviour. **Treatment** In Classical Greece some athletes ate testicles to enhance their performance. Because the liver deactivates digested testosterone, this is unlikely to have helped. However, around 400B.C., Hippocrates's Greek medical school on the island of Cos adopted the use of testicular tissue in medical treatment; provided it was administered as a suppository, this would have **Testosterone** released effective testosterone. The pomegranate skin that **Treatment**

**Oestrogen Treatment**

Soranus included in an abortifacient [see above] around 100A.D. released oestrogen, but not for treating an ailment. In China, complaints which modern medicine treats with oestrogen, were given treatments including tissue from placentas, which are rich in oestrogen. *Supplement for the Pharmacopoeias (Ben Tsao Shir Yi)* by Chen Tsarng Chi, published in 725A.D., contains the first mention of this new process.

**Steroids**

Another early treatment that was widely administered in the East and West was urine, which is rich in hormones. In China during the Sung Dynasty (960A.D.–1280), the distaste which this understandably evoked led to the artificial extraction of steroids, producing far more acceptable and effective hormonal medications. The first method was described in 1025A.D. by Jarng Sheng Dao in his book *Tried and Tested Prescriptions (Jing Yen Farng)*. The patient had merely to take five to seven pills with warm wine before breakfast to become a new man or woman. The extraction technique involved evaporating urine and sublimating the residue, mixed with charcoal, in an oven. The 80 g. of drug – derived this way from 700 l. of urine – contained various impurities. (In succeeding decades, improved processes were developed to produce virtually pure steroid. Yeh Meng De's *Water and Clouds Report [Shui Yewn Lu]*, published around 1110A.D., details two production methods, one involving the first use of saponins – extracted from soap beans – to precipitate steroids.)

**Endocrinology**

The reintroduction of hormonal treatment in Western medicine was associated with the foundation of endocrinology in the first three decades of the 20th century A.D. This new discipline is the work of numerous scientists, mostly German. The pioneers include Heinrich Otto Wieland, Adolf Windaus and Paul Hermann Diels. They examined the secretions of the endocrine glands and identified the steroid ring system, and in 1909 Windaus repeated the process of precipitation by saponins, as described by Yeh Meng De. The 'autumn drug' – as the Chinese came to describe steroids – was in fact first referred to in the *Huai Narn Dzu*, published during the Harn Dynasty in the 2nd century B.C. The description given there was not inconsistent with a steroid extract, but too little remains to determine whether the process was discovered back then, and merely reinvented in Sung times.

**Immunisation**

Immunisation was developed over a thousand years ago for combating smallpox. Its pioneers were specialists in the Taoist quest to get the body to produce its own elixir of immortality.

They were reclusive characters living in the Chinese province of Szechuan, mostly around Aw Mei Mountain. Deliberately treating healthy people with disease material was a difficult concept to sell to the wider community: their bizarre technique initially attracted little attention, and there is no record of its beginnings. The first mention is in the story of how immunisation became a recognised procedure. When smallpox killed the son of prime minister Warng Darn (957A.D.–1017), Warng published an announcement throughout China summoning doctors, experts and magicians to come forward with ways of preventing the disease. A Taoist from Aw Mei turned up – a nun or monk of the 'Three White Adept School of the Ancient Immortals', who explained the immunisation method. It consisted in those days of treating a plug of cotton with smallpox matter, and inserting it in a nostril, so that the pox would be absorbed through the mucous membrane and by inhalation. The success of immunisation depends on inoculating patients with material that triggers responses in their immunity systems, but does not cause full blown attacks of the disease. To achieve this the Chinese immunisers used various techniques of making vaccines out of dead and attenuated viruses. However it is not clear which of these techniques were being used as long ago as the 10th century.

Dogs' urine normally isn't enticing to flies. But in 1889, after removing pancreases from dogs, Oskar Minkowski and Baron Joseph von Mering observed that flies became attracted to the urine of their victims. This observation was the prelude to the discovery of insulin, because it demonstrates that something produced by the pancreas is essential to the metabolism of blood sugars. However, the actual identification and extraction of insulin had to wait for Canadian research in 1921. Dr. Frederick Banting (1891–1941) and his team at the University of Toronto Medical School first extracted insulin from a human pancreas in that year, and tested it on dogs, with the aim of discovering a diabetes treatment. The following year Banting and U.S.-born associate Charles Best published *Internal Secretions of the Pancreas* explaining their breakthrough; the year after that Banting and his British-born colleague John McLeod shared a Nobel Prize for the discovery of insulin. The first diabetic treated with insulin was a patient of Toronto General Hospital in 1922.

**Insulin Discovered**

Opium was first used as a medicine in Egypt during the Old Kingdom Period (c. 3500–c. 2500B.C.). One of the earliest books of prescriptions mentions a drink made from it.

**Opium**

**Morphine**
**Heroin**

Morphine was derived from opium by the German chemist Friedrich Sertürner (1783–1841) in 1805. It takes its name from Morpheus, the son of Sleep and maker of dreams in Greek legend. The German pharmaceutical manufacturer, Friedrich Bayer and Co. worked on morphine in the 1890s to develop a more effective analgesic for medical use. Their new product, heroin, was released in 1898.

**Aspirin**

**Salicylic Acid**

The father of German chemist Felix Hoffman suffered agonising rheumatism in the 1890s. The filial son worked to invent a painkiller without severe side effects, and in 1897 developed aspirin, from salicylic acid, extracted from willow tree bark. Aspirin is actually only the best publicised in a long series of formulas for making painkilling extracts from birch and willow bark, going back about 2000 years. Pure salicylic acid was first isolated by the Italian chemist Piria in 1838.

**Penicillin**

The Scottish bacteriologist, Alexander Fleming (1881–1955), discovered the anti-bacterial effect of the mould *penicillium notatum* by accident in 1928, whilst working at St. Mary's Hospital, London. The mould had infected a dish of bacteria in his laboratory and Fleming found that around each growth of mould the bacteria had died. Fleming could find no way to extract penicillin and apply it effectively against disease. In 1938 Australian scientist Howard Florey (1898–1968), a doctor from Adelaide, began a search at Oxford University for a means to exploit penicillin's medical properties. Florey and his team, including the talented biochemist Ernst Chain, who had fled Nazi Germany before World War II, stabilised the drug in August 1940. Only by following a complex freeze-drying procedure were they able to extract penicillin in a useable form.

**Pharmacopoeia**

The oldest pharmaceutical literature is a Mesopotamian clay tablet from about 2200B.C., in the Sumerian language, with fifteen prescriptions and observations on their use. Although none of the prescriptions would be found in a modern chemist shop, they are noteworthy for their pragmatic character, and free of mystical incantations.

**Medical Books**

Egyptian doctors began writing books on their areas of expertise from early in the Old Kingdom period (c. 3500–c. 2500B.C.). All that survives of them are small fragments in later digests, but we know from ancient records that amongst them were the first texts on ophthalmology and gynaecology.

A work on anatomy is said to have been produced as early as the reign of Atothis, a pharaoh of the 1st Dynasty, who may have lived in the 35th century.

An anonymous work from ancient Egypt, known today as the 'Edwin Smith Surgical Papyrus', is the world's oldest surgi- **Work on** cal text. It probably dates from Egypt's 19th Dynasty (c. 1350– **Anatomy** c. 1200B.C.), although it may be derived largely from work of the 3rd millennium. It considers in a scientific spirit, albeit with some factual inaccuracy, the effect of injuries to various parts of the human body. Amongst other things, it is the first **Work on** study to recognise that the motion of the limbs is controlled **Surgery** by the brain.

A manual of first-aid, appropriately titled *The Refuge of the Intelligent During the Absence of the Physician*, was written in **First-aid Guide** 13th-century Egypt by Shams al-Din al-Afani.

## 7. FARMING

This section deals with production technology. For farm produce see 'Foodstuffs and Beverages' [III, 2] and 'Materials' [XI, 4]. The tractor is treated in Chapter IX, section 1.

Remains discovered at Zawi Chemi Shanidar in the north of present-day Iraq reveal that animal husbandry was being prac- **Animal** tised by the nomadic people of the area by about 9000B.C. **Husbandry** They had already succeeded in domesticating the forerunner of today's sheep, although it was still fairly close to its goat cousins. In particular, it is unlikely that its short, lanky fleece **Sheep** was shorn, and it must have been bred for meat and milk rather than wool. (Though garments may well have been made from the sheepskins.) So – unless much older finds come to light in future – it seems likely that rearing of livestock started in the grasslands of West Asia some time in the 10th millennium B.C. Suitable areas were located in Iran, Iraq, southern Turkey, Syria and Palestine.

Agriculture – the world's most important technological revolution – began considerably later, but not far away, some- **Agriculture** where between the Mediterranean coast and southern Iran, probably around 8000B.C. Traces of domesticated wheat and barley [III, 2] have been recovered from sites dated to 7500–6500B.C. in present-day Turkey, Palestine and Iran, indicating by their wide spread that cultivation of crops began considerably earlier than the date of the remains themselves.

**Agriculture Manual**

In Mesopotamia in about the 18th century B.C., a work was composed in Sumerian verse with instructions on how to run a farm. It survives today written in cuneiform script on eight clay tablets from the city of Nippur. It begins with instructions on irrigation and goes on to preparation of equipment, soil cultivation, ploughing and sowing, nurturing of the crop, harvesting and threshing.

**Soil Analysis**

China's oldest prose book, the *Shu Jing* or *Classic of Documents*, includes a description of the typical soils of the nine provinces into which Northern China was divided. The first document in the section of the book dealing with the Hsia Dynasty (c. 2100B.C.–c. 1700B.C.) describes the economic features of China, province by province, including soil texture and often colour and richness. This is a very brief, early document, which may have begun as an oral tradition around 2000B.C. and later been written down.

**Soil Science**

Scientific analysis of soil does not appear until the 4th century B.C. where it occupies sections of the *Guam Dzu*, a book compiled mainly in the East Chinese state of Chi. One chapter of the *Guam Dzu* is a region-by-region analysis of soils, based on the depth of the upper and lower limits of the water table, topography, texture, colour, botany, transmission of sound when dry, effect on people's health, and salinity. Productive soils are rated on an objective scale from one to ten.

**Seed Drill Plough**

The seed drill plough was developed in the 3rd millennium B.C. in Southern Mesopotamia by Sumerian farmers. The ploughs consisted of one, and perhaps sometimes two or three prongs each, and seed reservoirs at about chest height, whence pipes conveyed the seed to the drills, which were adjusted to deposit them at the optimum depth under soil. They were drawn by teams of oxen and operated by anything up to four men each. One of these men had the task of feeding seed into the plough. According to the first agriculture manual [see above], it was important for the farmer to keep a close eye on this process, as well as to reset the plough for correct depth.

**Mouldboard Plough**

Before tractors [IX, 2] were invented, the biggest gain in powering agricultural implements was achieved with the mouldboard plough. By minimising friction it greatly reduces the amount of power required to draw the plough, so that a single animal can do the work of a team. Writers and artists are not much good at finding excitement in agriculture, so art and literature reveal nothing of the mouldboard revolution. But many iron mouldboards from the Former Harn period (206B.C.–9A.D.) have been recovered in China. Because their contoured designs are quite sophisticated, it is clear that flat wooden mouldboards (which have not survived centuries of decomposition) belong to the earlier Warring States Period (481–221B.C.). They were probably in use by 300B.C.

**Stump Jump Plough**

Robert Bowyer Smith owned a small farm on South Australia's Yorke Peninsula. The ground was littered with obstacles and ploughing was a nightmare. Working with his brother Clarence, a smith, Smith invented the stump jump plough and demonstrated the first model in 1876. Three plough shares, drawn along together but mounted independently of each other, carved parallel furrows. Each was designed to rise and ride over any obstacle it encountered, and then, under the impetus of a weight, to lock back into ploughing position. When the South Australian Parliament decided to reward the plough's inventor with money and land, a row blew up over who was justly entitled. Smith was eventually favoured in 1882.

**Harrow**

Harrows, with metal tines for breaking up clods and soil crusts, were first introduced in China in the 2nd century A.D.

**Rotary Hoe**

The rotary hoe was invented and constructed by a young apprentice engineer from Moss Vale, New South Wales, in 1913. Cliff Howard was disappointed by the performance of existing cultivator apparatus which was drawn through the earth by tractors or horses. His inspiration was to supply it with motion of its own by means of transmission from a tractor engine drive.

**Mechanical Reaper**

In Roman times the countries of northwestern Europe, which are now farmed as closely as cabbage gardens, were lightly populated and had many large cereal-cropping properties, like much of modern America and Australia. Their broad acres and shortage of labour encouraged mechanical harvesting, which was first achieved 2000 years ago with a simple mechanical reaper known as the *vallus*. This was a large frame on two wheels, pushed into a stand of wheat by oxen. Teeth projecting at the front guided the heads into channels, at the end of which edges ripped them off the stalks, leaving them to fall back onto the framework. The main limitation of the vallus was that it had no means for separating the grain from the chaff and trash.

**Winnowing Fan**

Winnowing fans, for automatic separation of grains from husks and chaff, were invented in China around the 3rd century B.C. (the earliest remains, including scale models, are from the Former Harn period). They consist of a rotary fan turning in a casing, which draws air through vents around its axis and blows it along a horizontal duct. Grain feeds into a vertical shaft intersecting the duct, and as it passes through the air current, the husks are blown off. The grain drops through an outlet near the fan while the husks come out an outlet at the end of the duct.

Winnowing fan.

**Combine Harvester**

In 1883 and 1884 seventeen-year-old Hugh McKay built the first harvester combining the actions of a reaper and a winnowing fan, at Drummartin in rural Victoria. He and his brother John worked in a shed on the family property and took apart bits of old machinery to reassemble into the new wonder. On its first run through a wheat crop in February 1884, the machine was a complete success – like the strippers it was to supersede, it took the wheat heads off their stalks; it then dropped the mixture of chaff, straw and grain onto riddles. A constant draft of air from a rotary fan blew away all the chaff and straw, leaving the grain ready for bagging. At first McKay could not afford to manufacture the machine for commercial use. But in 1894 he set up a workshop in Ballarat, Victoria. A visiting evangelist delivered a lecture called 'Sunshine' and McKay adopted the title as his brand name. Ten years later the Sunshine Harvester Works at Sunshine near Melbourne covered a ten-acre site, still in use today by the new Canadian owner.

A design for a sheep-shearing machine was patented in 1868 in Sydney by J. A. B. Higham, but his design – which involved a **Shearing** blade moving on a serrated plate – was not put into operation. **Machinery** Nineteen years later in 1887, a shearing machine designed by Frederick Wolseley – who later started the Wolseley motor car company – was successfully demonstrated in Melbourne. The machine had been engineered at Wolseley's sheep station near Walgett in New South Wales with the help of inventor John Howard and blacksmith George Gray. At the trial at Goldsbrough's Melbourne wool store, Hassan Ali operated the machine, taking on gun blade shearer Dave Brown. Brown finished first, but the machine took off more wool. Commercial production began the following year.

Insecticidal fumigants were first used in agriculture in North China in early Jo Dynasty times, prior to 1000B.C. Sprays, **Agricultural** aerosols, veterinary chemicals and other products came later **Pesticides** [see Insecticide, XI, 3]. The Jo Dynasty official fumigators had amongst their responsibilities the control of frogs and water-dwelling pests as well as insects.

    Those personages are known from a book referring to a **Veterinary** period over 3000 years ago. One of them was in charge of **Pesticides** eradicating internal pests by drenching animals against **Drenching** intestinal worms, using a vermifugal plant. The use of sheep dip to combat pests inhabiting the fleece can be traced back **Dipping** to ancient Carthage (in present-day Tunisia). The sheep were treated with a type of oil recovered from a spring in the vicinity of the city, which was remarkable for smelling like the sawdust of citrus wood. This practice originated perhaps around the middle of the 1st millennium B.C.

    The earliest recorded use of pesticides for ridding seeds of diseases or vermin before planting was in Greece in the 400s **Seed** B.C. There the philosopher Democritus is said to have **Pesticides** favoured soaking cabbage seeds in houseleek juice. Pesticides for treating cereal crop seeds must have developed – in the West and in China – not long afterwards: they are referred to in a Chinese agricultural book of the 1st century B.C. (with aconite as the toxin), and in Pliny's *Natural History*, published in Rome in the 1st century A.D. Both were probably referring to a process worked out before their time.

**Biological Pest Control**

Biological pest control normally entails the use of one species to curtail another. However the earliest recorded instance of the method is the use of a species to curtail itself. In Judea (present-day Israel) in Roman times, around 100A.D., people began collecting ants from their nests to take to other nests. In these circumstances the different groups of ants – recognising each other only as strangers – proceeded to kill one another. This is a fairly labour intensive and not particularly effective way of wiping out ants. Biological control using one species against another was introduced in the 3rd century A.D. to protect the mandarin crops of Southern China. Nests of citrus ants were sold in matting bags, available at the markets of Jiao Jir; these were attached by farmers to their trees, to keep down the other insect pests which threatened the harvest, but constitute the citrus ant's diet.

**Pelletised Seed**

The practice of encapsulating seeds in pellets before sowing is first noticed in China during the former Harn Dynasty, and must have been invented by about 200B.C. Active ingredients in the pellets included aconite, a pesticide, and silkworm droppings, which are a fertiliser, but being rich in collagen would have supported microbial activity that raises the temperature, thus stimulating germination.

**Pre-germination**

Germinating seeds prior to sowing them is recommended enthusiastically as an aid to productivity by Jia Szu Hseih in *Essential Techniques for the Peasantry (Chi Min Yao Sha)*, published in China in 535A.D. The advantages of pre-germination probably became clear as a result of the practice of soaking seeds adopted during the Harn Dynasty (206B.C.–220A.D.), which would have caused premature germination. It is not known at what time between the Harn and Jia's day pre-germination began to be done deliberately. Jia's book urges readers to sow pre-germinated rice seeds, and as long as the field for them is wet, hemp seeds.

**Double Cropping**

The first grain crops that could be planted and harvested on the same land twice a year were the precocious rices of Southeast Asia. They were grown in regions now occupied by Vietnam, and perhaps Laos and Cambodia. The oldest surviving reference to them is in Chinese records of the later Harn Dynasty (25A.D.–221), but they probably originated centuries earlier, without being recorded, because of the lack of written records in their homelands. In the Sung Dynasty, these fast maturing varieties of grain were interbred with higher yielding northern species, enabling an agricultural revolution that ultimately led to the population explosion of East Asia, and further breeding to achieve triple cropping.

In 1840 the German chemist Baron Justus von Liebig (1803–73), published *Organic Chemistry and its Application to Agriculture and Physiology*, explaining how soluble fertiliser can be manufactured by chemically treating naturally occurring minerals. In particular he demonstrated that phosphorus compounds become soluble when treated with acid, supplying phosphorus that can be absorbed immediately by plants. In England, John Lawes adopted Liebig's principle and patented the process of adding sulphuric acid to phosphate rock. In Deptford in 1842 Lawes began manufacturing in commercial quantities, producing the original superphosphate. **Soluble Fertilisers**

## 8. INDUSTRIAL METHODS AND PRODUCTS

Industries dealt with in other sections include printing [I, 1], distilling [III, 4], explosives [VI, 1], armaments [VI, 2], chemicals [VIII, 6, XI, 3 and XI, 4], textiles [XI, 4], paper [XI, 4] and minting [XII, 4].

Four main systems of mining have developed: surface working, open-cut mining, shaft and tunnel mining and deep drilling. The first three are so ancient that they go back well before any records which would make it possible to pinpoint their invention. **Mining**

The oldest system – working the surface – was practised by Stone Age people all over the world. Shallow pits were dug to get at good working stone such as flint by the first Stone Age cultures in Africa. Surface mining for clay began soon after the invention of pottery, probably around 7000B.C. in Southwestern Asia. The first mines for metal ores were lead mines, in the same region, in the 6000s B.C. **Surface Working** **Clay Mining** **Ore Mining**

Still later the principle was applied to extracting fluid products such as brine and pitch from the surfaces of lakes and swamps. Petroleum was first mined by people in Mesopotamia **Petroleum** in the 2nd millennium B.C. They called it 'stone oil' and gathered it from petrol springs and shallow ditches for use unrefined as a fuel. Most surface mines have been exhausted by long exploitation. However in the 20th century extensive mechanised surface mining has begun for aluminium ores: bauxite, the most common, is mined this way in America, Europe, Africa and Australia, causing massive destruction of native forests, especially in Australia.

**Open-cut Mining**  The second system – open-cut mining – was in use in Mesopotamia and Egypt early in the 4th millennium B.C., for quarrying stone.

**Shaft and Tunnel Mining**  The third system is shaft and tunnel construction, which enables minerals to be recovered from deep underground. We can only speculate about its beginnings, and suggest that it was first used for mining ores in Southwestern Asia, perhaps around 3000B.C.

**Tunnelling to 1000 m.**  A depth of 1000 m. was reached in 1875A.D. at the St. Vojtech Mine at Pribram, in the present-day Czech Republic. Another application of the shaft was in reaching brine, from which salt is extracted. The use of evaporators to extract pure salt from brine began in China about 600B.C. By about 400B.C. in the Szechuan region, brine was being extracted from deep wells for this process.

A Chinese salt factory beside a deep drilled gas well. Pipelines from the distributor in the foreground convey natural gas into the factory, to fire the evaporators. Brine and gas equipment, including an exhaust vent, can be seen on the left.

During the Harn Dynasty, in the 1st century B.C., deep drilling machinery, introduced in Szechuan, brought the **Deep Drilling** fourth mining system into life. The new technology was capable of boring 600 m. down for brine and natural gas. In the Sung Dynasty in the 1040s A.D. the narrow-outlet deep

A sedentary engineer instructs a workman preparing an animal-powered drill for deep drilling operations.

drilling system was invented. An iron drill bit with round blades penetrated hundreds of metres, digging a well less than 20 cm. in diameter. The well was lined with piping, and an inner pipe about 20 m. long could be lowered by a derrick. Valves in the inner pipe opened and closed when it was at the foot of the well, retaining fluid which was easily drawn up by animal-driven wheels.

Until 1511 A.D., the Chinese only drilled for brine and **Oil Well** natural gas. In 1512, during the Ming Dynasty, the first petroleum well was opened in Chia Jo, on the Szechuan oil basin. **Drilling to**

The first drill to descend 1000 m. was operating in the **1000 m.** natural gas field at Dze Liu Jing in Szechuan, between 1821 A.D. and 1850, during the Ching Dynasty.

**Potter's Wheel**
The forerunner of the potter's wheel is a flat turntable, which the potter revolves at intervals, to fix up work on one or another side. The true wheel also has a turntable, but it spins fast, while a regular circular pot is formed. It came into use in Mesopotamia at about 3600B.C. A potter's wheel recovered from almost that long ago is about 3 feet across and had a wooden handle for spinning.

**Concrete**
The Romans began to build in concrete in the vicinity of Rome itself soon after 200B.C., making ever-increasing use of it until their construction boom of the 2nd century A.D. They used concrete for water pipes, sewers, floors, walls, domed bath houses, skyscraping temples and humble drains. For their harbour works they used high-grade pozzolana cement, which sets as hard as rock even under water. Roman pre-eminence in concrete engineering was made possible by the numerous good cement quarries available in Italy, but the technique rapidly spread throughout the empire, so that nowadays excavations often strike Roman concrete.

**Reinforced Concrete**
By the 1st century B.C. the Romans had introduced concrete flagstones, cement bricks and reinforced concrete for use when extra strength was required.

**Spun Concrete**
The spun concrete technique, for making pipes and troughs, was developed in 1910 by Walter Hume in the Adelaide workshop of his pipe company. His method was to throw concrete on to the inner surface of spinning pipe moulds by centrifugal action. The result is a very strong non-porous pipe of a type that has now become almost universal. The technique was suggested to him by a boyhood memory of honey being spun out of honeycombs.

**Pre-stressed Concrete**
In 1926 two Melbourne engineers, Walter Robertson and Heaton Clark, founders of the Rocla pipe company, made the first pre-stressed concrete pipes, cast in vertical moulds. Pipe-making is a rather specialised application of the invention that has done so much to change the look of the 20th-century world. The French bridge engineer Marie-Eugène-Léon Freyssinet pioneered the use of pre-stressed concrete in architecture and general engineering. He began his work in 1928; the Gare Maritime at Le Havre, which was finished in 1933, is the first major building constructed by his method.

**Metallurgy**
Metal products were first made out of naturally occurring gold and silver, but only crude techniques were involved, such as

hammering and gouging. Metallurgical techniques were first required for the manufacture of lead.

Lead does not occur in a naturally metallic form, but the lead-rich ore, galena, has such a metallic look that it tempted prehistoric experimenters to extract the metal from it. This **Smelting** they first did in the 6000s B.C. by inventing smelting. Subjecting galena to the very high temperatures achieved in pottery kilns, they produced molten lead metal. Small simple lead objects dating from this time have been found at Çatal Hüyük **Lead** – site of a thriving prehistoric town in present-day Turkey – and at sites of similar age in Northern Mesopotamia (present-day Iraq). One of these countries is the first home of smelting over 8000 years ago.

Smelting probably pointed the way to another fundamental technique, casting. Metal cooling from its molten state **Casting** solidifies in the shape of the receptacle holding it, so early metallurgists began to make casts purposely to get the metal to set in desired shapes. This was first done probably in West Asia around 4500B.C. or a century or two earlier. But it was not until about 4000B.C. that moulds were used in any but the simplest shapes.

Because copper occurs naturally in a fairly pure metallic form people started working it before smelting began. Small copper **Copper** artefacts have been recovered from sites dating back prior to 6000B.C. At Çatal Hüyük, copper objects, including weights for cloth, have been unearthed from that period. Copper must have come into use after people noticed that hammering or scraping gives the dark lumps a bright metallic look. They then discovered that copper is malleable enough to work cold, and began making little tools, weights and pins. Considering both technological advancement and the availability of natural copper, West Asia is the most likely region of the first home of copper mining.

Bronze is an alloy of copper which was first made by adding tin to it. Bronze with sufficient tin is considerably bet- **Bronze** ter to work and use for most purposes than copper. However the earliest bronze-makers – in Mesopotamia and Asia Minor (present-day Iraq and Turkey) – evidently had no idea what they were doing, and added so little tin that their bronze offered minimal advantage over copper. Objects made of this shoddy bronze (often only one part tin in fifty) have been recovered from the ruins of Ur and other Mesopotamian sites dating back to Sumerian times, around 3500B.C. However the shortage of suitable tin ores in the area may mean that the earliest bronze was actually made further north. It took about a thousand years for good bronze (about one part tin in ten) to take over, setting the stage for the 'Bronze Age'.

**Iron** Limited amounts of iron metal occur naturally in meteorites. The first iron objects were worked from this source in the 4th millennium B.C. The oldest objects of smelted iron recovered by archaeologists were manufactured around 3000B.C. or soon after, and come from Mesopotamia and Anatolia, in present-day Iraq and Turkey. Ancient artefacts and the distribution of ore deposits make it likely that iron was first smelted shortly before 3000B.C. in Anatolia, west of the Taurus Mountains, in present-day Turkey or Armenia.

**Steel** By 1400B.C. this homeland of iron was subject to the Hittite Empire. With its superior ores it was the centre of experimentation in iron metallurgy, developing techniques very different to those used for bronze. This experimentation resulted at that time in the production of the first steel, for which credit is given to a people of Northern Anatolia called the Chalybes. For about two centuries, superior ores and technology gave the Hittite Empire a virtual monopoly on iron and steel production, and an export trade in iron.

However this trade did not extend as far as China, leaving the Chinese to invent iron smelting for themselves – which they were very slow to do. There is no trace of iron in China **Blast Furnace** from earlier than about 600B.C. Yet less than two centuries later, the Chinese had invented the blast furnace – a step that took twenty-seven centuries in the West. Prior to this invention iron had to be produced in the form of wrought iron, and steel was made by increasing its carbon content. The blast fur- **Cast Iron** nace enabled the Chinese to produce cast iron, which has a high initial carbon content. The oldest blast-furnace cast iron yet to be identified is a block dating from about 500B.C. found near the central coast of China. The secret of the Chinese success may have been that they had ores rich in phosphorus, or else added phosphorus to the blast furnace charge. Very gradually blast furnace design and operation improved, and the technology spread overseas, to India and Japan.

The Chinese made steel by decarburising cast iron. In the 2nd century B.C., to make this process efficient, they began delivering an oxidising blast of cold air to the hot cast iron. In China and Japan by the 1600s (at the latest) this led to a **Cast Steel** process for producing cast steel that included subjecting a

Blast furnace, with double-acting piston bellows.

molten mass of cast iron to a cold blast. (This is the first production of cast steel by any currently understood method. However modern Chinese archaeologists report that it was also produced during the former Harn Dynasty [206B.C.– 9A.D.] by a heat treatment for decarburising solid cast iron, which will need some explaining before we acknowledge it.)

There is an iron column in Delhi that has stood out in the open since about 400A.D. and shows no sign of rust or deterioration. It is 99.72% iron, 0.08% carbon, 0.046% silicon, 0.006% sulphur and 0.114% phosphorus. In being able to manufacture iron of such a composition, India's industry was about fifteen centuries ahead of Europe's – and the formula itself was only ever known by analysing the column. The reason for its invincibility is a matter of speculation; one suggestion is that the low sulphur content, and the absence of manganese, are responsible. The technique can hardly be much older than the column, because earlier specimens would have survived till now. Marvellous though this iron is, the invention of stainless steel makes it unlikely that any more will be manufactured.

**Rust-proof Iron**

Stainless steel is the name of iron-chromium alloys that resist corrosion. The first of these was produced experimentally in 1904 by the French scientist Léon Guillet. Curiously, Guillet failed to communicate the remarkable corrosion resistance of his new alloys, and his work was not immediately exploited.

**Stainless Steel**

From 1912 to 1914 Edward Maurer and Benno Strauss, at Germany's Krupp steelworks in Essen, developed austenitic stainless steel with a large amount of nickel in it. Its properties are ideal for industrial needs and it went into large-scale production.

**Brass** Brass is an alloy consisting mostly of zinc and copper. Early Greeks and West Asians almost 3000 years ago smelted brass from an ore with the correct mixture naturally occurring, without understanding its composition. The first brass mixed artificially came from Asia Minor (present-day Turkey) or the Aegean Islands, around 400B.C. Theophrastus (c. 383–287B.C.), head of the Lyceum in Athens, mentions the use of the zinc ore, calamine, for this purpose in his book *De Lapidibus*. (Brass was invented independently in India at a similar time, but the Indian brass is not dated accurately enough to know if it preceded the western.)

**Zinc Metal** A Greek geography book published in the Roman Empire in the 1st century B.C. mentions a metal called pseudo-silver, which must be zinc, because it is said to be a constituent of brass. That would mean zinc was first reduced to its metal state somewhere in the West – possibly Egypt or West Asia – perhaps around 100B.C. or earlier. The method was subsequently lost until 1797, except in India and China, where it was separately invented.

**Cupro-nickel** Cupro-nickel – formerly known as tooth-and-egg or paktong – is the substance from which coins are normally made. Its first identified use is in the coinage of the Hellenistic state of Bactria (in the north of present-day Afghanistan, on the overland trade route between China and Persia) around 200B.C. The source of the metal is still unknown, but it was probably imported from China, where it had just been invented. The Bactrian coinage appears to have had one part nickel in five, similar to early Chinese cupro-nickel, which the Chinese did not use for minting until the 500s A.D.

**Nickel Metal** Nickel, like zinc, was not produced as a pure metal till well after its use in alloys began. The Swedish chemist Axel Cronstedt (1722A.D.–1765) first reduced nickel separately in 1751 by extracting it from sulphides separated out of cobalt ore for the purpose of making cobalt blue pigment.

**Aluminium** The existence of metal in aluminium ore was suspected before anyone is known to have succeeded in extracting it. The suspicion was proved correct in 1825 by the discoverer of electro-magnetism, Danish physicist, Hans Christian Ørsted (alternatively Oersted, 1777–1851 [see Electric Motor, VIII, 9]). Ørsted did not develop a viable method of extraction; in 1846 the German chemist, Friedrich Wöhler, found that by heating a mixture of sodium and chloride of aluminium, he could extract the pure metal in the form of numerous tiny globules.

**Spinning Wheel**

The laborious chore of spinning yarn on hand-held distaffs was first supplanted by spinning wheels in China, either late in the Sharng or early in the Jo Dynasty (around 1000B.C.).

**Machine Spinning**

Spinning was revolutionised by the introduction of automated machinery. According to a Chinese book of the 14th century, a common one-spindle spinning wheel can turn out only 300 g. of silk yarn in a day and night. In the same time span, a single box-spinning machine could produce 60 kg. of yarn. This machine was introduced in the Sung Dynasty (960A.D.–1279) – the age of China's industrial revolution – and soon there were thousands of them. A typical hydraulically powered machine comprised thirty-two tubes, each with a spindle, mounted in a main frame 6 m. long, and driven by a 2 m. water wheel.

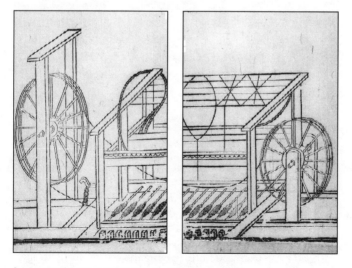

Spinning machinery contributed to the Industrial Revolution.

**Loom**

Simple looms were invented in prehistoric times in many parts of the world, including China, India, Southwest Asia, Egypt and South America. Of these, Southwest Asia is the earliest.

**Jacquard Loom**

Over thousands of years, developments in size, complexity and motive power have turned weaving into an efficient, complex and automated activity. The advent of the jacquard loom has facilitated mechanical production of cloth with intricate designs woven in. This machine was in use in China during the former Harn Dynasty (206B.C.–9A.D.) and it may have been invented earlier, in the 3rd century B.C. Jacquard looms have large frames and towers that support mechanisms for drawing up threads vertically. Their other essential feature is a memory system, enabling exact reproduction of intricate designs. The loom designed by France's Joseph Jacquard (1752A.D.–1834), achieved this by means of punched cards [VIII, 10]. Chinese looms use a memory frame with threads of varying length.

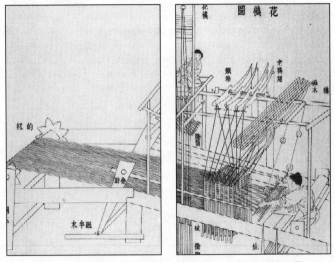

Jacquard loom – the first type of machine to require software [see VIII, 10].

**Cotton Gin**

The cotton gin was invented in China during the Sung Dynasty, to replace the laborious process of manual rolling. Cotton with seeds was passed through a pair of rollers, one metal, the other wood. These crushed the seeds, which dropped away from the fibre, leaving the cotton ready to spin.

**Sewing Machine**

In 1830, Barthélemy Thimonnier, a tailor from Saint Etienne, France, built a wooden sewing machine, consisting of a base surmounted by a hand wheel that moved a connecting rod up and down. This mechanism worked a double pointed needle.

Because his machine had no means of drawing the fabric through, the regularity of the stitches depended on the operator's skill. Thimonnier successfully put his machines into commercial use in Paris, although on one occasion he was attacked by a furious mob of seamstresses, who smashed up his machines in protest at the threat posed to their livelihoods.

Writing in the 13th century about Africa, Chinese author Jao Ru Gua refers to huge fish that are driven regularly onto the Somalian coast. **Commercial Whaling**

> They are over 200 feet in length and 20 feet high in diameter. The inhabitants do not eat their flesh, but cut away their brains and marrow as well as their eyes, to make oil . . . They mix this oil with lime to caulk their boats, or use it for lamps.

By the time Jao's book was published (1226A.D.), this earliest of all whaling industries may have been operating on the shore of the Indian Ocean for anything up to a few hundred years. Prior to that there is no record of any regular whaling operations – presumably for thousands of years people have been cutting up occasional beached whales. The early African whalers mainly sought the highly prized oil, but also traded in whale bones for building material and utensils. In the same region ambergris was gathered from the sea for pharmaceutical and cosmetic uses.

To judge from surviving literature, the systematic study of whales began long before the systematic exploitation. Information on whales in a Roman encyclopaedia – *Natural History* by Pliny (1st century A.D.) – makes it clear that Greek biologists had already discovered the main features of whales that identify them as mammals rather than ordinary fish. They noted in particular that whales give birth to live babies, that they suckle them with milk, that they have hair, and breathe with lungs. Theophrastus (370–285B.C.) is the first Greek scientist known to have made an investigation of whale biology. **Whale Biology**

Chilled food and drink initially depended on the availability of natural ice and snow. Because the greatest demand is in summer when ice and snow are rarities, insulated coolrooms were constructed, in which they were stored all through summer. The earliest coolroom on record is the one in the Southern Mesopotamian city of Ur (in present-day Iraq), during the reign of King Shulgi (c. 2250B.C.) in Sumerian times. **Ice House**

Artificial ice-making began with the use of specially shaped vessels in which water could be frozen by the chilling **Ice-making** effect of evaporation. They were porous pans which were filled with water and placed by night in shallow lined pits, so that ice could be gathered from them in the morning. The vessels were widely used in India and West Asia; and possibly first in ancient Mesopotamia, but their date is unknown.

**Refrigeration Plant**   Refrigeration plant using chemical refrigerants, like a domestic refrigerator [XI, 2], was the invention of a newspaper editor in Geelong, Victoria. James Harrison, editor of the *Geelong Advertiser*, and later the editor of the *Age* in Melbourne, noticed the chilling effect of a mixture of sulphuric ether and ammonia, which newspaper printers used to clean type. He developed an ether pump and a cooling coil through which the ether expanded. In 1850 he set up an ice factory on the banks of Geelong's Barwon River and was soon able to supply the whole city. Outside Geelong he sold very little ice because of consumer prejudice in favour of the natural product imported from America. However during the 1850s he successfully applied his technique to refrigerators and cool rooms.

**Refrigerated Ship**   In 1873, Harrison fitted out the first self-refrigerating ship for food transport, the *Norfolk*. On its first voyage with refrigerated meat from Australia to England, the plant was incorrectly operated and the meat spoiled, but subsequent ventures were highly successful.

## 9. ENERGY TECHNOLOGY

Engines are covered in this section, but their use for transport is dealt with in Chapter IX, sections 1, 2 and 3.

**Perpetual Motion**   The long and hopeless quest to achieve perpetual motion by mechanical means seems to have begun in the Chin Dynasty (3rd century B.C.), when the famous grave of the First Emperor was being constructed in North China. The decorators of the massive grave, which contains 6000 life-size pottery soldiers, provided it with a lamp that was supposed to burn forever, and a panoramic model of China with rivers of mercury that would never stop flowing. Whether the makers really expected them to work perpetually, or whether they were simply designed to impress by running until after the grave was sealed, is not recorded. However when the grave was located and opened in the 1970s, the light had gone out and the rivers had dried up.

Heron of Alexandria, the Greek who invented the steam engine and the automatically opening door, wrote in his *Pneumatica* (Alexandria, c. 100B.C.) of an Egyptian windmill very similar to the kind used today. It was fitted with angled vanes, and faced into the wind which drove it. **Windmill**

The water wheel was such a popular technological breakthrough that its invention was celebrated in poetry. The most immediate advantage of this multi-purpose mechanism was in replacing hard manual labour with automated operation in flour mills. For this the poet credits Demeter, goddess of grain: **Water Wheel**

Hold back the hand that works the mill; sleep long
    you grinding-women, though cocks announce the day:
Demeter has put your work out to the Nymphs
    who jump onto the very top of the wheel
and spin the axle which with twisting cogs
    revolves the Nisyrus millstones' hollow weights.
We taste the archaic life again by learning
    to feast on Demeter's produce without work.
                    (*Greek Anthology*, ix, 418, tr. Elliot)

This poem was written late in the 1st century B.C. by Antipater, from Thessalonika in Northern Greece. It appears from this and other sources that water wheels were introduced earlier in the same century.

Another kind of water wheel known as the noria was invented at about the same time. It is a brilliant device for pumping river water to a great height without any effort, and is still in use in some places for town and farm water. The wheel is driven by the pressure of the river current, turning it from underneath. At the same time containers on the wheel fill with river water, which they empty out at the top of the circuit of revolution, into an adjacent conduit. Both these wheels hail from the Mediterranean area, probably the eastern part of the Roman Empire, just over 2000 years ago. **Noria**

In 1796A.D. in France, Joseph Montgolfier, one of two brothers famous for their hot air balloon [IX, 3], invented another device for raising water under the power of its own flow. His 'hydraulic ram' develops high air pressure by directing gushing water in a sealed chamber. This pressure is then exploited to drive some of the water up to a height well above its natural level. **Hydraulic Ram**

The first domestic use of coal is unlikely ever to be known. Its use as an industrial fuel began in the Chinese iron industry **Coal**

during the former Harn Dynasty (206B.C.–9A.D.). Archaeo-
logical excavations of large steelworks at Tieh Sheng Go in
Northeastern China, which date from around the 1st century
B.C., have discovered coal to be one of the main fuels used.

**Briquettes** They have also revealed the earliest briquettes – cakes of pow-
dered coal combined with clay and quartz.

**Steam Engine** Heron of Alexandria – who invented the steam engine in
Egypt over 2000 years ago – had no known plans for putting it
to practical use. He saw it as a way to demonstrate the power
developed by expansion when water vaporises. Heron's engine
had a boiler from which two pipes carried steam into a spherical pressure chamber. Steam shooting out through jets
mounted outside the pressure chamber made it spin around. In
later times machines like this were used to keep spits turning,
the cooking fire being made to heat the boiler; but whether
anyone put the engine to practical use in Heron's time is
unknown. In fact it is not even known when his time was;
estimates range from before 200B.C. to after 200A.D. Somewhere around 100B.C. seems the most likely.

**Condenser** The engine is fully described in Heron's *Pneumatica*, a
scientific book dealing with the behaviour of fluid substances. It describes many of his inventions including
machines which take advantage of hot air to pump water,
make sounds and do tricks. Some of the hot air machines
include a condenser – a means of creating a relative vacuum
by cooling an expanded substance in a chamber. During the
16th or 17th century A.D., steam condensers were introduced in Europe for pumping water out of mines. The vacuum created by condensing steam acted directly on the water
to draw it up.

**Piston Rod** In Britain in 1712, Thomas Newcomen (1663–1729) was
**Steam Engine** the first to introduce steam to an engine with a piston in a
cylinder. Its piston rod was attached to one end of a pivoting
beam, with a pump rod at the other end, so that as the piston
rose the pump rod descended and vice versa. As the first recip-
rocating steam engine to transfer energy via mechanical linkage to a working machine, Newcomen's is the ancestor of
almost all subsequent steam power. Still its working stroke was
the stroke during which atmospheric pressure drove the piston
into the cylinder evacuated by condensation. It was not until
Leupold's steam engine of 1725 that steam under pressure was
intended to propel the working stroke.

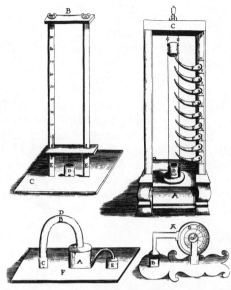

Gunpowder testers were the forerunners of petrol engines. This 1635 picture by John Babington shows – at bottom left – the first internal combustion engine in which the fuel is used for propulsive force (apart from guns). An explosion in chamber C drives water out of reservoir A, into a measuring vessel, E.

The original of all internal combustion engines is the gun [VI, 2] – the barrel works like the cylinder in a car engine. Looking for an engine with a piston rather than a bullet takes us back to the work of Leonardo da Vinci (1452–1519), the Italian artist who first designed a bicycle [IX, 2]. In 1508 he devised a weight-lifting engine, in which a gunpowder explosion in a cylinder would lead to a relative vacuum as the gases cooled. Under atmospheric pressure, the piston would be drawn up into the cylinder, raising a weight as it went. Leonardo was the first of several European inventors working with internal combustion gunpowder engines, but they all encountered problems, such as the difficulty of removing exhaust and residues. The first practical use of internal combustion had to wait for the genius of Swiss mechanic François Isaac de Rivaz (died 1828). He made an engine in 1804 powered by hydrogen gas ignited electrically. He got the idea for it from the work of Alessandro Volta, the Italian battery inventor [see below] who conceived a pistol using hydrogen exploded by an electric spark, instead of gunpowder. De Rivaz built road vehicles that travelled under the power of his hydrogen engines.

The four-stroke cycle for internal combustion engines is

**Internal Combustion Engine**

**Electric Ignition**

**Four-stroke Cycle** fully described in a pamphlet about gas cylinder engines published in France by Alphonse Beau de Rochas, in 1862. Beau de Rochas patented his inspiration early in that year, but it was not put to work until 1876, when Count Nicholas Otto (1832–91), a German engineer, built a four-stroke engine.

**Diesel Engine** In Germany in 1897, Dr. Rudolf Diesel (1858–1913), a German engineer born in Paris, completed the first workable diesel, from a concept he had patented in 1892. It was a stationary industrial engine: heavy in relation to its power, capricious and inefficient. But it could run well if kept at a steady speed and this limited success stimulated a string of improvements. Seventy years later the diesel engine had become the world's foremost source of motive power.

**Jet Engine** With the sponsorship of the Heinkel aircraft manufacturing firm, German engineer Hans von Ohain developed the jet engine in 1936 and 1937, at the Heinkel plant in Warnemünde, north of Berlin. Observing the success of this trial engine, German Air Ministry officials in 1938 gave the order to local firms to develop jet fighters [VI, 3]. Soon after came the jet bomber [VI, 3] and when the Second World War was over, the jet airliner [IX, 3].

**Electricity** In ancient Greece, the founders of the theory of atoms [VII, 4] conceived of electrical phenomena as the effects of currents – of highly mobile, infinitesimally small, weightless particles, which can travel through solid matter. They had no idea of how to generate or control these currents, but they likened them to the flow of water, and their inspired deductions produced a description consistent with modern understanding of the motion of electrons:

> There must be a fourth element, and this
> Lacks, so far, even a name; nothing exists
> More tenuous, more mobile; it is made
> Out of the smallest lightest particles,
> And it is this which first imparts to limbs
> Sense-bringing movements.

This description – by the Roman poet Lucretius in his *De Rerum Natura* – is based on the beliefs of the Greek philosophers Leucippus of Elea, and Democritus of Abdera, who worked in the 5th century B.C. The Greeks had no generators, and their observations are confined to electrical phenomena in nature: the mind and nervous system, and electrical storms.

Producing static electricity by rubbing was the earliest kind of electric generation. However the term 'generator' means a device that generates a charge by means of induction, rather than friction. In 1776, Alessandro Volta (1745A.D.–1827) invented a simple generator, which took its initial charge by friction, but subsequently kept up a supply of electricity by induction.

**Generator**

Volta was an Italian nobleman from Como who introduced the culture of the potato to Lombardy. Not content to let his fame rest on this achievement, he studied and criticised the pioneering work on electricity of his countryman Galvano. Volta's theory is that electricity is produced by contact of adjacent metals, and in 1799 he invented the battery, or 'pile' as he called it, with multiple metal plates, each formed of a sheet of copper and a sheet of zinc soldered together.

**Battery**

No one succeeded in deliberately producing artificial light from electricity until 1808, when the English scientist, Humphrey Davy (1778–1829), operated the first arc lamp. Two pieces of carbon joined to opposite ends of a battery almost touched, and the current crossing the gap between them heated them so they glowed.

**Electric Light**

Twenty years later Joseph Swan was born in England, during what he later referred to as the 'dark ages' when 'the common people, wanting the inducement of indoor brightness . . . went to bed soon after sunset'. One of his causes in life was to resolve domestic gloom which could not be comfortably countered by harsh arc lamps. In 1878 he produced the first successful specimen of the now ubiquitous filament lamp. Electric current lit up a carbon filament inside a glass bulb. A vacuum in the bulb prevented the filament burning away.

**Vacuum Filament Lamp**

The earliest electric motor was built in 1831 by its American inventor Joseph Henry (1797–1878). It was a tiny demonstration model, consisting of a rocker beam on a central pivot, powered by electromagnets in accordance with the principle of electro-magnetism detected in 1819 by Danish physicist, Hans Christian Ørsted (1777–1851). Its simple mode of operation is in essence the same as that of most subsequent more elaborate-looking motors.

**Electric Motor**

In December 1951, researchers at Argonne National Laboratory in Idaho, U.S.A., generated useable electricity from their experimental 150-kilowatt nuclear reactor. It was the first

**Nuclear Electricity**

practical demonstration of the capability of nuclear reactors to generate electric power supplies.

**Nuclear Power Station**
The first nuclear power station to feed a supply grid was opened by Queen Elizabeth at Calder Hall, in Cumbria, England, on 17 October 1956. Originally its main purpose was the production of plutonium for nuclear weapons. Electricity generation was a way to use waste heat, but soon became the principal object of the station.

## 10. INSTRUMENTS AND APPARATUS

For domestic and office appliances, see Chapter XI, section 2.

**Timepieces**
The most ancient timepieces took two forms. One, the clepsydra, was, in early models, just a leaking bucket with hour markings on the inside. As the water leaked out, its level dropped, and the time could be told by seeing which mark it came up to.

**Water Clocks**
These primitive water clocks were first used in Mesopotamia early in the 2nd millennium B.C.; unfortunately there is no way of knowing exactly when and where. Later clepsydrae had multiple chambers and siphons for the sake of accuracy, but the early bucket type was imprecise and inaccurate.

**Shadow Clock**
Accurate timekeeping at first relied on shadow clocks, and was therefore only possible when the sun shone. It shines almost all day in Egypt, where shadow clocks were first made, early or midway through the 2nd millennium B.C. A specimen surviving from the reign of Thutmose III (16th century B.C.), shows how a T-shaped upright casts a shadow on a horizontal bar marked with the uneven length hours of the Egyptian day.

**Sundial**
Greater accuracy and precision are possible with the sundial – another Egyptian invention, from a few centuries later. The oldest to be discovered is a small ivory disc, with a picture on the back, from the reign of Pharaoh Merenptah, in the 13th century B.C.

**Clock**
Compared to these early timepieces, the distinguishing feature of the clock is the escapement – the device for arresting its mechanical motion in order to fix the rate of progress. The escapement was invented in the Tarng Dynasty by Yi Hsing and Liarng Ling Dsarn, and incorporated in the huge water-powered clock which they constructed between 723 A.D. and 725 for the government in Charng Arn. The escapement worked by applying a brake to the mechanism, until water flowing at a controlled rate filled a measure, whereupon it

momentarily released the mechanism and the process began again. In this fashion the clock 'ticked' a few times each minute. A bell sounded on the hour and a drum every fifteen minutes. This clock was also fitted with a globe showing star positions, and moving Sun and Moon indicators showing dawn and sunset and the phases of the Moon.

The great clock built by Su Sung in the Sung Dynasty capital, Kaifeng (1088A.D.–1090), had multiple digital displays. Set **Digital Display** into the lowest storey of the three-storey clock tower was a series of windows in which figures appeared, giving information about the date and time. This mode of presentation may go back to the first clock [see above] completed in 725A.D. Whether a time display was included in it, or whether it was left to bells and drums to do the job is not known.

　　Some of the water clocks designed in Hellenistic times, and used in Mediterranean countries such as Egypt and Greece **Clockface** (probably from the 3rd century B.C.), were equipped with circu- **Display** lar clockface dials. The hours were marked by lines radiating out from the centre – and the dial was linked to a float in the water chamber. To make their task less straightforward, the Greeks and other peoples of the Eastern Mediterranean had hours which varied in length with the time of the year. The number of daylight hours was fixed, so in mid-winter they were much shorter than in mid-summer. For this reason a second face rotated behind the first to adjust the hour lengths as the date changed.

Because electric current causes quartz crystals to vibrate at a constant 32,768 cycles per second, they can be used to make **Quartz Crystal** extremely accurate escapements. Warren Alvin Marrison, a **Clock** clockmaker from Orange, New Jersey, U.S.A., and J. W. Horton took advantage of this in 1928 to build the prototype quartz crystal clock. They released their new invention to the public the following year.

The invention of the magnetic compass is based on the discovery of the lodestone – an iron-rich stone which, when sus- **Compass** pended turns to lie north-south. The earliest form of compass, invented in North China around 300B.C., was a spoon-shaped piece of lodestone balanced on a square board marked with directions. The bottom of the bowl part of the spoon served as a pivot while the handle rotated to point towards magnetic South. It was not until about 300A.D. that the Chinese developed the metal compass needle, which is more accurate because it encounters less friction than the spoon turning on a polished surface. Over 500 years went past after that before the compass was adapted to marine navigation [IX, 1].

**Abacus**  This machine, for which the Chinese always receive credit, has been identified in European sites from the days of the Roman Empire. These finds suggest that the abacus might have been invented in the West well before the earliest Chinese record of it, but we can't tell where or when. The specimens from Roman times are plates of metal or marble with slots for moving the counters up and down. The oldest Chinese reference is in a Harn Dynasty textbook of 190A.D., the *Account of Some Traditions of Mathematical Practice* by Hsew Yaw. According to the author, his own teacher had met a Taoist named Tien Mu Hsien Seng who explained 'ball arithmetic' to him. This book furnishes the first description of the type of abacus on which beads are moved along wires, as they are on the modern version.

**Computer**  The oldest known computer is one manufactured in 87B.C., probably on the Greek island of Rhodes. It comes from the wreck of a small ship, which sank off Greece shortly after 80B.C. Although its capabilities were not great by today's standards, the small hand-powered mechanism is quite intricate, and engineered with precision. Its function was to replace time-consuming astronomical and calendar calculations with an automatic method. In a case about 1 foot by 6 inches by 2 inches it had three dials, each with an inset dial like the seconds dial on a watch. Some dials had adjustable calibrated rings, some of which could be used to reset the machine from the Greek to the Egyptian calendar. Damage makes it impossible to tell exactly how it worked and the instructions on the door are no longer readable; but studies reveal thirty-one gear wheels and a drive shaft. The most intricate part of the mechanism is a turntable driven by the world's earliest differential gearing [VIII, 11]. Rhodes, where Posidonius had his school at this time, was a centre of astronomical studies, and computers like the one from the shipwreck were probably invented there around 100B.C.

**Software**  Before computers were invented, software was used in industry to programme machinery. It first appeared in jacquard looms [VIII, 8], in North China probably in the 3rd century B.C. Such looms could turn out cloth in an infinite range of intricate repeating patterns. The first step was to programme the loom with a master pattern consisting of vast numbers of silk threads in a frame – a job performed by the 'most ingenious craftsmen', working from patterns drawn by designers.

The British mathematician and engineer, Charles Babbage (1792–1871), designed computers in the 1830s, one of which he called the 'analytical engine'. Although he sunk vast funds into the project a successful working model was never completed. However he and his collaborator, Lady Ada Lovelace, the poet Byron's daughter, were responsible for a major breakthrough on the project. 'The analytical engine has no pretensions to originate anything', she wrote in 1843. 'It can do whatever we know how to order it to perform . . . it has no power of anticipating any analytical relationships or truths.' **Computer Programme**

To make it work Babbage, with Lady Ada's help, devised a system of computer programming using punched cards. Punched cards had previously been used to programme patterns into weaving equipment, including French jacquard looms. French inventor Basile Bouchon equipped a loom with a punched scroll in 1725A.D. The system was modified and cards replaced scrolls in 1728. **Punched Cards**

Z2, completed in 1938 or 1939, was one of a series of machines designed in the 1930s and during the Second World War, by the inventor of electric computers, gifted German statistician, Konrad Zuse (born 1910). Z2 was the first computer in the world to be fully digital and rely on electro-magnetic relays to the exclusion of mechanical linkages and valves. Zuse adopted the binary system [see VIII, 1] for the new computer, anticipating a method implemented in other countries in later decades. **Electronic Digital Computer**

The silicon chip – which is nowadays home to the microprocessor – was first put to use for integrated circuits in 1958 by researchers and technicians working for the American firm, Texas Instruments. They diffused impurities into different regions of a small slice of silicon to modify its conductivity and to put each region to work as a component in electrical circuitry. The different regions were connected by lengths of fine wire. The first silicon chip integrated circuit was comparatively simple, but with further development the number of components in each chip gradually increased. The challenge which brought the microprocessor into existence was that of building an entire calculating mechanism into a single chip. Several American firms aimed at this in the late 1960s. In 1969 Edward Hoff – an engineer at Intel Corporation with the job of designing components for a calculator – decided to put all the main circuits together in **Silicon Chip**

**Microprocessor**

a single chip instead of using a different chip for each circuit. His new design had separate chips for the programme and memory functions, and a single chip for all the central processing. This was released in 1971 as the Intel 4004 by Intel in conjunction with Texas Instruments. At the same time Gilbert Hyatt of Micro Computer Inc. was heading another team which developed a single chip micro-computer, completed in 1971.

**Robotics**

In the 2nd century B.C., Greek-speaking technicians began to create a lot of automated entertainments: elaborate machinery in which little robots acted out dramatic performances to the accompaniment of synchronised flames and smoke, sound effects, spraying fluids and shifting scenery. Foremost were Philo of Byzantium (present-day Istanbul) and Ctesibius and Heron of Alexandria, in Egypt. Of these, Philo – who is thought to have worked shortly after 200B.C. – was probably the earliest. Heron, inventor of the first steam engine [VIII, 9], may have lived a century later than the others. His book on the subject, *Automata*, still exists, unlike theirs. Using two robot performances as illustrations, he explains the complex range of machinery which made the robots work in time with each other and with the stage effects. Motive power was provided by a slowly descending weight, linked mechanically to complex arrays of gear wheels, cylinders, cords, lamps, pulleys, levers, reservoirs and containers of lead balls. The operator only had to set the works in motion and stand back, while concealed machinery propelled the little figures through all the episodes of a complex narrative.

**Responding Automata**

These and other early automata were preset to act on fixed patterns. The capability in such machinery to react to external stimulus came in Tarng Dynasty China, around 700A.D. It was a great help at palace garden parties. Five 2-foot tall robots travelled in a toy boat along a canal. One punted, two rowed, one poured wine, and one served. Their boat stopped at each guest's place, and the server handed the guest a full cup. When the guest gave the cup back, the little robots refilled it automatically. Underwater machinery set in the canal drove the mechanism, which was probably hydraulically powered. We no longer have the inventor's name, nor any indication of how he got the machinery to respond to an external factor. An intermediate stage had previously been reached in the 2nd century A.D. with the differential gearing [VIII, 11] of the Chinese 'south-pointing carriage'. The pointing figure reacted to the unpredictable motion of the wheels to achieve what can actually be called a passive response, and kept pointing south wherever he was driven.

The discovery of the camera obscura is the first major step towards the photographic camera. A camera obscura is a chamber with light entering only through a tiny hole at the front. An upside-down image of whatever is in front of it appears on the inside back surface of the chamber. In the *Maw Jing*, a philosophical book from North China, in a section on optics added around 300B.C., there is a description of this device with an explanation of how it works and why the image is inverted. The anonymous writers are the first known to have experimented with the camera obscura, but it may have been invented shortly before their time, anywhere in North China. **Camera**

**Camera Obscura**

It was improved in Italy by Daniele Barbaro of Venice, in 1568A.D., who added a lens to focus the image coming through the pinhole. **Camera Lens**

In Britain, about 1800A.D., Thomas Wedgwood added the final essential component of a camera – the film. He described his method in an article in the *Journal of the Royal Institution* published in 1802. Wedgwood treated white paper and white leather with nitrate of silver to make them light sensitive, and exposed them in the camera obscura where they took photographic images. Although in this way he was using a camera in the true sense, he had no way of fixing the image so that it would not disappear on exposure to general light. **Film**

This objective was accomplished in France in the 1820s by Nicéphore Niepce of Chalon-sur-Saône. Niepce (1765–1833) made hundreds of camera images of the view from his attic window over many years. He experimented with varnishes to fix the image and developed the first negative to positive system. His method of fixing images seems to have failed as often as it succeeded, but the success he had makes him the first person to have taken photographs. **Photographs**

Niepce's nephew, Claude Niepce de St. Victor, began work on colour photography around 1850, and in 1852 produced a set of colour photographs of real and artificial flowers, coloured engravings, and gold and silver lace. He used silvered plates treated with chloride of copper. Unfortunately colours fade fairly quickly with this method, known as the heliochrome process – so we can't tell how good his colours were. **Colour Photography**

The history of moving pictures goes through dozens of minor firsts rather than a single conspicuous invention. The capability **Cinema** of taking movie film developed well before any successful technique for projecting it on screen. That breakthrough came to the French brothers Auguste and Louis Lumiere, early in 1895. They were scientifically trained, but also owned a photography business in Lyons. They launched their invention in Paris in March, by screening a short film shot in 1894 at their Lyons workshop. Their film had a line of punched holes running down each side, to help the projector move it at a regular speed and arrest the motion for each frame.

**Telescope** Late in the 16th century A.D., two Italians tried placing a pair of lenses together in a tube for viewing distant objects. Giovanbaptista Della Porta and Raffael Gualterotti achieved such weak magnifications that their inventions cannot be called telescopes. But around 1605, the Italian device, or at least the idea, turned up in the Dutch city of Middelburg – site of a leading lens factory – and there impressed the first telescope maker with its potential. What then happened is a mystery, until September and October 1608, when four Dutch telescope makers came out of the woodwork within a few weeks of each other. Each had achieved impressive results by better matching and placement of the lenses. Hans Lipperhey (1560–1619) of Middelburg applied to the Netherlands federal administration, the States General in The Hague, for a patent. In Germany, an anonymous Dutchman at the Frankfurt Autumn Fair offered his telescope for sale. Sacharias Janssen of Middelburg, and Jacob Metius of Alkmaar (who would certainly have been a visitor to Middelburg in his occupation of spectacle maker) both came forward with telescopes of their own, during the inquiry into Lipperhey's application. Unless new evidence comes to light, the name of the first inventor cannot be chosen out of these four. All we can say is that in 1608 or one of the few years before it, one of them succeeded in making the first telescope.

**Binoculars** Lipperhey was not granted a patent because others also had telescopes. But his enterprise in going to The Hague won him a 900-guilder contract with the States General. This government order specified that he was to deliver binoculars, on the same principle as his prototype telescope. He made and delivered the first three pairs in 1608.

**Astronomical Telescope** The Dutch telescopes and binoculars worked by pairing a concave with a convex lens. In the astronomical telescope, both lenses are convex. This model was invented by Johannes Kepler, a German astronomer working in Prague, in 1610.

Radio waves reaching the Earth from galaxies, nebulae, quasars, pulsars, gases and ordinary stars can be measured in **Radio** order to augment discoveries made with the naked eye and **Telescope** optical telescopes. The first radio telescope large enough to do this was constructed by Grote Reber (born 1911), an exceptionally keen young amateur astronomer, in his backyard at Wheaton, Illinois, U.S.A., in 1937–38. It had an iron parabolic dish, 9 m. in diameter. The radio waves it received were recorded as a line on a graph, but the operator could also listen to its reception with earphones.

The other fundamental instrument of radio astronomy is the interferometer, which detects and isolates radiation from **Interferometer** outer space, using antennae. The first was the 'sea cliff type', built on coastal ridges and cliff tops in order to correlate direct beams with rays reflected from the sea. Australian physicist Joseph Pawsey, head of the Radiophysics Laboratory of the C.S.I.R. (now CSIRO), and his staff, founded the first of these in 1945, on Collaroy Plateau above Sydney's Northern Beaches. In that year it became the first observatory to ascertain that the Sun's radio intensity is out of proportion to its optical strength, and directly linked to sun-spot activity. Bernard Mills (born 1920), also working with the CSIRO, **Cross** designed the first cross interferometer, the Mills cross at **Interferometer** Fleurs near Sydney, built in 1953. Cross interferometers consist of two long lines of antennae intersecting at right angles; each leg of Mills's first device was 1500 feet long. Their great size and dual alignment enable them to register radio images as distinct as the optical images received by conventional telescopes.

The thermometer was invented in Italy about 1600A.D. In 1612, Sanctorius – a doctor who had been teaching at the **Thermometer** University of Venice – wrote:

> We have an instrument with which not only the heat and cold of the air are measured, but all the degrees of heat and cold of all the parts of the body.

His thermometer had a bulb at the top for taking the temperature, and a tube standing in fluid. The height of fluid in the tube indicated the temperature. A document from Rome dated 1611 has descriptions and drawings of two thermometers, one with gradations marked on it. Sanctorius wrote that he used the thermometer with his students, but he never claimed to be the inventor, nor indicated whether he knew anything of the designs from Rome. The thermometer was unknown to Galileo in 1592, when he reinvented the much less useful 'thermoscope'.

**X-ray** The X-ray was discovered in the course of research carried out over several minutes on 8 November 1895, by Prof. Wilhelm Röntgen (1845–1923) at Wurzburg in Germany. During experiments in a darkened laboratory with a cathode ray tube, Röntgen noticed green light coming from a piece of cardboard some distance from the tube. Although the cardboard was coated with a luminescent preparation, there was no light source to make it glow. Röntgen placed his hand in the way of the tube, and saw the shadow of his bones on the cardboard. He called the rays which were penetrating his flesh X-rays, because he didn't know the name of them. Nor does anyone else, but their applications were discovered quickly enough. Before the end of the year they were used for clinical photography in Vienna, the first diagnostic application. The first Australian patient to have his fracture X-rayed was Adelaide schoolboy William Lawrence Bragg (1890–1971).

**X-ray Crystallography** That X-ray was taken by his father, William Henry Bragg (1862–1942), a British-born scientist who was working on X-ray research at the time. A few years later, in 1908, father and son both travelled to Britain. There, early in 1913, the elder Bragg succeeded in detecting the reflected rays in an ionisation chamber. This enabled him to make the first X-ray spectrometer. His son joined him and together they used the new technique to examine crystal structures. Their exhaustive work throughout 1913 created a whole new science of X-ray crystallography. In 1915 they became the first parent and child team to share a Nobel Prize, when their work was rewarded with the prize for Physics.

**Diving Gear**
**Snorkel**
**Breathing Tube** The equipment available to divers has gradually become more sophisticated. Snorkels go back to the Stone Age. Long breathing tubes conveying a constant air supply from the surface were well known in Greece by the 4th century B.C. Aristotle in his book *The Parts of Animals* describes an elephant's trunk for his readers by comparing its action to that of a diver's tube. The diver's helmet and the caisson, or diving bell, are first described in a Greek book, *Physical Problems*, of about 200B.C.

**Diver's Helmet**
**Diving Bell**

**Pumped Air** Breathing tubes provided with air pumps, which enable divers to go very deep, are first mentioned in an Arabic work on hydraulic engineering written around 1000A.D.

In 1942 the French marine biologist and naval officer, Jacques Cousteau, and control valve engineer, Emile Gagnan, together designed a portable air supply for divers – the aqualung. It was the first appliance that provided a variable volume of air regulated by the diver's breathing, and adjustable pressure to prevent lung collapse at great depths.

**Aqualung**

Al-Biruni's great scientific book on geology, *Kitāb al-jamāhir*, has elsewhere been referred to for its pioneering insights into plant nutrition and coral [VIII, 5]. As befits a marine biologist, al-Biruni (973A.D.–1051) took a great interest in diving, and his practical comments on it in the book include guidance on the diving months and seasons, harmful sea animals, and spots free of the shark menace.

**Diving Guide**

Calipers are a Chinese invention, probably from the Warring States Period (481–221B.C.), designed to make measuring quicker and more accurate. The oldest set still in existence is from 9A.D. The gradations are in inches and tenths of inches. It was equipped with a finger hole and a locking pin – refinements which may not have been included on the first caliper gauge.

**Caliper Gauge**

# 11. MACHINE TECHNOLOGY

The wheel was a much later invention than people generally think. Cavemen would not have been able to make one, let alone work out what to do with it. The earliest evidence archaeologists have been able to find of vehicles with wheels is from Mesopotamia, (present-day Iraq). This suggests that wheels came into use on carts there in the early to mid-4th millennium B.C.

**Wheel**

Toys or models with clay wheels have been found in Mesopotamia which may date back up to 6000 years ago. Some cultures are known to have developed wheels for children's toys before they had them on working vehicles, so it is possible that the first wheel amused a Mesopotamian toddler around 4000B.C.

**Wheeled Toy**

Working wheels in the early days were made of solid wood or joined planks cut into circular shapes. The first spoked wheels, introduced in Mesopotamia around 2000B.C., brought in a revolution in lightness and efficiency.

**Spokes**

The counterweight was first employed on a simple water lifting machine, the shadoof. The counterweight of stone, clay,

**Counterweight**

timber or other material was set at one end of a long timber arm. At the other end was a container for drawing water, and between them a fulcrum. The water is quite easy to raise because gravity operates to lower the counterweight at the same time. Shadoofs are still used on the Nile River. However, representations of them on cylinder seals from Mesopotamia (present-day Iraq) dating before 2000B.C. are the oldest evidence of counterweights, suggesting they were developed there before in Egypt.

**Screw** The screw was first used in presses to increase the pressure that an operator could exert over a large surface. Screw presses became popular for producing oil and wine, but they were already in use in Asia Minor (present-day Turkey) in the 6th century B.C., for compacting cloth. The first description is given by the Greek natural philosopher, Heraclitus, who lived in Ephesus at that time, and wrote of the screw press as an illustration of helical motion.

**Archimedean Screw** The Archimedean screw – a screw used for conveying material – was certainly in existence by Archimedes's time, but derives its name from his interest in it, not because he invented it. It is usually in the form of a very long screw set within a pipe for use as a pump. As the screw is rotated, the pipe takes up water at the bottom and ejects it at the top. Its inventor is not recorded, but probably lived in the Eastern Mediterranean around 300B.C.

**Piston Pump** The piston pump, which operates by means of two pistons going alternatively up and down in cylinders, and feeding an outlet vessel, was invented about 300B.C. by Ctesibius, a Greek engineer living in Alexandria. (In China his principle was already in use at this time on bellows for smelting metal, and allegedly in chemical weapons [VI, 2].)

**Rotary Pedal Propulsion** Long before bicycles were thought of, pedal drive was put into use on water pumping machinery by the Harn Dynasty engineer Bi Larn. He was commissioned in the 2nd century A.D. to build an elaborate water supply system for the capital of China, Law Yarng. His equipment included such exotic machines as the spread-eagled toad (gear-wheel assembly), the heavenly pay-off (noria [VIII, 9]) and the square-pallet chain **Square Pallet Chain Pump** pump. This last invention, operated by a pedal-driven shaft turning an upper sprocket wheel, is still in use today. The chain carries a series of pallets that push water upwards through a conduit from the bottom (unpowered) chainwheel to the outlet. The principle of chain drive around chainwheels – used today for escalators, bikes, photocopiers and a variety of industrial machines – was first applied with these pumps.    **Chain Drive**

The eccentric lug converts round-and-round motion to back-and-forth motion, or vice versa. It can be seen in action on steam locomotives, on which a piston connected to a point beside the wheel hub makes the driving wheel rotate. But its first use was in the iron foundries of Narn Yarng during the later Harn Dynasty. The inventor Du Shu was a government official who, for humanitarian reasons, wanted to save the back-breaking work of metallurgical bellows. In 31A.D. he replaced the manual operation with a mechanical reciprocator driven by a water wheel with an eccentric lug.    **Eccentric-lug Linkage**

Last century, on steam engines, the eccentric lug superseded the ingenious sun-and-planet linkage which was actually a later invention. English engineer James Watt had invented it because James Pickard had taken a patent on the eccentric-lug system for steam engines in 1780, and an alternative method had to be devised.    **Sun-and-planet Linkage**

Gear wheels were manufactured in Northern China early in the Warring States Period (481–221B.C.). Ratchet wheels are a later refinement – also Chinese – from about 300B.C. A 3rd century B.C. specimen has been recovered from Shansi in Northwestern China. It is about an inch in diameter and has forty ratchet teeth. Going by archaeological finds gear wheels in a double helix pattern (with cogs like chevrons) appear to originate in China late in the 3rd century B.C.    **Gear Wheels**

**Ratchets**

**Double Helical Gears**

Cams in China came into use about 200B.C. The oldest specimens belong to crossbow triggers of the Harn Dynasty. The first 'three-dimensional cams' are the helically grooved swashplates that came into use in Western Europe in the 15th century A.D.    **Cams**

**Swashplates**

In motor vehicles differential gearing delivers greater driving motion to the outer wheel in a turn, so the inner wheel won't skid or take the vehicle out of control. However the first differential machinery was used for assimilating information; it referred motion from the axles rather than to them. The oldest computer [VIII, 10], made on the Greek island of Rhodes in 87B.C., includes a differentially driven turntable. It reconciled data relating to the synodic cycle of the Moon from one gear    **Differential Gearing** train, with calendar data from another. The turntable moved at a rate dictated by half the algebraic sum of the two inputs. The mechanism was probably developed around 100B.C. The first vehicle with differential gearing was an ancient Chinese curiosity, the 'south-pointing chariot' – probably the handiwork of the great scientist Jarng Heng, in about 120A.D. Atop the chariot stood a statue with an extended arm pointing south. Whether the chariot turned right or left or went round in circles, the statue continued resolutely pointing south.

**Roller Bearing**

**Ball Bearings**

Vehicles in Shansi, in Northwestern China, were being fitted with roller bearings for greater smoothness and efficiency from the 4th century B.C. Ball bearings were used by the Italian artist Benvenuto Cellini (1500A.D.–1571) to mount rotating statues that turned freely on being spun.

**Gimbals**

The non-spilling ink pot invented by the Greek scientist Philo of Byzantium (c. 200B.C.) is the first device known to have used the ingenious principle of gimbals. (A mounting of three concentric hoops, each pivoted on the next, and swinging on an axis perpendicular to the next one's, holds an object in the centre perfectly upright through any amount of shifting.)

**Pneumatic Suspension**

The brilliant British pioneer of steam locomotion, George Stephenson (1781–1848), invented pneumatic suspension as a means of preventing derailments. In 1816 he built an engine with axle bearings that could move up and down within guides. Attached to the axles were pistons that travelled in cylinders mounted under the boiler. Steam from the boiler under pressure in the cylinders kept the wheels in contact with the tracks. Stephenson built several engines on this plan from 1816 to 1822 for use on colliery railways.

## 12. COMMUNICATIONS TECHNOLOGY

Printing is treated in Chapter I, section I.

**Telecom-munications**

In the 20th century B.C., Bannum, an officer and spy from the Akkadian city of Mari on the Euphrates River, reported his observations on transmissions through the communications network of a neighbouring country:

> Yesterday I departed from Mari, and spent the night at Zuruban. All the Benjaminites raised fire signals. From

> Samanum to Ilum-Muluk, from Ilum-Muluk to Mishlan, all
> the cities of the Benjaminites of the Terga district raised
> fire signals in response, and so far I have not ascertained
> the meaning of those signals.

From prehistoric times until the advent of radio [see below] fire signals were used to send messages faster than documents could be transported. By their arrangement and timing, a wide variety of messages could be dispatched. This alone cannot be called telecommunication, which involves long distances as well as speed. However, the Benjaminites had instituted chains of relay stations to carry messages over a long distance – so effectively that a whole district could receive the message in one night. The other early reports of extensive fire signalling come from Mari, and Northwestern Mesopotamia is the probable birthplace of telecommunications.

The only invention of great importance to telecommunications during the next 3500 years was the telegraphic code, **Telegraphic** first devised in China during the Warring States Period **Code** (481–221 B.C.). It became possible to send messages over thousands of kilometres in all weather, at any time of day, by means of beats along lines of drum stations, each one in earshot of its neighbours. Most stations were located on main roads, and travellers could hear messages overtaking them. This was the forerunner of Morse Code, invented in the U.S.A. in the late **Morse Code** 1830s by Samuel F. Morse, for electronic rather than percussive use.

Work on static electricity which led to the invention of the so-called 'Leyden jar' in 1745 A.D. sparked a new interest in **Electronic** the possibilities of telegraphy. In France, the Abbé Jean- **Transmission** Antoine Nollet (1700–70) – a physicist and biochemist – linked up 200 monks of the Carthusian order in a circuit greater than a mile in length. Each monk held wires connecting him to the next monk on each side. As a charge passed down the wires, every monk received an electric shock, proving to the Abbé the feasibility of electric telecommunication, and impressing him with the rapidity of electric impulses.

After the Abbé's experimental transmission several short point-to-point lines were installed, with minimal impact on communications. The first to use electromagnetic transmission rather than static electricity was one which Baron von Schilling of Russia installed in St. Petersburg. Von Schilling explained his system to William Fothergill Cooke, who subsequently teamed up with Prof. Charles Wheatstone to improve

**Electric Telegraph Network** the method and begin building telegraphs in Britain. Their first line was laid for the Great Western Railway from London to West Drayton in 1838. This only went 21 km., but over the next few years the pair linked other centres, forming the Electric Telegraph Company in 1846. Britain thus had the world's earliest electric network. As they created it, Cooke and Wheatstone squabbled like schoolboys over who should have the credit for their breakthrough, each arguing that the other's part was the minor one.

**Telex** In 1841 Wheatstone made a receiver that could print telegraph messages in type – the first telex machine – but it did not go into general use.

**Overseas Submarine Cable** Before long attention turned to international extensions of the system. In 1850 John Brett and his brother Jacob began laying a cable across the English Channel to mainland Europe, by paying it out from a tug boat so it would lie on the bottom. Their first attempt was not a success, but in the following year they tried again and completed the cross-Channel link.

**Satellite Telecommunications** In 1960 the United States space administration, N.A.S.A., launched a novel type of satellite, *Echo 1*. It took up an orbit comparatively close to Earth, about 1600 km. up. Once in position it grew to a diameter of 100 feet, by inflating its own balloon made of a plastic material called mylar. The mylar had a reflective coating of aluminium. Radio signals beamed from Earth to *Echo 1* bounced off the satellite's surface and could be received on Earth far from the original transmission. *Echo 1* successfully transmitted voice, music and pictures between America and Europe, but in 1968 it disappeared from the sky.

**Telephone** In his native Germany, between 1860 and 1864, Johann Philipp Reis (1834–74) – a former trader who had taken up teaching – made and demonstrated a series of similar devices, all of which he called telephones. In doing so he came up with a model that was capable of transmitting some of the features of human speech over a distance. The receiver he used included a needle wrapped in a wire helix which was rapidly magnetised and demagnetised by pulses travelling along the line from the transmitter whenever someone spoke or sang into it. In this way the receiver reproduced the pitch of the voice, though the series of sounds heard by the listener could not be described as articulate speech.

**Speech Transmission** On 14 February 1876 the U.S. Patent Office received documents from two arch rivals seeking to protect 'speaking telegraphs' for which they furnished diagrams and descriptions.

One of them, Alexander Graham Bell, made a set of telephone equipment straight afterwards and on 9 March succeeded in transmitting articulate speech with it, for the first time on record. Intriguingly Bell's equipment resembled the design submitted by his rival Elisha Gray – incorporating a transmitter with liquid in it – and departed from the design in Bell's patent application. Gray first transmitted speech with a similar device in June or July that year.

Originally telephones were connected in pairs, until Bell and the Bell companies introduced exchanges in 1877 so that callers could choose to be connected to particular lines. The experiment began in several towns in the Northeastern United States, where vertical switchboards were installed with linkages for connecting each incoming line to any other. They were manually operated, and the caller had to 'ring off' at the end of the conversation by operating his bell to signal that the lines were to be disconnected. **Telephone Exchange**

The earliest mobile phones were specialised devices to assist telephone technicians on the job. Mobile phones for public use were introduced in the 1960s, by the Société Nationale de Chemin de Fer, France's government rail authority, on prestige long-distance express trains. **Mobile Telephone**

In 1974 a solar-powered telephone was connected to the Australian phone system at Wilkatana near Port Augusta, South Australia. This was the first of such phones now common in outback areas, out of the reach of wiring. The modest power requirement came from solar generators and accompanying storage batteries. The telephone messages were relayed by the first 'digital radio concentrator system' based on widely spaced radio repeater towers, and invented in 1978 by Telecom Research Laboratories, Melbourne. **Solar-powered Telephone**

The fax machine familiar in modern offices is a comparatively crude variant of equipment that has been in use for many decades to transmit newspaper photographs. Prof. Arthur Korn invented the prototype system in Germany in 1902 and first succeeded in transmitting a picture along telegraph lines from Munich to Nuremberg in 1904. The first known overseas transmission is a photo published in London's *Daily Mirror* after being faxed from Paris in 1907. **Fax**

Radio waves were generated artificially in Germany in 1887 or 1888 by Heinrich Hertz (1857–94), by setting up and moving electric currents. Hertz found that he could cause a spark **Radio** across a gap in an electric circuit by activating another circuit a short distance away. He rightly identified this as transmission by electromagnetic radiation. His work had been anticipated in an 1873 book *Electricity and Magnetism* by Scottish physicist James Clerk Maxwell (1831–79).

**Wireless Transmission**

Hertz was not convinced of the communications significance of his discovery, but from then until 1895, a number of experimenters examined wireless transmissions under test conditions. Earlier still, David Hughes, inventor of the microphone [XI, 2] had found that he could sometimes hear sounds from the microphone through the earphone even after disconnecting its wires. He described the phenomenon as aerial transmission. Most successful of the experimenters was the Italian electrical engineer Guglielmo Marconi (1874–1937), who began making radio equipment in 1894. In 1895 he made an antenna and found he could pick up radio signals with a receiver behind a hill. A long-wave transmission by Marconi in 1895 over about a mile can be regarded as the first over a distance great enough to take radio beyond the test stage into the class of practical communications. Marconi went to Britain and established a radio-telegraphy company there. In December 1901 he established the first trans-Atlantic radio link, successfully transmitting signals in both directions. He shared the Nobel Prize for Physics in 1909.

**Overseas Wireless Transmission**

**Television**

Television was developed by a large number of people over several decades working concurrently in Russia, Western Europe, Britain and the U.S.A. Being first does not necessarily mean being most advanced in development. In 1926, the first transmission of a television image was achieved experimentally by a Scot, John Logie Baird (1888–1946), and his team, in London. The image was transmitted by medium-wave radio, and projected crudely but discernibly in pinkish neon light in the receiver. Later in the same year they made their first colour transmission – made possible by equipping the scanner with colour filters.

**Colour Television**

**Regular Broadcast**

The first daily public broadcasts were begun in August 1928 by two American radio stations, using a technique similar to Baird's. The previous month, commercially manufactured television sets, from Newark, on the outskirts of New York, had gone on sale.

# IX

# TRANSPORT AND TRAVELS

This chapter covers both the means of transportation and the great expeditions and journeys. In fact prehistoric man travelled to every land except Antarctica – as is proved by aboriginal settlement all over the world. But those journeys were never recorded, and were mostly made in short stages, which are not recorded here.

## I. SHIPS AND WATER TRANSPORT

Boats, rafts, sails, oars and paddles are all prehistoric inventions of unknown origin. Naval vessels including submarines, and marine warfare, are dealt with in Chapter VI, section 3.

Ships were being built in Egypt for the Nile River traffic by the beginning of the Old Kingdom period around 3500 B.C. **Ships** Large cargo carrying river boats had been built entirely of papyrus, but the introduction of wooden frames at about this time meant that a well-shaped hull could be constructed and

People on one of the first seagoing ships showing their relief at making it back to port. (An Old Kingdom inscription from Egypt)

larger vessels, genuine river-going ships, could be launched. Seaworthy ships came into use soon after, although it is not clear whether the earliest were built in Egypt or on the Asian coast of the Mediterranean where suitable wood was plentiful. The shores of the Persian Gulf are another possibility.

**Ocean-going Fleet**   Records dating from about 3000B.C. contain the oldest reference to an ocean fleet: forty ships that sailed from the coast of present-day Lebanon to Egypt.

**Fore and Aft Sail**   The fore and aft sail, with its capability of sailing into the wind, was invented by a Stone Age people, who in this respect were far in advance of their civilised contemporaries. While the Egyptians and Mesopotamians were making do with the poor manoeuvrability of square riggers, and the Chinese could hardly sail at all, natives of Southeast Asia equipped their canoes with fore and aft sails. These people, known to ethnologists as Austronesians, lived in Malaya and on the Indonesian Archipelago. They had probably worked out how to rig a square sail at a fore and aft angle by 2000B.C., after which they would have developed the distinctive triangle-like sails seen on Polynesian canoes.

**Catamaran**   In the same period, these people invented the catamaran, by replacing the stabilising outriggers of their canoes with a second hull. Within a thousand years their descendants had used it to discover and colonise islands throughout the Indian and Pacific Oceans – from Micronesia in the East to Madagascar in the West.

**Multiple Fore and Aft Rig**   Sailing ships driven by fore and aft sails are recorded by the Chinese writer Warn Jen in his book, *Study of the Peculiarities of Southern Countries* (3rd century A.D.). These were ships from Southeast Asia, and Warn's description is the oldest of the multiple fore and aft method:

> their ships sometimes rig four sails, which they carry in a row from bow to stern . . . the four sails do not face directly forwards, but are set obliquely, and so arranged that they can all be fixed in the same direction, to receive the wind and spill it.                                    (tr. Needham)

Earlier still, square-rigged ships in the Mediterranean Sea in Roman times carried small fore and aft sails at the bow but their main sails were square-rigged.

**Rudder**   The oldest known rudder has been recovered from a Harn Dynasty tomb at Canton, of about 100A.D. The rudder is attached to a 2-foot model ship made of clay. Its design is fairly

sophisticated because it is centrally positioned under an operating gallery, and is balanced by having part of its blade forward of the rudder post. But older Chinese ship models always
feature less efficient steering oars rather than rudders. This
means that despite the sophistication, the rudder must have
been a recent invention in 100A.D. – from some earlier decade
in the 1st century, on the rivers and coasts of China. There is
a possibility that the rudder was invented earlier still in Egypt,
where it could have been useful in the Nile River current. The
Greek writer Herodotus describes the steering equipment of
Egyptian ships as running straight through the keel as a central rudder might, but too little is said to be sure.

An anonymous Latin book, *De Rebus Bellicus* (*On Military
Matters*, Byzantium, present-day Istanbul, c. 370A.D.) includes **Paddlewheeler**
a design for a side-wheel driven paddlewheeler. Inside the ship
an ox goes round and round, driving the wheels. It is uncertain when and if the design was executed in practice, so the
first operating paddlewheelers may have been the little fleet
used by Chinese admiral Warng Jen Aw to attack the Chiarng
barbarians in 418A.D. They were worked by men on tread-
mills, and struck awe into the barbarian observers by moving
along without sails or oars.

The sternwheeler, with a single huge wheel at the back,
comes seven and a half centuries later, in the fleet of Sung **Sternwheeler**
Dynasty admiral Shir Jeng Ji. He commissioned a 100-tonne
warship with a single twelve-blade paddle wheel. The ship,
built in 1168A.D., was powered by men on a treadmill, and saw
service on the Yangtze River.

The paddle wheel has now been superseded by the screw, a
more efficient device of propulsion. The realisation that the **Screw
Propulsion**
turning motion of a screw can drive a boat forward in water was
voiced in Europe and China in the 18th century, and first put
into practice on Chinese model boats of that time. The oldest
known record is Col. Mark Beaufoy's description in 1818 of a
Chinese model operating in Switzerland, about 1780:

> This model had underneath its bottom a spiral, which was
> turned when wanted with considerable rapidity by clock-
> work put in motion by a spring similar to that of a watch.
> The vessel being placed in a tub of water and the helm put
> over more or less, according as the tub was large or small,
> the boat continued running in a circle until the clock went
> down.

Historically, much more use has been made of screws in the West than in China; it is possible that European missionaries, some of whom worked in China and were very brilliant, had a hand in the invention.

**Steam Vessel** Ferdinand Verbiest, inventor of the motor car [IX, 2], was a true enthusiast of steam power, and in the 1660s in Peking, began work not only on a car, but on the first steam-driven boat. Early in the 1670s he finished the boat, which had four steam-driven paddle wheels, turned by linkages to a driving wheel. A jet of steam blowing out of the boiler caused the driving wheel to rotate and thereby turn the paddle wheels.

**Hydrofoil** Ten years after making the first aeroplane flight [IX, 3] Clément Ader (1841–1925) of France built the first hydrofoil – a boat with wings at water level. Air released under pressure formed a cushion beneath the wings so the boat could travel with a greatly reduced water contact area. In 1900, when Ader first demonstrated his 'hydro-glisseur', as it was named, he hoped to attract support for its commercial development, but as none was forthcoming he took the idea no further.

**Hovercraft** In Britain in 1955, Christopher Cockerell (born 1910) made and demonstrated a successful working model of a hovercraft. This was not the first demonstration of the idea, but the test run of his design improvements that made full-scale hovercraft practicable. As a result the British Government supported Cockerell and the Saunders and Roe company, in efforts to develop hovercraft. Saunders and Roe Number One, 'SR-N1', measuring 31 feet by 25 feet, was completed and launched in 1959. In July that year it made the first crossing of the English Channel, from Dover to Calais.

**Wave-piercing Catamaran** Hydrofoils and hovercraft are being superseded by the more conventional and efficient wave-piercing catamaran, consisting of a high superstructure with a centre hull, mounted above two long slender side hulls which carry only engines and fuel. It was invented by marine architect Philip Hercus, of International Catamarans, Hobart, in 1982. One of these craft broke the thirty-eight-year-old trans-Atlantic passenger record in 1990.

**Transom-ended Ship** The first vessels were designed so that the left and right sides came together at the bow and stern. But in ancient Egypt there was a kind of ship known as the Horian, in common use by the 6th Dynasty (c. 2700B.C.), in which the sides were separated at the bow and stern by cross beams – the 'transoms' familiar in later nautical architecture. Such ships are blunt at the ends rather than pointy.

From around 1000B.C., inflatable vessels were used by Armenian traders sailing down the Tigris and Euphrates Rivers in Mesopotamia to commercial cities in the south. The current was too strong for the traders to be able to sail back up river, so at their destinations downstream they used to deflate their craft, sell off the frames, and return by donkey, carrying the collapsed air cells, which were made of animal skins. A properly outfitted Mesopotamian inflatable carried on board a full cargo, and at least one donkey for the return trip.

**Inflatable Craft**

Metal was initially used in ship-building not for structural strength, but to protect wooden hulls against deterioration caused by borers and other pests. The practice of covering entire hulls in lead sheathing began in the Eastern Mediterranean, where Phoenician and Greek merchantmen made frequent voyages in insect-infested waters. It appears to be an invention of the 5th or 6th century B.C. The hull of a Greek wreck of the early 4th century B.C. found at Kyrenia shows the technique used: the hull is made of wood completely covered in lead sheeting, attached by copper nails. Heavy iron panels on 'ironclads' [VI, 3] in military use were introduced in China in the 11th century A.D.

**Metal Construction**

A Ming Dynasty book of 1628, *The Best Designs in Armament Technology*, includes a picture and description of a Chinese articulated ship of the previous century. The ship, which was jointed in the middle, was designed as a mine layer. The explosive mines were stored in the front section, which could be detached in an emergency and left behind by the rest of the ship. Soon after, the military design was adapted for civil purposes, and jointed vessels came into use as canal transports, first in China, then elsewhere.

**Articulated Ship**

On 3 May 1844 the Brown and Bell shipyard in the United States launched the *Houqua*, a long, slender sailing ship with a very pointed bow and a fairly flat bottom. Sailing with square-rigged sails on tall masts, she broke all records for the journey from New York to China, and ushered in the age of

**Clipper Ship**

**Clipper Hull**

the majestic clipper ships. The innovative hull design had been produced as a model in 1843 by Capt. Nathaniel Palmer (1799–1877), previously a claimant to the honour of having first sighted Antarctica [IX, 4]. A similar hull style had been used by Algerian privateers of the 17th and 18th centuries, in their *chebeks*, notably successful fore and aft rigged vessels.

**Luxury Liner**

Sea travel was usually basic in ancient times; apart from a few cabins on cargo ships, there were just cramped sleeping areas below and above deck. *Syracusia*, launched in about 250B.C., was probably the largest merchant vessel built to that time, and offered comfort and facilities previously available only to royalty. Her lower-deck promenade gave access to the holds; the deck above had spacious cabins and suites, opening on to a middle promenade. Above that was another promenade and a deck with open walks, a gymnasium, library, heated freshwater baths, fish pond, large garden beds with a watering system, stabling for twenty horses, and a shrine. Nine-foot statues supported upper works, including eight turrets with cranes on top, and an array of mechanical weapons such as spear throwers, and grappling cranes. The timber used would have been enough for sixty warships and was held together with 10-pound bronze rivets. The hull was covered in pitch-coated canvas, with a smooth sheathing of lead panels; 300 tradesmen, with assistants, worked twelve months to build her. *Syracusia* was commissioned by Hieron (308–216B.C.), king of the Greek city of Syracuse, in Sicily, and built there by Archesius of Corinth. Project manager was the Syracusan scientist, Archimedes (287–212B.C.), who designed the launching gear and weaponry. Instead of having boats slung along her sides like a modern liner, *Syracusia* had hers in tow, including a pinnace of 90 tons, some 45-ton boats and several smaller cutters. For her maiden voyage she was loaded with 90,000 bushels of grain, 600 tonnes of wool and 1000–2000 tonnes of fish and mixed cargo. The only harbour outside Syracuse that could handle such a big vessel was at Alexandria, capital of Egypt. There was then a grain shortage in Egypt, so Hieron renamed his ship *Alexandris*, and gave her and her cargo to Egypt's king, Ptolemy.

*Syracusia* was unique, and Mediterranean passenger services remained an adjunct of small and medium cargo vessels.

**International Liner Service**

Regular international sailings by luxury liners did not begin until about the 11th century A.D., when a new travel concept was introduced, on the heavily trafficked routes between China and India, through Southeast Asia. Chinese tycoons built up fleets of huge junks with practical aids like compasses and water-tight compartments, plus luxuries like portholes, and stewards to bring food and drinks. A Moroccan traveller, Ibn Battutah, who was going to China in 1342 from Calicut on India's West Coast, describes one of these liners:

> The vessel has four decks and contains rooms, cabins and saloons for merchants. The cabins have chambers and toilets; they have doors which can be locked and keys for the occupants. Passengers take with them their wives and concubines . . . The sailors have their children living on board ship, and they cultivate garden herbs, vegetables and ginger in wooden tubs.

Well before the days of Antarctic exploration, ice was a problem for shipping on transport canals. In North China (as later in Northern Europe) it could prevent the progress of conventional vessels, and ice-breakers were required to prepare the way. They went into service first in the later part of the 11th century A.D. under instructions from the Chinese Prime Minister, Warng Arn Shir. They were treadmill-powered paddle-wheelers, with automatic ice-smashing hammers mounted at the bows. **Ice-breaker**

Shipping containers were initially transported on ordinary ships with other cargo, and on conventional ships modified to carry them. M.V. *Kooringa*, built by the New South Wales State Dockyard at Newcastle, in 1964 was the first purpose-built container ship with fully cellular cargo space. She was built for the Melbourne–Perth service of the Associated Steamship Company. **Container Ship**

Prehistoric navigators on rafts and boats determined their position by observing the coastal topography. At first no one who ventured out into the open ocean knew where he was going. The first important breakthrough came with celestial navigation. It seems likely that in Eastern Mediterranean waters in the middle of the 3rd millennium B.C., seagoing vessels began to carry experts who knew the positions and regular motions of the Sun, Moon and stars. With this information, except when it was overcast, they could reliably identify their position and direction. **Navigation**

**Celestial Navigation**

Over the centuries science gave navigators many ingenious inventions: star charts, measuring cards, astrolabes and quadrants. All of these are simply aids to improve celestial navigation. But around 900A.D., something altogether different was added to the navigator's equipage – the marine com-

**Compass Navigation** pass. First installed on Chinese ships sailing on the Pacific Ocean, the marine compass suddenly made it possible to determine travel direction even on the cloudiest night. By then the compass [VIII, 10] had been in land use for centuries, but the marine compass is an improved version that stabilises the needle to give readings on a moving ship.

Stars and compass solve the navigator's problem of working out the vessel's position and direction. His other major

**Great Circle Method** challenge is to plot the best course from position to destination. The Portuguese mathematician, Pedro Núñez, worked out the best system in 1537A.D. This is 'great circle navigation', by which a ship's course is made to approximate an arc along the Earth's full circumference between any two points. Because the Earth is curved, this entails a shorter journey than following a straight bearing. Núñez made it possible by devising practical ways to plot the lines.

Until the 18th century, though navigators at sea could

**Chronometric Navigation** establish their latitude with precision, they had to rely on crude approximation to work out their longitude, i.e. how far east or west they were. Longitude can be precisely determined by comparing local time with the time at another place of known longitude kept by a chronometer; however, no early clock kept time at sea accurately enough for it to be rated as a chronometer. In 1714 the British Parliament legislated to offer a £20,000 prize – a rich fortune – to the first inventor of a marine clock sufficiently accurate to pinpoint longitude within half a degree. The winning clock would keep Greenwich Mean Time (the time for 0° longitude) on ships making long voyages east and west. John Harrison (1693–1776), who had completed his first plan for a marine clock in 1728, finished what might be called the first chronometer in 1735; it was not proved to the accuracy standard required for the prize, but did secure him funding for further development. In 1759 he finished 'Clock no. 4'. The Board had it tested on two Atlantic crossings with satisfactory results, and Harrison-type chronometers went into general use almost immediately.

Satellite navigation is just like celestial navigation except

**Satellite Navigation** it relies on artificial satellites instead of stars; it replaces eyesight with all-weather radio reception, and offers greater precision. It was introduced internationally after successful tests in 1971–72.

Locks enable navigation canals to operate through changes in altitude, by regulating the water level between sections of different height. The precursors of true locks were flash locks, with one set of gates at the lower end of a long stretch of canal. This fairly simple method of adjusting water level was probably in use in Egypt around 300B.C. or earlier, and perhaps also in North China. In Egypt, during the reign of Ptolemy II (285–246B.C.), an 'ingenious lock' was installed in the canal from the Nile River to the Red Sea [see below]. The choice of the word 'ingenious' by the Greek historian Diodorus suggests that it may have been the first pound lock, the more sophisticated double-gated type. If not, the world had to wait until 983A.D., when Chiao Wei, the Assistant Commissioner of Transport for Huai Narn, designed a lock with two gates about 75 m. apart. When transport barges entered, it could be sealed off and have its water level gradually adjusted to match that of the next section of the canal. The first such lock went into operation that year on the portion of the Grand Canal under Chiao's control.

**Canal Locks**

**Flash Lock**

**Pound Lock**

When work started last century on the Suez Canal, which carries ships from the Indian Ocean into the Mediterranean, the engineers reopened large tracts of an ancient Egyptian ship canal, for the purpose of getting fresh water to the construction site. This old canal in its full extent achieved the same result as the Suez Canal today – linking the two great oceans in navigation. It was first opened during Egypt's Middle Kingdom period, the 12th Dynasty (c. 2000B.C.). During the 26th Dynasty, Pharaoh Neckho had it restored and opened to large vessels in the 7th century B.C. The restoration and enlargement work was not completed during his reign but under the Persian rule of Darius (521–485B.C.). The traces which remain today show a canal 150 feet wide and about 17 feet deep. The lock installed in it in the 3rd century B.C. may have been the first pound lock [see above].

**Indian Ocean Connected to Mediterranean**

The first long-distance navigation canal, the Grand Canal of China, was constructed during the Sui Dynasty in the reign of Emperor Sui Yarng Di. The section linking the Yellow River system with the Yangtze was completed in 605A.D. It was 200 feet wide, with parallel highways and willow trees planted along the banks. The northern section, opened in 608, continued the canal to the neighbourhood of present-day Peking. In 610 the whole project came to completion with the opening of the southern extension to the city

**The Grand Canal**

of Harng Jo (Hangchow or Hangzhou) and slightly beyond, to a point about 1600 km. away from the northern terminus.

**Pacific Ocean Connected to Atlantic**
After many plans and proposals, construction of a canal through the Isthmus of Panama was begun by French engineers and promoters in 1881A.D., but ended in financial ruin in 1889. In 1903 the United States negotiated the Canal Zone Treaty with Panama and began building the canal, which was opened for traffic in 1914. It ran through six locks, from the vicinity of Colon on the Atlantic to Panama City on the Pacific through the U.S. administered Canal Zone, a distance of 82 km.

## 2. LAND TRANSPORT

The first alternatives to pedestrian transport on land were pack animals. Riding of horses and camels came later, but in prehistoric times, from which no trace remains. For bridges, see Chapter V, section 2.

**Horse Book**
Kikkuli, a Hurrian (from present-day inland Turkey) wrote a manual on horses around 1400B.C. The land of the Hurrians was part of the ancient Hittite Empire, and his book was written in the Hittite tongue. Topics covered include breeding and veterinary care, together with a day-by-day course in the use of horses for light chariots.

**Shaft Harness**
Before the invention of shaft harness, horses could only draw small loads. As soon as one gathered speed with a heavy load, the harness would squash his windpipe. But shaft harness directs the load through the chest onto the horse's skeleton, making it possible to haul several times more weight. When the new system was invented around 400B.C., it was the greatest stimulus to horse-drawn transport since carts first came into use. The new harness was first used in North China; the inventor is thought to have been Wen Dzu, the brother of a duke. North China was still on the cutting edge of horse and cart technology about 800 years later when it was the scene of **Collar Harness** the earliest collar harness. This is the system generally in use now, a refinement of the shaft system to make it more efficient and manageable.

**Motor Car**
The Belgian Father, Ferdinand Verbiest (died 1688), and his colleague, Philipe-Marie Grimaldi, were two Jesuits who worked in Peking for the Chinese Government. They designed and built a little car, about two feet long, driven by a

simple steam engine. A jet of steam – through a canal running from the coal-fired boiler – turned a small wheel which was connected to the driving axle. Verbiest began working on the project in 1665. On its first test run in Peking in 1671 the miniature car went for two hours. Despite the success of the trial no follow-up work was done either in China or Belgium, so the first Verbiest remained the only one.

In late-18th and in 19th-century Europe, steam vehicles were manufactured for practical use, taking advantage of engines far superior to Verbiest's. But Siegfried Marcus (1831–98) – a German mechanic working for the Austrian Court in Vienna – had a different idea. Over a decade or so from 1864, he built a number of vehicles with simple petrol engines. He took advantage of two inventions: the magneto for providing a spark – his own invention – and the internal combustion engine [VIII, 11]. It would be too charitable to call his first vehicle a car. It was a handcart body with a single-cylinder engine that was started up with its wheels jacked off the ground. When the engine was running he dropped the wheels and the thing took off, out of control, on its maiden voyage, which ended with engine failure after about 200 m. Later vehicles sported a conical clutch, a seat over the centrally mounted engine, and a steering wheel. Marcus had not heard of the four-stroke cycle [VIII, 9], and his engines worked at low revs like a steam engine. But with all the other fancy new gear, he had the world's first petrol car. In 1875 he went for a drive of many kilometres through outer suburbs. His jaunt, and his marque, came to an end when police ordered the little wooden car off the streets. It has been claimed that Marcus actually worked years later, and that his first long drive was late in the 1880s. If so it remains possible that vehicles built by Benz and Daimler in 1885 were the first petrol cars.

**Petrol Car**

Gottlieb Daimler's petrol engine – invented in Cannstatt, Germany in 1885 – was closer to present-day car engines, although ignition was by a tube of hot metal rather than a spark. It was a fast-revving four-stroke motor with a superior surface-type carburettor, in which the engine drew air bubbles through a petrol reservoir. In that year Daimler (1834–1900) fitted such an engine between the wheels of a simple wooden bike, with a leather belt to power the rear wheel. On 10 November 1885 his son Paul rode it from Cannstatt to Untertürkheim and back.

**Motorcycle**

The 1895 Panhard-Levassor, built in France with a Daimler engine, was fully enclosed, with the engine mounted at the

**Saloon Car**

front, concealed by panels, and a passenger compartment with seats and windows behind. This is the world's first saloon car, the direct ancestor of most cars on the roads today.

**Tractor** Long before they were put into agricultural use, tractors were designed for hauling artillery pieces. The first was built in 1769 by the French artillery officer Nicolas Cugnot. It was a heavily built three-wheeler, with a large kettle-shaped boiler forward of the front wheel that supplied steam to a piston cylinder. Cugnot's tractor was a pretty hopeless design; having most of its weight at the front made it very hard to control, and it crashed into a wall. His second tractor the following year hauled about 4 tonnes at 3 km/h.

**Railway** The first railways were built with timber rails and timber sleepers to service mines, quarries and docks. Some were portable, and none was durable enough to leave its traces for archaeologists to discover. For this reason, there is no way of telling where the first one was built. However, the date can be estimated on **Rutway** the basis of rutways, which used the same kind of technology. They have lasted to the present day because the vehicles, instead of travelling over rails, ran along ruts carved permanently into stone. The oldest to be discovered is on the Mediterranean island of Malta, constructed early in the 2nd millennium B.C. The first railway must have come into use at roughly the same time or soon after, but this is only conjecture. It is unlikely that flanged wheels were then in existence. More probably, bars fixed on each rail guided the vehicles and kept them on track. Rutways were preferred where a suitable stone base was available, and they are mainly found around ancient quarries.

**Main Line** All the earliest railways and rutways were short routes carrying specialised local traffic. The first line for carrying general through traffic was the *Diolkos* across the Isthmus of Corinth in Greece. It ran past the city of Corinth, from Lechaeon on the Corinthian Gulf, for 7 km. to Cenchreae on the Saronic Gulf. It was opened in the 590s B.C. by Periander, tyrant of Corinth. The traffic was too heavy for wooden tracks; instead a strong stone rutway was used, with a gauge of approximately 1½ m. The line is notable for some important innovations: a double-**Double Track** track section, and bogies. These are the multi-wheeled trucks **Bogies** that are used, two to a carriage on modern railways, to take the weight of long vehicles, and enable them to get around bends in the track. On the *Diolkos* they were used to carry small and medium-sized ships from one gulf to the other, saving them the long journey around the Peloponnese. The *Diolkos* has now been superseded by a ship canal through the Isthmus.

The railway standard gauge, 4 feet 8½ inches, was originally a gauge applied to cart and chariot wheels in the Roman Empire. The wheel ruts cut into ancient highways conformed to various local and temporary standards, but during the Chin Dynasty (221–206 B.C.), China's First Emperor, Shir Huarng Di, proclaimed a standard gauge for the whole of China and the foreign territories under his sway. Ruts on this gauge were built into the national highway system to make carriage transport more efficient; ever since, China has enjoyed a standard gauge. One province long remained on a broad gauge; axle-exchange stations on its borders serviced carts going from one province to another over the break of gauge.

**Standard Gauge**

The great Irish inventors do not weigh in heavily with transport firsts, which makes the work of Louis Brennan all the more noteworthy. In 1896 he began inventing a railway with only one rail; he obtained a patent in 1903, and built a model in 1907. The trains were to be equipped with gyroscopes to prevent them toppling over. To his dismay, Brennan learnt that a German newspaper proprietor, August Scherl, would be demonstrating just such a train at the Berlin Zoo on 10 November 1909. Brennan hastily prepared to match this, and the two first true monorail systems were thus demonstrated on the same day. In 1910 Brennan demonstrated an impressive monorail car that dwarfed Scherl's humble prototype; he also signed an agreement granting Scherl his patent rights for Germany, and won a prize at the Japan–British exhibition in 1910. In the previous century the French engineer C. F. M. T. Lartigue and his firm had built pseudo-monorails for North Africa, France, Russia and Latin America. Without gyroscopes Lartigue trains could not balance themselves and relied on extra horizontal wheels that ran against guide rails to avoid toppling. The Lartigue railway from Ballybunion to Listowel in County Kerry opened in 1888, and may have inspired Brennan in his remarkable labour.

**Monorail**

The first steam locomotive was built by English engineer, Richard Trevithick (1771–1833), for a short wagon-carrying railway at Coalbrookdale in central England. Little is recorded of its performance, but Trevithick's next engine, which went into service the following year, proves the calibre of his works.

**Locomotive**

It made a successful journey at about 8 km/h, along a 14 km. line in February 1804, at the head of a train carrying 10 tons of iron. The engines were too heavy for the primitive rails of that period. Although Trevithick's design had an inefficient flywheel drive system, it was more sophisticated than many later models – the boiler had an economical heat distribution via a horseshoe-shaped flue, and tractive effort was via smooth wheels rather than toothed ones.

**Electric Locomotive**  In Scotland in 1842 Robert Davidson demonstrated the world's first electric locomotive – a battery-powered machine that hauled a load of 6 tons at 4 miles per hour over a short section of the Glasgow–Edinburgh line.

**Internal Combustion Locomotive**  In 1892 a small industrial locomotive was built at Esslingen Engine Works in Germany. It was a stubby little contraption powered by a Daimler petrol engine, one of the early designs by German motor car builder, Gottlieb Daimler, who invented the motorcycle [see above]. At this time the diesel had only just come into use for stationary industrial engines, but ultimately it, rather than the petrol engine, was adopted for rail traction.

**Diesel Locomotive**  The first diesel locomotive was jointly manufactured in 1912 by two German firms, Diesel-Klose-Sulzer at Winterthur and Borsig of Berlin. It turned in a disappointing performance for the buyer, Prussian State Railways, because the mechanical transmission was ill-suited to applying the engine's 1000 horsepower to a heavy stationary train. In Sweden in the same year two firms, Atlas and A.S.E.A., completed a passenger railmo-

**Diesel Electric**  tor for the Södermanland Midland Railway, in which for the first time, electric transmission was substituted for mechanical – a solution that gave the world the familiar diesel electric. For the precursors of the engines driving the various locomotives, see Chapter VIII, section 9: Piston Rod Steam Engine; Internal Combustion Engine; Diesel Engine; Electric Motor.

**Mainline Electrification**  In 1895 the Baltimore and Ohio Railroad in the U.S.A. electrified a 5½ km. section of line running through the city of Baltimore, Maryland: a reaction to complaints about the smoke from steam trains in the city. An overhead direct current system was used, installed by the General Electric Company. A fleet of 1440-horsepower engines worked the line.

**Railway Passenger Service**  The first railway to operate a regular passenger service was known initially as the Oystermouth, but as the Swansea and Mumbles Railway after its opening to passenger traffic in 1807. It ran from Swansea on the South Coast of Wales, around the adjacent bay to the Mumbles, on a nearby promontory. Passengers were conveyed in horse-drawn carriages along iron plate rails. Later, well into the steam age, this line was notable for carrying huge double-deck trams, but today only buses run on the route.

The technology of underground railway construction developed very early for use in mines. Passengers had to wait until 10 January 1863, when London's Metropolitan Railway opened for business, the brainchild of solicitor Charles Pearson. It was a dual-gauge line running from the Great Western Railway's Paddington terminus to Farringdon Street. Its standard gauge track matched most British surface lines, while its broad track was uniform with the Great Western's 7-foot gauge. The Metropolitan remains in operation as part of the huge London Underground system that developed around it. **Underground Passenger Railway**

Gradually underground railways were opened in other large crowded cities, some of which posted notable firsts. In Istanbul (formerly Constantinople) in 1875, a funicular [IX, 2] system was introduced on the Tünel underground railway, which climbs the steep slope from the Golden Horn to Pera. On the Paris Metro in 1957 trains with rubber tyres were introduced on specially converted lines fitted with concrete runners; these trains also have flanged steel wheels. In Sydney, double-deck carriages went into service underground in 1964, taking advantage of the existing high tunnels which also accommodated overhead wiring. A few years later the introduction of double-deck power cars in Sydney enabled the running of trains on which all eight cars are double-deckers. **Underground Funicular** / **Rubber Tyred Underground** / **Double Deckers Underground**

Construction of the first railway across America, from the Missouri River to California, began during the Civil War, by companies supported by the Federal Government of the northern states of the U.S.A. Work started at both ends in 1863, though the war was long ended when the lines from east and west reached each other in Utah in early 1869. However the two companies responsible – the Central Pacific building from the west, and the Union Pacific from the east – refused to notice that their task was complete, and kept on laying track as though the job were unfinished. By the time the Government stepped in and made them acknowledge that the link had been completed, 362 km. of duplicate track had been laid. On 10 May 1869 a track-joining ceremony was conducted at Promontory Point, Utah. The Central Pacific president's hammer was **Across America** specially wired up so that when he raised it to drive in the golden spike, bells would ring out in San Francisco and Washington; however he missed the spike, and others had to drive it in and inaugurate the linking of Atlantic and Pacific coasts with less far-reaching sound effects.

**Across Asia** Construction of the Trans-Siberian Railway began at Vladivostok on the Pacific coast of the Russian Empire in May 1891, and at Chelyabinsk, over 7000 kilometres to the west, in the Ural Mountains, in July 1892. The link was completed during the Russo–Japanese War of 1904–5, by the temporary closure of the gap in the line at Lake Baikal, where ferries had been used to carry the trains. This gap was filled by the laying of rails on the ice on top of the lake. Carriages were hauled over the lake by horses, locomotives being too heavy. However in the same year, the eastern leg of the line through Manchuria was cut off from the coast by the Japanese. The replacement route further north was not complete until 1916.

**Across Australia** In 1912 the Western Australian Government Railways had an isolated rail network running 611 km. east from the coast to Kalgoorlie. Work began in September that year on Commonwealth Railways' Trans-Australian line, to join it with the nearest part of the eastern states network, South Australian Railways at Port Augusta. Construction continued during the First World War, until the final spike was driven in, with little fanfare, on 17 October 1917. The first 'Trans-Australian' passenger train left Port Augusta five days later and reached Kalgoorlie in under two days. One of its passengers was Commonwealth treasurer, John Forrest, later Baron Forrest of Bunbury, who forty-seven years earlier had led the first overland expedition from Perth to Adelaide. The journey from the Pacific to the Indian Ocean still required in 1917 six changes of trains, over five separate government railway systems: standard gauge from Sydney to Albury, broad gauge to Melbourne, broad gauge to Adelaide, broad to Terowie, narrow to Port Augusta, standard to Kalgoorlie and narrow to Perth.

**To Three Oceans** In 1970 trains began to run on the newly standardised route through Broken Hill, and since then the 'Indian Pacific' has run through from Sydney to Perth. In doing so it became the first train to take passengers to the coasts of three oceans: the Pacific at Sydney, the Southern at Port Pirie, and the Indian at Perth.

The first channel tunnel, linking Britain to mainland Europe, along the floor of the English Channel between Dover and **Channel** Calais, was completed in 1994. Engineering work started in **Tunnel** 1987; work on the present design began with the setting up of the Channel Tunnel Study Group in 1957, and the initial proposal was put in 1802 by Albert Mathieu-Favier.

Double-deck cars were manufactured for the Lyons and St. Etienne Railway, the line that carried France's first steam **Double-deck** locomotive in 1829. They were used to carry the second-class **Carriages** passengers in horse-drawn trains; over part of the line even horses were dispensed with and trains coasted down the gentle slope. These early double-deckers were unenclosed, as befitted second class at that time.

The innovative railway on which they ran had the first locomotive with a multiple flue boiler – the one supplied in 1829 by Marc Séguin, nephew of the Montgolfier brothers who made the first balloon flight [IX, 3]. (Such boilers had previously been used in the Roman Empire, but only for heat- **Bogie Carriage** ing.) Early in the 1830s the same line introduced the world's first bogie carriage, an invention that gave much improved ride qualities. Bogies [see above] had previously been used in ancient Greece, but not for passenger carriages.

The first sleeping cars, fitted with bunks for the passengers, were provided on the Cumberland Valley Railway in the **Sleeping Cars** inland of the United States in 1836.

Two dining cars went into service on trains running between Baltimore and Philadelphia in 1863. They were origi- **Dining Cars** nally ordinary sitting cars, but were converted for their new purpose.

The most distinctively North American oddity in passenger train design is the upper-storey observation lounge known as a scenic dome or vista dome. Yet in the 19th century, one **Scenic Dome** had to go to Russia rather than America for the joy of travel- **Car** ling in one. The design was pioneered there at the Alexandrovsky engine and carriage works, in a composite sleeping and lounge car which entered service in 1867. A spiral stairway led from the lower level lounge to an upstairs observation lounge amply supplied with windows and upholstery, which took up the middle third of the carriage roofline.

Baths, and probably showers, were installed in some private **Showers** V.I.P. carriages last century. For normal fare-paying passengers **on Trains** showers were first laid on in 1918 on the 'Trans-Australian', by Commonwealth Railways, between Perth and Port Augusta, on the first railway across Australia [see above]. The few showers were installed in existing sleeping cars. Sleeping **Private** cars with an ensuite shower for each two-berth compartment **Showers** were added to the Melbourne–Adelaide 'Overland' over several years beginning in 1950. This broad-gauge express was then jointly operated by Victorian and South Australian Railways. The cars were built at the Islington Workshops of South Australian Railways. But passengers in single-berth compartments still have the inconvenience of a trip down the corridor **Showers in** for their showers. Showers for sitting car passengers were **Sitting Cars** introduced when the standard-gauge 'Ghan' from Adelaide to Alice Springs replaced the former narrow-gauge train in 1980.

Machines for measuring road mileage came into use in Egypt **Odometer** in Hellenistic times, around 200B.C. They worked on a system of reduction gearing, so that the toothed odometer wheel made one whole revolution after several hundred revolutions by the main carriage wheel. At the end of each mile travelled a pebble was released, and at the end of the journey a count of the number of liberated pebbles could be made, to get an exact total. These machines were purpose-built road measurers but by the 1st century B.C. you could have your chariot or carriage fitted with its own odometer. The operating principle was the same, but the mile pebbles travelled down a pipe underneath the vehicle and made a ringing noise in a bronze receptacle, letting the traveller know that another mile had passed.

The earliest device for carrying a vehicle with reduced fric- **Sledge** tion is not the wheel but the sledge. A pair of early sledge runners found at Heinola, Finland, has been conjecturally dated to the 8th millennium B.C. The wooden runners, shaped like skis, are evidence that sledge transport in Northern Europe may date back 10,000 years or more, to a stone age time when much more of the Earth was under ice than is today. Skiing [X, 2] appears to be at least as old, and may have inspired sledging.

Perhaps wind power will never be an important way of pro- **Sailing** pelling wheeled vehicles, but there is a long history of experi- **Carriage** ment in Europe and China. Gao Dsarng Wu Shu invented the first sailing carriage in China in about 550A.D. It was claimed to have a capacity of 30 people and to travel over 100 miles in a day. The reader might consider exercising scepticism on this point – although such a performance is technically conceivable, it would be an unusual road which allowed such a large vehicle scope for tacking to catch the breeze. Gao's invention was probably more a scientific curiosity than a practical conveyance.

The wheelbarrow was invented in China during the Harn Dynasty (206B.C.–220A.D.), and in its early days was used for **Wheelbarrow** military transport as well as civil purposes. Then, as now, the Chinese wheelbarrow had a single large wheel directly under the load, instead of out at the front like one of ours. It is extraordinary that the Chinese design is not in use everywhere because it saves the pusher from having to lift the weight of the load.

Leonardo da Vinci's idea for a bike.

Although the bicycle is a simple, highly advantageous invention, ancient masterminds spent lifetimes on more compli- **Bicycle** cated, less practical ideas, without even thinking of it. Eventually an impractical visionary turned his mind to the principle for long enough to design one. Leonardo da Vinci (1452A.D.–1519), the Italian artist from Vinci near Florence, conceived a machine very like a modern bicycle, with two equal-size wheels, handlebars and pedal, crank and chain drive to the back wheel. It was probably never built in Leonardo's time. The first working bicycle was Kirkpatrick Macmillan's machine of 1839. Compared to Leonardo's this Scottish design was rather crude – pedals pumped back and forward by the cyclist turned the rear wheel by means of eccentric lugs.

**Cable Car** The cable car made a humble start in 1774 in the West Chinese province of Szechuan. The acting administrator of Jao Hua district arranged for a 160-foot long cable to be run across a ravine and tightened by windlass. This supported an iron cage that was hauled in one direction or the other by long cords. The intention was to hasten the delivery of documents through the rugged region. At each end there were signal towers, and post horse stations.

**Funicular** The funicular came into operation on the banks of the Yangtze River in China in the next century. It was used first for taking coal down from hilly country to the riverbank for shipment. The descending car, with its greater weight, pulled the other one upwards. The two cars were attached to a cable that passed around reels at each terminus.

## 3. AIR AND SPACE

For military aviation, see Chapter VI, 3. Space rockets are included in this section, but the earliest rockets of various types are dealt with in Chapter VI, 2, with other weapons.

**Kite** The oldest reference to kites is in the *Harn Fei Dzu*, the book of the Chinese legalist philosopher, Harn Fei (died 233B.C.). He mentions two kites, one of them 'a bird made of bamboo and wood' which stayed up for three days. It was built by Gung Shu Parn. The other took Maw Dzu, the philosopher [see Utilitarianism, VII, 1], three years to construct, but crashed after the first day's use. Both gentlemen lived around 400B.C., and though it is possible that neither of them made the first kite, or perhaps any kite at all, kites must certainly have been invented at about this time or shortly beforehand.

**Train of Kites** From then on kite design increased in variety and complexity, and by the 3rd century A.D. trains of kites were being designed to carry people aloft. One system described by the writer Kaw Hung called for fourteen individual kites of three types; it was claimed that by exploiting wind resistance they would carry a man 20 km. upwards, but some readers may be sceptical about that.

**Manned Flight** There is no record, till much later, of anyone actually going up on a train of kites. However the first manned kite flight on record is in 559A.D., during the period of disruption when barbarians from the North ruled parts of China. The king of one of these states, Northern Chi, decided in the

interests of aeronautical research to launch some of his prisoners from atop the Tower of the Golden Phoenix, to see how
far they might go. The Tower was about 100 feet tall – it
seems that most of the prisoners landed soon and unhappily,
but Taw Ba Huarng To, a nobleman of the Toba tribe, made
a flight of 3 km. to the Purple Way, a nearby thoroughfare.
Each prisoner was equipped with a 'paper owl', which was
probably a kind of kite with a ground operator. (A similar
result might have been achieved with a well designed and
skilfully operated hang glider.)

Unfortunately these early records of various flying contraptions are rarely specific about the way they worked. It seems **Hang Glider**
that a device demonstrated to Warng Marng, Emperor of China
from 9A.D. to 23, was the first successful hang glider. It consisted
of two large wings. The inventor had told Warng Marng he
could fly it 500 km. from the city of Charng Arn to spy on the
military preparations of the Huns. In the event he was able to
go several hundred metres before crashing. Warng Marng, an
admirer of science, honoured the inventor for his ingenuity,
although he realised there was no practical application.

The box kite, which contributed much to the develop-
ment of early aeroplanes, was invented in Sydney by Lawrence **Box Kite**
Hargrave (1850–1915), early in the 1890s. At Stanwell Park,
now a popular hang-gliding site south of Sydney, in November 1894, Hargrave took off in a seat mounted under three
box-kite gliders and lifted into the air with the wind as his sole
motive power.

A model aircraft called the 'Flying Dove' was built and flown
in about 380B.C. by Archytus, a Greek from Tarentum in **Artificial Flight**
Southern Italy. It was propelled by compressed air or vapour,
on a similar principle to that which makes a party balloon fly
around when released.

In the 2nd century A.D., the Chinese scientist Jarng
Heng was enthralled by the dream of flight. He wrote poetry **Mechanical**
about space travel and on one occasion after an unhappy bout **Flight**
with his political opponents, looked forward to aviation
research for a break:

> Certain base scholars used to report evil of me to the
> Emperor, but I decided not to worry about such affairs or to
> study their 'unique arts' [of civil service intrigue]. Yet
> linked wheels can be made to turn of themselves so that
> even an object of cardboard may be made to fly all alone in
> the air. With drooping feathers I have returned to my own

home; why ought I not adjust my mechanisms and put
them in working order?                          (tr. Needham)
Jarng Heng was the inaugurator of mechanical flight – he
made a wooden model aircraft with wings and a spring-
powered mechanism in the body. It flew a long distance,
driven by a propeller or ornithopter. Both Archytus and Jarng
Heng understood a lot about flight, but lack of a suitable
motor restricted them to models, leaving manned flight [see
below] to much later pioneers.

**Hot Air Balloon**

The principle of the hot air balloon was exploited in an enjoy-
able trick practised in ancient China, and described in a book
from the 2nd century B.C., *Huai Narn's Ten Thousand Infallible
Arts*. It explains that eggshells can be made to take off and fly
through the air, by having tinder ignited inside them. Once
the combustion has filled the empty eggshell with hot air and
smoke, it becomes light enough to float away. (There is no
point trying this on ordinary chook eggs. The shell has to be
large, light and empty.) Later on, the Chinese in country areas
started entertaining themselves by making balloons out of
oiled paper on bamboo frames. On a little platform at the bottom they kindled a fire of pine needles. After a short time the
balloons would lift off and float through the night air, resembling red stars. This is probably a custom many centuries old
but remains undated.

**Balloon Passengers**

At Versailles, near Paris, in September 1783, a large balloon constructed by the brothers Montgolfier, paper manufacturers, and heated by burning hay, carried a duck, a sheep
and a cock aloft in a suspended basket, and safely lowered
them again. In Paris in November, Pilâtre de Rozier and the
Marquis d'Arlandes made a 25-min. trip in a Montgolfier hot

**Manned Flight**
**1. Hot Air Balloon**

air balloon. The following month Jacques Alexander César
(1746–1823) and his mechanic, Robert, took to the air in a
similar-looking balloon filled with hydrogen; theirs was the

**2. Gas-filled Balloon**

first of many flights made in contraptions filled with gases
lighter than air.

**Dirigible**

Balloons can only travel where the wind takes them;
navigation through the air requires motive power and a design
suitable for steering. These requirements led to the invention
of the dirigible. In France in 1784 Meusnier recommended an
elongated balloon with a series of propellers. In 1843 the first
model dirigible, designed by Monck Mason, was launched
inside a hall in London. Its clockwork propellers took it the
length of the hall. Dr. William Bland, a member of the New

South Wales parliament and former convict, drew up elaborate plans for a full-size version in Sydney in 1851. He christened it the 'Atmotic Ship'; he never built it, but sent the plans to London for the Great Exhibition. At Versailles in September 1852, a full-sized dirigible (44 m. long) finally came into operation – the hydrogen-filled airship of Henri Giffard. On its inaugural demonstration flight the airship's 3-horsepower steam engine, turning a single large propeller, drove it at 8 km/h for a distance of 27 km.

On 9 October 1890 the first manned aeroplane took off at Armainvilliers, near Paris, and flew approximately 50 m. before returning to the ground. In the pilot's seat was its French inventor, Clément Ader (1841–1925). Ader's flight was made possible by his years of work developing a spirit-fired steam engine with a much higher power-to-weight ratio than any other of his time, higher in fact than any achieved in petrol aviation engines until 1907.

**Manned Aeroplane Flight**

The design of his aircraft 'Eole' differed from other early designs in many respects, the most obvious being its incorporation of a fuselage, or closed-in body, in which Ader placed two portholes.

**Fuselage**

The wings were modelled on bat wings, and were curved in the manner of aerofoils to improve the lift they could impart. By means of cables running from the cockpit to articulated joints in the wing struts, *Eole*'s pilot could adjust the angle of the outer wings – the first use of the principle of ailerons for controlling flight. It is not very likely that the availability of such controls made a practical difference on the first flight, there being little scope for manoeuvres in 50 m., or even on *Eole*'s second flight, of 100 m. in 1891.

**Ailerons**

Propulsion came from a single helical propeller with curved arms, on each of which multiple vanes were fixed; Ader later built a two-engined plane with a pair of propellers, which flew 300 m. in 1897. An amusing sequel to Ader's achievements is the way popular books in English resort to twisted phraseology to disparage them. Linecar and Green in *Early Aeroplanes* declare that Ader's plane 'never really flew'; *The Guinness Book of Records*, observing that 'the flight was neither sustained nor controlled', dismisses it as a 'hop', as does the *Encyclopaedia Britannica*, which reserves the term 'flight' for a similar feat by Americans thirteen years later. Such blusterings do not belong in a book of firsts, nor, dare we suggest, in future editions of the works quoted?

**Two-engined Plane**

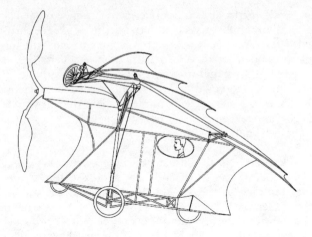

The first aeroplane, as reconstructed by Jacques Lissarrague, from Clément Ader's drawings.

**International Passenger Service** In March 1919 the French company, Farman, an aeroplane manufacturer, began a regular passenger aeroplane service between Paris and Brussels.

**Cross-Channel Flight**
**Cross-Channel Passenger Service** Louis Blériot (1872–1936), French manufacturer of the Blériot XI monoplane, flew one of his products across the English Channel on 25 July 1909, covering the 38 km. in 36½ minutes. He won a prize of £1000 offered by the London *Daily Mail*. The First World War delayed the inception of regular passenger flights over the Channel, which began in August 1919.

**Trans-Atlantic Flight**
**Trans-Atlantic Non-stop Flight** A flight across the Atlantic between North America and Europe – from Newfoundland to Portugal – was completed in May 1919 by Lieut. Commander Albert Cushing Read of the U.S. Navy, and his crew, travelling in a Curtiss NC-4 flying boat. They made a landing en route, at the Azores. Next month British Airforce officers, Capt. John Alcock and Lieut. Arthur Whitten Brown made the first non-stop Atlantic crossing from Newfoundland to Ireland, flying a Vickers-Vimy biplane.

**Europe–Australia Flight** In March 1919, when the Australian Government offered a generous £10,000 prize to the first airman to fly from England to Australia, it laid down some restrictive terms. The crew had to be all Australian, the aircraft manufactured in the British

Empire, and the journey completed in thirty days. One entrant was Charles Kingsford Smith, who later made the first flight across the Pacific [see below]. At the instigation of Prime Minister Hughes, the nomination of Kingsford Smith and his associates was rejected, because of their youth and inexperience in navigation. But the prize inspired aviation's most keenly fought race for a first; six Australian crews took off at various dates; simultaneously Lieut. Poulet of France set out to fly to Australia. The Australian crews did not fare well: two disappeared, two withdrew and one was delayed well beyond thirty days. The remaining crew, four men led by Ross Smith (1892–1922) – a veteran of the Gallipoli campaign and of the Australian Flying Corps – had left England on 12 November 1919. Co-pilot and navigator was his older brother Keith. The Smiths overtook Poulet in Burma, and reached Darwin on 10 December, undisputed winners, in a time of 135 hours.

**Flight Around the World**

Two U.S. army Douglas DWC aircraft flew around the world in 1924: *Chicago*, crewed by Lieut. L. H. Smith and Sgt. L. L. Arnold, and *New Orleans*, crewed by Lieut. Eric H. Nelson and Sgt. J. Harding. The flight began in April 1924 and ended 175 days later, on 28 September, at Seattle U.S.A. The circumnavigation was completed in 57 stages, and 351 hours' flying time.

**Flight to the North Pole**

The polar regions of our world have long had a conspicuous way of bringing forth codswallop from the hardy souls who report on their experiences there. But never has more hot air issued from their gloomy confines than when the famous American naval commander, Richard E. Byrd, paid visits. It was mostly vented by Byrd himself in the form of verbiage relating to his expeditions – excruciating but generally harmless. However on 10 May 1926 he and his pilot, Floyd Bennett, deceitfully led the world to believe they had flown to the North Pole on the 9th; new American research has deciphered a rubbed-out entry in their navigational notes and established that they actually turned back with engine trouble over 200 km. short of the Pole. Byrd's deception won him a medal from President Coolidge, a triumphal procession, and a volley of accolades rightfully belonging to his Norwegian rival, Roald Amundsen (1872–1928), who flew over the Pole two days later. Amundsen – who had been first to reach the South Pole [IX, 4] fifteen years earlier – flew in an airship, the *Norge*, accompanied by Umberto Nobile, Lincoln Ellsworth

**Crossing of the Arctic Ocean**

and Oscar Wisting. After taking off from Spitzbergen they passed directly over the North Pole on 12 May 1926, and flew on to Alaska: completing their flight across the Arctic Ocean – another first – but one for which Amundsen received due credit.

**Flight Across the Pacific**

The flight across the Pacific from America to Australia was the longest and most challenging crossing facing aviators, with its great distances between tiny island landfalls. On 31 May 1928 the Fokker tri-motor monoplane, *Southern Cross*, took off from Oakland Airfield near San Francisco, carrying the Australian aviator and First World War veteran, Charles Kingsford Smith (1897–1935), his co-pilot and countryman Charles Ulm, and two Americans, navigator Harry Lyon and radio operator James Warner. Their longest hop was over 5000 km. from Hawaii to Fiji in shocking weather, taking 33 hours. They reached Brisbane on 9 June, and Sydney the next day, greeted by a crowd estimated at 300,000. Two months later Kingsford Smith and Ulm in *Southern Cross* made the first non-stop flight across Australia, from Point Cook, Victoria to Perth, and a month after that, the first flight across the Tasman Sea, from Sydney to Christchurch.

**Trans-Tasman Flight**

**Flight in Antarctica**

Kingsford Smith had bought *Southern Cross* from fellow Australian and Arctic aviator, Hubert Wilkins (1888–1958), who was planning at the time to take aircraft to Antarctica. With the backing of American media tycoon William Randolph Hearst, Wilkins could afford more expensive planes which he liked much better than Fokker tri-motors. He bought two Lockheed Vega monoplanes, and took them to Deception Island aboard a Norwegian whaling ship, the *Hektoria*, sailing from New York in September 1928. On 16 November Wilkins's Canadian deputy Ben Eielson took off in one of the planes from the beach on Deception Island, circled a few times and landed again safely. On 20 December they made a 70-mile flight over Graham Land, the first in a series of exploratory surveys of the Antarctic Peninsula. Because from the air glaciers resemble iced-over channels, Wilkins mistook the Peninsula for a series of islands, until John Rymill's later sledge-borne surveys corrected him.

**Flight to the South Pole**

American explorer Richard E. Byrd took a large expedition to Antarctica in 1928, the same year as Wilkins's journey, sponsored by Hearst's media rival, the *New York Times*. Byrd, who wanted to be the first to fly to the South Pole, was afraid that Wilkins had undeclared plans for the same objective and might beat him there. However Byrd was not ready to fly any of his three aircraft till 1929, and had to wait till winter was gone to attempt the Pole. On 28 November 1929 a crew of four Americans took off from Byrd's base 'Little America', near the Ross Sea: Bernt Balchen, pilot; Byrd, navigator; June, radio operator, and McKinley, photographer. Their plane was a Ford tri-motor called *Floyd Bennett*. They ascended to the Polar Plateau by jettisoning supplies, and reached the Pole early on the morning of the 29th. Without landing they turned around for an uneventful flight back to base. Wilkins had not been there already, because despite Byrd's fears, he had not planned a flight to the Pole.

The notorious De Havilland Comet first flew in 1949 in Britain. It reduced travelling times but tended to crash with **Jet Airliner** depressing frequency, because a design flaw caused metal fatigue. This was not detected unfortunately until after it went into commercial airline service in 1952.

The primaeval helicopter was a Chinese hand-held toy: a simple rotor with blades, which could be made to spin by twisted **Helicopter** cords fast enough to take off and fly. Later, with the aid of gunpowder, they could go quite high, but they were only decorative fireworks. Around about 300A.D. helicopter rotor blades had been fitted by an anonymous Chinese inventor to a 'flying car' made of the lightest timber. The rotor was driven by leather straps. Such a contraption could certainly have taken off, but without an engine, it could not have carried a passenger or stayed aloft.

The German Fa-61 helicopter, designed by Professor Heinrich Focke, took to the air in 1936. Focke's machine was **Motorised** the first motorised helicopter, capable of carrying a passenger, **Helicopter** to fly successfully. Focke was a designer and part owner of the Focke-Wulf aircraft company, but because he was regarded as politically unreliable by the Nazi government, he was not allowed to participate in military aircraft design. For this reason he turned his hand to helicopters, whose military usefulness was not envisaged till well into the Second World War. The Fa-61 had twin rotors mounted on outriggers and could reach 122 km/h and an altitude of over 3000 m.

On 4 October 1957, *Sputnik I* – designed by Sergei Korolyov (1907–66) and his team – was launched by rocket, from the **Spacecraft** Soviet Government space base, or 'cosmodrome', Baikonur, in

Kazakhstan, to become the first craft sent beyond the Earth's gravitational pull and into orbit. It reached a height of 946 km. Instruments mounted on *Sputnik I* measured electron densities, and upper atmosphere temperatures and the findings were radioed back to Earth automatically. *Sputnik* burnt up on 4 January 1958 as it re-entered the atmosphere.

**Spacecraft Passenger**
*Sputnik II*, launched on 3 November 1957, carried Laika, a samoyed husky dog, the first animal to travel in space. She travelled in an air-conditioned compartment with a food supply suspended in gelatin. Sensors wired to her 5 kg. body gathered information about her pulse, breathing and movement in a weightless state. Her successful adjustment to space conditions was an important observation leading to the go-ahead for the Soviet Government's manned space flight programme.

**Moon Rocket**
On 14 September 1959, the unmanned Soviet craft, *Lunar II*, reached the Moon, in the region known as Mare Serenitatum (Sea of Tranquillity).

**Man in Space**
Flight Major Yuri Alekseyevich Gagarin (1934–68), a Russian pilot, became the first man in space on 12 April 1961, when his craft *Vostok I* – the lead portion of a multi-stage rocket designed by Korolyov – orbited for 90 minutes before returning him safely to the atmosphere. Gagarin ejected shortly before its landing and parachuted safely to Earth.

**Woman in Space**
The first space woman was Jr. Lieut. Vladimirovna Tereshkova (born 1937) who left Baikonur Cosmodrome aboard *Vostok 6* in June 1963, and remained aloft almost three days, before a safe return.

**Spacewalk**
On 18 March 1965 Lieut.-Col. Aleksei Arkhipovich Leonov (born 1934) became the first person to get out of his craft (*Voskhod II*) while it was in space. To describe his excursion as a walk is somewhat misleading, but he did move around a bit.

**Men on the Moon**
The spate of Russian firsts in space was galling to Americans in the 1960s, and led to a policy designed to win the U.S.A. a first more glorious than any since Gagarin's flight. President Kennedy declared that the U.S.A. would land a man on the Moon by 1970, and saw to it that his aim received ample government support. Although he did not live to see the dream realised, the prediction came true with time to spare. On 21 July 1969, *Apollo 11* – launched from Cape Canaveral, Florida, U.S.A. – landed on the Mare Serenitatum. The first man to get out and walk on the Moon was Neil Armstrong (born 1930), commander of *Apollo 11*. He was

joined by Edwin Eugene Aldrin (born 1930), who had accompanied him in the landing module. The other member of the *Apollo* party, Michael Collins, remained aloft, in the command module.

The more modest achievement of landing a vehicle on the Moon was successfully accomplished in November 1970 when a Soviet craft deposited the radio-controlled motor car *Lunokhod I* on part of the lunar surface known as the Mare Imbrium. In 1970 and 1971 earthbound controllers drove it a total of 10½ km., taking readings from its monitoring equipment in various locations.

**Vehicle on the Moon**

The first space station, known as *Salyut I*, was launched by the Soviet space administration from Baikonur Cosmodrome on 19 April 1971. As a space station it was to remain in space while other craft travelled to and from it. On 23 April *Soyuz XI* arrived, carrying three cosmonauts, and docked successfully at the 18-tonne *Salyut*. The crew worked at the station for 570 hours, before returning Earthwards. (Regrettably all three died because of a misfortune on re-entry.)

**Space Station**

## 4. EXPEDITIONS AND DISCOVERIES

What amounts to discovery depends on the definition. Here we only count expeditions which find something and bring back information to the world at large. This counts out castaways, and explorers whose findings were successfully kept secret. Most lands were located by ancestors of their indigenous peoples long before known explorers got to them, but those primaeval settlers are excluded for the same reason.

Unfortunately some readers will be very irritated by the conclusions and conjectures given here about first discoveries. Nothing of practical importance turns any longer on these discoveries – they are simply historical curiosities. So the religious fervour which goes into debating them is entirely inappropriate, as well as an impediment to getting at the truth. The priority of the discovery of the Americas, Australia, New Zealand and the Polar regions gives rise to much controversy. But as almost all the conflicting opinions are based on unproved assumptions, no one is entitled to be doctrinaire about them. In controversial cases the conclusions adopted in this section are those which are most likely to be true, according to a careful and impartial consideration of a wide range of evidence.

The first ascents of famous mountains are included here; there are enough of them to fill a whole book, so only the tallest in each continent appears.

Around about 600B.C., perhaps a few years earlier, the Egypt-
**Cape of Good** ian pharaoh, Neckho, dispatched a group of ships, manned by
**Hope Rounded** Phoenicians (residents of present-day Lebanon), to sail round
Africa. They travelled south from Egypt's Red Sea coast, along
the East Coast of Africa. They rounded the Cape of Good
Hope, sailing from east to west, noticing as they did so, that
the Sun was on their right. This phenomenon was remarkable
to mariners who had never been to the Southern Hemisphere
before. They continued northwards along Africa's Atlantic
**Africa Circum-** coast, entered the Mediterranean through the Pillars of Her-
**navigated** cules (the present-day Straits of Gibraltar), and returned to
Egypt having completed the circumnavigation. On two occa-
sions they had put ashore for winter on African soil, and
**Southern** grown crops. They arrived back in the third year – the first
**Hemisphere** expedition to go to and return from the Southern Hemi-
**Explored** sphere, bringing a description of its findings.

Crates of Mallos (2nd century B.C.) was a Greek scholar who
**Southern** worked at Pergamon in present-day Turkey and who visited
**Hemisphere** Rome and broke his leg in the main sewer there. He was
**Studied** deeply interested in the Southern Hemisphere, and on his
famous terrestrial globe [V, 3] the southern continents were
roughly guessed at. He also knew from the work of earlier
scholars that the southern climatic zones mirror those of the
North. He posited that the central Torrid Zone is chiefly occupied by ocean and that south of it lay lands inhabited by
'Aethiopians', resembling the natives of ancient Ethiopia, as
well as by other unknown races.

If Christopher Columbus had paid closer attention to ancient
**America** Greek books he might have read that a huge continent across
**Discovered** the Atlantic Ocean would interfere with his plan to sail west
from Europe to Asia. The Greeks knew of America because of
its discovery by the people of Carthage, Phoenician seafarers
from North Africa. The reference to a land mass extending
from north to south in the Atlantic between Europe and Asia,
in Strabo's *Geography* (Rome, 1st century B.C.), is probably
based on the writings of Eratosthenes (276–195B.C.), who also
worked out the distance round the Earth [see Measurement of
the Earth, VIII, 3]. The Carthaginians discovered America
about 400B.C. The oldest record of their discovery is in Aristotle's work *On Marvellous Things Heard* (Athens, 4th century
B.C.), which speaks of a land many days' sailing beyond the
Pillars of Hercules (the Straits of Gibraltar), supporting

timber of all kinds, and penetrated by navigable rivers. According to Aristotle, Carthaginian authorities prohibited travel to this new world.

The Carthaginians were prosperous and successful navigators who frequently mounted large Atlantic naval expeditions, especially along the coast of Africa. One of their notable accomplishments was to sail to the Canary Islands, which square-rigged ships from Africa can only reach by going west into the open sea and then doubling back. This journey takes the ship comparatively close to America, into part of the Atlantic where the winds and currents tend south and west towards the North Coast of South America. That is probably how the Carthaginians discovered it. Because Carthage's population was fully committed in supporting trade and colonies in Spain and on the Atlantic coast of Africa, it made sense for her to prohibit travel to America; American resources might have done more to benefit Carthage's eager Greek and Phoenician rivals than Carthage herself. Information about the land over the Atlantic is given by several ancient authors after Aristotle, but the second group to visit America, Norse seamen in the 11th century, commanded by Leif the Lucky, knew nothing of these records.

**Canary Islands Discovered**

The coast of North America was sighted in 985 A.D. by an Icelandic trader, Bjarni Herjolfsson of Herjolfsness. Bjarni was sailing to Greenland to find his father Herjolf, who had just left with Eirik the Red's expedition for the settlement of Greenland [see below]. He was blown off course towards America. He sighted the coast of Canada's maritime provinces and sailed in close without making any landing. Then he made his way to Greenland and joined his father. His lack of curiosity was much remarked on at the time.

**North America Sighted**

About 1000 A.D. Leif the Lucky, son of Eirik the Red, set out from Greenland in a single ship with thirty-five crew to explore America. They landed first in Labrador, which they named 'Markland', and after a short visit sailed on southwest to present-day Maine (in the U.S.A.), which they named Vinland, where they explored and stayed for winter. The following year Leif and his party returned to Greenland. News of their discoveries encouraged other Norse travellers to sail there and establish settlements. The Norse settlements did not last, and America was left alone until 1397. On April Fools' Day that year Henry Sinclair, Earl of the Orkneys, and his offsider, Antonio Zeno of Venice, sailed west and reached

**Landings in North America**

Nova Scotia, where they spent the winter. The next European arrivals were the Spanish expeditions to South and Central America – those of Columbus on his third transatlantic trip, and of Hojeda, both of which reached the mainland in 1499.

**South America's East Coast Explored**

The main length of South America's East Coast was explored by two navigators in the service of Spain, Pinzon and Solis, between 1500 and 1514. In 1520 the Portuguese navigator, Fernando de Magalhaens, known to his Spanish employers as Magellan, located the Straits of Magellan. His ships, travelling from east to west on the first circumnavigation of the Earth, [see below], sailed through the Straits, successfully completing the first rounding of the tip of South America.

**Tip of South America Rounded**

**America's Pacific Coast Sighted**

The discovery of the western side of America is the joint achievement of many explorers. In 1513A.D., Vasco Núñez de Balboa (1475–1517), Spanish governor of Darien, set out to cross the Central American isthmus, drawn by reports of a great western ocean. On 25 September, looking down from a mountain top behind Panama, he saw the Pacific Ocean, and thus proved that America has a west coast, which till then was in doubt. He called the Pacific Ocean 'the South Sea' because it lies south of the isthmus. Notable amongst those who rapidly extended knowledge of the coast is Francisco Pizarro (1471–1541), a Spanish desperado who made three voyages southwards between 1524 and 1532. Accompanied sometimes by his brother Gonzalo, and Diego de Almagro and Hernando Luque, Pizarro went to Peru and overthrew the Inca empire.

**North America's West Coast Explored**

Sponsored by the Spanish conqueror of Mexico, Hernán Cortés, in 1539 Francisco de Ulloa sailed north from Acapulco on the Mexican south coast, up to the mouth of the Colorado River, establishing that Baja California is a peninsula, and making an important start on northern exploration of the West Coast. Exploration of the western extremities of North America had probably already begun, by Japanese ships sailing north along the Pacific coast of Siberia and thence across to Alaska. Early Japanese maps showed the Bering Strait in sufficient detail to establish that Asia and America are separate continents.

**Alaska Discovered**

**Iceland Discovered**

Around 320B.C. the Greek scientist, Pytheas, from Massilia (present-day Marseilles, France), led a research expedition from Gades (present-day Cadiz, Spain), far into the North Atlantic. He sailed out of the Mediterranean Sea, and north up the West Coast of Great Britain. Immediately north of

Britain he discovered the Orkney Islands, and sailing north-west from there for six days, he came to an island which he called 'Thule', that we now identify with Iceland. After leaving Iceland he found his northward progress barred by the Arctic ice pack. At approximately the position of the Arctic Circle – the furthest north any discoverer had been, he turned away. He described the Arctic Circle as the northern tropic – i.e. the southernmost point at which the 24-hour polar night [VIII, 2] occurs. He next explored the Baltic Sea, after which, sailing along the east coast of Britain, from the point where he had previously left it, he completed the first circumnavigation of that island. His trip contributed much useful information to science, including observations of dramatic North Sea tides helping to confirm the theory of lunar determination of tide.

**The Arctic Circle Reached**

**Baltic Sea Entered**

**Britain Circum-navigated**

In the 2nd century A.D. and earlier, diplomats and business-men from Java and other islands southeast of Asia travelled to and from China in well laden ships. It would be very strange if people from these countries – who were easily able to make the 4000-kilometre trip through hazardous waters to China – had not also, at least once or twice, made the safe crossing of 1300 or 1400 kilometres, to Northwestern Australia. In those days the Indonesian Archipelago housed a number of small civilised states populated by native Malays, and Indians whose families had recently arrived by sea from India itself. The people of these kingdoms were well organised, prosperous and adventurous, and expert mariners. Yeh Tiao, the Javan ruler whose diplomatic mission visited China in 132A.D., would, for instance, have had no trouble arranging journeys to Australia. The likelihood of early discovery by the Malay states would explain the old East Asian tradition of a large land mass far to the southeast of China. At an unknown date Australia's coast came to be of economic interest to the Malays for its *bêche de mer*, a sea slug [III, 2] that fetched a high price in China as a delicacy. Until recent times they regularly sent fleets to Australia to gather this product, and early last century the English explorer, Matthew Flinders, encountered such a group off the northern coast, and interviewed the captain.

**Australia Discovered**

If the Malays were the first to discover Australia, the Chinese were probably second; they had huge fleets in Indonesia from late in the Sung period to early in the Ming (12th to 15th centuries). A hostile expedition to Java in the 13th century consisted of 1000 vessels. A Chinese expedition in this period is likely – perhaps interested in *bêche de mer*, and perhaps

**Australia's East Coast Discovered**

responsible for placing a Chinese figurine found last century, deep in the roots of an old banyan tree in Darwin. A third group, Spanish, Portuguese or Asian may have discovered and charted the East Coast, in about 1500. The French 'Dauphin Map' of 1536 appears to have been based on a Portuguese chart, but it is uncertain whether the East Coast was known from European or Asian exploration especially as there is a significant lack of European place names on it.

**Australia's South Coast Discovered**

The Dutch, who came in 1606, are probably the fourth or fifth national group to discover Australia. But Peter Nuyts and the crew of the Dutch trading ship, *Gulden Zeepaerdt*, in 1627, were the first who were adventurous enough to discover and explore the South Coast, which they sailed along as far east as present-day Ceduna. During the 17th century various Dutch ships gradually explored different parts of the West Coast, most of which they had discovered by 1640.

**Australia's West Coast Discovered**

**Tasmania Discovered**

In 1642 Anthonie Van Diemen, the governor in Batavia (present-day Jakarta) for the Dutch East India Company, sent Abel Tasman, with two ships, to explore Australia. Tasman discovered Tasmania and sailed around its south coast. This way he proved that Australia is not part of the great Antarctic continent that many Europeans believed in. Tasman continued east to explore New Zealand, then returned to Batavia, travelling north of New Guinea. He thus became the first navigator to circumnavigate Australia, but since he did not follow the Australian coast, credit for that achievement might better go to Matthew Flinders, who sailed the *Investigator* around the continent from 1801 to 1803.

**Australia Circumnavigated**

**Greenland Discovered**

About 900A.D. the Icelandic navigator Gunnbjorn Ulfsson was carried far to the west of Iceland by an unfavourable wind. He saw land in the distance, the East Coast of Greenland. In 978A.D. Snaebjorn Gulti led an Icelandic colonising expedition which landed on this coast, but immediately suffered an appalling winter, and returned without exploring or learning the extent of Greenland.

**Greenland Explored**

At about this time Thorgest of Breidabolstead in Iceland borrowed some bench boards from Eirik the Red of Eirikstead, but did not return them when asked. There ensued an acrimonious quarrel, for Eirik's part in which, the Thing of Thorsness voted to outlaw him. Eirik decided to search for new land in the West, and with his crew set sail in 981 or 982. They spent three years exploring the southern sections of the East and West Coasts, locating suitable sites for agricultural settlements. Like many explorers Eirik had the mind of a real estate agent, and he named the new land Greenland to tempt settlers from Iceland; the name offered far more in encouragement than truthful information.

Back in Iceland in 985 Eirik persuaded twenty-five shiploads of settlers to follow him, on the expedition which **Greenland** sailed that year to establish Greenland's first permanent set- **Settled** tlement, in the area known as Julianehaab.

The circumnavigation of the Earth is a great achievement in its own right, and offered a marvellous opportunity for expan- **Earth Circum-** sion of knowledge. But it was a scary, difficult project and no **navigated** one got round to it, until the motives of gain and power were added to the calculations. Fernando de Magellan (Magalhaens in his native Portuguese, born 15th century A.D.) served the Portuguese Empire in the Far East, where it was enriched by trading in spices from Malacca and neighbouring islands, and in manufactured products from China. Portugal's King Manoel I couldn't stand Magellan, refused him promotion and made it obvious that his career prospects were not good. So in 1517 Magellan made his abode in rival Spain, and instructed the Spanish authorities that the riches of Malacca and China were on the Spanish side of a demarcation line which Spain and Portugal had agreed on as the way of dividing their claims on world territory and trade. King Ferdinand supplied five ships and 236 men, and Magellan sailed west from San Lucar on 20 September 1519, to South America. The flotilla progressed slowly southward along the American East Coast, and on 26 November 1520 reached the opening of the Strait of Magellan, which links the Atlantic and Pacific Oceans, around the southern tip of South America.

One of his ships had been wrecked and another deserted **Strait of** the expedition and went home. With the remaining three, **Magellan** Magellan sailed through the strait named after him, with the **Discovered** coasts of Tierra del Fuego, now discovered for the first time, on **Tierra del** his left. Although this was later thought to be part of a conti- **Fuego** nent, Magellan recognised it as an island or islands, by the **Discovered** roar of the sea from beyond. They entered the Pacific Ocean, which they crossed from east to west in three months, twenty days – the first European expedition to complete the crossing. Shortly before Easter 1521 Magellan reached the Philippines, where he began to stir up trouble amongst the local kingdoms. He was killed while attacking the island of Mauthan on behalf of the king of Subath. So many Spaniards were killed by the natives that they could no longer man three ships, so they burnt one, and fled in the other two into the Indonesian Archipelago. In the Moluccas they loaded up with a cargo of cloves, but only one ship, the *Victoria*, was seaworthy enough to sail home. In this they crossed the seas on the forbidden, Portuguese, side of the line of demarcation, and reached the Cape Verde Islands after rounding the southern tip of Africa. Thirteen Spaniards were there imprisoned by the Portuguese; the remaining eighteen fled aboard *Victoria* and reached Spain on 6 September 1522 under the command of Juan Sebastian d'el Cano, one of the surviving officers, three years after setting sail.

**New Zealand Discovered** In 1576 the Spanish pilot Juan Fernandez set sail from Chile, beginning his journey at about 40° South latitude, on a westerly and southwesterly course. He returned to report that he had discovered an unknown coast, which appeared to be continental, with large river mouths in it. It was a fruitful country with hospitable people, well built and dressed in cloth. This was probably the East Coast of New Zealand, which was inhabited by the Maoris, and had been unknown till then, except to Pacific islanders. According to the Spaniards in Chile later on, they did not follow up the discovery for fear that other nations would take advantage. Most of the few commentators who have taken notice of Fernandez's report believe he came to some tiny island or group in the mid-Pacific. But that is only because his stated journey time – one month – is hardly enough to reach New Zealand. However there were very few islands in his way, and no other land that matches his description as New Zealand does, so alternative explanations are all pretty far-fetched. More likely one month is an understatement, or he had a very fast trip, or both. (If Fernandez's discovery is really a fabrication, then Tasman takes the credit instead [see Circumnavigation of Australia, above].)

**New Zealand Circum- navigated** After Abel Tasman discovered the West Coast of New Zealand, many people suspected that it was the coast of Terra Australis, the huge southern continent conjectured by geographers. So in 1768, when James Cook of the British Navy sailed in *Endeavour* out of the Thames to observe the transit of Venus in Tahiti, he carried secret instructions to search for land in the south. After leaving Tahiti, *Endeavour* went south into open sea, then west, until in October 1769 she came to Poverty Bay on the east coast of New Zealand's North Island. Cook sailed around the North Island in an anti-clockwise direction and passed from the west through the strait that separates the North and South Islands. He then sailed north to establish that the North Island is not connected to any other land. On sighting Cape Turnagain, which he had seen at the start of his circumnavigation, he turned south and made a clockwise circumnavigation of the South Island. When he got back to the western mouth of Cook Strait, it was March 1770, and *Endeavour* had completed a figure-eight circuit around New Zealand, proving that it is only a pair of islands.

In 1829 Captain John Ross of the British Navy sailed in command of an exploratory expedition financed by his friend Sir Felix Booth, in search of the Northwest Passage. He discovered the northernmost promontory of the American continent and christened it Boothia Felix. Second in command was Ross's nephew, James Clark Ross (1800–62). On 31 May 1831 this nephew found the North Magnetic Pole, at that time located on Boothia. The expedition did not succeed in finding the Northwest Passage, but young Ross's work so impressed the Admiralty that he was made a captain and put in charge of a magnetic survey of Britain and Ireland. **North Magnetic Pole Reached**

In 1878 Prof. Adolf Erik Nordenskjöld (1832–1901) led a Swedish expedition from Tromsö in Norway to sail through the Northeast Passage – the sea lane to the Far East from the Atlantic which it was hoped might exist to the north of Russia. Numerous Dutch, English and Russian expeditions had previously sought a way through without success. Nordenskjöld had twice before gone part way. On this occasion he was almost in the Bering Strait – the final leg – when the waters froze on 25 September 1878 and trapped his ship *Vega* for the winter. Not until July in the following year did the ship get free and pass through the Straits into the Pacific Ocean. Her journey finished at Yokohama in September 1879. **Northeast Passage**

The Northwest Passage is the corresponding way from the Atlantic to the Pacific, north of Canada. By the time of Nordenskjöld's journey no ship had been through it, but a British ship's crew under Commander Robert McClure (1807–73) had completed the journey from west to east. In 1850 their ship, the *Investigator*, had her way blocked by sea ice amongst the islands north of Canada. In April 1853 McClure saw a man approaching the ship, who turned out to have come from a group of British ships which had entered the region from the east. *Investigator*'s company abandoned ship and headed over the ice to join the *North Star*, which transported them out the **Northwest Passage Surveyed** eastern end of the Northwest Passage. McClure got back to England in September 1854, having thus made the Northwest Passage by a combination of ship and foot travel.

**Northwest Passage by Ship**

The first ship to make the Northwest Passage was *Gjoa* under the command of Norwegian explorer, Roald Amundsen (1872–1928). *Gjoa's* east–west journey began in 1903 and finished in 1906. Amundsen had already been amongst the first party to winter in Antarctica [see below] and in 1926 led the first flight across the Arctic [IX, 3]. With him on *Gjoa* was Helmer Hanssen, who joined him on the first trip to the South Pole in 1911 [see below].

**North Pole Reached**

Three claims by American expeditioners to have reached the North Pole – Dr. Frederick Cook's (1908), Admiral Robert Peary's (1909) and Admiral Richard Byrd's (by air, 1926) – are probably all fraudulent. Cook already had the bogus first ascent of Mt. McKinley to his credit [see below] and was later convicted of fraud in another matter. His claim to have got to the Pole is not as incredible as Peary's and Byrd's, but is unsupported by navigational records, and relies on improbably rapid ice traverses. Consequently Roald Amundsen and his party, who reached the Pole by air on 12 May 1926 [IX, 3], were probably the first to go there by any means. They apparently gave credence to Peary's claim and made no effort to land anyone at the Pole. Members of a party from the U.S.S.R. which arrived on 23 April 1948 were probably the first men to reach the Pole at surface level: Pavel Geordiyenko, Mikhail Yemel'yenovich Ostrekin, Pavel Kononovich Sen'ko and Mikhail Mikhaylovich Somov.

**Southern Ocean Entered**

According to Polynesian tradition recorded on Raratonga, the company of the catamaran *Te Ivi-o-Atea* saw 'wonderful things' on a journey beyond Rapa (Opara Island):

> the rocks that grow out of the sea in the space beyond Rapa; the monstrous seas; the female that dwells in those mountainous waves, whose tresses wave about in the waters and on the surface of the sea; and the frozen sea of arrow-root, with the deceitful animal of that sea who dives to great depths – a foggy, misty and dark place not seen by the Sun. Other things are like rocks, whose summits pierce the skies, they are completely bare . . .

This is Polynesian imagery for the phenomena of sub-Antarctic waters south of the Pacific – the female with tresses, bull kelp; the frozen sea of arrowroot, pack ice; the animal that dives, the elephant seal; and the bare things like rocks, icebergs.

*Te Ivi-o-Atea* was built in Fiji in the 600s A.D., according to one theory, but the dating cannot be relied on, and it may have been considerably later. Her builder was Ui-te-Rangiora, who then sailed her south to become pioneer navigator of the frigid Southern Ocean. Polynesians in catamarans accomplished spectacular feats of exploration, but they are usually excluded from our book because word of their finds hardly travelled beyond their island communities. However Ui-te-Rangiora's feat was imitated by other Polynesian mariners, and there is a good chance their collective knowledge of the Southern Ocean spread all the way to Europe in 1510, when Ludovico di Varthema's *Itinerary* was published in Rome. That book includes a brief account of an extremely cold region with a four-hour day, which Varthema quotes from a Chinese junk captain. According to the captain that region was navigated not by the Chinese but by races who live beyond Java, suggesting that he knew the Southern Ocean from Polynesian informants from waters to the east.

A Chinese atlas based on a map made in 1315A.D. appears to show a number of islands, in the region of the Crozets and Kerguelen groups, southeast of Africa. These islands may have been located not much earlier by seal hunters searching for new sealing grounds in the far south. However it is not possible to tell from the map whether the discoverers were Chinese, island people or Africans.

**Sub-Antarctic Islands Reached**

Captain James Cook, on his second great voyage, aboard the *Resolution*, accompanied by the *Discovery*, led the first expedition across the Antarctic Circle in 1772. He went on beyond 71°S without coming within sight of land. However ice phenomena convinced him that a continent lay over the horizon and at one point he saw what may have been a distant range reflected in the sky by ice crystals. When heavy sea ice forced Cook to turn back at his southernmost point, a young wag in his crew, George Vancouver, clambered out to the end of the bowsprit and made a pardonable song and dance about having travelled further south than anyone else ever had.

**Antarctic Circle Reached**

Decades passed before anyone came close enough to see the continent of Antarctica. Then suddenly in 1820 and 1821, three expeditions – American, Russian and British – made sightings which have since been claimed as first discoveries. By a three-day margin over the British, the honour belongs to the Russians, led by Admiral Thaddeus von Bellingshausen, in *Vostok* and *Mirnyi*, who came within sight of the coast of present-day Dronning Maud Land on 27 January 1820.

**Antarctic Mainland Discovered**

Bellingshausen did not go ashore, or even claim that a continent had been sighted.

Antarctica remained a place which was never visited **Winter in** more than briefly until the 1897–99 expedition led by Belgian **Antarctica** naval officer, Adrien de Gerlache de Gomery. It sailed there from Antwerp in the *Belgica*. Her multinational company included Roald Amundsen of Norway and Frederick Cook of the United States. The expedition was not prepared mentally or materially for more than a summer cruise, but *Belgica* was stuck in pack ice when the sun disappeared for the winter of 1898. They spent the winter drifting with the pack ice in the Bellingshausen Sea. One man died without medical cause, and others got sick or went mad. Most had recovered when they got back to Belgium in 1899.

Carsten Egeberg Borchgrevinck (1864–1934) came to Aus- **Base on** tralia from Norway aged 24. In 1895 he joined Henryk Bull's **Antarctica** summer trip to Antarctica and became convinced that the continent could be explored from an all seasons land base. At the time there were no buildings and it had only been visited briefly from ships. After returning to Australia and visiting Britain, Borchgrevinck obtained funding from his new employer, the British publisher Sir George Newnes. His ship *Southern Cross* sailed from Hobart in December 1898, with 'The British Antarctic Exhibition', a company mainly of Norwegians, but including the Australian scientist Louis Bernacchi, two Finnish dog handlers and over seventy sledge dogs. At **Antarctic** Cape Adare by the Ross Sea, they set up a base with two pre- **Continental** fabricated huts – named Camp Ridley after Borchgrevinck's **Traverse** English mother. In February a party with dog sledges travelled to the head of Robertson Bay and climbed the ridges adjacent to the Sir John Murray Glacier, the first of the many overland journeys which have since revealed the details of the Antarctic interior. In March the ship sailed away, leaving ten men to spend winter 1899 at Camp Ridley. *Southern Cross* returned to collect them and their pioneering collection of scientific specimens in January 1900. Back in England later that year Borchgrevinck met a lukewarm reception; Britain's Royal Geographical Society eventually gave him a medal in 1930.

A spate of Antarctic expeditions followed Borchgrevinck's. **South** One was the 1907 British Antarctic Expedition led by Ernest **Magnetic Pole** Shackleton (1874–1922), which aimed to reach the South **Reached** Pole. Icy seas prevented his ship *Nimrod* from mooring at a convenient base and Shackleton's party had to settle for Cape Royds on the Ross Sea coast. The four-man polar group, including Shackleton himself, turned back 180 km. short of its objective. But three other expeditioners notched up a definitive first. The leader, Edgeworth David (1858–1904), professor of geology at Sydney University; Douglas Mawson, lecturer at Adelaide University, and Alistair Mackay, surgeon with the British Navy, set out from Cape Royds in September 1908. Their destination, the South Magnetic Pole, was located at that time in George V Land. A sledge-hauling motor car had left depots of stores 16 km. and 24 km. out, but overheating prevented it from doing more. Without depots they lived on food hauled by themselves, and some seal meat. Despite agonising deprivation they reached the Magnetic Pole in January 1909, and headed for the coast where *Nimrod* was to pick them up on her way home from Cape Royds. When she collected them they had travelled 2028 km. pulling their supplies on sledges without any dogs or ponies to assist.

Antarctica's first motorcar: the Arrol-Johnston which overheated, while conveying supplies for the first expedition to the South Magnetic Pole.

Roald Amundsen was a Norwegian explorer who had led the first expedition to go through the Northwest Passage [see above]. In 1909 he aspired to go north again and be first to reach the Pole. He won support from his government, and **South Pole Reached** private backers, including Fridtjof Nansen, who contributed his ship, *Fram*. When Amundsen heard that the journey to the North Pole was already accomplished, he decided the South Pole would have to do, and secretly changed his plans. Then he learnt that Britain's Royal Geographical Society was organising an expedition under the leadership of Capt. Robert Falcon Scott (1868–1912), with the aim of being first to reach the South Pole. Not much geography was expected to be learnt there; a previous British expedition under Shackleton almost reached it and revealed that the region was only an ice desert. But the Society's president, Sir Clements Markham, declared that it would furnish a good opportunity for young British men to perform 'feats of bravery and derring-doe'. After setting sail in 1910, Amundsen wrote letters to Nansen and to his king, apologising for the deception, and a telegram to Scott, to let him know that he was racing him to the South Pole. On 4 January 1911, Scott's ship *Discovery* reached Cape Evans where his party landed to establish its Antarctic base. *Fram* did not reach her destination till 14 January, but the Bay of Whales where Amundsen made his base was almost 100 km. nearer the Pole than Cape Evans. The competitors spent the rest of summer establishing depots of stores along paths they planned to follow. Amundsen's southernmost depot was 770 km. from the Pole; Scott's was over 1000 km. They all returned to their coastal bases for winter. Next spring Amundsen and his men set out on 8 September. Scott's main party did not get started until 1 November; his men used ponies, motor sledges and a few dogs to help tow supplies, but on the final leg the men pulled their sledges to the Pole unaided. Relying on plenty of dogs for haulage, the Norwegians – Amundsen, Bjaaland, Wisting, Hassel and Hanssen – reached the Pole comfortably first, on 14 December 1911, over a month before Scott's party. Scott and his four companions died on their way back, from hunger, exhaustion, cold and perhaps melancholy. For once though, posterity has put aside its preoccupation with firsts, and the heroic tragedy of Scott has made a loser more famous than his rival.

**Antarctica Crossed**
Antarctica was crossed on the surface from coast to coast via the Pole in 1957–58. The Commonwealth Trans-Antarctic Expedition, led by British geologist, Sir Vivian Fuchs, was supported by the governments of Britain, South Africa, Australia and New Zealand. In October 1957, New Zealand adventurer, Sir Edmund Hillary – who four years earlier had been the first

to climb Mt. Everest [see below] – led a party south from McMurdo Sound on the Ross Sea, in sledge-hauling tractors. Their purpose was to lay supply depots between the Pole and McMurdo Sound. In November, Fuchs's party set out in Sno-Cats from the Weddell Sea Coast, reaching the Pole two weeks after Hillary. They all then travelled to McMurdo, via the depots laid by Hillary.

**The Sahara Crossed**

From around 1000B.C. there was a regular trade between the tribes of the African interior and the civilised nations of the Mediterranean, carried out by native caravans going most of the way, but transferring the goods to merchants from the coast at staging points. Much later, probably around 500B.C., the people of Carthage, on Africa's northernmost tip, decided to make for themselves the long journey across the Sahara to the rich lands of tropical Africa. They developed three main routes from the Mediterranean coast – one southwest to Senegal, one south to the Niger and the other southeast to Sudan. The date and identity of the pioneer of each route is unknown, although the ancient books speak of one Mago who boasted of having crossed the Sahara three times without drinking. His exploits present both a dating problem and a credibility problem.

**Asia Crossed**

From the beginning of history, Asia has been comparatively well known, and crisscrossed by countless travellers on long journeys. However it does not appear that any individual made the whole crossing from east to west (or vice versa) until 97A.D., when the Harn Dynasty diplomat Garn Ying reached the Black Sea, at the end of travels from his native China. Garn Ying worked with the Chinese general, Barn Jao, who seventeen years earlier had set out from China with a few hundred soldiers, and by diplomatic mastery, brought all the kingdoms of Central Asia under Chinese rule. At the end of his campaign he reached the Parthian Empire, the only power standing between China and the Roman Empire. Barn Jao marched unopposed into Parthia with an army of 70,000 men recruited mainly from Central Asia. They stopped at the sea (probably the Caspian Sea, perhaps the Persian Gulf). But Barn Jao wanted to establish a direct link with the Roman Empire, and sent one of his men, Garn Ying, with a small group, to visit Rome. The Parthians would not have been pleased by this development; it threatened their grip on the lucrative overland trade between the two great powers, and Parthia's continued independence. So when Garn Ying reached the Black Sea, which separates Asia from Europe, to join a ship for Rome, they exaggerated the difficulties of the voyage and astutely discouraged him – 'if the Harn ambassador is willing to forget his family and his home, he can embark'.

**Contact between Rome and China**

So the not-so-intrepid Garn Ying promptly set out on the first west–east journey across Asia, leaving direct Rome–China contact to the following century, and to Roman initiative. The Roman envoys sent by Emperor Marcus Aurelius arrived in Law Yarng, capital of China, in 166A.D., having travelled to China by the sea route around the Malay Peninsula.

**South America Crossed**

Gonzalo Pizarro joined his famous brother Francisco on the 1532 Spanish expedition from Central America to Peru [see above]. On the overthrow of the Inca Empire, Francisco appointed Gonzalo to govern the former Inca territory of Quito (present-day Ecuador) near the Pacific Coast, and urged him to mount an eastbound expedition in search of a rumoured country of spices. Amongst the 350 Spaniards with whom Gonzalo set out in 1540 was Francisco de Orellana. They found the 'Land of Cinnamon' on the eastern slope of the Andes, but then continued in search of gold which was reputedly to be found further on. In a state of deprivation they reached the Napo River, where Pizarro deputed Orellana to take a party downstream in a roughly made river boat, and bring back supplies. The boat carried them to the Amazon, and Orellana – considering there was no way back against the current – chose to abandon Pizarro, and sail with his fifty men, down the river to the Atlantic. In this they succeeded; that native Americans had preceded them in going from coast to coast is quite feasible, but unrecorded.

**Australia Crossed**

Early in 1838 Edward John Eyre (1815–1901) set out from Sydney, droving a mob of cattle to South Australia. He reached Adelaide in July, and after making a variety of excursions to the North, decided to continue west, setting out from Spencer's Gulf early in 1841. Ignoring numerous suggestions that he give up the idea, he travelled with an old companion, Baxter, two local Aborigines, and Wylie, a Western Australian Aborigine, across the desert of the Nullarbor Plain. He was intent on reaching the nearest western settlement, Albany on King George's Sound. Midway across, the South Australian Aborigines killed Baxter and ran off with most of the supplies. Eyre and Wylie staggered on, mopping up dew with a sponge for drinking water. When they were almost dead they reached Thistle Cove, where a whaling ship happened to be anchored. After recuperating on board, they refused the offer of a lift, being determined to finish the trip by land. They arrived in Albany in July 1841. Twenty years later Robert Burke and William Wills completed the south–north crossing of Australia from Melbourne to the Gulf of Carpentaria. They died of thirst and hunger on the way home.

**Australia Crossed South–North**

Europe's highest mountain was first scaled by Dr. Michel-Gabriel Paccard and his porter, Jacques Balmat, who reached the summit, 4807 m. up, on 8 August 1786. Paccard planned the route of their ascent with the help of telescopes, and chose a way up via the Taconna Glacier. Both climbers were equipped with shoe nails and crampons, but not with safety ropes which were standard equipment on more recent climbs.

**Mont Blanc Climbed**

Compared to the other peaks mentioned here, Mt. Kosciusko (2230 m.) presents more of a picnic opportunity than a mountaineering challenge. The real achievement of Count Paul von Strzelecki (1796–1873) is in locating it and ascertaining its pre-eminent height, rather than the climb itself. The great Polish explorer reached the summit of Australia's tallest mountain in 1840. It is highly likely that it had already been visited by Aborigines long before. It is perhaps a pity that no Aborigines were around to tell Strzelecki the mountain's name. They left him free to give it a name of his own, commemorating the unpronounceable 18th-century Polish general, Tadeusz Kósciuszko. 'The particular configuration of this eminence struck me so forcibly', he wrote, 'by the similarity it bears to a tumulus elevated in Kraków over the tomb of the patriot Kosciusko, that . . . I could not refrain from giving it the name Mt. Kosciusko.' This is not quite satisfactory, as Kósciuszko was actually interred in Cracow Cathedral.

**Kosciusko Climbed**

Kilimanjaro, the highest mountain in Africa, is regarded by mountaineers as a tedious climb. Two Germans – Hans Meyer and L. Purtscheller – discovered this in 1889, when they became the first men to reach the summit of Kibo, the highest of Kilimanjaro's peaks.

**Kilimanjaro Climbed**

A hundred years ago, Matthias Zurbriggen was one of history's most indefatigable mountaineers. In 1887 he was one of the first party to reach the top of Stecknadelhorn. He later went to New Zealand and climbed Mt. Cook and the Tasman

**Aconcagua Climbed**

Glacier. In 1892 he joined the first expedition to the top of Pioneer Peak in the Himalayas, and in 1897 he was in the Peruvian Andes with Edward Fitzgerald's expedition. During the course of this expedition he climbed to South America's highest point: the summit of Mt. Aconcagua – perhaps the most strenuous of his many conquests.

**Mt. McKinley Climbed**

In 1913 when Hudson Stuck, Harry Karstens and a party of four others set out to scale North America's highest peak, two claims to have climbed it had already been made. Frederick Cook's 1906 ascent was taken seriously, but decades later proved to be just as bogus as his claim to have reached the North Pole (referred to above). A less plausible claim was made in 1910 by a group of prospectors, who accepted a local publican's $500 challenge to them to climb Mt. McKinley. Six prospectors set out but three went home after a brawl at the base of the mountain. Peter Anderson, Billy Taylor and Charley McGonagall camped 9000 feet below the summit with very little food and equipment. By their own account, they went from this camp to the summit and back in a single day. Of course they were not believed. In 1913, when Karstens and Stuck really did reach the southern peak of Mt. McKinley, they were surprised to see – on the nearby northern peak – the flagstaff which the brave trio had indeed planted three years earlier. Although the three prospectors in 1910 were the first to climb Mt. McKinley, the southern peak is higher by 300 feet, so the 1913 expedition was the first to North America's highest point.

**Everest Climbed**

Serious efforts to climb Asia's tallest mountain began in 1921 when Tibetan authorities gave permission for parties to climb the north face of Everest. Several expeditions probed the route, but entry was closed after the Second World War, before anyone had reached the top; a new route had to be surveyed up the south face after the Nepalese government gave permission in 1951. In May 1953, two members of the second south face expedition set out to reach the summit. On 29 May, the New Zealander, Edmund Hillary (born 1919), and the Sherpa, Tenzing Norgay, reached their goal, the highest place on Earth. In a small hole, Tenzing placed food offerings to Chomolungma, the god who dwells on the peak, and alongside Hillary placed a small crucifix.

# X

# SPORT AND
# RECREATION

Some sports began so the players could have fun; others derived from fighting. Some were originally acts of religious devotion, some started out as ways to keep the body in shape. It was by making rituals out of them that people turned exercise, worship, fighting and play into sport. The original sources were very different but the outcomes are alike. Sport is now the strongest expression of the enthusiastic craving for ritual common to all people.

## I. COMPETITIVE SPORT

Some of the most prestigious sports had humble inaugurations and no one at the time could see that they were worth documenting. Others began in prehistoric communities which left no trace of their origin. The result is a long list of sports concerning which it is no good trying to pinpoint a first. These include (in approximate chronological order): wrestling, running, weightlifting, javelin, jumping, canoeing, archery, sailing, bowls, rowing, wood-chopping, horse racing, jousting, chariot racing, polo, fencing, lacrosse, karate, shooting, water polo, bicycle racing, table tennis, motor sports.

During Egypt's 18th Dynasty (c. 1600–c. 1350B.C.) it was customary for the pharaoh to perform athletic feats that required **Sporting** strength, skill and training. Each reigning pharaoh aimed to **Records** improve on the performance of his predecessor, and to verify their performances, the first accurate sporting records were kept. Around 1550B.C., in front of a large crowd, Tuthmosis III shot an arrow at a standard copper plate of 3 fingers' breadth, so that 3 hands' breadth came through. This record stood for about ten years before Amenophis broke it.

**Professionals**

There were professional sportsmen in prehistoric times – champions competing on behalf of wealthy sponsors. (The advent of professionals in some major sports is entered under their separate headings.) Really large earnings were first made in chariot racing. The first known sports millionaire was Crescens, an African driver in the Roman circus, who died

**Sports Millionaire**

aged twenty-two in 124A.D. The purchasing power of the sestertius was slightly greater than a dollar. Crescens had won 1,558,346 of them in prize money.

**Sports Multi-millionaire**

Crescens's later contemporary, Gaius Apuleius Diocles, a Spaniard, was the earliest multi-millionaire sportsman. He came first 1462 times: 81 times for the Whites, 205 times for the Blues, 216 for the Greens, and 960 for the Reds. Diocles was the first racing charioteer to drive a seven-horse team, which he did in one race for a 50,000 sestertii prize. His winnings had totalled 35,863,120 by the end of his twenty-four-year career. In 146A.D. he retired to the country and became a family man.

**Starting Gates**

Starting gates were invented by Cleoetas in about 500B.C. or just after, for the Olympic Games. They were designed to make race starts fairer, with all gates springing open at once when the starter pulled a rope. An intricate mechanism of cords travelled in concealed channels. In the hippodrome at Olympia, one set of gates was used to start chariot races. In the stadium, they were used for runners instead of a starting pistol.

**Referee's Whistle**

Until 1884, umpires and referees had to yell when it was necessary to stop play. Since this often happened when the players were already shouting a fair bit, the task was an exhausting one. A sheep farmer from the Canterbury district of New Zealand's South Island, W. H. Atack, was a rugby referee who pondered the problem. While doing so his hand strayed into his pocket and felt his dog whistle. 'The inspiration came to me', he later wrote, 'that it would be a fine thing to use the whistle to stop the game.' He tried it, with instant approval from players and other referees.

**Olympic Games**

The first Olympic Games were (more truthfully, the first Olympic Game was) held at Olympia in the Greek state of Elis in 776B.C., during the period known as the 1st Olympiad. They were convened by Iphitus of Elis, who judged the only event, the *stade* foot race, a 185 m. sprint (the length of the stadium at Olympia). First place went to Coroebus of Elis. The **Olympic** Games were held every four years from then on, until the **Sprint** Roman emperor Theodosius banned them in 393A.D. Over the centuries their character changed considerably; initially the Games were a Greeks only, men only exercise, with few events. The following list records the first introduction of **Olympic** some interesting events: **Champions**

|  | Date | Winner |
|---|---|---|
| **370 m.** | 724B.C., 14th Olympiad | Hypenus of Pisa |
| **2220 m.** | 720B.C., 15th Olympiad | Acanthus of Sparta |
| **Pentathlon** | 708B.C., 18th Olympiad | Lampus of Sparta |
| **Wrestling** | 708B.C., 18th Olympiad | Eurybatus of Sparta |
| **Boxing** | 688B.C., 23rd Olympiad | Onomastus of Smyrna |
| **Chariot Race** | 680B.C., 25th Olympiad | Pagondas of Thebes |
| **Pancratium** | 644B.C., 33rd Olympiad | Lygdamus of Syracuse |
| **Horse Race** | 644B.C., 33rd Olympiad | The horse of Crauxidas of Crannon |
| **Race between Armed Men** | 516B.C., 65th Olympiad | Damaretus of Hemaea |

An ancient Greek girl demonstrates the outfit worn in early women's events.

Olympia was a sports complex in the countryside near Elis, where games had been played well before the first Olympiad. At the time, the Olympics were regarded as a

**Museum of Sport** revival of ancient sports. Olympia grew into an open-air sports museum – the world's first – as the grounds filled with statues of successful athletes and horses, inscriptions of results and

**Games Village** lavishly carved friezes depicting great events. The facilities included a stadium for track and field events, hippodrome for equestrian games, gymnasium for indoor competition, and houses for the athletes.

The true Olympics had no women's only events. These

**Women's Events** were held in a separate function, the Heraean Games, conducted every four years in the Olympic stadium by a local group known as the Sixteen Women. These games originated at an unknown early date, possible as long ago as the 1st Olympiad. Maidens of all ages were invited to compete. They wore skirts of almost knee length that left the right shoulder bare.

In the real Olympics, women gained notable victories over

**Woman Champion** male competition in the equestrian events, breeding and training champion horses and teams. Cynisca, sister of King Agesilaus of Sparta, was the first female victor, probably in the 390s B.C., when her team won the chariot race; her statue was put up amongst those of the male champions of past ages. In the

**Woman First Champion** 129th Olympiad (360B.C.), when the race of chariots drawn by pairs of foals was run for the first time, the inaugural winner was a woman, Belistiche, representing Coastal Macedonia.

As time went on, the Games came to be attended by a

**Junior Events** widening range of competitors, and Egyptians and Romans became prominent participants. Still, admission to the ancient Olympics was a privilege, and they were never properly international like the modern Games. But in another department the ancient Games went beyond the modern ones – by providing junior events for athletes eighteen and under, which proved very popular. These began in the 37th

**Junior Champions** Olympiad (632B.C.). That year, Hipposthenes of Sparta was the first victor in junior wrestling, while Polynices of Elis won the first junior running race. The Heraean Games had junior

**Girls' Events** events for girls, perhaps dating back to about the same period.

The first attempt to restart the Olympics during the reign of

**Modern Olympics** Greece's King Otho in the 19th century was bungled, and failed. In 1893 Baron de Coubertin called delegates from many countries to a congress in Paris, which decided unanimously to revive the games, and to accept the Greek delegate's invitation to hold them first in Athens. The Greek Government was reluctant, but Crown Prince Constantine launched a massive fund-raising drive, and miraculously all was ready for the new games on Easter Monday 1896. Hundreds of athletes came, but it would be an exaggeration to call them the world's élite: some were tourists who decided to represent their countries whilst in Athens; the largest contingent was the Greeks, described even by sympathisers as very poor athletes.

Festivities closed on the sixth day when King George presented to each winner a silver medal, a diploma, and an olive **Olympic** branch, and to the second place-getters, bronze medals and **Medals** laurel sprigs. The budget did not run to gold for first place, but after each event the champion's national flag was raised, as it continues to be. (When Australia, which had no flag, won its **Silver** first event, games organisers made do with the Austrian flag.) **Medallists**

| | Event | Winner | Country | |
|---|---|---|---|---|
| **Running** | 100 m. | Thomas Burke | U.S.A. | 12 sec. |
| | 400 m. | Thomas Burke | U.S.A. | 54.2 sec. |
| | 800 m. | Edwin Flack | Australia | 2 min. 11 sec. |
| | 1500 m. | Edwin Flack | Australia | 4 min. 33.2 sec. |
| | Marathon (42,195 m.) | Spiridon Louis | Greece | 2 hr. 58 min. 50 sec. |
| | Hurdles (110 m.) | Thomas Curtis | U.S.A. | 17.6 sec. |
| **Jumps** | High jump | Ellery Clark | U.S.A. | 1.81 m. |
| | Long jump | Ellery Clark | U.S.A. | 6.35 m. |
| | Pole vault | William Welles Hoyt | U.S.A. | 3.30 m. |
| | Hop, step and jump | James Conolly | U.S.A. | 13.71 m. |
| **Throwing** | Shot put | Robert Garrett | U.S.A. | 11.22 m. |
| | Discus | Robert Garrett | U.S.A. | 29.15 m. |
| **Cycling** | 333⅓ m. time trial | Paul Masson | France | 24 sec. |
| | 2,000 m. sprint | Paul Masson | France | 2 min. 52 sec. |
| | 10 km. track race | Paul Masson | France | 24 sec. |
| | 100 km. track race | Léon Flameng | France | 3 hr. 8 min. 19.2 sec. |

|  | Event | Winner | Country | |
|--|-------|--------|---------|--|
|  | 12 hr. race | Adolf Schmal | Austria | 300 km. |
|  | Road race (87 km.) | Aristidis Konstantinidis | Greece | 3 hr. 8 min. 19.2 sec. |
| **Fencing** | Foil | Eugene-Henri Gravelotte | France | |
|  | Masters foil | Leon Pyrgos | Greece | |
|  | Sabre | Ioannis Georgiadis | Greece | |
| **Gym-nastics** | Horizontal bar | Herman Weingärtner | Germany | |
|  | Parallel bars | Alfred Flatow | Germany | |
|  | Long horse vault | Karl Schumann | Germany | |
|  | Pommelled horse | Jules Zutler | Switzerland | |
|  | Rings | Ioannis Mitropoulos | Greece | |
|  | Team horizontal bar | | Germany | |
|  | Team parallel bars | | Germany | |
|  | Rope climbing | Nicolaos Andriakopoulos | Greece | |
| **Shooting** | Rapid fire pistol | Ioannis Phrangoudis | Greece | |
|  | Free pistol | Sumner Paine | U.S.A. | |
|  | Military revolver | John Paine | U.S.A. | |
|  | Free rifle | Pantelis Karasevdas | Greece | |
|  | Three positions | Georgios Orphanidis | Greece | |
| **Swimming** | 100 m. freestyle | Alfréd Hajós | Hungary | 1 min. 22.2 sec. |
|  | 500 m. freestyle | Paul Newmann | Austria | 8 min. 12.6 sec. |
|  | 1200 m. freestyle | Alfréd Hajós | Hungary | 18 min. 22.2 sec. |
|  | 100 m. freestyle for Greek Navy | Ioannis Malokinis | | 2 min. 20.4 sec. |

|  | Event | Winner | Country | |
|---|---|---|---|---|
| **Tennis** | Singles | John Pius Boland | U.K. (Ireland) | |
| | Doubles | Boland and Traun | Ireland, Germany | |
| **Weight-lifting** | One hand lift | Launceston Elliot | U.K. | 71 kg. |
| | Two hand lift | Viggo Jensen | Denmark | 111.5 kg. |
| **Wrestling** | Greco-Roman | Karl Schumann | Germany | |

Gold medals were awarded at the Paris games in 1900 and at all subsequent Olympics. Gold medallists for each sport first included in the Olympics are as follows:

**Gold Medallists**

### Paris 1900

|  | Event | Winner | Country | |
|---|---|---|---|---|
| **Equitation** | High jump | Dominique Maximien Gardéres on Canela | France | 1.85 m. |
| | Long jump | Constant van Langendonck on Extra Dry | Belgium | 6.1 m. |
| | Prix de Nations jumping | Aimé Haegeman on Benton II | Belgium | 2 min. 16 sec. |
| **Soccer** | | | U.K. | |
| **Archery** | Au cordon dore, 50 m. | Henri Heronin | France | |
| | Au chapelet, 50 m. | Eugène Mongin | France | |
| | Au cordon dore, 33 m. | Hubert van Innes | Belgium | |
| | Au chapelet, 33 m. | Hubert van Innes | Belgium | |
| | Sur la peche a la herse | Emmanuel Foulon | France | |
| | Sur la pedre a la pyramide | Emile Grumiaux | France | |
| | Game shooting (with gun) [sic] | Donald Mackintosh | Australia | |

| | Event | Winner | Country | |
|---|---|---|---|---|
| **Yachting** | ½ ton | Texier | France | |
| | ½–1 ton | Currie, Gretton and Hope | U.K. | |
| | 1–2 ton | Hermann and de Pourtalés | Switzerland | |
| | 2–3 ton | Exshaw | U.K. | |
| | 3–10 ton | E. and F. Michelet | France | |
| | 10–20 ton | Billard and Perquet | France | |
| | Open | Currie, Gretton and Hope | U.K. | |
| | | | | |
| **Cricket** | | U.K. | | |
| | | | | |
| **Croquet** | Singles – 1 ball | Aumoitte | France | |
| | Singles – 2 balls | Johin | France | |
| | Doubles | Johin and Aumoitte | France | |
| | | | | |
| **Golf** | Men | Charles Sands | U.S.A. | |
| | Women | Margaret Abbott | U.S.A. | |
| | | | | |
| **Polo** | | Foxhunters Hurlingham | U.K./ U.S.A. | |
| | | | | |
| **Rugby** | | | France | |
| | | | | |
| **Tug of War** | | | Sweden/ Denmark | |
| | | | | |
| **Rowing** | Single sculls | Henri Barellet | France | 7 min. 35.6 sec. |
| | Coxed pairs | | Nether- lands | 7 min. 34.2 sec. |
| | Coxed fours | | France | 7 min. 11 sec. |
| | Coxed eights | | U.S.A. | 6 min. 9.8 sec. |
| | | | | |
| **Water Obstacle Race** | | Frederick Lane | Australia 38.4 sec. | 2 min. |
| | | | | |
| **Water Polo** | | | U.K. | |

## St Louis 1904

| Event | | Winner | Country | |
|---|---|---|---|---|
| **Decathlon** | | Thomas Viely | Ireland | |
| **Boxing** | Flyweight | George Finnegan | U.S.A. | |
| | Bantam-weight | Oliver Kirk | U.S.A. | |
| | Feather-weight | Oliver Kirk | U.S.A. | |
| | Lightweight | Henry Spanger | U.S.A. | |
| | Welter-weight | Albert Young | U.S.A. | |
| | Middle-weight | Charles Mayer | U.S.A. | |
| | Heavy-weight | Samuel Berger | U.S.A. | |
| **Lacrosse** | | | Canada | |
| **Diving** | 10 m. platform | George Sheldon | U.S.A. | |

## Athens 1906

| | Event | Winner | Country | |
|---|---|---|---|---|
| **Walking** | 1500 m. | George Bonhag | U.S.A. | |
| | 3000 m. | György Sztantics | Hungary | 15 min. 13.2 sec. |
| **Pentathlon** | Long jump, discus, stade foot race, javelin, wrestling | Hjalmar Mellander | Sweden | |
| **Canoeing** | 1000 m. kayak | Delaplane | France | 5 min. 53.4 sec. |

## London 1908

| | Event | Winner | Country | |
|---|---|---|---|---|
| **Hockey** | | | U.K. | |
| **Skating** | Men's figure skating | Ulrich Salchow | Sweden | |
| | Women's figure skating | Madge Syers | U.K. | |

| Event | Winner | Country |
|---|---|---|
| Pairs | Anna Hüber and Heinrich Burger | Germany |
| Special figures | Nikolai Kolomenkin (alias Panin) | Russia |

## Antwerp 1920

| | | |
|---|---|---|
| **Ice Hockey** | | Canada |

## Berlin 1936

| | | |
|---|---|---|
| **Basketball** | | U.S.A. |
| **Handball** | | Germany |

## Tokyo 1964

| | | | |
|---|---|---|---|
| **Judo** | Lightweight | Takehide Nakatani | Japan |
| | Middle-weight | Isao Okano | Japan |
| | Heavy-weight | Iao Inokuma | Japan |
| | Open | Antonius Geesinck | Netherlands |
| **Volleyball** | Men | | U.S.S.R. |
| | Women | | Japan |

## Seoul 1988

| | | | |
|---|---|---|---|
| **Table Tennis** | Singles | Yoo Nam Kyu | South Korea |
| | Women's singles | Chen Jing | China |
| | Doubles | | China |
| | Women's doubles | | South Korea |

## Barcelona 1992

| | | | |
|---|---|---|---|
| **Badmin-ton** | Singles | Alan Budi Kusuma | Indonesia |
| | Women's singles | Susi Susanti | Indonesia |
| | Doubles | | South Korea |
| | Women's doubles | | South Korea |

| | Event | Winner | Country |
|---|---|---|---|
| **Baseball** | | | Cuba |

### Atlanta 1996

| | Event | Winner | Country |
|---|---|---|---|
| **Beach Volleyball** | Men | Kent Steffes and Karch Kiraly | U.S.A. |
| | Women | Jackie Silva Cruz and Sandra Pires Tavares | Brazil |
| **Softball** | | | U.S.A. |

The Winter Olympics were first conducted as a separate event in late January and early February 1924 at Chamonix, France, although ice-skating had been introduced to the Olympic Games at London in 1908 [see above]. In the Chamonix games, Norway's Thorleif Haug won both the 15 km. and 50 km. cross-country ski races, as well as the combined skiing and ski jump competition. **Winter Olympics**

The sport of boxing began in Egypt during the New Kingdom period over 3500 thousand years ago. The oldest depictions are on an 18th Dynasty (c. 1600–c. 1350B.C.) tomb, amongst reliefs illustrating celebrations of Pharaoh Amenophis III's thirtieth year on the throne. The pictures show various boxing manoeuvres, captioned with words like 'pounce' and 'defence'. **Boxing**

How to box: some guidelines from the 18th Dynasty.

**Boxing Gloves**

From the 9th century B.C. or earlier the Greeks dispensed with 'bare knuckle' boxing and began to tie protective straps of hide or leather around their hands. From about 350B.C. these were replaced with gloves of a complex design. An inner glove of soft cloth left the fingertips bare; outside it, thick leather pads were arranged, stitched into position to prevent their edges cutting the opponent's flesh. Leather straps bound them to the lower arms. Because boxing was an important sport in the Olympic Games [see above] from 688B.C. onwards, and in other prestigious meetings, training became highly organised. Training aids such as ear guards and punch-ing bags were first invented for Greek boxers.

**Ear Guards**
**Punching Bag**

**Marathon**
**Running**

Shulgi, a powerful and imaginative king of Sumer who reigned for nearly fifty years in the 23rd century B.C., was a great enthusiast – a crank really – for road travel. Apart from widening the footpaths and straightening the highways, he set up the first hotel chain [V, 1] along them to make travel eas-ier. He was also an athlete, and decided to go in for marathon running. His first great run was from Nippur to Ur, in South-ern Mesopotamia. The distance is about 170 km., but the exact mileage depends on how straight he had made his high-way. Crowds cheered the King in cities along the route, and he decided soon after to run back to Nippur again. Although a fierce hailstorm hindered this run, Shulgi made good time – he astonished people by celebrating the 'eshesh feast' on the same day in both Ur and Nippur. Such a lot of running purely for athletic performance was even stranger then than now. But governments had employed messenger runners since early times; 1600 years after Shulgi, one ran from Athens to Sparta, in Greece, taking news of the Persian invasion at Marathon. This is how marathon running got its name.

**Relay Races**

Relay races were introduced at Greek athletic meetings, prob-ably during the 6th century B.C. Runners exchanged a flam-ing torch, and it was a rule of the competition that the flame must remain alight.

**Four Minute**
**Mile**

The earliest recorded mile in four minutes or less was run by an English sprinter, Roger Bannister, at Oxford in 1954. He crossed the one mile (1609.34 m.) line in 3 min. 59.4 seconds.

**Discus**

Unfortunately the disarray of Indian records makes it impossible to tell whether discus throwing took place first in India or in

Greece. Greek athletes were throwing discuses made of copper by about 1000B.C. The Indian god Krishna is sometimes depicted with a discus, and in Northeastern India (or in present-day Pakistan) the custom may date back several centuries before 1000B.C.

**Motor Racing Grand Prix**

Preparations for the first Grand Prix motor race were completed on a truly grand scale in 1906 by the Automobile Club de France, on a 103 km. circuit of closed public roads east of Le Mans. The Club built tunnels under the track, a planked roadway round the town of St. Calais, depots, grandstands, and 65 km. of palisade fencing to restrain spectators. Competitors raced over six laps of the circuit on each of two days, 26 and 27 June 1906. The long rough circuit was savage on tyres and race rules provided that only drivers and their on-board mechanics could make tyre changes. Only teams using the new detachable rim system for tyre changes had a chance, and in an anti-climax the Grand Prix became a two-horse race between the Fiat and Renault teams. Hungarian Renault driver Ferenc Szisz averaged 101 km/h overall – despite breaking a rear spring on the second day – and won the race; Paul Baras in a Brasier drove the fastest lap, averaging 118 km/h.

**Volleyball**

The *Odyssey*, written about 900B.C. by the Greek poet Homer, includes the first account of a volleyball game, played by Nausicaa, beautiful princess of Phaeacia. Nausicaa was a bit like one of our modern girls – according to Homer she got up early one morning and interrupted her father in an important meeting to see if she could borrow the car. She said she wanted it because the laundry needed doing. Her father doubted this but let her take it anyway. Nausicaa and her friends, after attending to the dirty clothes, had a picnic at the beach and finished up with a game of volleyball:

> Over the green mead the sporting virgins play
> (Their shining veils unbound.) Along the skies,
> Toss'd and retoss'd, the ball incessant flies.       (tr. Pope)

This ball game was one of many sports popular with the Greeks of Homer's time which later on lost their following and had to be reinvented for the modern world. Nausicaa's fame helped the game's prestige, and about four centuries after Homer, when the playwright Aeschylus staged his *Nausicaa*, he played the game himself on stage with great skill. (Whether Nausicaa had ever played it is doubtful – she lived before Homer's time and the *Odyssey* is a fictionalised account.)

**Hockey**  The Greeks were playing hockey by early in the 5th century B.C., using sticks with curved ends, and abiding by rules which must have made it a game of skill rather than a primitive free-for-all. Knowledge of the game they played comes only from a carving discovered in a 5th-century wall in Athens, showing two players in what looks like the once ubiquitous bullying-off posture, while others stand by.

Hockey outfits have changed more than the equipment since 500B.C.

**Football**  Football developed in two stages. Skilful games governed by codes of rules are from the latter stage. The first stage, of primitive contests between rival mobs, was disorderly, poorly documented and generally injurious. Football's first home was China. Some say it was invented 5000 years ago by the Yellow Emperor, but this is only a colourful story; the most ancient game was probably mob football developed by common people. The skilled, regulated type was invented before the 3rd century B.C.; by then it was in use to keep soldiers fit.

**Pointy-ended Ball**  **Round Football**  Traditional Chinese balls were shaped like modern ones, and made by joining sections of leather together. They were not spherical because they were meant to be kicked through the air rather than along the ground. During the Tarng Dynasty (618A.D.–907), the game played by kicking a round inflated ball along the ground supplanted the true sport, although even then aerial kicks were retained.

Rules changed with time but the earliest recorded code involved two equal teams, tall goalposts planted very close together, and a scoring system of goals and behinds, as in Australian Rules football. The game became almost respectable during the reign (32–6B.C.) of Emperor Cheng Di, who remained a keen player despite his wife's efforts to make him give it up. The serious regard for skills and rules which marks

football in its mature stage is clear in the first football poem, **Football Poem**
by an enthusiast:

> A round ball and a square wall
> Suggesting the shapes of the Yin and the Yang;
> The ball flying across like the moon,
> While two teams stand opposed.
> Captains are appointed and take their places,
> According to unchanging regulations:
> There must be no partialities.
> But there must be determination and coolness,
> Without the slightest irritation at failure . . .
> And if all this is necessary for football,
> How much more so for the business of life!      (tr. Giles)

Whether anything better than mob football was played in the
ancient West has not been ascertained. The Roman game of
*harpastum* developed clear rules, but those rules limited ball
play to handling, as in netball, so it doesn't count. After
Roman times, mob football was widespread, and many centuries went past with no sign of development in skills and rules.

Eventually radical progress began in one country, which
invented several codes and laid the groundwork for all the **Rugby**
types of football now popular around the world. This was England, where football games played in the leading schools
began to take on an increasing regularity and order early last
century. Foremost of these was Rugby School near Warwick,
which by about 1820 had adopted a ball-handling style of
game governed by rules which must have made it close
enough to rugby football, as we now understand it, to be worthy of the name. Credit for the game is usually given to
William Webb Ellis, a pupil in 1823 believed to have been the
first to pick up the ball and run with it – as though before that
they had been playing a game like soccer. However, by 1823,
rugby already had a marking rule: a player who caught the ball
on the full was entitled to retire and take a kick, his opponents
coming no closer than the 'mark' where he caught it. Ellis's
innovation was to keep the ball and run forward with it,
instead of stopping to take his kick. That idea of playing on
may have converted the old game – dominated by fairly static
mauls and long kicks at goal – into a running game like today's
rugby – but it hardly justifies denying that the game played
immediately before was also rugby.

As the most sophisticated of the school games, rugby
spread to the universities, and eventually all over Britain, **Rugby**
promoted by former pupils. By the start of 1871, rugby in **International**

Scotland was strong enough for exponents there to challenge England to a match, which was played between twenty-man sides before a crowd of 4000 at the Edinburgh Academy's ground in March. The Scots, with a big home ground advantage on the very narrow field, won by one goal to nil. Though it was a contest between two British countries, in rugby parlance the game was the first international. The current international competition between all leading rugby countries, the World Cup, was first run in 1987, and won by New Zealand.

**World Cup**

Rugby league was begun in Lancashire and Yorkshire in 1906 by the Northern Rugby Football Union – a group of professional clubs, including some that had broken away from the purely amateur English Rugby Union in 1895. For the 1906 season the Northern Rugby Football Union promulgated new rules, introducing thirteen-man sides and other features that distinguish the game from rugby union.

**Rugby League**

A New Zealand representative professional rugby side went on an international tour in 1907. It first took on a side representing the newly formed New South Wales Rugby League in Sydney, but since no one there knew the new British rules of 1906, their three-match series was played to rugby union rules. However, the New Zealanders, going on to represent their country in Britain against the Northern Rugby Football Union, learnt the new thirteen-man game for the first international series late in 1907. Star of the New Zealand team was New South Wales's Dally Messenger, whom New Zealand had recruited in Sydney on the way through. Great Britain won the first match 14–6, before 8000 spectators in Leeds, but New Zealand took the series two matches to one.

**International Rugby League**

Despite this, league never became popular in New Zealand, and in Australia it was confined to Queensland and New South Wales. Interstate matches between New South Wales and Queensland tended to be uninspiring from 1908 to 1980, mostly because the wealthy Sydney competition always drew the best players to New South Wales. In 1980 a new principle was adopted under which representative footballers play for their state of origin. At the first such match, under lights at Lang Park in Brisbane, Queensland won 20–10. From 1981 onwards all representative games between the two states have been played in the annual State of Origin Series, the most popular rugby league competition.

**State of Origin Match**

Football in Australia was played by Aborigines in prehistoric times. In the 19th century in Southern Australia, the Aboriginal game, played with balls of possum hide, was noted for its high marking duels. If this feature contributed to the high marking style of modern Australian Rules it is probably the only link between the two games. The main proponent of the new game was Thomas Wills (1835–80), a sportsman from Western Victoria who had been to Rugby School. Wills acknowledged that rugby is a suitable game for schoolboys – who have time to recover from injuries – but wanted to develop a safer kind of football for men who had to be back at work on Monday. On Saturday 7 August 1858, Melbourne Grammar School played Scotch College in parkland beside the Melbourne Cricket Ground, the rules being worked out as the match went on. The umpires were Wills and John Macadam, a scientist after whom the macadamia nut is named. This match was played by teams of forty, and five hours of play brought it to a 1–1 draw, which was not resolved by two scoreless tiebreakers played later. Over subsequent weeks the game developed in regular social matches in the same park, promoted by *Bell's Life*, a sporting and cultural magazine, and the nearby Parade Hotel. In May 1859, Wills and six others met in the Parade Hotel and drafted a brief set of rules, which must have been based on the previous season's experience, the first edition of 'Victorian Rules', as the game used to be called. Later amendments made it a less bunched and slow-moving game, and therefore quite unlike rugby, which it still resembled in 1858.

**Australian Rules**

The first interstate match was Victoria's defeat of South Australia in 1879 – called an inter-colonial match at the time, because it predates Federation. In the same year, the world's first organised night football match was played, under electric floodlights at the Melbourne Cricket Ground, with a white ball. A crowd of about 12,000 watched Collingwood Artillery play East Melbourne.

**Interstate Match**

**Night Football**

The game's most important competition, the Victorian Football League (now officially named the 'Australian Football League'), was first played in 1897, when Essendon, coached by G. Stuckey, won the premiership flag. The League had formed in 1896 when eight leading clubs withdrew from the Victorian Football Association (V.F.A.) to set up the V.F.L. The V.F.A. had its first season in 1877, but two sides playing in the V.F.L., Melbourne and St. Kilda, could trace their participation back to the 1858 season, as could the now defunct South Yarra.

**V.F.L.**

**V.F.A.**

Night football at the Melbourne Cricket Ground, 1879, from *The Australasian Sketcher*.

**International Series**
Although Rules is the most popular sport in those parts of Australia which are its traditional homeland, it is not often played anywhere else. Consequently international matches are rare. The first British rugby union side to tour Australia in 1888–89 is notable on two counts: one for giving the locals a hiding in rugby; the other for learning to play Rules very well. The British had nine wins and ten losses at the Australian game, against a variety of leading sides.

**Gaelic Football**

**Hurling**
The Gaelic Athletic Association was established in Ireland in 1884 to do something about the incursion of English games. Its plan was to revive ancient Irish sports by codifying them and fitting them to the needs of spectators and modern players. The Association had a major success with hurling – a game that had been played in Ireland (and England) since an unknown but very early time. Realising that old Irish football was an unskilled mob game that could never compete for popularity with rugby and soccer, the prudent gentlemen of the Association, led by civil servant Michael Cusack created a new game – first played in 1885 – which some enthusiasts could believe was Irish football revived. It is apparent – though not proven – that the game combines principles adopted from several non-Irish codes: from soccer, its round ball; from rugby, its goalposts and an offside rule; and from Australian rules, most of its other rules. Their knowledge of the Australian game might have come from Thomas Smith, who had been on the original rules committee in Melbourne in the early 1860s, and from Irish soldiers in British regiments who played football in Melbourne in 1868 and 1869, after service in the Maori

wars. One of the regimental footballers had already proclaimed a Gaelic modification of the Australian code when H. C. A. Harrison, the Melbourne captain, complained that kicking in the shins is against the rules: 'To Hell with your rules! We're playing the . . . Irish rules!'.

**Soccer**

The name soccer is built on the third, fourth and fifth letters of 'association football' the code of England's Football Association, established in 1863. Before that, soccer was already being played – as a game without a name – having taken shape at the same time as rugby, in English public schools of the early-19th century. Unlike Rugby, some of these schools had games in which the ball was normally dribbled and kicked off the ground. Conspicuous among them were Charterhouse and Harrow, which used round balls and had rules against handling. Often these games were played by mobs with frequent body contact. But a game at Harrow with eleven men a side is on record as being played by 1814, and could well be the prototype of all soccer.

This distinctly British invention has never caused popular excitement amongst other English-speaking peoples; but Great Britain and most non-English-speaking countries have vigorous national soccer competitions which are passionately supported. The parent of all these is the F.A. Cup. It was introduced as the Football Association Challenge Cup in 1871, mainly at the instigation of Charles William Alcock of the Wanderers club. The new cup was the prize in a fifteen-team knockout competition, won by the Wanderers, captained by Alcock.

**F.A. Cup**

The main international soccer competition is the World Cup, which was initially proposed at a meeting in Paris in 1928 by Jules Rimet and Henri Delaunay. The French were motivated in part by what European soccer administrators regarded as British disdain for the soccer powers in foreign countries. Uruguay, the leading soccer nation of the day, hosted the first World Cup competition in 1930. The Estadio Centenario in Montevideo was built for the purpose, and representative teams from South America and Europe (but not Britain) joined in. In the final, Uruguay defeated Argentina 4–2 in front of 90,000 spectators, including 20,000 who had made the journey from Argentina.

**World Cup**

Modern types of football were first promoted in North America in the 19th century by universities and schools. A characteristic of American culture has since been the developmental

**American Football**

role of the universities (collectively referred to as colleges). Universities in Canada played rugby in those days; in the United States it was soccer, except at Harvard, which played 'Boston football', a code that allowed ball handling. Princeton met Rutgers in the first inter-college match at New Brunswick, New Jersey, in November 1869. It was a soccer-type game, but with twenty-five-man sides. (The present National Collegiate Athletic Association [N.C.A.A.] was formed in 1905 as the Inter-Collegiate Athletic Association.) In 1874 a touring Canadian side from Montreal's McGill University converted Harvard to rugby, and in 1879 the other major universities followed suit. The following year they introduced a new rule dispensing with scrums and allowing the attacking side to retain possession. It was the first major reform in a long series that turned American football into the very boring game it is now. The architect of the most important changes was Walter Camp, 'the father of American football'. Late in 1905 came a sweeping innovation that marks the beginning of today's game: the forward pass – banned in other rugby codes – was expressly permitted, and has since become the principal way of gaining ground.

**Inter-college Match**

In the following years American football caught on increasingly outside the universities, and developed into a professional spectator sport. In 1919 Joseph F. Carr, manager of the Columbus Panhandles club side, encouraged a number of important clubs to form a national league. In July they became the National Football League, and launched the first N.F.L. annual championship series. The 1919 series was won by the Canton Bulldogs.

**N.F.L.**

Early in 1967 the first A.F.C.–N.F.C. Championship – better known as the Superbowl – was played. The Green Bay Packers (1966 N.F.L. champions) defeated the Kansas City Chiefs (1966 American Football League champions) 35–10.

**Superbowl**

The inventor of golf faced an exacting task. He had to work out a slow-moving sport without scope for tactics or team-work; with no interaction between the opponents except on a social level; a sport in which vigour and aggression could not be turned to advantage; one that would neither require nor promote physical fitness; one in which the scorecard would be more interesting than the play. Golf is obviously the work of a genius who ought to be famous rather than forgotten. This is not said only in jest. Virtually every other sport which involves scores or goals began and continued as a form of

**Golf**

confrontation; physical interference with the opponent or the ball was usual and often violent. Golf is a striking departure. The earliest golf on record was played around 950A.D. when a district official in China got his daughter to make holes in the ground and hit a ball into them one after another. He is not described as the inventor of the new Chinese game, but his daughter's lesson came near the start of its development, which could well have begun in the early 900s.

**Golf Book**

The first book dealing with golf specifically is the *Warn Jing* ('Ball Classic'), published in 1282. Together with old pictures, it makes it clear that golf in those times closely resembled today's game. It was generally played on lawns with small holes in them, sometimes identified by markers. Players had sets of clubs which came in three basic types – metal headed, plain and spoon headed. The game had a wide following ranging from emperors – who had coloured clubs and kept their balls in silk bags – to small children.

**Professional Golfer**

But old Chinese golf records lack one thing that makes the game so keenly contested nowadays: they make no mention of anyone deriving financial support from golf. That was a Scottish innovation in 1682, when the Scottish-born Duke of York (later crowned James II of England and VII of Scotland) was living in Edinburgh, as the royal commissioner to the Parliament of Scotland. The Scotch had developed the game to a sophisticated level after discovering an early form in France in the 1400s. Two visiting English noblemen had the audacity to tell the Duke that England is the homeland of golf. A debate ensued, and a challenge to settle the issue on the golf course at Leith – with a large sum wagered on the outcome. The two visitors would represent England, and the Duke was to name a Scottish champion as his partner. So John Patersone, a shoemaker, partnered the future king, in a joint victory for Scotland in the first international match. A half share of the Duke's winnings made Patersone's fortune, part of which he spent building a house in Edinburgh.

**Ice Hockey**

The ancient Scandinavian game of *knattleikr* is the first form of ice hockey of which any evidence remains. It is described in Icelandic sagas, including the story of *Gisli the Outlaw* (early-13th century A.D.). Not much is known about the game except that it was played with a wooden ball and that the saga heroes used to throw their opponents on the ice when the occasion offered. Ice hockey was popular last century in Canada, which is where the modern game was first played in 1875. In March that year two nine-man teams from the Montreal Football Club lined up against each other at the Victoria Ice Rink, Montreal. The main thing that distinguishes their game from earlier versions is that boundary lines limited play to a narrow area. In 1879 and 1880 rules like today's were established by players from Montreal's English-speaking university, McGill.

**Stanley Cup**

**Professional League**

The most prestigious award in ice hockey, the Stanley Cup, was donated by Lord Stanley, Governor General of Canada, in 1893. It was not tied to a particular league, but was presented annually to the most outstanding team. In 1910 it became the trophy of the annual professional league playoffs. However the first professional league had been established in 1905 – the inspiration of an American dentist in Houghton, Michigan. It was the grandly named but shortlived International Hockey League. There were teams from the cities of Sault Ste. Marie and Pittsburgh, and a few other towns in the United States.

**Tennis**

The ancient game of handball was popular in many Mediterranean countries, and by the 1300s it had spread widely in France, where it was named *paume* after the palm of the hand. Tennis began when people started playing paume with racquets, in France early in the 15th century. The racquet may have taken its name from *racachier*, an old Picardian word for 'to return the ball'. Early tennis was played to a wide assortment of rules, both outdoors and indoors. However during the 17th century tennis in France split into two forms with distinct rules: lawn tennis, played outdoors in an open area, was called *longe paume*; *courte paume*, played on a walled-in court, is what is now called royal tennis.

**Lawn Tennis**

**Royal Tennis**

**Wimbledon Championships**

The All-England Croquet and Lawn Tennis Club decided to hold a championship in 1877 because it needed to raise funds. So it proclaimed a tournament to be held at Wimbledon on the outskirts of London in June and July, with a silver cup for the winner. Twenty-two gentlemen entered and the Club made a modest profit. The first Wimbledon champion, Spencer Gore, was an experienced player of racquets, a game resembling squash. The transition at Wimbledon was not all plain sailing for him: he complained that 'we detested the tennis scoring . . . which puzzled us pretty considerable'.

**Wimbledon Women's Title**

In 1879 the first doubles tournament was held in conjunction with the annual championships, but the Club rejected a proposal to offer a cup for a women's championship. Five years later that omission was rectified, and Miss M. Watson won the inaugural women's title in 1884.

The U.S. championships were first held in 1881 (won by R. Sears); the Australian championships began in 1905 (won by R. Heath). In 1925, the French championships (first held in 1891) were opened to international competition, and won by R. Lacoste.

**Grand Slam Championships**

Squash is an offshoot of racquets – a game related to tennis that was played in Britain at Harrow school, one of the homes of soccer [see above]. By about 1850 boys at the school had started playing squash, on a smaller court with a softer ball than racquets. The usual explanation is that players waiting their turn on the racquets court used to hit the ball around in a nearby walled area. Because this area was small they used a squashy ball, which rebounds slower, and so squash was born. The first set of common rules was published in 1922 by a sub-committee of Britain's Tennis and Rackets Association.

**Squash**

In the Middle Ages, when most of Europe was languishing in poverty and ignorance, progress was taking place in two small pockets, which was later to have international repercussions. In the cities of North Italy there was an intellectual and cultural revival which sparked off the Renaissance. In England and the Low Countries, sportsmen were developing a game in which a player with a piece of bent timber defended a hole or a wooden frame from a ball thrown by his opponent. A crooked or twisted staff called a *cryec* was used as a bat, and gave the game its name.

**Cricket**

An aggressive field placement in the 1300s. At left is a streaker with some nuns in a wheelbarrow.

There is no record of the first cricket match but around 1200A.D. is the most likely date. On 10 March 1300, Prince Edward (Edward I), then aged sixteen, and his offsiders, spent

**Famous Cricketer**

a lavish 100 shillings on a sports day at Westminster, which included cricket and other games. The entry for that day in the royal wardrobe accounts is the first record of cricket, and supplies the name of the first notable cricketer.

In early times bats were long and curved, wickets wide and low, bowling was underarm, grounds were rough and rules widely varying. However by the 18th century many fundamentals of the modern game had developed. The first cricket poem was written in Latin by William Goldwin in 1706. **Cricket Poem** Called *Certamen Pilae*; *Anglice*, it tells of a village match that begins with a heated argument over the rules. A retired player, invited to settle the matter, lays down the following rules: there are to be two wickets, each with two stumps and 'a milk white bail' ; the batting side is to be selected by a toss of a coin; overs are four balls each, and batsmen can be out caught, bowled or run out.

For all its similarities, this is still not modern cricket, **Modern** which really began with the introduction of overarm bowling **Cricket** early in the 19th century. Willes (of Kent), Broadbridge (Hambledon) and Walker (Sussex) are the first known over-**Overarm** arm bowlers. Willes's sister Christina is said to have invented **Bowling** the technique because her skirt interfered with underarm action; she bowled her brother out first time, and the lesson was not lost on him. However although she may have coached him in a novel technique, it is likely that some now anonymous early bowlers had already experimented with overarm balls. Batsmen complained, timidly and correctly, that overarm bowling is dangerous, and a controversy persisted until 1835, when cricket's leading authority of the day, the Marylebone Cricket Club, voted to allow it.

Informal matches have been played by mixed sides and **Women's** women's teams for centuries. The first women's representative **Cricket** cricket on record was a match between 'eleven maids of Bromley' and 'eleven maids of Hambledon, all dressed in white', on 26 July 1745, which Hambledon won by eight runs.

In the mid-1700s English noblemen who had their own **Professional** cricket sides began recruiting top players on a professional **Cricket** basis. The custom spread to clubs and local teams, and the Hambledon Cricket Club, cricket's leading authority in the late 18th century, laid down a standard scale of payments.

**County** The earliest known game of English county cricket is a **Cricket** match between Kent and Surrey, advertised for 29 June 1709, to be played at Dartford for £50. This must have been one of the first, if not the first such contest. Soon afterwards, a number of southern counties began playing each other in an irregular but permanent representative competition. In 1744 James Love praised it in *Cricket: An Heroic Poem*:

> Fierce Kent, ambitious of the first Applause
> Against the World combined asserts her Cause
> Gay Sussex, sometimes triumphs o'er the Field,
> And fruitful Surrey cannot brook to yield.

In 1751, before American independence, the first international cricket match was played in America between a team from London and a team from New York. Almost a century later there was still enough interest in the sport in North America to promote the first international series, played in 1844 between Canada and the U.S.A. **International Match** **International Series**

Cricket matches between Australian states began before Federation, when they were still known as colonies. The present interstate competition, the Sheffield Shield, began in 1892. Tasmania, the last state to be admitted to Shield competition, was the first to host an inter-colonial match: in 1851, when Launceston Cricket Club played at home to Melbourne Cricket Club. The first match between representative sides was in 1856, when New South Wales defeated Victoria at the Melbourne Cricket Ground. **Interstate Cricket**

In the first test match at the Melbourne Cricket Ground in March 1877, Australia defeated England by 45 runs (a margin it repeated in the 1977 centenary test). Australian batsman Charles Bannerman, who retired injured on 165 runs, recorded the first test century in this game. **Test Match** **Test Century**

Cricket's most coveted prize, the Ashes, has a notional rather than a physical existence. Some observers thought the seven-run victory of Australia, captained by W. L. Murdoch, over England at the Oval in London on 29 August 1882 marked the end of England's 700-year cricketing pre-eminence. In this match Frederick Spofforth took four of England's last six wickets for two runs. Next day *The Sporting Times* wrote of English cricket: 'The body will be cremated and the ashes taken to Australia'. **The Ashes**

Polocrosse was played in the Eastern Roman Empire (also known as the Byzantine Empire, in present-day Greece and Turkey) during the 12th century A.D. Amongst the players was the emperor, who rolled his pony during a game. Two teams played on a level field with an apple-sized leather ball, and sticks fitted with a net made of gut, their aim being to score the most goals. **Polocrosse**

**International Polocrosse**   Polocrosse was reinvented in the 20th century, and international competition began at the 1976 Australian Championships, when Australia, New Zealand and New Guinea played a series of games.

**Baseball**   In 18th-century England, the names 'base-ball' and 'rounders' were given to the parent game of today's baseball, softball and rounders. The oldest mention is in *A Little Pretty Pocket Book* (London, 1744A.D., with a U.S. edition in 1787). By the 1740s the main principles were in place, so it is likely that the game had a tradition going back into the previous century. It probably derived from a game in the cricket family, because early cricket was sometimes played with only one batsman at a time. Cricket needed open country; baseball was better suited to situations where time and space were limited, and could be played in town.

Baseball, illustrated in *A Little Pretty Pocket Book*.

**Rounders**   An early use of posts, rather than bases, to mark the corners of the square running track (known in baseball as 'the diamond') may explain the name rounders. Batters scored by running round all the posts to 'home'. Nevertheless, rounders is often played with bases.

**American Baseball**   In the Northeastern United States, two sorts of baseball were popular in the first half of the 19th century. The 'New York game' followed British rules, with the batter at one corner of the diamond. In the 'Massachusetts game' the batter stood between fourth and first bases. In 1845 a party of New York gentlemen founded the Knickerbocker Base Ball Club, and laid down a set of rules. They played their first official game at their field on the Hudson River at Hoboken, New York, in 1846, against the New York Base Ball Club, and lost 23–1. The New York game as refined by the Knickerbockers ultimately became America's national game, and ousted rival versions internationally. Knickerbocker rules provided for nine-man teams, 'three out all out' dismissals, and a winning score of twenty-one runs.

**Professional Team**

The Knickerbockers were resolute amateurs, who resisted moves to commercialise the game. Their aristocratic influence waned as baseball's popularity increased. Popular clubs began fencing their fields and charging admission. Throughout the 1860s this produced a gradual spread of professionalism. Cincinatti, Ohio – disgusted at the terrible performance of its baseball players – raised the first entirely professional team, for the 1869 season. The Cincinatti Red Stockings included only one local, and players earned salaries ranging from $600 to $1200 for the season.

**College Baseball**

The earliest official inter-college match was played in Massachusetts in 1859. In that year Williams College accepted a challenge from the students of Amherst College, on condition that Amherst accepted its challenge to play chess as well. Thirteen-man baseball teams were selected by student ballots, and joined battle at Pittsfield, on the ground belonging to the town's baseball club. In a 3½-hour game played to Massachusetts rules, Amherst won 73–22. Next day Amherst won the chess as well.

**Women's Baseball**

Although women played baseball socially in its early days in England, stuffy opposition to women's sport prevented the development of women's teams in America until the 1860s, when a number of the more advanced women's colleges formed baseball clubs. Vassar College, which opened in 1865, offered its girls a bowling alley, croquet, riding and baseball, despite wowseristic opposition. (In 1866 Vassar had two clubs, the Laurel Base Ball Club and the Abenakis Base Ball Club.)

**National League**

In men's baseball the tide of professionalism led to the formation of the National Association in 1871, to run competitions between America's leading clubs. In 1876 this was replaced by the National League. Its eight clubs held monopolistic rights to particular territories, from which players were drawn.

**American League**

The present American League was set up in competition by B. B. Johnson and his associates in 1901. But in 1903 the

**World Series**

two leagues entered an agreement, which, amongst other things, established the World Series, which was first played in that year between the premier sides of each league.

**Basketball**

**Choule of Oise**

An early version of basketball survives in the French department of Oise, under the name *choule*. Each choule team attempts to send a round ball of about 15 cm. in diameter through a circle of stretched paper, 9 or 10 m. up a mast. Like many extinct European ball sports, the game has antecedents in ancient pagan celebrations. It is played at Easter time between husbands and bachelors; the classification of players, time of year, the ball and the goal can all be thought of as elements in traditional fertility symbolism. However because folk fertility rites continued after Christianity came in, these clues cannot fix the date of the game's beginnings. It might be a thousand years old or it might have evolved last century from a game quite unlike basketball. No such doubts surround modern basketball, which was first played in December 1891 at the International Y.M.C.A. Training School at Springfield, Massachusetts. It is unrelated to choule, having been invented at his desk by an instructor at the school, James A. Naismith (1861–1939). Naismith – a Presbyterian minister from Canada – took up a challenge from his boss to create an indoor winter training game. He devised basketball to suit a clinical set of requirements. His game would be easy to learn. It would be one in which skill is important, but strength is not necessary. It had to be suitable for men and women, but required no fertility symbolism. It had to be a team sport but not a contact sport. When it was first played the goals were baskets, attached to the gymnasium balconies.

**Netball**

Netball has rarely been played in America, but to begin with it was based almost entirely on various basketball rules and methods brought to Britain from the United States. In the 1890s Martina Bergman-Osterberg's Physical Training College was at the forefront of basketball for women, and kept on modifying its game with the latest American developments. Naturally enough, after the Ling Association was formed in 1899 to promote physical education for British women, Martina Bergman-Osterberg's people had a major impact on its work. In 1901 a sub-committee of the Association revised the basketball rules for women, building in a new set of American modifications. The 1901 reforms included reducing the ball to soccer-ball size, raising the posts to 10 feet, and adding nets to the rings. Rules have since been amended by other countries, but the 1901 British game was the first netball, from which the rest has sprung.

## 2. PHYSICAL PASTIMES

Swimming is a prehistoric invention developed spontaneously **Swimming** all over the world. There is no substance in the idea that the stroke known as overarm or the australian crawl – which is **Overarm** invariably used in modern freestyle events – is a recent discovery. Amongst Egyptian hieroglyphs from the Old Kingdom Period (c. 3500–c. 2500B.C.) is one that clearly depicts a swimmer using overarm technique; it might have originated in Egypt 5000 years ago, but just as possibly have been used by others well before that. But it is far more likely that the Egyptians have a real world first in their formal learn-to-swim **Learn-to-swim** classes conducted in the Middle Kingdom Period (c. 2150– **Classes** c. 1950B.C.). The first record of them is by Kheti, a prince of Siut, who wrote that when he was little the Pharaoh made him go to swimming lessons with the royal children.

Diving in was made into an athletic display by the Classical Greeks. Depictions of people diving appear on a number **DivingHigh** of Greek objets d'arts from the 400s B.C. onwards. Amongst them is a picture of the high-diving board, a Greek invention **Diving** of the Classical period. **Board**

Boxers in Northeastern Italy began to use hand-held weights in their training programmes at least as early as the 12th cen- **Weight** tury B.C. Judging by illustrations on bronze vessels of that **Training** time, the weights were purpose-made in the modern dumbbell shape, and used in arm exercises just as they are today. (Similar weights from a later period appear in the picture illustrating the first bikinis [XI, 5].)

Kung fu began early in China's Ming Dynasty (1368A.D.– 1644) as a system of gymnastic training primarily intended to **Kung Fu** benefit health. Because many exercises involved opponents tackling each other, it developed into a competitive martial art. *The Manual of Nourishing the Life by Gymnastics*, a book of **Kung Fu** uncertain date, probably around 1400, is the earliest of many **Manual** kung fu textbooks.

Kung fu is one of a series of martial arts for individual combatants without weapons, which began over a thousand years

**Judo**  ago in China and spread early on to Japan, where karate and ju-jitsu evolved. The most recent derivative of the tradition is judo – 'the gentle way' – developed by Jigoro Kano, who opened a judo academy in Tokyo in 1882, when he was only twenty-three. The term *judo* was already used for a method in ju-jitsu, which Jigoro learnt as a teenager. He worked out his new system, based on ju-jitsu, in the early 1880s, and it proved instantly successful when his academy opened. Four years afterwards his graduates defeated ju-jitsu exponents in a public match.

**Tae Kwon Do**  Korea also had a martial arts tradition. During the Koryo dynasty (918A.D.–1392) tae kwon do was instituted for training soldiers. It was a standardised formal version of combat sports which had existed in earlier times, modified under Chinese and perhaps also Japanese influence.

**Tai Chi**  Breathing and blowing, inhaling and exhaling, spitting out the old and drawing in the new breath, imitating in gymnastic the steps of the bear, the fluttering and expanding of the wings of birds, the ablutions of the duck, the stooping of the gibbon, the glare of the owl and the concentrated stare of the tiger . . .

This is how a Chinese book of the 2nd century B.C. describes the earliest system of tai chi exercises. The measured imitation of animal postures and the control of breath was then a trendy new way to achieve inner peace and physical health, and govern the life force. The authors of the book, the *Huai Narn Dzu*, whilst furnishing the oldest description, were not impressed by tai chi. Its motions, which were supposed to cultivate the body, could only end, they said, in confusion of the mind. The name tai chi and the movements practised nowadays are thought to have been introduced by Jarng Sarn Feng in the 1100s A.D.

**Board Riding**  Early in 1779, the great British navigator Captain James Cook saw surfboards in use in Kealakekua Bay, Hawaii:

Twenty or thirty of the natives taking each a long, narrow board, rounded at the ends, set out together from shore. The first wave they meet they plunge under, and suffering it to roll over them rise again beyond it and make the best of their way by swimming out into the sea. The second wave is encountered in the same manner with the first . . . As soon as they have gained by these repeated efforts, the smooth

water beyond the surf . . . their first object is to place themselves on the summit of the largest surge, by which they are
driven along with amazing rapidity towards the shore.

The Polynesian inventors of this pastime kept no written
records and the date of its beginning is unknown; so is the
identity of the Pacific island on which it was first practised.
Reports brought from Tahiti by travellers on HMS *Bounty*
establish that body boards were in use there in 1887, but as
Hawaii seems to have been where surfing was most popular
and developed, perhaps board riding was invented there.

Surfing became primarily a spectator sport at the annual
mid-autumn aquatic carnival during the Sung Dynasty **Surf Carnival**
(960A.D.–1279) at Harng Jo (Hangzhou or Hangchow) in
Southern China. The highlight was provided by a natural phenomenon known as a 'bore', a huge incoming wave always on
the verge of breaking, which surged up Harng Jo Bay and into
the Chien Tarng River, growing taller as the estuary got nar-
rower. Tens of thousands of fans watched the dauntless 'wave
riders' who rode the bore several kilometres from the sea to the
shallows upstream, their red and green flags often disappearing
in the foam. Spectators from overseas, from all over China, and
especially from the large city nearby crowded the hazardous
banks in defiance of regulations. One year they broke down a
safety fence and many drowned. The year 1072A.D. was more
auspicious – China's favourite poet wrote verses for the surfers
to chant, and brought prestige to the event with his enthusiasm.

The surf reel was tested by lifesavers at Bondi Beach, Sydney, on 23 December 1906. The first lives saved with it, **Surf Reel**
eleven days later, were those of two young boys. One of them,
Charlie Smith, survived to become the aviator Sir Charles
Kingsford Smith. In 1928 he made the first flight across the
ocean from which the surf reel had plucked him twenty-one
years earlier [IX, 3]. After many battles the sea eventually
claimed him in 1935, when his plane was lost in the Indian
Ocean off Thailand.

For all its modern popularity, skiing is an incredibly ancient **Skiing**
activity. It goes back too far beyond historical record for a
'first' to be assigned to it. The oldest evidence is a small picture scratched on rock, discovered in Rödöy, Norway. The
image looks remarkably like a man on two long skis, with high
raised tips. He is bent like a skier at the hips and knees. Specialists have dated it tentatively in the 'Upper Palaeolithic'
period, which would make it over 10,000 years old. If this is

correct, the ski has been around more than twice as long as the wheel. The oldest remains of actual skis, dated at about 2000B.C., come from Kalvträsk in Sweden. They were 204 cm. long, 15½ cm. wide, and pointy at both ends.

**Ice-skating**
There is some evidence hinting that Norway was also the home of ice skating. Specially carved reindeer jaw bones from about 3000 years ago may have been used as the blades of skates. More recently and certainly ice skating was practised by nomadic peoples northwest of China, known as the Wooden Horse Turks, who were observed by the Chinese during the Tarng Dynasty (7th to 10th centuries A.D.). The *New History of the Tarng Dynasty* explains that they 'commonly go very fast over the ice by binding boards over their feet; and then treading with a propulsive motion of the base of the spine they suddenly shoot forward a hundred paces with great rapidity'.

**Skating Rink**
In the 19th century, lots of people who had no need to travel this way began to skate in circles just for the sake of it. Residents of London, where nature failed to supply skateable ice, felt their deprivation so keenly that in 1876 they were provided with the Glaciarium, the first artificial ice-skating rink. It had spectator galleries, and walls decorated with alpine and forest scenes.

**Parachute**
The ancient Indian book *Prabhavakacavita* describes the inventive exploit of two nephews of the philosopher and encyclopaedist Haribhadra. Around 800A.D. they climbed to the top of a very tall tower and jumped off, descending safely by means of special 'umbrellas' that they had brought for the purpose.

## 3. GAMES, TOYS AND HOBBIES

**Chess**
Chess was invented in the Indus Valley, in present-day Pakistan, about 4500 years ago. The chessmen used included elephants, knights, chariots and ships. These have been found at archaeological sites in the Harappa district. Square ceramic boards divided into sixty-four squares have been found in the same area.

**Playing Cards**
Playing cards originated in China around 700A.D. In Chinese publishing at the time, paged books were taking over from scrolls – and the example of pages suggested cards to someone with too much imagination and spare time. In the 8th century, cards rapidly became a popular pastime. They were played at respectable dinner parties and by members of both sexes; but

it was a lady, in about 800A.D., who wrote *Card Games*, the **Book on Cards**
first book to be published on the subject.

After paper money [XII, 4] became widespread during the
Sung Dynasty (960A.D.–1279), the Chinese invented cards
which looked like banknotes. These formed a pack in four
suits: coins, strings, myriads and tens of myriads – all of them **Suits**
money denominations. Some early packs had forty-one cards,
numbered two to nine in three of the suits, and one to nine in
the fourth. Later, specially ranked cards, comparable to jacks,
queens or kings, were added.

It is no coincidence that the backs of European playing
cards are decorated with geometric line patterns – they derive
from Chinese banknote designs, which spread first to the cards
of China and then to those of the Islamic world in West Asia
and Egypt, where the modern-style fifty-two card pack was **Pack of**
invented. The Egyptian pack had four suits: cups, coins, swords **Fifty-two**
and polo sticks – each suit had numbered cards one to ten as well
as a deputy, a viceroy and a King. A complete pack survives from
about 1400A.D., but an older Egyptian card fragment suggests
that the four by thirteen system dates back to about 1200A.D. **Spades,**

The four modern suits were invented in France in about **Hearts, Clubs,**
1480. *Pique* was spade, in the shape of a metal-tipped wooden **Diamonds**

Early Chinese cards established the style for their western descendants.

shovel. *Carreau* is our 'diamond', but in meaning, a four-sided paving tile. *Coeur* means heart. *Trèfle* means clover, but this is club in English because it resembles the nobbled club on old Spanish cards. These simplified designs may make playing quicker, but they were probably created to make cards cheaper to manufacture. Cards were made from stencils or by wood-block printing. Simple designs and the two colours (red and black) which became standard, were easier to reproduce.

**Joker**   A joker was added to North American packs in the mid-19th century to suit euchre players. It started to be used in other games, and eventually two jokers became standard because of the rules of some modern games.

**Pinball Machine**   In the 1400s A.D., European inventors discovered that they could achieve marvellous things with spring mechanisms. Among their contributions to the world were spring-driven clocks and pinball machines. The pinball machine appears to have been born early in the century; Spain may be its original home because the oldest specimen is in Barcelona (at the Grupo Invenciones du Museo Tecnico). This machine, built in 1449, is a wooden cabinet about 80 cm. tall, with a spring at the bottom that propels three balls upwards. As the spring is released, three figures put out their right hands; the aim is to get as many balls as possible to land in the hands.

**Amusement Parlour**   In 1850 the Chinese Government mounted an exhibition in Peking of Chinese game-playing machines from the previous six centuries. Sixteen years later the exhibit was repeated by Peking's Imperial Museum, which charged visitors for the privilege of playing the machines. A monthly average of 5000 customers was recorded, spending over 15,000 taels (a sum that amounts to millions of today's dollars in spending power).

**Casino**   In early times gambling was permitted indiscriminately, and casinos only arose once governments imposed legislative restrictions on gambling, with the intention of combating a social evil or raising revenue. The casino idea began in India about 2000 years ago. Although the date and location of the first one is not recorded, Kautilya in the *Arthasastra*, his manual on administration, written not much later, describes the principle of their operation. Casinos were to be controlled by the Superintendent of Gambling, who provided equipment and accommodation, ensured fair play, and could levy five per cent of winnings as revenue.

Neville Chamberlain – not the British Prime Minister notorious for his trust in Adolf Hitler, but his countryman who **Snooker** became General Sir Neville Chamberlain – invented snooker in 1875 when he was serving as a subaltern with the Devonshire regiment stationed in India at Jabbalpore. There he added coloured balls to the billiard table at the Ootacamund Club, and fixed rules and positions for the balls.

The first crossword puzzle was published in the *New York World* of 21 December 1913. It was devised by the English-born American, Arthur Wynne, and consisted of thirty-two clued words.
**Crossword Puzzle**

Origami is the Japanese name for the art of folding paper into ingenious decorative shapes, sometimes resembling people **Origami** and animals, or into water bombs for use in school grounds. The technique actually began in China, during the Tarng Dynasty (618A.D.–906).

1902A.D. was a seminal year in toy bear development. In Germany, Margarete Steiff, manufacturer of stuffed pigs, horses, **Teddy Bear** donkeys, monkeys and camels, was presented by her imaginative nephew with the mohair prototype of a toy bear with moveable limbs. Later that year American President Theodore Roosevelt ('Teddy') went hunting in the wilds of Mississippi, without much success. A young bear was captured in his camp, presenting the president with an opportunity. But in response to his tender feelings Roosevelt declined to shoot the animal, and the survival of 'Teddy's Bear' rebounded to his credit in the press. In New York a Russian confectioner, Morris Michtom, and his wife made the first teddy bear to a design resembling Margarete Steiff's, out of brown plush, with moveable limbs. Michtom began marketing his invention the following year, with presidential permission, as the teddy bear.

In 1761 a London engraver and cartographer, John Spilsbury, was taken with the notion that children ought to find their **Jigsaw Puzzle** education entertaining. He put this into practice in the field of geography with an invention he called the 'dissected map'. He pasted maps onto boards, and cut around the borders of the countries with a fine saw so that the map could be contained in a box full of jumbled pieces.

**Kaleidoscope**  The first kaleidoscope was made in Edinburgh in 1816 or 1817 by Sir David Brewster (1781A.D.–1868). Brewster was an editor and scientist who also wrote a treatise explaining the operation of the kaleidoscope.

**Boomerang**  Remains of a return boomerang discovered at an Aboriginal archaeological site at Wyrie, South Australia, are known by carbon-dating to be over 10,000 years old. Prior to this time there were non-return boomerangs in Australia and Europe in use for hunting animals; they were sophisticated enough aero-dynamically to make curved flights to targets behind obstructions, but the Wyrie design is the oldest discovered that could have come back to the thrower.

## 4. ENTERTAINMENTS

See also Dramatic Arts [II, 2] and Music [II, 3].

**Bullfighting**  Bullfighting became a spectator event in Roman times. It was staged first at the games put on by Julius Caesar in 45B.C. The method used had been developed by the Thessalians of Northern Greece – horsemen who captured bulls by riding up beside them and grabbing their horns.

**Cockfighting**  Organised cockfighting appears to have begun in Southeast Asia about 1000B.C. as a religious ceremony. For reasons which ought to have been clearer to the divinities than they were to the cocks and are to the reader, cockfighting had a beneficial effect on the fertility of the land and people, long before it became a crowd puller as secular entertainment.

**Gladiators**  The Romans were not the inventors of gladiatorial contests. They merely copied the idea from their old neighbours the Etruscans, who used to rule Northern Italy before the Romans dealt with them. Initially, Etruscan religion appears to have called for human sacrifices at funeral ceremonies. Eventually as they became more refined, in the 500s B.C., Etruscans developed the substitute of having a blindfolded gladiator with a club fight for his life, in honour of the deceased, against a wild animal. By around 500B.C. they had fighting pairs of gladiators, who were usually prisoners of war. This was tried out at a Roman funeral in 264B.C. Rome's contribution was to turn gladiatorial combat into a spectator sport and commercial activity. During the 2nd

Punic War (219–201B.C.) the Romans began to stage contests purely for entertainment. Gladiatorial bouts lost their religious significance, and often even their fatal conclusions.

**Birthday Party**

In primitive times and amongst the earliest civilisations, people did not bother to keep a record of their birthdays. Even in the 13th century Marco Polo considered it remarkable that the Chinese could remember their dates of birth. Birthdays were first recorded because of the astrological belief that they determine personal fortunes. It was only later that the real reason was discovered for remembering them – having parties. In the first half of the 1st millennium B.C. some of the less polished peoples of Western Asia started to celebrate birthdays with enthusiasm. Amongst them were the Persians – conquerors of West Asia – whose parties were described by the Greek historian Herodotus, in the 5th century B.C.: 'Of all the days in the year the one which they celebrate most is their birthday . . . they eat little solid food but an abundance of dessert, which is set on the table a few dishes at a time.'

**Birthday Cake**

The birthday cake originated a century or two later in separate circumstances. Greek worshippers of the Moon goddess, Artemis, offered round honey cakes in a ceremony on her birthday, which recurred every month (with the renewal of the Moon). Lighted candles set atop the cake were originally inspired by the light of the Moon and stars, but they were adopted along with the cake for the commemoration of birthdays in general.

**Aviary**

Individual caging of birds goes back to time immemorial. But the first aviary containing a range of all kinds of birds was established in Italy in the mid-1st century B.C. by Marcus Laenius Strabo of Brundisium. He used multiple cages to contain his large flock and began a popular aviary-keeping tradition in the Roman Empire.

**Aquarium**

The Sumerians in Mesopotamia began to build aquariums around 2000B.C. The first on record is a lavish construction described by its owner in a poem addressed to his fish. Sixteen species of fish are recommended for inclusion, amongst them the barbel, the carp, the sturgeon, the catfish and the eel.

**Dancing Horses**

Horses were trained to dance to pipe music in the Greek city of Sybaris, Southern Italy, around 600B.C. The Sybarites used the dancing horses as an entertainment at feasts. According to one account of their fate, the enemy Crotonites learnt the music, and wrought havoc in action against the Sybarite cavalry by piping the dance and setting the Sybarite horses dancing on the battlefield.

**Firework Display** Long before the invention of gunpowder [VI, 1] the Romans entertained themselves with firework displays – ornate presentations of flammable materials which appear to have begun around 300A.D. The earliest description, by the Latin author Claudian, refers to a display with whirling firewheels and dropping fountains.

**Bungers** Earlier still, the Chinese enjoyed the explosive sound effects of fire, with a primitive version of the bunger. They used to put sealed sections of bamboo in fires, so that the air and moisture inside would enlarge till they exploded; such bungers are first recorded during the Harn Dynasty (206B.C.–220A.D.), in the 1st century A.D. or earlier. By packing bamboo tubes with gunpowder they produced modern-style bungers, probably in the 10th century A.D.

**Gunpowder Fireworks** Another Chinese innovation – since adopted universally – was the introduction of gunpowder to display fireworks. By the 11th century, Chinese displays included plays that simulated people in motion, with facial features, clothes and hair, in a wide range of colours. Such sophistication must have been based on development of gunpowder displays going back at least to the previous century.

**Merry-go-round** Prince Bhoja, the scholarly ruler of Malwa (reigned 1018A.D.–1060) in Northern India describes a mechanical rotating amusement ride in his book on engineering. He calls this merry-go-round a *rathadota*.

**Loop-the-loop** No aviator had ever attempted a loop-the-loop before one was successfully performed on 27 August 1913 by Lieut. Peter Nesterov of the Russian Imperial Airforce. He took his Russian-built, French-designed Nieuport biplane into a steep climb then wheeled it over backwards and returned to his starting point, completing the manoeuvre without killing himself. His death followed the next year during the First World War, when he initiated Russia's first air combat by flying head on into an attacking German plane.

**Pole Sitting** Pole sitting is in this section because of its obvious suitability to the needs of people with too much time on their hands. It might just as well appear with 'Religion' because of its origin in Christian worship. It could also be in 'Finance' because in America it has been adapted to the profit motive, and vindicates the principles of the free enterprise society. Handsome monetary rewards indicate the value which that society sets on the pole sitters' service. In consequence the modern record is held by America (399 days). Gain is a weak motive compared to faith, and in the 5th century A.D., Christendom recognised no loftier demonstration of devotion than the practice of ascending a tall pillar and remaining there exposed to the elements. The most devout person in those days was St. Simeon Stylites of Syria, the first pole sitter and the best. After a practice stint at low height, he extended his pillar to a precarious 60 feet, went to its summit and sat there. Many copied his example, but never has his thirty-year endurance record been matched or even threatened. When he died, the Patriarch of Constantinople, with 6000 men, escorted his coffin to the capital.

**Beer Can Regatta**

The first properly organised regatta for rafts and boats constructed out of empty beer cans was held in Darwin in 1973. From then on the Darwin regatta has been an annual event. The Darwin-built *Can-Tiki*, constructed in 1978 out of 15,000 beer cans, was the first long-distance ocean-going vessel to exploit this new method of construction. On her maiden voyage she sailed 4024 km. from Darwin to Singapore.

# UTILITY AND LUXURY

This is the chapter about the day-to-day things which can be hard to live without, but are difficult to get excited about. Naturally many items in this category were first used in distant prehistoric times, leaving no traceable first.

## 1. HOUSE AND FURNITURE

Very very old inventions which are still around after all this time are usually more important to our lifestyle than recent inventions. The house is a good example. The first house might have been built about 10,000 years ago, but since that time houses have been an unfailing success story. Today people want them as much as ever, and those who have them like to spend lots of time in them. The same goes for various household fittings and contents. Some are such old and commonplace inventions that their origin will never be known – locks, steps, ovens, baths, cupboards and so on. The bed is one of the earliest inventions that can be assigned a particular time and place. Almost everyone nowadays spends more time using a bed than anything invented in the 20th century, or even in the last 5000 years.

**Bathroom**

The houses excavated at the ancient site of Mohenjo-Daro on the Indus River in present-day Pakistan, and at Harappa on the same river further north, may date back to 3000 B.C. A surprising feature of houses even at this early stage is private bathrooms – fitted out with inlet water pipes, and drains. These bathrooms were tiled and equipped with such conveniences as baths and washstands. The existence of such facilities, even in some very humble abodes, leaves a favourable impression of the hygienic standards of this ancient civilisation – which is more than can be said for their drains; these merely led the dirty water a short distance away from the houses into soak pits, which must have resulted in a smelly city.

The kind of toilet known as a water closet, which is flushed with water from a cistern after use, was first installed in houses **Flush Toilets** in the ancient cities on the Indus River in present-day Pakistan. The two pictured here have been uncovered in the ruins at Mohenjo-Daro, where flush toilets date back to about 3000B.C.

They built a toilet to last in the Indus Valley. The two along the back wall have a sewer behind and ablution areas in front.

'They are not careful about cleanliness and do not wash themselves with water when they have done their necessities; but **Toilet Paper** they only wipe themselves with paper.' So wrote an Arab visitor to China in 851A.D., giving the outside world its first description of toilet paper. The Chinese began to manufacture it in the 5th century A.D. Like the people on T.V. advertisements they were preoccupied with softness, and made paper from rice straw and special grass crops for the best results. Statistics about supplies for the palace in 1393A.D. give a good idea of the shape – there were 720,000 sheets 2 feet by 3 feet, as well as 15,000 sheets cut to 3 inches square and perfumed, for use by the imperial family.

Bodily hygiene was a preoccupation in many ancient cultures, but the technical simplicity of the tub meant that showers **Shower** were unthought of until relatively late. The Greeks began installing them in the 5th century B.C. or thereabouts. The earliest picture is on a vase that depicts a number of unclad ladies under adjoining showers. The water issues in fine sprays from a variety of imitation animal heads mounted on decorated columns. The picture appears to show heated towel rails, and the pipes carrying the shower water to each column. Greeks and Romans preferred to wash in lavishly equipped public baths. Showers in private bathrooms were non-existent or rare until the advent of Sergius Orata (c. 90B.C.), a Roman property developer. He installed showers in a lot of houses before putting them on the market. He also introduced oyster farming [V, I].

**Central Heating**

Archaeologists at Mohenjo-Daro, on the Indus River in present-day Pakistan, have discovered a public bath complex, built c. 2500B.C. or soon after, with the world's oldest central-heating system. Heat came from a furnace with hot air ducts under the floors. This is known as a hypocaust and works by keeping the floors warm, without blowing hot air into the rooms. Other novel features of this remarkable establishment are the first swimming pool [V, 1] and a hot air bath, which functioned as a sauna.

**Sauna**

**Bed Divan**

In prehistoric times, the privileged élite who first began to sleep on anything fancier than the floor, made themselves at home on benches or divans. Divans were ledges of mud brick built onto house walls, which became seats and work areas by day. One of the first towns, at Çatal Hüyük (in present-day Turkey), in about 6000B.C., offered divan space for almost everyone. But the first beds, freestanding and purpose built, did not appear until the 4th millennium B.C., when the early Egyptians began to make them. At first they were designed with the head end higher than the foot. Each consisted of a timber frame with skins or hides stretched across, and a footboard at the end. The oldest specimens come from the centuries just before Egypt was united in 3500B.C.

**Camp Bed**

Ancient Egypt is also the home of the portable camp bed. The oldest specimen is from the 18th Dynasty, found in the tomb of Pharaoh Tutankhamen (14th century B.C.), but the invention may go back to any time in the preceding millennium.

**Water Bed**

One of Queen Victoria's physicians, Dr. Neil Arnott, devised the water bed – not specifically to make Her Majesty more comfortable, but to help patients confined to bed who had trouble rolling over. The medical advantage which appealed to Dr. Arnott was that blood flow to parts of the flesh pressing into the mattress is not restricted, as it is on normal bedding. His bed was a watertight trough the same size as a normal bed and six or seven inches deep, sealed on top with a loose rubber membrane. Observers of the time would have been surprised could they have seen how little medical use and how much domestic use the water bed gets today.

The Egyptians began making armchairs early in the Old Kingdom period, no later than the 4th Dynasty (about 3000B.C.) – **Armchair** whence the oldest remains come – and perhaps in the previous century. The design is totally obsolete, because the armrests come out from the chair back at armpit height. They were made of decorated wood, with legs like animal legs.

During the 4th, 5th and 6th centuries A.D., China was weak and disunited, and barbarian tribes from the North were able **Swivelling** to occupy and rule large parts of the country. The swivelling **Chair** chair was one of several interesting innovations that resulted from the blending of the barbarian lifestyle with Chinese technical sophistication. The North Chinese state of Chao was ruled by a Hun named Shir Hu. Owing to the overindulgence that goes with supreme power, Shir Hu got so big and fat that he was too heavy to sit on a horse and couldn't go hunting. So they mounted a chair on his chariot that could swivel around like a modern office chair – making it much larger, of course, to accommodate his gross dimensions. It was a great success because he could face his quarry while shooting.

## 2. EQUIPMENT AND APPLIANCES

For scientific and medical apparatus see Chapter VIII, Science and Technology, particularly VIII, 2; VIII, 3; VIII, 6 and VIII, 10. For radio equipment see VIII, 10, and Flying Doctor, IV, 3. VIII, 10 also includes clocks and computers. For telephones and television see VIII, 12; and for farming equipment VIII, 7. Slide projectors are in II, 1, record players in II, 3.

In prehistoric Anatolia (present-day Turkey) obsidian was used to make the first mirrors. Specimens which date back to **Mirror** 6000B.C. have been recovered from the ancient town excavated at Çatal Hüyük, but no such mirrors are found amongst the older layers of the town.

**Glass Mirror**

In the 2nd millennium B.C. bronze mirrors became very widespread, a large tin content being used to make them highly reflective. Glass mirrors, however, are comparatively recent, the work of an anonymous inventor in Italy in the 1300s. They were made by smoothing tinfoil on to a sheet of glass, and adding mercury, which formed an adhesive amalgam with the tin.

**Magnifying Glass**

The Greeks made simple lenses of natural crystal and glass, and eventually of glass filled with water, beginning at least as long ago as the 400s B.C. Initially lenses were designed to make fire by concentrating light, but naturally their magnifying effect was quickly discovered and they were produced for people who wanted help examining small writing. Specimens have been unearthed from various parts of the former Roman Empire, and there are several mentions in Greek and Latin literature.

**Rotary Fan**

**Cooling Fan**

The rotary fan was first employed as a component of the winnowing machine [see Winnowing Fan, VIII, 7] invented for Chinese farmers by about 200B.C. In this machine, a constant gust of air, from an enclosed fan, blows the husks away from grain. The first use of the fan as a cooling device was the idea of an engineer, Ding Huarn, who flourished around 180A.D. He set up a mechanism of seven fans each 10 inches in diameter, connected by a single drive belt or shaft and turned by an operator. It is recorded that this device could make people so cool in a hot hall that they began to shiver.

**Refrigerator**

Refrigerators were made in Geelong in the 1850s by James Harrison, the pioneer of refrigeration [VIII, 8] by means of the evaporation of ether and ammonia. However their purpose was to make ice for commercial sale. The first domestic refrigerators for use by ordinary householders in their kitchens were manufactured by the French firm Carré and Co., which released them for sale early in the 1860s in France, and other European countries. They were easy to get, portable, cheap and effective, but it can hardly be said they were easy to use. By heating and cooling cylinders, the operator caused the evaporation of ammonia within, and rapid chilling which produced ice. One device could produce a kilo or two of ice per hour in this way.

The thermostat was devised in 1609 by a Dutch scientist working in England, Cornelius Drebbel (1572–1634), who **Thermostat** incorporated it in an incubator he invented that year. The incubator was a sealed, water-jacketed box within a cabinet that was heated by coal fire. Alcohol in a tube – mounted inside the water jacket – expanded with heat and propelled mercury through a pipe to the exterior. A rod with one end in the pipe was attached to a damper that regulated the air inflow to the fire. When its temperature fell the alcohol contracted, drawing the mercury back inwards; this caused the rod to fall, opening the damper so the fire would burn hotter. Drebbel, who worked under royal patronage, subsequently applied the same mechanism to chemical furnaces. It was one of his many pneumatic inventions, the best known of them being the sub-marine [VI, 3].

Scissors were invented in Northern China during the Warring States Period (481–221B.C.). The oldest surviving specimens, **Scissors** however, come from the Roman Empire, so the West was not far behind China in their manufacture.

Ctesibius, the Greek inventor who gave the world the air gun [VI, 2] and a musical organ [II, 3], also did a lot of work on **Cuckoo Clock** clocks. He had a clock which kept time by measuring the flow of water from a series of tanks. His most refined timepiece was a singing bird operated mechanically (probably by water clock), which called the hours. Ctesibius worked in Alexandria (Egypt) early in the 3rd century B.C.

In 1898 Valdemar Poulsen (1869–1942), of Copenhagen, began making 'telegrafones': machines which would give a **Answering** pre-recorded message to people ringing up others who were **Machine** not at home, and record a message they wished to leave. Poulsen's machine was one of the earliest applications of magnetic sound recording, using a reel of magnetised wire. A few years later he developed a model with magnetised steel tape **Tape Recorder** instead of wire: the first tape recorder. Some of the features which have encouraged so many phone users nowadays to install answering machines were missing from the telegrafone – including an amplifier which makes messages easy to hear.

A Melbourne blacksmith, Gilbert Toyne, invented the rotary **Rotary** clothes hoist in 1924. His design never went into production, **Clothes Hoist** and the type seen now in millions of backyards is the 1946 design of Lance Hill from Adelaide, who added the crank-operated raising mechanism.

**Aerosol** Originally, spraying of chemicals under pressure was achieved by a pump action can which atomised the fluid contents as they left the nozzle. But in 1926 Norwegian inventor Erik Rotheim developed the aerosol, a spray can that works by the internal pressure of a liquid or gas in the same cylinder as the substance intended for spraying. Its first commercial application was for insecticide, in America during the Second World War.

**Vacuum Cleaner** The vacuum cleaner is the product of pioneering research in 1901 by Herbert Cecil Booth, an English engineer of rides for amusement parks, and bridges. Booth's research consisted of sucking on armchairs and carpets, through a handkerchief placed over his mouth. Encouraged by the success of this test he built *Puffing Billy*, the first vacuum cleaner, completed early the following year. It had a 5-horsepower electric motor, sucking air through a cloth filter. Booth and his employees were able to vacuum Westminster Abbey in time for Edward VII's coronation later that year. He brought out a domestic model in 1904, but his greatest success was in going from house to house with big three and four-hose petrol vacuums mounted on carts.

**Self-cleaning Floor** Self-cleaning floors are not used these days, but they are given a mention here because porous paving remains a good idea. They originate in the dining rooms of ancient Greece, perhaps in the 5th century B.C. A firm base is first smoothed out below floor level, inclined to a drainage point. Over it is laid a mixture of gravel, lime and ashes to a depth of half a foot, which is levelled and smoothed with a whetstone, drying to resemble black pavement. Any spilt fluid disappears instantaneously, and as flooring it had the advantage of not being too chilly underfoot in cold weather for slaves who had to stand on it barefoot.

**Keyboard** The earliest description of a keyboard is given by the Roman author Vitruvius in his *Ten Books on Architecture*. It was part of the mechanical water organ, a Greek invention of the 3rd century B.C. [see Organ, II, 3]. The keys activated slides, which opened and closed holes in the organ, to produce musical notes.

The pram was an invention of China's Tarng Dynasty period (618A.D.–906). A picture from the 850s reveals that the early **Pram** designs were low slung and cradle-shaped, with four wheels.

The Greek scientist, Heron, famous for inventing the steam engine [VIII, 9] and automatic doors [V, 2], designed many **Coin-operated** lesser marvels including the coin-operated drink-vending **Vending** machine. A five-drachma coin in the slot at the top caused **Machine** the machine to dispense a cup full of fluid from an outlet near the bottom. The design is described in detail in his book, *Pneumatica* (Alexandria, 1st century B.C.). It could not give change and did not even have a coin-return chute.

Theatres in ancient Greece were equipped with bronze sounding vessels in strategically located recesses under the seats at **Public Address** various levels. The vessels were arranged on principles of **System** musical harmony, to sound on seven separate notes in the double octave, whenever the speaker's voice struck those notes. They made it possible to hear words loud and clear even at the back of the theatre. We first hear of such vessels at Corinth in the 2nd century B.C., but they must have been used earlier, perhaps in the 4th century B.C. To adopt this aid to clear hearing, modern theatre architects need only follow the instructions of the Roman author Vitruvius in his *Ten Books on Architecture*. (In the 5th century B.C. the Chinese used similar equipment, but not for addressing the public. Buried under fortifications, it detected the approach of hostile forces excavating trenches and mines.)

The microphone was invented in Britain in 1878 by Prof. David Hughes. Hughes ran an electric current from a battery **Microphone** through a length of carbon wired to the sound receiver. He recommended willow charcoal, tempered in mercury when white hot, as the ideal conductor.

The first xerographic (dry) photocopy was made in 1938 in a laboratory near New York, by American research physicist, **Xerographic** Chester Carlson (1906–68). Carlson had long been exasperated **Copying** by the unsatisfactory performance of the wet chemical system of existing copiers, and devised a system in which light is used to overcome a positive electric charge. The image is reproduced because areas least exposed to light retain the charge which attracts the toner – the dry ink powder. Carlson had difficulty finding financial support. Eventually he succeeded and in 1947 he established the Xerox Corporation, to sell photocopiers commercially.

**Word Processor** The first word processor on the market was designed and manufactured in the U.S.A. by the IBM company. Released in 1964, it resembled an ordinary electric typewriter in appearance, and printed out by the typewriter system of letter keys striking the paper. Unlike later word processors it had no display screen. The content and the layout instructions were entered on magnetic tape.

## 3. USEFUL PRODUCTS

**Soap** Sometimes the first is not the best, and in fact distinctly inferior to the result achieved with later refinements [consider Traffic Light, V, 1; Blood Transfusion, VIII, 6; and Jet Airliner, IX, 3]. Soap is a very good example of a poor start. It was made in Southern Mesopotamia in the 23rd century B.C.; the active constituent was ash with a high potash content, made from rushes of a local species. This was combined with oil and fine clay, and made into cakes.

**Insecticide** The first chemical treatment against insects was fumigation. Fumigant insecticides date back in China to shortly before 1000B.C. In the early years of the Jo Dynasty (c. 1100B.C.– **Fumigation** 256B.C.) the government employed eradicating officials. One specialised in combating internal pests by administering worm potions; the others were the Frog Controller and the Exterminator, both of whom used toxic smoke to counter vermin. The Exterminator's responsibility included insect pests in general, which he fought with the smoke of the *marng dsao* plant.

**Mozzie Coil** A simpler and more domestic form of fumigant which will be familiar to readers in afflicted areas is the mozzie coil – a piece of incense that drives away mosquitoes. These came into use in mosquito-infested South China during the Sung Dynasty (960–1280A.D.).

**Rub-on Insecticide** Rub-on insecticides in the form of ointments and resins made from plant materials were introduced in China by the 2nd century B.C., for both people and animals. By that time, external insecticide treatments were already in use on live-**Insecticidal Spray** stock in North Africa [see Sheep Dip, VIII, 7]. Spray-on insecticides, which were initially water-based and contained active ingredients infused from plants, were also pioneered in China at about the same time as the rub-on variety. Aerosols [X1, 2] came much later.

**Pyrethrum** Pyrethrum, which became the dominant insecticide when it began to be used in Europe last century, was first employed over 2000 years earlier, in China in the 2nd century B.C. At first the Chinese took advantage of its insecticidal effects only by powdering chrysanthemum flowers, rather than extracting the active component from them.

**Ink** Writing was originally done by scratching lines on hard surfaces, or pressing shapes into clay. The Egyptians invented ink before they had papyrus paper, prior to 3000B.C. Later with the introduction of papyrus, ink became their standard writing substance. Egyptian ink was a liquid, usually dyed with soot from burnt bone.

**Indelible Ink** The jet black, indelible ink known as India ink was first manufactured in China, the product of a careful mixture of pigments and specially treated binding agents. It originated in the Harn Dynasty (206B.C.–220A.D.). It can be soaked for weeks without washing out and is perfectly black.

**Graphite** Graphite, the mineral used in pencils, was called stone ink by the Chinese, who started using it probably during the Harn Dynasty.

**Printer's Ink** Printer's ink can be made to a variety of recipes. The first ink made specially for printing probably dates back almost as long as the invention of printing itself. Chinese ink blocks are not suitable for printers, and a thick ink paste was produced instead, at least as long ago as the Tarng Dynasty (618A.D.–906).

**Invisible Ink** Invisible ink is referred to in a story from the Sung Dynasty. A certain Warng did not like the influential Chin Guei (1090A.D.–1155) and wrote 'Death to Chin Guei' in what he was told was invisible ink. The words became uncomfortably black after water was poured on, and the ink maker had to be bribed not to show them around.

**Correcting Paint** During the Tarng Dynasty (618A.D.–906) a new item was added to the Chinese stationery range. It came in the form of a stick, like a crayon, and could be painted over any mistake on a sheet of paper, to mask it with an opaque film. In those days the Chinese always used yellow paper for their documents and correspondence, so the correcting paint was in a matching yellow. The effective ingredient was the mineral *dzu huarng* ($As_2S_2$), insoluble in water and easily pulverised for inclusion in the stick.

**Glue**   People worked out how to write before they could make glue, but still no one was interested enough to write up the invention of glue. The only way to put a date on such comparatively boring and unnoticed inventions is to rely on archaeological remains and passing references in writing about other things. In this way it is known that glue was invented in Egypt in the Old Kingdom Period before or during the 4th Dynasty (c. 3000B.C.).

**Matches**   The first matches, manufactured in China in the 6th century A.D., were an insignificant contribution to human welfare. They were little pine sticks impregnated with sulphur, which burst into flame on the slightest touch of fire, but had no other way of being lit. Between the 6th and the 19th centuries various ways of making matches ignite were explored, but none of them involved striking.

**Friction**   In 1827 the English chemist John Walker invented 'fric-
**Matches**   tion lights', the first matches of the modern type, lit by striking. They were sticks 8 cm long, dipped in a paste of chlorate of potash, sulphide of antimony, gum arabic and water. They were first sold at Walker's chemist shop in Stockton.

**Lighters**   Lighters were invented around 1200A.D. by Arab military technicians. This is well before the introduction of cigarettes, and their lighters were only meant for lighting incendiary weapons such as Greek fire [see Flame Thrower, VI, 2]. The flasks used as containers were probably too large to be comfortable in a modern pocket. In a book called *Stratagems and Wars, Instruments of War, the Siege of Fortresses, the Way of Striking the Sword, Throwing Arrows and the Manufacture of the Burud* there are several formulae of that time for lighter fluid. The author of the book may have had a part in inventing lighters.

## 4. MATERIALS

Earthenware, glass, woollen fabric and leather are amongst the many materials with unknown origins in prehistoric times. Concrete and metals can be found in VIII, 8.

**Felt**   A 5000-year-old human mummy, discovered in 1991, preserved in ice on the mountainous Austrian–Italian border, comes with its own set of equipment. As well as a knife, axe, bow and arrows, and leather clothing, the man had a felt hat. This is the oldest felt specimen in the world, and points to an invention of felt by pastoral people in the mountains of Europe during the 4th millennium B.C.

Cotton was domesticated and woven into cloth in the Indus Valley in present-day Pakistan, before 3000B.C. Archaeolo- **Cotton** gists have discovered traces at Harappa and Mohenjo-Daro, dating back to early in the 3rd millennium B.C. Since cotton working is quite tricky and these sites are far apart, it probably came into use in the region hundreds of years earlier, at an unknown birthplace.

In 1958 archaeologists unearthed the remains of a bamboo basket that contained the oldest fragments of silk fabric ever **Silk** discovered. They have been dated, with limited reliability, to the period 2850–2650B.C. They come from a site at Chien Sharn Yarng in present-day Southeastern China, and are of pre-Chinese manufacture. The fragments are made of the thread of domesticated silkworms, and one is finely woven with up to seventy-two threads per centimetre. This level of development points to an invention of silk cloth, in this area, between 3000 and 2500B.C.

Depending how it is used, the hemp plant *Cannabis sativa* serves mankind either as a hedonistic indulgence or as the **Hemp** least exciting of necessities. For the former of these, see the entry on Cannabis Smoking [IV, 4]. As to the other, it consists in the use of hemp fibre as a textile in cloth and rope. Hemp material was first made in Eastern Asia in the 3rd millennium B.C. A 4000-year-old scrap has been found in territory that belonged to the Chi Jia people who lived northwest of the Chinese; it is referred to also in Chinese records covering the early 3rd millennium.

    The same record mentions ramie – fabric made from the plant *Boehmeria nivea*; the oldest remains come from South **Ramie** China, made in c. 2750B.C. before that area fell into Chinese hands.

Asbestos fibre was worked by the people of coastal China in the 5th or 4th century B.C. In particular they took advantage **Asbestos** of its indestructibility in flame to make lamp wicks; at the same time or shortly after, it was woven into cloth.

**Nylon** Nylon was invented in 1937 by Dr. Wallace H. Carothers (1898–1937), a research chemist with the American chemical firm E. I. du Pont de Nemours and Co. Carothers had been working on long-chain polymer fibres in imitation of silk for almost ten years at the firm's laboratories. After disappointment with its work on polyesters, his team pioneered the development of artificial molecules known as polyamides. From amongst the polyamides he left behind on his death, the Du Pont company selected the sample called 'fibre 66' for commercial development, christened it nylon, **Nylon** and released it publicly in 1938. The first nylon product, **Stockings** women's stockings, went on the market in October that year.

**Kevlar** Kevlar is the extremely strong woven synthetic material used for hulls and sails, radial tyres and bulletproof vests. It was invented by Dr. Stephanie Kwolek, of America's Du Pont chemical company, in 1976.

**Lacquerware** In the eastern part of what is now China, lacquerware was made long before the Chinese existed. The earliest lacquer article recovered by archaeologists is a wooden bowl of about 5000B.C. from the coastal province of Chekiang, south of the Yangtze River, coated inside and out in bright red.

**Plywood** The invention of plywood in ancient Egypt is known by a specimen discovered by archaeologists dating from soon after 3000B.C. It comprises six plies of different kinds of wood.

**Paper** In a Chinese dictionary published during the Harn Dynasty (206B.C.–220A.D.), there is a definition of the word paper, 'a mat of refuse fibres', which proves that by then even dictionary writers understood what was going on. The first paper was manufactured in the early years of the dynasty, the 2nd century B.C. The earliest fragments which have been found are all rough and thick, and made of hemp.

**Paper Book** Later during the Harn Dynasty, in 76A.D., an edition of *The Spring and Autumn Annals with Tso's Commentary* was distributed to students – the first book made of paper, which by then had improved in quality.

**Coloured** Chinese manufacturers began producing coloured papers **Paper** during the Jin Dynasty in the 200s A.D. A range of colours was achieved using dyes from various sources. The Amur cork tree was processed to produce an insecticidal dye. Paper impregnated with this came out yellow, and proof against bookworms, silverfish etc.

In the 2nd century B.C. when King Eumenes II, of Pergamon in present-day Turkey, was building up the new and magnifi- **Parchment** cent Pergamene Library, the jealous Egyptian Government put a temporary embargo on papyrus export. The Pergamene Library was threatening the pre-eminence of the Library of Alexandria, so the intention was to prevent books being copied in large numbers elsewhere, by restricting the supply of the only practicable writing material, papyrus. Pergamon overcame Alexandria by developing parchment, a new material prepared from animal skin. It wasn't the first time skins had been used as stationery, only the invention of a new treatment to suit them better to the purpose. (Shortly afterwards, when papyrus supply resumed, parchment proved uneconomic and less suitable for books; however in Europe in the Dark Ages it became the standard material.) Next century the library at Alexandria had its eventual triumph, when Cleopatra's Roman boyfriend, Mark Antony, gave her 200,000 volumes from Pergamon to restock the Alexandrian collection.

Porcelain is also called china because that is where it origi- nally comes from. It was very difficult to invent, because firing **Porcelain** temperatures well over 1000°C are required, together with precision in mixing the components. The result is a harder, finer and more vitreous product than ordinary glazed pottery. It was first made in North China early in the Later Harn Dynasty during the 1st century A.D.

The oldest descriptions of pyrex are in Chinese books of the 1100s and 1200s A.D., which admire its resistance to breaking **Pyrex** in heat. Pyrex in China was imported from the Arab countries, where it was probably invented in the 12th century, or perhaps slightly earlier. According to the Chinese, the Arab manufacturers added 'southern borax' to give their glass the elasticity required to resist heat.

Very early glass-makers must have been familiar with the possibility of producing long fibres from glass. But the date and **Fibreglass** location of the first manufacture of fibreglass into a distinct material are not recorded. The earliest known is the fabric made of woven glass fibres presented to the French Academy of Sciences in 1713 by the brilliant scientist and inventor,

René de Réaumur. Réaumur did not claim that his specimen was the first. In Europe in the following century, again at an **Fibreglass** unknown time and place, fibreglass insulation was introduced **Insulation** on industrial boilers. It was known in Britain as slag wool, because it was made from the slag of blast furnaces, which is a kind of glass.

**Plastic** Plastic was first made in Britain in 1845 by Alexander Parkes (1813–90). His product, called Parkesine, was produced by mixing nitro-cellulose with plasticisers and solvents. From this he made a range of articles including combs, billiard balls and plaques. Parkesine attracted attention at the International Exhibition in London in 1862, but Parkes's manufacturing company failed – according to him because of Parkesine's tendency to explode, according to detractors because his stinginess was impairing the quality. Renamed 'celluloid' the plastic enjoyed a long commercial life in America, after Parkes had to stop making it.

## 5. FOR THE PERSON

Most common sorts of clothing, cosmetics and jewellery date back to very ancient unrecorded origins. The inventions in this section are the unusually recent – all 4000 years old or less.

**Japanese Fan** The paper fan, folded in a zigzag pattern for easy putting away, is popular in many countries where it was not first invented, especially Japan. In China, non-folding fans of paper or cloth are far more common, but it was invented there in the 10th or 11th century A.D., during the Sung Dynasty.

**Swimming** Most ancient races would have regarded the habit of wearing **Costume** costumes to go swimming as very odd, since they generally went into the water naked. However, the fashion houses of early Egypt did not miss the chance to exploit female vanity and included swimwear in their ranges. There is an anonymous Egyptian poem about their advantages, written in about 1200B.C.:

> Love, how I'd love to slip down to the pool,
>     bathe with you close by on the bank.
> Just for you I'd wear my new Memphis swimsuit,
>     made of sheer linen, fit for a queen –
> Come see how it looks in the water!

Couldn't I coax you to wade in with me?
  Let the cool creep slowly around us?
Then I'd dive deep down
  and come up for you dripping,
Let you fill your eyes
  with the little red fish that I'd catch.     (tr. J. L. Foster)

The bikini caught on during the Roman Imperial Period (27B.C.–410A.D.), not that it was then popular, as far as we know, for bathing. Apparently it was mostly used in sports, dancing and fitness classes. Here's a picture of a pretty young thing working on her biceps, as seen by the mosaic maker in the 'Room of the Ten Girls' at Maximian's villa in Sicily (3rd century A.D.). **Bikini**

Bikini.

Women's cork-soled shoes with thick heels and soles were adopted for winter wear in the Roman Empire about 2000 years ago. **Cork Soles**

The Ansell Rubber Company of Melbourne began making washing-up gloves out of latex (a rubber product) in 1925. **Washing-up Gloves**

The company also produced latex gloves for medical use, made by the same process.

**Zip** The first zip was invented in 1891 by a mechanical engineer, Whitcomb L. Judson of Chicago. Judson's system comprised rows of hooks and eyes that locked as a slide ran along them. He established a zip-manufacturing business but his invention was never a great success. In 1906 a Swedish employee, Gideon Sundback, designed a new zip with interlocking teeth which has entirely supplanted Judson's original system.

**Sunglasses** Discs of coloured glass and rock crystal were used in ancient times for looking at things through bright sunlight and studying the sun. But it is not until about 1100A.D. – during China's Sung Dynasty – that any record appears of paired lenses in spectacle frames. It is likely they came into use during the century or two before that, as a form of eye protection. But the book that first mentions them describes a far more august function: Chinese judges wore sunglasses in court so that litigants and witnesses would not be able to see their reactions to the evidence being given. The judges' sunglasses were made of transparent quartz, the colour of tea.

**Spectacles** Spectacles, with convex lenses for curing long-sightedness, were manufactured first in Northern Italy around 1280A.D. They may have originated in the city of Florence, or more probably Pisa. Although Allesandro della Spina, a Florentine monk, is often given credit, it seems likely that it really belongs to an anonymous layman.

**Bifocal Glasses** In 1784A.D., roughly eight years after drafting the U.S. *Declaration of Independence*, American scientist and statesman, Benjamin Franklin (1707–90), invented bifocal glasses. They resembled ordinary glasses, but with two different adjacent lenses for each eye.

**Watch** The clock [VIII, 10] was invented almost 1300 years ago and the details are still on record. Considering that the first clock took up a small building, the first watch represents quite a feat in miniaturisation. Considering that it was only invented 500 years ago, it represents quite a failure in documentation that the details are not available. The date must be shortly before 1500A.D. The technical capability to make a watch may have existed in France, Northern Italy or Germany, perhaps at Nuremberg in Germany or Blois in France.

Visiting cards first became the fashion in China during the
Harn Dynasty (206B.C.–220A.D.). Paper in those days was **Visiting Cards**
pretty awful, so the cards were made on little strips of wood,
two to three inches wide, with characters painted on a white
background. Information on the cards included the subject's
name, town and title.

Spanish invaders of the Aztec empire in Mexico in the 16th
century saw cigarettes being smoked there, which consisted of **Cigarettes**
tobacco rolled in corn husk or thin bark. Cigarette-smoking is
a very old custom with its origin in South or Central America. The 16th-century Spaniards quickly took to using paper
wrappers instead.

Perfume distillation is first discussed in a tablet text excavated
by archaeologists in Northern Mesopotamia (present-day **Perfume**
Iraq). The tablet is inscribed in cuneiform script in the
ancient Akkadian language. Although its date is probably
around 1200B.C., it is likely that perfume manufacture began
in Mesopotamia several hundred years earlier, like many other
achievements in the same area.

Cultured pearls are made by artificially introducing an irritant
together with some oyster tissue into a living oyster. A method **Cultured**
of achieving this, so that fully developed pearls can be har- **Pearls**
vested after two years, was mastered in the 11th century A.D.
during the Sung Dynasty. The inventor was Hsieh Gung Yen,
a government official working at Kaifeng.

# XII
# LAW AND FINANCE

At first there was no law except the law of the jungle. The stronger party could do whatever he wished, unless the weaker successfully appealed to some non-legal motive for restraint. Laws have existed only since the relationship of sovereign and subject was established in distant prehistoric times. To protect weaker subjects, the sovereign makes laws which are binding on the strongest subjects as well as the rest. To protect the regime, the sovereign makes laws which enforce the obedience and contribution of all subjects. Consequently laws relating to crime, property, judicial procedure, administration, the status of subjects and taxation have existed since time immemorial. Legal firsts are only recorded for the special areas that have come up since writing was invented, because of developments in economic and social structures, religious beliefs, and the pressures put on resources by industrial societies.

## I. LEGISLATION

Many laws originated in custom and in decisions that were memorised but not recorded. Although these methods of establishing laws are still in use, written legislation has been building up for nearly 5000 years and now deals with most subjects. As well as the secular records treated in this section, laws originate in religious texts such as the *Ten Commandments* [VII, 7] and the *Koran* [see Islam, VII, 5], and in the philosophic commentaries on the *Koran*.

**Statute** Long after the invention of writing [I, 1] the law was still recorded only in remembered traditions rather than documents. Eventually rulers began to issue decrees dealing with specific legal topics and then to commit them to writing. The process began in Sumeria in Southern Mesopotamia (present-day Iraq) early in the 3rd millennium B.C. One of the achievements of Urukagina, the first social reformer, was to re-establish the old statutes of the state of Lagash around 2700B.C. This is the earliest reference to statutes, which must have come into operation in the Sumerian cities within the previous century or two. Although the first statutes must have been simple enactments on single topics, within a few centuries of Urukagina's time the Sumerians were drafting more complex legislation, covering a wide variety of subjects. The oldest known today is the law of King Ur-Nammu of the city of Ur from about 2300B.C. It covers many aspects of procedure and substantive law. The first law code, encapsulating an entire legal system, is a later specimen of the same Mesopotamian tradition.

This code was sponsored and enacted around 1900B.C. by **Law Code** Hammurabi, King of Babylonia. Towards the end of his forty-three-year reign he had copies set up on stone monuments throughout his empire. Two-hundred-and-eighty-two sections, brilliant in their thoroughness and simplicity, record laws in plain Babylonian about diverse matters: justice and litigation; crimes; property; commerce; finance; the family; succession (inheritance); professional liability; agriculture; wages and charges; and slavery. Hammurabi's aim was to establish a uniform and permanent system of justice, but he achieved something else, unheard of to modern legislators: he published his laws so that the ordinary people could find out what they were and understand them easily. He wrote:

> Let the oppressed man who has a cause go before my statue
> . . . and then have the inscription on my monument read
> out and hear my precious words, that my monument may
> make clear his cause to him, let him see the law which
> applies to him, and let his heart be set at ease . . .

Statutes and codes are classed as legislation, one of the main written sources of law. The other is court decisions **Case Report** which are treated as authority by courts handling comparable cases later on. These are written up in case reports. The oldest report was made around 2000 B.C., shortly before Hammurabi's time, at Nippur in Sumeria. The case in question was referred from the city of Isin to the Citizens Assembly at Nippur, a superior court that could pronounce sentence. Like modern case reports, the Sumerian report begins with a statement of the facts, proceeds to a summary of the arguments on both sides and concludes with the court's findings. Three of the accused had murdered a man; the fourth accused was the victim's wife, Nin-dada. The killers told her what they had done, but she did not inform the authorities. The court held that Nin-dada was not to be punished, despite her concealment, because she had no part in the murder itself. Like most reported decisions this one has an ambiguity in the reasoning, which leaves room for conflicting interpretations. Archaeologists have found a number of tablets containing this report, proving that it was widely studied.

**Written Constitution**

The oldest written constitution was issued from Hattusas (in present-day Central Turkey), capital of the ancient Hittite Empire. It was proclaimed by King Telepinu, who ruled in about 1500B.C. It allocates specific functions to the ruling council of state – the Pankus – and lays down a strict order of royal succession. However it would be wrong to describe

**Constitutional Monarchy**

Telepinu as the first constitutional monarch; the rulers of Mesopotamian cities in the 4th millennium B.C. had strictly limited powers based on unwritten constitutions. A good example is the state of Kish, whose bicameral parliament is described elsewhere [IV, 1]; similar constitutions prevailed in a number of neighbouring states of that time.

**Civil Damages for Torts**

In the earliest legal systems all the remedies for wrongs, apart from breach of contract, included a punitive element. One of the great advances of early Babylonian law, preserved in Hammurabi's *Code* (c. 1900B.C. [see above]), was to provide for purely civil judgments against wrongdoers, which compensated the plaintiff for damage suffered and nothing more. These only applied in cases where the legislators did not consider a penalty or punishment appropriate – for instance when negligently maintained irrigation works cause damage to an adjoining crop, or where two vessels collide accidentally.

**Medical Liability**

In about 1900B.C., Hammurabi's law code for the Babylonian Empire laid down the first written stipulations penalising medical incompetence. The laws applied only to unsuccessful surgical operations. Under section 218 of the *Code*, a surgeon who causes his patient's death or destroys his eye is liable to have his hand cut off in reprisal. In fact in such cases the negligent surgeon would negotiate a settlement with the plaintiff (either the victim or his surviving family), and thereby buy his way off mutilation. Other clauses deal with operations on slaves; the surgeon who kills a slave is obliged to replace him, but does not lose his hand.

The oldest of all defamation laws only protects the reputations of high priestesses and married ladies. In Hammurabi's *Code* (Babylon, c. 1900B.C.), section 127 enabled such a plaintiff in the Babylonian Empire to bring an action against someone who had 'caused the finger to be pointed' at her. Such a slanderer was punished by being cast down and having half his head shaven. A defence to this defamation action was to prove the accusation true. **Defamation Law**

The laws of ancient Babylonia, contained in Hammurabi's *Code* (c. 1900B.C.) are quite explicit about the rights of an adopted child. Though natural parents have no right to reclaim the child, by section 186 of the *Code*, an adopted child who persists in searching for the natural father and mother may return to them. Apparently the operation of this law extended to include recently adopted infants who gave sufficient signs of missing their natural parents. **Adoptee's Right to Reunion**

At first, legal systems had no provision to enforce the will of a deceased individual as to the disposal of the estate. Whatever was left at death simply went to another member of the family, or was divided between family members according to an established formula. As soon as wills began to be recognised and enforced, lawmakers encountered the problem that some testators choose to cut off deserving or dependent relatives from their share. The solution of laying down legal guidelines to protect the interests of disinherited survivors, but otherwise recognising the testator's will, was first enacted in Hammurabi's *Code*, the law of the Babylonian Empire, around 1900B.C. The succession law, in sections 162 to 177 of the *Code*, gave a married man the choice of leaving his widow an amount adequate for her maintenance or of following a fixed formula to determine her provision. By this formula she was entitled to the use of the family home until her death; also to a fair portion of the estate, and the dowry she had brought to the marriage. Children were entitled to equal shares, although daughters also received dowries, unmarried sons were due extra, and favourites could be given more than their share. To disinherit a son, the father had to bring two successful court actions establishing that the son was unworthy. **Testator's Family Maintenance**

Sharng Yarng – who founded the philosophy of Legalism [VII, 2] in the 4th century B.C. – implemented a plan of compulsory registration of carts, carriages and goods wagons. It was part of **Vehicle Registration** the sweeping programme of reforms he introduced while prime minister of the state of Chin in Northwest China.

**Liquor Laws**

These days, laws regarding drinking establishments deal with things like toilets, ventilation, opening hours and age limits. In the Babylonian Empire, the first liquor laws had quite different preoccupations. One provision obliges the publican (assumed to be a woman) to accept payment in grain if requested. Another prohibits a priestess from opening a pub, or going into one for a drink – on pain of being burnt to death. Yet another compels the publican to bring to the authorities any criminals who band together in her house. These and other liquor laws are preserved in Hammurabi's *Code* (Babylon, c. 1900B.C.).

**Environment Protection Laws**

The earliest environment protection laws have perished and their beginnings can only be surmised. The environment minister [IV, 2] appointed by the Chinese ruler Shun, about 2200B.C., must have had legal authority to carry out his work, but what his powers were is unknown.

**Conservation Measures**

The first protection measures were designed to conserve useful forests, wild animals and fisheries. There were two types – one restricting the killing of young, such as the rule about throwing back small fish – and the other imposing closed seasons, to confine hunting, fishing, chopping and burning to certain times of year. Since prehistoric times, Stone Age customs have included observances like these. By the 2nd millennium B.C. in the West and in China, many of them must have been enshrined in legal regulations.

**Drinking Water Safeguards**

Laws for the protection of drinking water also date back to very early times. The oldest to have survived comes from the Hittite Empire (in present-day Turkey), around 1500B.C. – a time when Hittite law reformers were very keen on reducing penalties. Section 25 of the *Hittite Code* reduces the penalty for fouling stored water to 3 shekels, payable to the injured party. The old law had required that an additional 3 shekels be paid to the state. This legislation suggests that legal safeguards for clean water originated early in the 2nd millennium B.C.

**Wildlife Sanctuary**

The earliest permanent (rather than seasonal) prohibitions on killing wildlife, were applied in limited areas, not to protect the wildlife but to reserve the pleasures of hunting for kings, rather than ordinary people. A breakthrough came in China during the 12th century B.C., when the 'Spirit Park' of the Jo Dynasty was established [see National Park V, 1], allegedly to preserve the beauties of nature for the benefit of everyone.

Noise pollution was the next distinct area to be targeted by law. In the 6th century B.C. at the Greek city of Sybaris in Southwest Italy, laws were enacted prohibiting noise-producing activities in the town area. They covered trades such as those of carpenters and blacksmiths, but even went so far as to prohibit roosters. The aim was to eliminate disturbances to sleep. **Noise Legislation**

Laws to control polluting substances come relatively late in the piece. The earliest evidence is from the 4th century B.C. for land pollution in mainland Greece, and the 3rd century B.C. for water pollution in North China. **Pollution Laws**

Throughout Egypt, during its rule by the Ptolemaic Dynasty, there was a prohibition on cutting down any tree without official licence, no matter whose land it was on. This is the first example of what is today called a tree preservation order. It probably came into effect in the 3rd century B.C. and lasted until the Roman takeover in the 1st century B.C. **Tree Preservation Order**

In 242B.C., the Emperor of India, Asoka, laid down detailed laws for the protection of animals throughout his vast empire. An ardent Buddhist, he ruled by the principle of respect for all living creatures, and encouraged his subjects not to kill or eat animals. He also built a list of protected species into his legislation. In India's state forests it was illegal to kill any animals. But to kill one of the protected species was a punishable offence, even outside the forests. The oldest list comes from Asoka's 5th Pillar Edict, passed in 242B.C., but it may be an amended version of a list from earlier in his reign, which began in 273B.C. One animal that is conspicuous for not being protected is the cow, which is today the most sacred in India. **Listing of Protected Species**

At some stage, probably in the 2nd century B.C., the Roman Senate was seised with the idea of protecting the whole of Italy from exploitation. One result was that it enacted a ban on mining throughout the country. It is not clear now whether this was meant to close existing mines or merely to prohibit new developments. However the law was not formally repealed, and in the following centuries, new mining developments went ahead in disregard of its provisions. **Mining Embargo**

In ancient times the movement to preserve historic buildings was a reaction to economic decline. As things went downhill and times got harder in the Roman Empire, developers began to covet old buildings as useful sources of building **Preservation of Historic Buildings** materials. In the later part of the 4th century A.D. the Roman Government passed a series of laws prohibiting damage to or demolition of historic buildings throughout the Roman Empire, and requiring local authorities to take steps for their preservation.

**Blanket Fauna Protection**

In the 7th century in Arabia, the Prophet Muhammad introduced a package of restrictions to provide all-out protection for animals, not just those in forests and sanctuaries or on the protected species list. He expressly prohibits:

- hunting for sport
- causing creatures to die without sufficient reason
- killing an animal that is not harmful, except in order to obtain necessities, or to end its misery
- urinating into animals' holes or water sources
- cutting trees in the desert which provide shelter or sustenance to people or animals.

Muhammad set up wildlife sanctuaries, and his ad hoc orders were recorded and used as precedents. In one case he ruled that a man who had taken fledgling birds must return them to their mother; in another that a fire lit over an anthill must be extinguished.

## 2. CRIME AND PUNISHMENT

Homicide, treason, trespass, assault and battery, larceny, kidnapping, rapine and most other serious crimes have been prohibited under threat of punishment since primitive times. Subsequently all sorts of minor criminal offences have been created and a number of more notorious ones, some of which are treated in this section.

**Infanticide**

In some ancient societies, exposure or killing of newborn babies was an accepted method of family planning. The oldest express prohibition of this practice is in Chinese law of the 3rd century B.C. Whether or not they had too many children already, parents were prohibited from killing their newborn baby – unless it was deformed. Our knowledge of this prohibition comes from case reports of the time, which may be following a precedent set a century or two earlier.

**Rape**

Under the earliest legal systems, rapists only had to fear the private vengeance of the victim's family, or the punishment for assault or trespass. The first law identifying rape as a distinct crime is section 130 of Hammurabi's *Code*, the law of the ancient Babylonian Empire from about 1900B.C. Section 130 only deals with the rape of a married woman who has not yet moved in with her husband. What the Babylonian courts did to rapists in other circumstances is not known, but rape under s.130 is punishable with death.

Many ancient Greek men, including most of the famous ones, were enthusiastic homosexuals, especially when there were **Homosexuality** pretty pubescent boys around. Such relationships were condoned by respectable society and thought to strengthen social bonds. For precisely this reason dictators who took over power in certain Greek city states from about 600B.C. onwards were the first to make laws against homosexual intercourse. They believed it threatened the security of their governments by creating strong loyalties outside the authoritarian structure, and by inspiring self-sacrifice. The first of these rulers on record is Polycrates, dictator on the island of Samos in the 6th century B.C. He carried his campaign against homosexuality so far as to burn down the local wrestling school, which must have been a good pick-up joint.

Laws against female homosexuality have been less common. Their oldest appearance is in the *Manu Smriti*, an Indian **Female** law book over 2000 years old. Its contents come from *Dharma* **Homosexuality** *Sutras* (holy law texts) written in North India probably before 200B.C. and perhaps as long ago as Polycrates's time. The vaguely worded prohibitions are set out in Ch. VIII of Manu's book, sections 369 and 370. Punishment for an infringement varies with circumstances, but may be a fine, ten strokes of the rod, head shaving, loss of two fingers or being made to ride a donkey through town.

Laws protecting animals from cruelty were framed in Northern India approximately 2000 years ago, if not slightly longer. **Cruelty to** No actual legislation survives from this period, but specimens **Animals** remain in Kautilya's *Arthasastra*, a manual of government from that time. His version provides a fine for a person who inflicts pain on a quadruped: 2 panas for a minor animal and 4 panas for a bigger one.

In Arabia in the 7th century A.D., a legal obligation was imposed on owners of animals to provide adequately for their **Neglect of** care and feeding. The Prophet Muhammad regarded proper **Animals** care as a duty of the Islamic faith, and his immediate successors made it law that an owner who cannot afford to look after his animals properly must sell them.

**Anti-vilification Law**

A prohibition on vilifying people on grounds of nationality, disabilities, occupation, education, habits and bodily characteristics is described in the *Arthasastra*, an Indian manual of government about 2000 years old. It does not say, however, when such legislation was enacted, nor whether it was general practice in the Indian states. The *Arthasastra* recommends a fine of 3 panas in a case where the abusive expression is intended at face value, such as deriding a blind man as so and so 'the blind'. Where the intention is ironic, such as calling him the man with the beautiful eyes, the fine is 12 panas. Taunting someone with embarrassing or odious disabilities such as leprosy, insanity or impotence also merits 12 panas. Fines were to be reduced where drunkenness, carelessness, loss of sense etc. were responsible, and varied according to the offenders' social status.

**Transportation**

The criminal punishment of transportation, which has been responsible for developing numerous sparsely settled parts of the world, was introduced by the early Chinese ruler Shun, who instituted a system of five graded punishments. Transportation to work in remote areas was conceived as a mitigation of the death penalty; the first transported convict on record is Huarn Do, a corrupt minister who had served under Shun's predecessor Yao. Around 2200B.C. he was sentenced and transported to Chung Sharn in present-day Honan province, then a remote outpost of the Chinese Commonwealth. Other convicts were sentenced at the same time but their names are not recorded.

**Criminal Compensation**

The criminal law of the Hittites, who ruled in present-day central Turkey during the 2nd millennium B.C., was more concerned with compensating victims than punishing the culprits. An example is the law framed around 1500B.C. concerning personal injuries:

> If one man injures another and the latter falls sick, he shall tend the aforesaid man. He shall give someone in his place who shall work in his house. As soon as he is well he shall give him six shekels of silver, likewise the doctor's fees.

The Hittite criminal law had once been punitive, like most others, and became compensatory as the society progressed. This change in emphasis was partly the deliberate work of King Telepinu (c. 1500B.C.) and his legislators, who drafted a revised legal code. For example, their penalty for stealing beehives is compensation to the owner; whereas under the old law it was to require the culprit to be stung by the bees.

Imprisonment was first adopted as a sentence for convicted criminals by the founders of China's Jo Dynasty around **Imprisonment** 1100B.C. Their penal theory was nothing if not optimistic. The prison was intended to be a centre of moral education, where intractable people were taught to be good. For serious crimes the maximum sentence was three years. Offenders who reformed and became good during their sentence were released to live in normal society. Those who failed were put to death when the sentence finished. The system was considered liberal and benign when introduced, offering criminals, as it did, a chance to reform instead of execution.

In 1890 in New York state, the first operational electric chair claimed its first victim – convicted murderer William Kem- **Electric Chair** mer. Although the new item of prison furniture had been promoted as a humane way of ridding society of undesirables, its first kill was excruciatingly slow, and the prisoner must have been looking forward to death with increasing enthusiasm as the process drew on.

## 3. COMMERCIAL LAW

Governments in the old Sumerian cities of Southern Meso- potamia began to issue lists of prescribed charges, rates, and **Wage and** prices, amongst their earliest legislation. The practice proba- **Price Fixing** bly began early in the 3rd millennium B.C., although the oldest list of several which have survived comes from the city of Ur, during the reign of King Ur-Nammu (around 2300B.C.). Typically regulations of this type fix the cost of grain, oil and wool, rates of pay for labourers, doctors' bills, and hiring fees for work animals and equipment.

Simple contract law dates back earlier than the oldest records. The law of agency is a refinement that acknowledges the **Law of Agency** authority of the agent to contract on behalf of a principal, who bears a risk and enjoys an entitlement to profits on the transactions involved. Sections 100 to 107 of Hammurabi's *Code* (c. 1900B.C.), the laws of the ancient Babylonian Empire, are the first enactments dealing with agency. Although badly damaged they reveal in some detail the relationship between principal and agent and their obligations to each other. Agency was an established practice when the *Code* was drafted, and probably dates back in Mesopotamia to 2000B.C. or earlier.

**Limited Liability**

Shareholders in the public companies of the Roman Empire in the 3rd century B.C. enjoyed limited liability, which is to say that all they stood to lose if the business failed was the amount they had already invested in the company, while their other assets remained immune from the claims of creditors. Nowadays almost all business corporations are privileged with limited liability. In the 3rd century B.C., only the limited group with public status could claim it, although shares were available to a wide range of investors. The principal business of these companies was to bid for tax-collecting rights at auctions held by the state every five years. Successful bidders were granted revenue-collecting monopolies in various territories, and kept the excess of their collections over their bids as profit. The large capital they commanded, and their offices in several countries, enabled the companies to prosper in other lines of business also. Their privileged status carried special obligations, particularly regarding their constitutions and the depositing of securities.

**Debt Relief**

Under the laws of the Babylonian Empire, enacted about 1900B.C., an extension of time and remission of interest were granted automatically to a debtor who could not repay because of the effects of a natural calamity such as flood or drought.

**Moratorium on Debts**

This relief, provided under section 48 of Hammurabi's Code, was only applicable in cases of hardship, and it was probably open to lenders to contract out of section 48 in advance. The first recorded general moratorium on debt repayment was granted by the Babylonian government, probably around 1800B.C. It operated in favour of people from many walks of life who were relieved of their repayment obligations, at least in the year of its issue.

**Product Guarantee**

Ships and transport boats came with a one-year warranty in the Babylonian Empire. Under section 235 of Hammurabi's Code (c. 1900B.C.), the owner could have a vessel repaired free of charge by the manufacturer if it developed a defect within the first year after purchase, due to faulty caulking or pitching. Similar guarantees were given by sellers of slaves, against them getting epilepsy in the first month. Sometimes guarantees were spelt out in sale contracts, but even if they were not, consumers could invoke the Code to ensure their protection.

**Patent Law**

The earliest patent law on record was framed to encourage inventiveness on the part of chefs and caterers. It was passed in about 600B.C. in the Greek city state of Sybaris in Southern Italy, whose people were notorious for their sybaritic luxury. The law gave anyone who invented a delicious new dish the exclusive right to manufacture it for a twelve-month period after its first release.

Until 1709A.D., protection against the copying of literary works only availed governments which declared exclusive **Copyright** rights in some of their own works, and people, usually printers, who had been granted exclusive licences on a job-by-job basis. In 1709 the English Parliament legislated to grant authors of books a monopoly on the right to publish them for a maximum of twenty-eight years from the date of publication.

A cooling-off period is the time during which the law allows the purchaser of property to back out of the arrangement after **Cooling-off** the deal has been done. Nowadays there is a twenty-four-hour **Period** cooling-off period in many jurisdictions for buying land. Buyers of goods in India 2000 years ago were allowed ten days to change their minds, according to section 222, ch. VIII of the *Laws of Manu* drafted in Northern India about that time, and based possibly on an earlier law dating back as long as 2500 years ago. Sellers, too, could rely on the law and take back things they had changed their minds about selling, up to ten days after the transaction.

The Aedilician Law of Rome was the first comprehensive system of consumer protection. It is based on the *Aedilician Edict* **Consumer** issued in the time of the eminent jurist Salvius Julianus (c. **Protection** 140A.D.). The edict makes it the seller's responsibility to draw the buyer's attention to any defects in the quality, title, dependability and warranties of new and used goods or properties for sale. 'The motive', says the edict,

> is to defeat the artifices of sellers, and to assist buyers whenever they are cheated by sellers. It is however to be understood that a seller, even though he was unaware of the existence of faults . . . must still be held liable. Nor is this unfair, for the seller was in a position to inform himself.

Despite its strictness the law allows freedom of contract to the parties to a transaction, subject only to faults having been sufficiently publicised, and to the seller's incapacity to exclude liability for undisclosed faults of which he is actually aware. Remedies open to the consumer include cancellation of the original sale and damages payable by the seller. These remedies avail not only the purchaser but anyone to whom he has given or sold his acquisition. The law was administered by officials called curule aediles, who were also empowered to penalise sellers and to keep defective goods off the market.

**Consumer Courts**

Going shopping can be a strenuous experience, and shoppers, especially among the less affluent, can wind up appearing rather dishevelled, and wearing shoes covered with dust or, to use an Old French term, 'piepoudre' (foot powder). If, to top this off, they have been cheated or mistreated by a retailer, they may lack both the stamina and the presentability necessary to take their case through the ordinary legal system. For this reason, in English markets and fairs they were given recourse to Courts of Piepoudre. These courts had jurisdiction to settle disputes between buyers and sellers, and were conducted with a minimum of formality and waiting time. There were piepowder courts operating in the 12th century, perhaps earlier, mainly dealing with disputes between traders. From about 1280A.D. to 1360 the English Parliament passed a large number of statutes governing price, measure and quality of goods, and restricting monopolistic arrangements, deceptive trade practices and harsh contracts, so the Piepoudre Courts took on an active consumer protection role at this time.

# 4. MONEY AND BUSINESS

This section deals with financial business, but the business of turning money from recreational pursuits is dealt with elsewhere: see Millionaire Entertainer [II, 2]; sport professionals and millionaires [X, 1]; professionalism in Football, Ice Hockey, Cricket, Golf and Baseball [X, 1]; and Casinos [X, 3]. For tax avoidance, tax gathering and fund-raising activities, see: Door Knock Appeal [IV, 4], Firewalking [IV, 4] General Anaesthetic [VIII, 6], Pole Sitting [X, 4] and Limited Liability [XII, 3].

**Coinage**

It's commonly thought that cash economies arose as soon as simple bartering ceased to be the main system of exchange. The truth is very different. Ancient Mesopotamian trade was based on sophisticated credit and banking systems over a thousand years before cash was first invented. Cash of a sort came into restricted use in some countries in the 2nd millennium B.C., in the form of cowrie shells, but had little economic impact. Major transactions continued to be reckoned in units of metal weight, whether or not the metal physically changed hands. By the 7th century B.C. coins were being issued. In Lydia (in present-day Turkey) they were small metal pellets stamped with a simple design; in China they were cast in stylised shapes of knives and spades, as well as simple discs like modern coins. Lydian coins go back no earlier. Chinese minting may have begun early in the Jo Dynasty, perhaps before 1000B.C., but there is very little evidence for it.

**Notes**

Carthage, the Phoenician city which ruled a powerful empire in Western Europe and Africa, issued a leather currency in the 3rd century B.C. These notes were sealed leather envelopes, with a small solid object inside, and had the value of one *stater* each.

**Paper Money**

Paper currency was first issued by an agency of the government of China's Sung Dynasty in Cheng Du, Szechuan Province, in 1023A.D. Chinese notes printed in the 11th century were made of specially manufactured paper to discourage forgery, and bore serial numbers. To make the counterfeiters' task harder, colour printing [I, 1] was introduced in 1107.

**Plastic Money**

In January 1988 the Australian Reserve Bank in Canberra released the first batch of plastic ten-dollar notes, incorporating a see-through section and a holographic image on a metallic background. The intention was to produce a more durable note than the common paper type and, with the holograph, to make forgery difficult.

**International Currency**

In a few decades up to 300B.C. the Alexander drachma became the fixed unit of currency for dozens of empires and petty states, from present-day Pakistan to Italy. When Alexander the Great (356–323B.C.) decided to institute a world currency, he adopted the 'Attic standard' – the monetary values of the city of Athens. Although every state went on minting its own money, many brought theirs into line with this standard, and money minted in one country became freely interchangeable with the money of all other users of the Alexander drachma. The group included Macedonia, free cities in Greece and Italy, many countries on the Northern Mediterranean and the Black Sea, and the empires of the Seleucids, Pergamon and, after 268B.C., Rome. Some important exceptions were Egypt, the Carthaginian Empire, the Rhodian Empire and Marseilles. These adopted the Phoenician standard, and by the 3rd century B.C., nearly the whole Western World was using one or other of the two international currencies.

**Bills of Exchange**

Bills of exchange developed in Mesopotamia around 2200B.C. and quickly came to play a vital part in the commerce of the Babylonian world. Like today's bills they were payable either to the original creditor or to another party on a date previously fixed. Some were redeemable by any bearer and did not even carry the creditor's name. The most important change in the system is that bills nowadays are written on paper, rather than clay tablets.

**Loan Secured on Profit**

In Mesopotamia as long ago as the 3rd millennium B.C., financiers were prepared to advance funds in exchange for the right to take possession of a borrower's harvest. In Hammurabi's *Code* (Babylon, c. 1900B.C.) the lender's rights were restricted and the principle of using profit as security for borrowings was formalised. Section 49 of the *Code* provided that the lender was only entitled to take possession of as much of the yield as represented the loan plus interest, and that the borrower was to retain property in the land and crop.

**Bank**

The Egibi Bank was founded in the New Babylonian Empire during the reign of Nebuchadnezzar (605–562B.C.). It outlived the destruction of two empires, to thrive under Persian rule in the 5th century B.C. Many of the bank records have been recovered, and they reveal that it employed numerous clerks in a network of branches. Its activities included credit management and tax collection. The Murasu Bank of Nippur in Southern Mesopotamia may be equally old, though its records do not go back so far. Japanese though it sounds, it was apparently set up by Jews, during the Babylonian Captivity complained of in the Bible.

**Central Banking**

The first large centralised bank was the national bank of Egypt, established c. 300B.C. by Egypt's Greek-speaking Ptolemaic Government. Its head office was in Alexandria, but it must have had hundreds, if not thousands, of branches, including village sub-branches, and more important offices in prefectural towns. It had a monopoly of all of Egypt's internal banking arrangements, a typically socialist feature of the Ptolemaic regime.

**Socialised Banking**

**Automatic Teller Machine**

In 1969 an automatic teller, made by the De La Rue company, was installed at a branch of Barclay's Bank in the London suburb of Enfield. Bank customers were issued with paper vouchers encoded with punched holes. The machine compared the encoded information with a personal identification number which the customer was obliged to tap in on a small keyboard. The service was supposed to operate 24 hours a day, seven days a week, but technical teething troubles at times prevented this. The machine delivered cash in seconds, but withdrawals could only be made in multiples of £10.

In the Old Babylonian Empire, if the culprit could not be tracked down, the victim of a robbery was automatically cov- **Theft** ered for the loss by the local government authority. No pay- **Insurance** ment of premiums was involved, except indirectly by the taxpayer, and the victim could claim whether or not a resident of the area. It must have been a system designed to encourage good policing by the local authority, by threatening financial calamity. The oldest reference is in section 23 of Hammurabi's law code (Babylon, c. 1900B.C.). Section 126 of the same code sets out a penalty for false claims.

Life insurance began in Rome, probably in the 1st century B.C., offered by an organisation called *Collegium Tenuiorum*. A **Life Insurance** sample policy provides for a participant in the scheme to pay 100 sesterces to join, with a monthly contribution of 5 asses and a payment to his heir of 300 sesterces on death. Suicide vitiated the entitlement, and in time policies were extended to cover mishaps other than death.

Roman soldiers were paid an extra regular amount, the *donativa*, on top of their ordinary wages. Half of this was held **Superannuation** back and paid into their super scheme. They then received a lump sum payout on leaving the armed forces. This scheme probably began around 100B.C.

Scientific life insurance and superannuation schemes depend on mathematical calculations that value life on the basis **Actuarial** of probable life expectancy at each age. These figures are now **Valuations** worked out by specialists known as actuaries. They were first devised by Jan De Witt (1625A.D.–1672), grand pensionary of the States-general of the Netherlands. De Witt is more famous as the champion of the republicans in Dutch politics than for his report to the States-general on the calculation and payment of annuities, which contains his actuarial computations.

Third-party insurance for drivers of vehicles covers them for **Third-party** claims made against them by other people injured due to neg- **(Driver)** ligent or culpable driving. The first such policies were issued **Insurance** in France in 1829 by the La Parisienne insurance company.

**Consumer Guide**

For the guidance of the perplexed consumer in the tough world of shopping, Lynceus of Samos produced a handy little book in Greek, *How to Buy in the Market* (Samos, 4th century B.C.). It no longer exists, but readers could try out the following helpful tip, which has survived from Lynceus's work:

> You will find it useful, when standing at the fish counters and facing the market men, who with stony glare refuse to come down in their price, to abuse their fish roundly, quoting Archestratus, the author of *High Living*, or one of the other poets . . . You will scare away many customers and bystanders, and compel the dealer to accept your terms.

**Business Studies Course**

Bai Guei, a wealthy investor in Central China, was known to his own times (c. 400B.C.) as 'the father of business management'. He built his fortune speculating in commodity prices, and investigated business principles, so he could seize every opportunity for profit, and train people in business success. His student entry standard is revealing of his principles:

> If they don't have enough intelligence to respond to change, enough courage to make firm decisions, enough humanity to be able to give, or enough strength to be able to keep what they have, then although they may have a desire to learn, I don't teach them if they ask me.

# CHRONOLOGICAL TABLE OF ENTRIES

To place everything in this sequence, firsts with precise dates are listed with others that have to be estimated roughly. This makes it possible to see the order they happen in – but only approximately.

    The first historical events that can be dated to particular years were in the 900s B.C. All historical dates throughout the world before that are approximations or conjectures. The earlier they fall, the less reliable they are, because the original annals have been lost.

    For events before 1600B.C. in Western countries (including Egypt and Mesopotamia), the date estimates in this book are earlier than those which are often used. The longer ago the times, the greater the discrepancy, up to 5000 or 5500 years ago. Events of that era are dated about five centuries earlier here than in most current histories and reference books. Even with such an adjustment, the dates given may not be early enough.

    History goes back to the 4th millennium B.C. For the prehistoric period, before that, the dates are no earlier in this book than most others, but estimates vary widely.

HELLENISTIC
AGE
BEGINS

——————————————— 300B.C.

3rd
century

# INDEX